can't be more. Yet, there is! Amy has a resolve unlike anyone I have ever known. Her inspiring story shines hope for those struggling to overcome life's most difficult challenges.

Keep this book on the bed side table as a reference and resource. Give this book as a gift to anyone who needs a companion. Bless your family and friends with Amy's amazing tale of adventure, betrayal, pain, resolve and triumph. Let them know, they are not alone.

—Eileen Bild
CEO
Ordinary to Extraordinary Life

I0458726

PRAISE AND REVIEW FOR
WHITE HERON: A CREATION STORY

In this captivating masterpiece, Amy invites us into her intricate yet refreshingly grounded world of perspectives. I was immediately drawn into a thought-provoking dialogue surrounding the nuances of complexity and complication — a distinction that sets the tone from the onset for the profound insights to come.

Her assertion that they are "complex" rather than "complicated" reveals a deep self-awareness and appreciation for the multifaceted nature of their experiences and learning. This openness to embracing the richness of life's lessons is both humbling and inspiring, reminding us that true wisdom often lies in the ability to find simplicity amidst complexity.

What truly resonates is Amy's reverence for individuality and respect for diverse belief systems. Her stance on understanding and accepting others, even in the face of disagreement, is a powerful testament to the universal values of empathy and open-mindedness. This perspective is a much-needed antidote to the polarization and intolerance that pervade our modern discourse.

This book captures a unique blend of spirituality, mythology, and personal experiences, blurring the lines between fiction and non-fiction. This intriguing fusion promises to take readers on a deeply personal yet universally relatable journey of self-discovery and enlightenment.

Overall, I found this extraordinary work of art to be a tantalizing opportunity for each of us to step back and challenge our assumptions, broaden our perspectives, and ultimately, remind us of the beauty and simplicity that can be found in life's complexities.

—Dennis J. Pitocco
Publisher & Editor-in-Chief
BIZCATALYST 360°

This powerful and purpose-driven work takes the reader into the personal experiences of a woman driven by love, truth, faith, spirituality, wellness, courage, and authenticity.

We all have at least one of those qualities and can relate to them in any aspect of Amy's story. Those qualities make us incredibly human and unique.

Most people squelch those qualities and show up how the world thinks they should be, essentially becoming someone else's vision of who they are meant to be.

Amy shows up as purely Amy. She courageously shares the ups and downs and the ins and outs of her life, allowing readers to learn from and utilize what they have learned to overcome their own challenges, personality quirks, flaws, or whatever they feel they need to change.

This testimony is an invitation to unlock your power and honor the uniquely authentic person you are.

—Teresa Velardi
https://linktr.ee/teresavelardi

Life is a series of conversations and experiences that ultimately help us define who we are and create the life we want. There are people in the world whose life journey is filled with an incredible amount of trials and tribulations, loss and success. Amy is such a person. Her story interweaves spirituality, real life events, and her own insights with teachings stimulating the reader on multiple levels. Personally, an awakening may occur for the reader as each chapter unfolds creating a trail of new perspectives. You may feel deeply connected to Amy's experiences and begin to question yourself and your relationship with the world around you including the people, places and things that have altered your existence. Thus, leading to a greater understanding of life and its meaning. Every step along the way Amy miraculously pushes through to the other side. You continuously think to yourself, there

WHITE HERON
A Creation Story

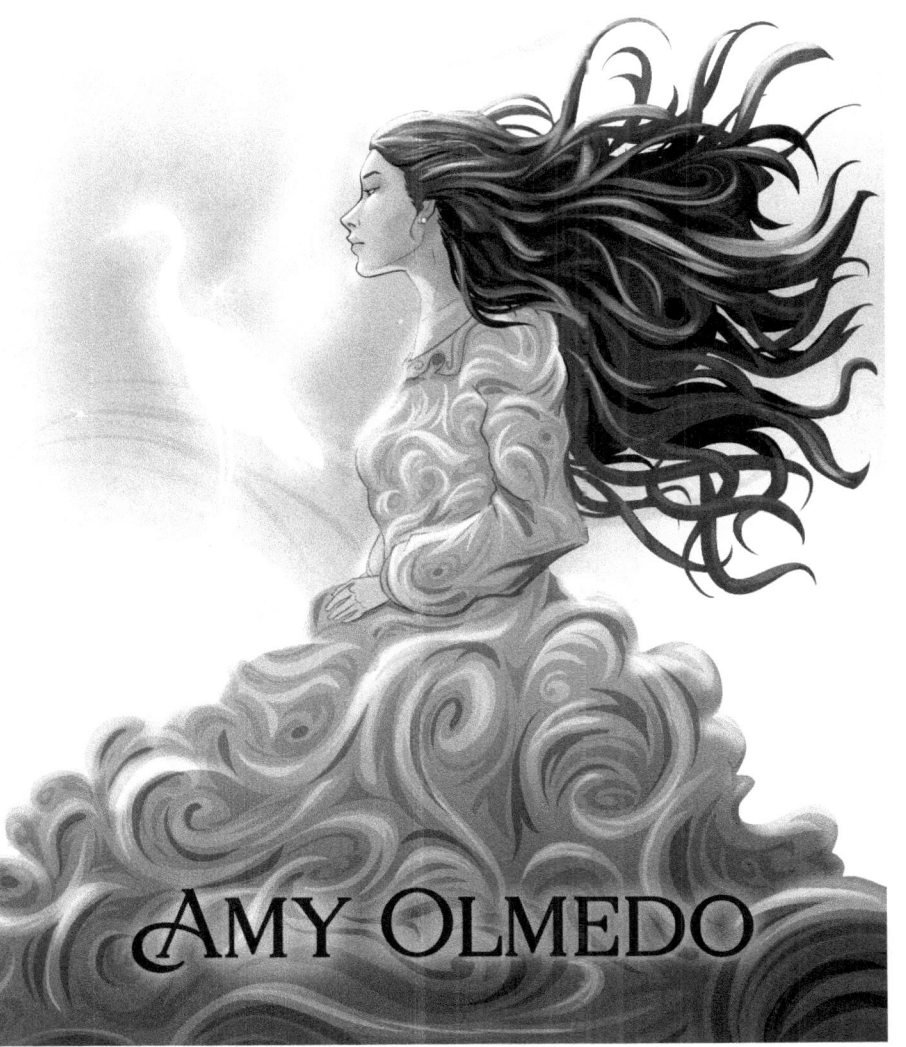

AMY OLMEDO

Published in the United States of America
All rights reserved worldwide

Authentic Endeavors Publishing
Scranton PA 18505

White Heron: A Creation Story

ISBN: 978-1-963849-73-8 (Paperback)
        978-1-963849-74-5 (Hardback)
        978-1-963849-75-2 (Ebook)

Library of Congress Control Number: 2024926265

Interior Design by Amit Dey

AUTHENTIC ENDEAVORS
PUBLISHING

www.AuthenticEndeavorsPublishing.com

DEDICATION

To My Children:
"The White Lotus" and "The Leather-back Turtle"

TABLE OF CONTENTS

PROLOGUE

I abruptly awoke at midnight. My brain was running on high as I tried to tie the beginning and the end of my story together in an enticing way. I tossed and turned for several hours before saying, "Spirit Blue Elixir." Instantly, this legend was created in my mind. For the next couple of hours, I dictated my thoughts to my phone via text messages. When I came to a stopping point, I put my phone down, cuddled up into my blanket and drifted off to sleep. I hope you enjoy it.

The Legend of The White Heron

Long ago, when the Earth was still in-formation, a rich and glorious land was filled with prehistoric plants, animals, fungi, and humankind's earliest forms. We called this fertile land Pangea, and the gods and goddesses kept close watch over our evolutionary experience from the heavens above.

Heron, a distant star, exploded into a supernova and sent stardust down, covering most of our Earth. Clusters of heavenly dust settled along our land's internal waterways. The Rivers of Intuition, Integrity and Imagination unveiled their importance as the oceans subsided.

Over time, this Heron stardust transformed deep within the waterlogged soil, and large winged creatures began to emerge. Their legs and necks were long and elegant so they could traverse the newly formed wetlands with grace and prosperity.

One day, Ducha Inžinier, the god of mathematics, science, and engineering, and his spouse, Dea Farfalla, the goddess of peace, love, and language, saw a pale blue egg sitting in the marsh and decided to build a nest upon a nearby tree branch to keep it safe from predators. The sticks, moss, and leaves created a soft platform where the egg could be nurtured.

Soon, a great blue heron hatchling broke into the world, and the gods were so pleased that they bestowed the name, Amy, which means "love in all of its heavenly forms," upon her sweet and gentle soul.

As Amy flourished, few could understand her existence because she seemed so much different than the rest of creation. Thus, much turmoil grew, and day after day, everyone tried to force her to conform and emulate the other creatures. She became a quiet and curious hunter of truth and wisdom.

When the feathers of her youth molted, Amy desired knowledge beyond the marsh. As she took flight, there was much chaos throughout Pangea, but she felt comfortable and confident in her explorations. Feeling the breath of life intensify from beneath her wings was glorious.

As the plumage on her head and shoulders elongated and glistened, her strong bill visibly brightened to mimic the sun's warmth. It was time for Amy to find a mate. As the seasons progressed, a dense fog clouded the land, and a black heron took notice of this young maiden. Daniel, which means "God shall be my judge," was mesmerized by her beauty, wisdom, and grace and desired to be by her side.

Black herons have a unique hunting style, and Daniel obnoxiously flaunted his cloak. He arched his wings into a large canopy over the water's edge and placed his head deep inside. This dark refuge diminishes reflections in the water, making prey more apparent. Once inside, predators could neither see nor steal his catch. However, Amy was not impressed by this pompous display of affection and continued in another direction.

Daniel had an adventuresome spirit and was determined to follow his instinctual calling and mate for a lifetime. So, he devised a plan to allure this great blue heron to be the love of his life.

Daniel, who had also descended from the Heron stardust, sought guidance from the gods who had nurtured him since his creation. Diwa Madilim, the god of dark medicine, martial arts, and warfare, and his spouse, Dukh Sonechko, the goddess of fertility and the harvest as well as caregiver of souls on the verge of life and death, encouraged him to drink a spirit blue elixir to transform the appearance of his plumage from black to blue. Initially, this elixir made him feel as powerful as the gods and opened his heart to the land's magic and all the opportunities their wealth and knowledge could afford.

Amy was captivated by Daniel because she did not know of any other great blue herons that existed in Pangea. Gloriously, on the Summer Solstice, a white lotus emerged within their nest. They called this heavenly blossom Mohala Lani, symbolizing a special blessing bestowed upon souls during the trials and tribulations of great transformation.

For several years, these two herons lived in harmony, cherishing Mohala Lani as she joyfully basked in the glory of each passing day. But their hearts longed for a son to fulfill their world of dreams.

Eventually, the heavens heard the cry of the great blue heron and bestowed a clutch of tiny eggs on a sandy beach near the marsh. Amy was so excited to see over one hundred of these white spherical wonders and hoped at least one would join their happy family. During the first phase of the Flower Moon, the hatchlings emerged as sea turtles and instinctively crawled toward the brightest light.

However, the largest sea turtle was torn between the moonlight over the land and the ocean. So, he crawled into the nesting grounds of the great blue herons for comfort. Daniel and Amy were delighted to keep him and named this gentle giant Honu ʻili because his hard-shell exterior was more like leather, and his natural ability to dive deep into the turbulent oceans seemed eternal. They knew Honu'ili was destined to travel far and wide in search of his true calling.

As the years passed, Daniel needed more and more spirit blue elixir to maintain his colors. The more he drank, the darker his plumage became. To his dismay, it was not the shiny black plumage that had adorned him in his younger days but a dark and envious shade of green.

You see, the god who created that elixir knew it would turn to poison, causing the family to live in a constant state of dis-ease. When Amy realized Daniel was not genuinely blue, she pleaded to the gods, *"Please, allow my love to amend his ways and become blue once again."*

But the gods were not pleased and secretly added molten fire to the elixir, causing the poison to transcend.

When Amy demanded that her family be set free, Daniel and the gods clipped her wings and imprisoned her. They warned, *"If you tell the truth about our dark magic, there will be great suffering across the land."* But Amy was determined to be set free and take flight in her dream again.

While Amy created and executed an escape plan, Daniel demanded another elixir from the gods, wanting it to be more potent than ever before. As Daniel ingested this new elixir, it instantly turned to poison and mutated his soul. This dis-ease was unprecedented, creating wild-fires that scorched the Earth, leaving nothing behind.

Not fully understanding the power of the darkness within his words, he cast a spell that forced Amy into another prison and stole a piece of her soul. He knew he could not tolerate losing everything as he vowed, *"I will torture you every day until the day I die."*

As seasons passed, Amy protected Mohala Lani and Honu 'ili, hoping the dark spell of imprisonment would be broken and they could return to the light. Their suffering caused great dis-ease. One day, a magician appeared and asked Amy to perform the work intended for the great blue heron. She worked day and night throughout the seasons of her soul, but alas, the spell remained.

As Mohala Lani's petals unfolded and shone forth, and Honu 'ili explored the spiritual connections between the creatures of the lands and oceans, Daniel became preoccupied with worldly endeavors. Amy saw an opportunity to escape and quickly retreated into solitude along a blackwater river. Its wide mouth opened to ominous sandbars lying beneath the shallow ocean floor, known to instill fear. Although her shackles remained, she felt a certain sense of freedom and discerned that he would not look for her in such a desolate place.

Each day, she quietly searched for answers to questions yet unknown. Initially, this river basin seemed bleak and barren until the sights and sounds of the tides transformed their meaning and appearance. During high tide, there was much work to be done in the busyness of the land. But during low tide, Amy became curious, unearthed remnants of her past, and asked the gods, *"Who am I?"*

Just then, the magician reappeared as fierce and blustery winds encompassed Amy, transforming her into a pure and elegant White Heron. Finally, the spell was broken. Slowly, creatures emerged from the oceans and forests, bringing forth gifts that helped to mend her broken wings, allowing her to fly higher than she ever expected. As she soared through the heavenly skies, she witnessed sacred trees standing in the distance. These majestic souls were weeping red tears as the intense orange horizon signaled the end and the beginning of a new era. Amy closed her eyes in sorrow as gratitude filled her heart. She knew she needed to create a special place where every creature, near or far, could come to heal, transform and progress. This had always been her dream.

As she landed in a mystical sanctuary still in-formation, she saw the magician standing amongst a field of wildflowers. When she approached this being immersed in sunlight, she asked, *"Who are you?"* The magician reverently bowed to her soul and replied, *"I am you inside of me. You have just forgotten to remember. Welcome home, my beautiful child. It is extra-ordinary to hold you in my arms once again."*

Disclaimer

Before we get started with the rest of the story, there are a few things to consider.

In the next section, I will explain how I think and why. A friend of mine once noted, *"You are extremely complicated."* However, I firmly disagreed and described myself as *"complex."* While these two words may seem synonymous at times, they have distinctly different connotations. I have had an extra-ordinary number of learning experiences in my life, and I value all of them.

Further, once you gain understanding and insight into my knowledge and wisdom, you will eventually conclude that my methodology is simple. Everyone is unique and inherently possesses gifts from God. I firmly believe in the notion *"To each their own,"* which means I need to understand and respect others whether or not I agree with them. However, if their belief system is filled with anger, hatred or resentment, I simply choose not to participate in the conversation. But they are entitled to have their opinions. Last, I will disagree even under the best circumstances if one wishes to impose their values and beliefs upon others. People base their truth on their experiences in life, not mine.

When asked if my book is fiction or non-fiction, I was unsure how to answer that question. This story is filled with spirituality, mythology, knowledge, and my experiences. In my mind, all of these things equate to my wisdom and my life.

If, by chance, anyone recognizes themselves in my writing, it may be purely coincidental, or it may be related to my personal experiences throughout my life. I have made every effort to ensure the information contained in this book is accurate and correct according to my memories and life experiences. Any information concerning health or medicine presented in this book is my opinion and does not constitute medical advice. I am not a medical professional. The content of this book is for informational purposes only and is not intended to diagnose, treat, cure, or prevent any condition or disease. Please seek advice from your healthcare provider for your personal health concerns.

Now that we have the sticky stuff out of the way, there is one more thing I need to mention so you do not get confused by my writing. When I use hyphenated words, they usually have a double meaning. Some people may refer to certain compound words as coupling, portmanteau, or a double entendre.

For example, the word disease means an illness characterized by certain symptoms occurring in people, plants, and animals. In modern medicine, disease indicates scientific abnormalities in the structure and function of our body and bodily systems, especially when it has a known cause.

If I put a hyphen in the middle of dis-ease, it transforms into lacking ease. It describes feelings lacking in comfort, situations causing stress, or exchanges where one is at a disadvantage. If you find yourself feeling physically uncomfortable or experiencing emotional distress, watch out. Eventually, the dis-ease may manifest in your body and cause a physical disease. Then, when you go to the doctor, the origin of the problem may not be apparent, and the prescribed treatment may be futile.

Another word I often use in this story is extraordinary, which usually has the connotation of being very unusual or remarkable in a positive manner. One may remark that a famous personality has had an extraordinary life and wishes they could experience fame and fortune.

When I put in a hyphen in the middle of extra-ordinary, I am referring to experiences outside of *"ordinary life."* However, ordinary life is open to interpretation. What may be extra-ordinary to me may seem like a normal everyday experience to you. Let's say you are a sky-diving instructor. I would imagine jumping out of a plane on a clear day, with no wind and no obstructions, would be considered normal. I can assure you, if I ever jump out of a plane, it will take something extremely extra-ordinary.

When you get to my hyphenated words, stop and consider their meanings. Logically, if you discern the statements in two different ways, they will have two distinct meanings. Those meanings are open to your interpretations because you may disagree with mine.

There is one more hyphenated word I use quite often. I think we all know information is a set of facts that are provided or that we surmise about a person, place, or thing. However, I feel when our brains are still in an information gathering session and processing the facts, the conclusions are or at least should be forming or in-formation. In other words, we should be gathering and synthesizing our knowledge. We owe it to ourselves to uncover, discover or rediscover our truth.

CHAPTER 1

FOUNDATION OF MY WISDOM

An Ocean of Words

I am very particular about my word choice, and I always have been. Choosing the optimal word when speaking or writing makes a world of difference. I do not choose words to make myself sound intelligent. Moreover, I just prefer to use the optimal word for a given situation. The word may be high level and obscure, or it may be fun and jovial. Possibly, it's a goofy word that I just made up. Life is supposed to be understood and enjoyed, and words can bolster the experience. If you know me, you will come to love my use of the language. Hopefully, some of my words will be new to you or used in a different and thought-provoking way.

The following three concepts are essential because they affect our daily lives. However, these concepts are often overlooked, disregarded, or taken for granted. If you want to understand yourself and your world better, look through these concepts and decipher what they mean to you. If they are unclear or you render them useless, just tuck them into the back of your mind.

Ocean of Words: I remember reading a book years ago that aligned the wisdom of Jesus and Buddha while formulating their teachings with natural metaphors. I will attempt to paint a picture of the ocean and the waves in your mind. The only caveat is that the ocean is filled with words, and the deeper you dive into those waters, the more words you will know, and the more you can synthesize those words into new thoughts and ideas.

The vast ocean of words I have accumulated helps explain how Amy came into being and helps me search for my Why, or should I say, *"Why do I get out of bed in the morning?"*

My story is still in-formation. It may make you laugh or make you cry. Hopefully, you can relate to the fear and the folly. Most importantly, I hope it will help you to pay attention. Life is going to happen whether you notice it or not. Choose to live the best life every day. Your words will depend on it. The conundrum remains: Do our words happen upon us on purpose or accident? I venture to say both.

In theory, we should be able to explain how every word, shining like stars in the sky, was thought into existence. Please close your eyes for a few minutes and imagine yourself swimming through a vast ocean of words. Swim as deep as you can before you return to the surface to inhale your next breath.

As you dive down, notice how the same words have emerged from the ocean but in a different pattern. There may be new meanings, and your curiosity develops so you dive deeper and attain new knowledge again. Hold your breath and exhale as wisdom flows through your soul.

Suddenly, you feel a sense of ease and comfort swimming in your ocean, but the thrust of waves comes along with it. Some are large, and some are small. The ocean cannot exist without waves, and the waves cannot exist without the ocean. Cherish each wave because you will never see the same wave twice. Each new wave is in-formation in your ocean of words.

Every word or idea in the world is already in-formation. This process is omnipresent, completely independent of the faculty or power of human will (volition) and action. In-formation actually in-forms the recipient. It is a real and effective factor that delegates the parameters of life. You will have the opportunity to induce, as well as deduce, a new form of knowledge.

I believe we are all born with an innate ability to understand that we are all connected to each other, nature, and the heavens within multiple realms of existence. Every word we learn has the potential to help us to forget our connections. Then, something out of the ordinary happens, and we begin to remember that we need to understand once again.

When we reach that pivotal moment, there is no turning back. Every experience we have endured until that point is the foundation of our learning experience. Every word we use aids us in discovering our experience and helps us to become the person we were meant to be in this world.

Years ago, I remember reading that the sound [M] is phonetically found in 96% of languages worldwide. Why did I remember this fun little fact? Because it is one of the first and easiest sounds a baby can utter. No wonder so many languages contain the sound [M] to distinguish *Mother*.

Think about the internet: a small set of algorithms governs a finite and surprisingly simple set of words. These rules inform the sets of words to initiate a process that orders and organizes those words to create more complex structures and interrelations by allowing the process to unfold over time.

When we want to create a new theory based on everything we have ever learned, we proceed in a corresponding manner. We naturally compare and contrast the words we have learned. How we relate these words makes it clearer to ourselves and hopefully, to our recipients. In addition, our genetics and environment need to be added to the equation of connections.

Genetic Predisposition: I participated in a brief discussion in college about the confluence of biology, psychology, and sociology that come into play upon a person's unique and adjustable personality. The genetics of where we are born is the simplest and the most complex system because we are distinctly human. All the other measurable and immeasurable factors that influence who we are need to be addressed.

The easiest way to visualize the concept would be to draw a perpendicular ruler, meaning the numbers go from bottom to top. To make it easy, let's say the scale randomly measures any one of our attributes from 1 to 100. Then add a horizontal line, let's say around 50, representing the genetics of the specific egg and sperm that fertilized and brought us into creation.

Atop this genetic line is an adjustable transparent square that extends from a range of 40 to 60. This range allows us to thrive within a certain predetermined range of existence. As you read, consider a set of identical twins. Technically, each child should be identical, but often, they are not.

Next, adjust the transparent range by considering each and every moment inside our birth mother's womb as well as the actual birth process. Subsequently, you must adjust the range for all other physical, psychological, sociological, and environmental issues. All of these factors can either elevate or lower our number. If one twin had optimal conditions and the other was deprived, they would develop much differently. Please note that this isn't a critical assessment or a competition. It is simply being truthful with yourself.

For example, if you take your height as a factor and you were genetically predisposed to be about 5 feet tall. You may be exposed to optimal growth conditions and reach 5 feet 2 inches tall. But, if you suffer from food deprivation or adversity, you may only reach 4 feet 10 inches tall. But nothing will enable you to reach a height of 7 feet tall. This is an easy factor to understand.

When you take intelligence as a factor, we will discuss ten agreed-upon genetic predispositions in the next section. Numerous caveats influence every disposition of intelligence and alter how it is exhibited. We could be here for days and never really determine at what number you were conceived or *why*.

Quantum

Quantum is the smallest measurable unit of energy, and quanta is the plural form of the word. The origin is Latin and simply means "*How much?*" In scientific research, quantum refers to the minimum amount of measurable energy required for a change. The how much part is important because it must be identified and replicated. If we were communicating in Spanish and wanted to know how much of something we needed, we could simply ask, "*Quanto?*" the potential answer would be intrinsically understood.

But what if we had no idea what or how much to measure? What if the word or energy we were searching for to explain the change wasn't tangible? If we were speaking in French and wanted to communicate that there is a certain immeasurable amount of quantum required for an energy shift, one could simply say, "*Je ne sais quoi*," which literally means, "*I don't know what (to quantify).*"

This captivating expression captures a quality or quantity of energy that cannot be described, named, measured, or expressed. It evokes an energy that sets something apart from the rest and is usually used positively. Today, it is one of the oldest French expressions still in use and most likely dates back a couple thousand years.

It's used to capture an indescribable charm or appeal, a unique distinguishing feature, or to name some unnamable quality. It encapsulates the notion that certain qualities are beyond words—thus leaving a whimsical flair, fascination, or intrigue in the recipient's mind.

Is that certain unnamed something called magic, or do we just not understand the law that created that energy and therefore cannot name it just yet?

Quantum allows us to draw upon an extensive repertory of rules if we understand the laws of nature, the laws of the natural world with or without human intervention, with or without a researcher having to prove something through scientific analyses. Many researchers who believe in magic or potentially the presence of God are immediately shunned within the scientific community. In my experience, many leaders in scientific research have an unidentifiable entity that guides them, like Je ne sais quoi.

Remember, life is not a competition. At the end of the day, the person who knows the most words or how to quantify those words doesn't win in the game of life. They just have an impeccable memory.

But don't get me wrong, there is a necessary and distinct problem with words. We use them to develop the narratives of our lives. Thus, our narratives become reinforced over time, and these stories become our reality, whether based on our truth or on a truth that does not belong to us. Therefore, I have tried not to label my experiences with words for most of my life because they limit my perceptions and opportunities to learn, expand, and synthesize the in-formation I receive.

However, writing a book based on my life experiences became tricky. Since I have tried not to label everything with words and was forced to use words, it took me a while to find the words I felt comfortable using. Why? Because I did not want my words to be placed into a box to be used as comparisons or weapons. I simply want my words to be heard and contemplated for your own collection of knowledge and wisdom.

Cognitive Dispositions

Life is big, but our aptitude for intelligence is bigger. Understanding what you know is great. Understanding what you don't know is spectacular. Understanding that you don't know what you don't know drives insurmountable curiosity.

Cognitive Dispositions (*Can be measured*): Genetic predisposition is a person's inherent or dominant quality coupled with learning, experience, and motivation to expand. This quality can be placed or arranged in accordance with the abilities of other people. Typically, it can be measured or quantified (*quanto – how much?*)

The facets of human intelligence (*intellectual capacity*) can be broken down into ten categories:

1. **Verbal Linguistic Intelligence** (*The Art of Language*): These people have well developed verbal and written skills. They know how to listen and are sensitive to the sounds, meanings, and rhythms of what we speak. They are gifted with words, and they make those utterances receivable to the next person. They can attach feelings and thoughts into words to make others comprehend. These people are drawn to reading, writing and public speaking activities. Whether a teacher or a preacher, their words can be very persuasive.

2. **Mathematical Logical Intelligence** (*The Art of Numbers*): These people can think conceptually and abstractly. They can discern problems logically and recognize numerical patterns. They are excellent at math and working with numbers. Their reasoning skills can be used to talk themselves out of trouble. They are naturally drawn to games involving strategy. They can solve math problems in their head and can crunch numbers.

3. **Musical Intelligence** (*Musical Arts*): These people have a rich understanding of the sound and structure of music. They are more sensitive to sounds in our environment and pick up on noises other people may not know. They may have an amazing sense of rhythm and the ability to recognize tone and pitch. Their brains have a natural proclivity to think in sounds and patterns. They are naturally drawn towards music and help to create the instrumental words and sounds that fill our lives.

4. **Visual-Spatial Intelligence** (*Visual Arts*): They turn pictures or images in their mind into reality. They can think in images and pictures and visualize accurately and abstractly. They gravitate towards painting, constructing, fixing, and designing objects. They can see things in three dimensions. They are very

creative, have vivid imaginations, and possess artistic ability. They have excellent spatial reasoning, make good architects, and excel at design and map reading. They draw for fun, are good at puzzles, recognize patterns, and interpret visualizations well.

5. **Bodily-Kinesthetic Intelligence** (*Physical Arts*): These people are naturally skilled in mind-body coordination, can control their body movements, and skillfully handle objects. They have an excellent sense of timing and fine and gross motor skills. They use their bodies to convey feelings and ideas, solve problems, or create something meaningful. These people learn by doing rather than through hearing or reading. They may excel as athletes, dancers, mechanics, artisans, yogis, or tradespeople.

6. **Interpersonal Intelligence** (*People Skills*): First of two in emotional intelligence. These people can detect and respond appropriately to the moods, motivations, and desires of others. They can see things from perspectives outside of themselves. They are usually very empathic and naturally gravitate towards counseling or leading others. They are good at reading people and social situations and understanding verbal and non-verbal cues. They may be adept at creating healthy relationships and resolving conflicts. It may seem like they have never met a stranger.

7. **Intrapersonal Intelligence** (*Self-awareness*): Second of two in emotional intelligence. These people understand themselves and the human condition. They are in tune with their feelings, values, beliefs, and thinking processes. Although they may exhibit a deep understanding of themselves, they can be very shy. They are highly adept at introspection and see great value in strengths and weaknesses. Besides their normal day job, they may be spiritual leaders, counselors, and writers.

8. **Naturalist Intelligence** *(The Natural World)*: These people deeply appreciate the natural world. They may be able to recognize and categorize plants, animals, and other objects in nature and feel a sense of connection. They may have a green thumb and can make any garden flourish. They love being outside and exploring the environment. They are sensitive to subtle environmental changes and understand patterns and relationships in nature. They thrive in the great outdoors.

9. **Existential Intelligence** *(The Spiritual World)*: These people desire to tackle deep questions about human existence, such as the meaning of life. Why are we here? What is the point? They are deeply philosophical and love to look for questions with answers bigger than themselves. They possess a strong moral compass exhibited by believing in God, energy, light, love, or a higher power. Call it what you like but these people are highly spiritual and purposely gather wisdom throughout life.

   Note: A person with superior intelligence in any of the above categories may lack common sense. Likewise, a person with superior common sense may not be very intelligent in one or more categories. Sometimes, these correlations may go hand in hand but are quite different.

10. **Practical Intelligence** *(Common Sense)*: This is when we exercise sound, realistic, and sensible judgment concerning everyday matters. It is derived from a combination of intellectual abilities and life experiences. Some people, like outliers and nonconformists, may refer to this phenomenon as street smarts. A low degree of common sense inevitably causes friction in life. In contrast, a high degree of common sense makes situations in life much easier to understand and endure.

Everyone is born with a disposition to develop common sense. As life progresses, you can learn and experience more about the world. This useful knowledge provides insight into what just seems to make sense. Can you build upon past experiences and learn how to relate and adapt? If yes, then common sense will eventually evolve into practical wisdom.

Adversity Early in Life?

Wait, wait, wait! One more thing is of tremendous importance to your ability to thrive in this world. This factor cannot be discounted and impacts most, if not all, people worldwide. Adverse childhood experiences are often overlooked or undervalued when ascertaining the origin of issues about the ability to learn and thrive. In my opinion, adverse experiences cause major lifelong complications for you, your children, and your grandchildren.

This is a lot of in-formation I would love for you to contemplate so you can begin to understand my view on the complexities of life. I don't want you to wake up one morning, look in the mirror, and think, *"Oh my God, it's me! I am the one (please insert whatever word you call yourself) who didn't seem to understand. I've had the ability to change my life this whole time!"*

Pointing Out the Obvious

Knowledge + common sense + life experience = a wise and powerful story. So, when you read my tidbits of wisdom throughout this book, take them for what they are: my opinions. Then, go out and discern the *in-formation* for yourself. You are worth it.

Pointing out what seems obvious or common sense, which the other person doesn't understand, can be seriously annoying. These people make your life so much more difficult and frustrating than necessary. You think, *"Come on, this is not rocket science people. Why can't you just understand?"*

Further, when any conclusion you come to can be seen as obvious, including the exact opposite conclusion, there is a problem with the concept of the obvious. Think about this for a moment.

Once you know an outcome, hindsight allows you to go back and identify a string of obvious factors to deduce what occurred. We can only identify these factors after the fact and not during. But have you ever noticed how some people still can't comprehend the individual steps that lead to a conclusion?

Pandemonium: For some people, common sense entails controlling a situation. They feel that if they are not in control, there is an uproar of chaos, disorder, and noise at their level of consciousness. They may think, *"If I am in control, I create the outcome. I always land on my feet, so I must be right. If I am not in control, there will be pandemonium. My control is justified."* The end justifies the means. Is that a correct assumption, or the situation would have worked itself out anyway?

Conversely, I feel that attitude in no way entails a commonsense perspective. I feel like telling them to get over themselves and appreciate the gifts everyone has to offer. But if or when the outcome is desirable, they will think their control is correct, and I will still believe they are mistaken. Therefore, our common sense definitions will never align even under the best circumstances.

The sequence of events tells us *how* but not *why*. Those who do not learn from the past are destined to repeat it. Don't let your past determine your future. Using common sense to rewrite your future does not make you a coward; it makes you a warrior. When we do not have intuition or common sense in an area, we search for new in-formation. The internet can give us hundreds of thousands of so-called facts to prove almost any desired outcome.

Philosophical abstractions are not as powerful as emotion and experience. Talk to people with words they can understand. Embrace intuition and common sense and learn to trust those feelings deep inside your head, heart, and gut. Those feelings are a ray of light that helps to burn off the morning fog of doubt and allows you to proceed clearly through the day.

Let's go back to Common Sense and break it into various categories. I will give some *real-life examples that may help prompt your memory when trying to discern the problem or discrepancy. Honestly, I am not sure why they call it common sense because it makes it sound ordinary, but it is actually extra-ordinary. Everyday life would be much easier if people employed or searched for common sense, even in uncommon areas.

*Once, I was running a huge project, and the chief executive officer had a glorious array of questions as well as suggestions for each member of the group to proceed properly. Everyone had a blank face and was hiding their underlying frustration. After the meeting, I explained what he wanted in normal people's words, and everyone cheerfully agreed. Later that week, the CEO asked me why he experienced such consternation from the group. I simply replied, "Your knowledge and common sense in executing the project isn't common at all. It far exceeds most people's knowledge and ability to use that knowledge." He pulled his head back and looked very confused.

Then, he asked why everyone was doing exactly what he asked. I replied, "I explained what you meant in normal people's words. It was extremely helpful and put everyone on the same page. They were more than happy to comply." He still looked mildly confused, albeit relieved.

Stating the obvious is not always obvious. The most obvious and practical course of action comes from exercising logical judgment. Just because something works "in theory" does not mean it will work in "real life." Self-evident and conventional wisdom is an exercise we need to practice and refine. Just like playing a sport or a musical instrument, our skill level will decrease without practice.

Plus, common sense and conventional wisdom mutate and evolve over time. What our ancestors did hundreds of years ago does not match what we do today. Even what our parents or grandparents did won't get us through life successfully.

*"I don't profess to be profound, but I do
lay claim to common sense "*
Emily Dickinson

Some people aren't very good at thinking about consequences before taking action. They tend to rely too much on the input of others or the information they are exposed to daily rather than using their own judgment, experience, and logic or searching for something more.

Black & White Mindset: People with a low degree of common sense believe everything has to be one way or another. *"I am right; you are wrong."* There is no gray area in which to find alternatives. Many people who possess higher degrees of education are of this mindset. They are excellent at memorizing vast amounts of information and regurgitating it to others. While their information may be beneficial, using the acquired knowledge and skills in the real world may or may not translate. However, this dichotomy is arrogant, naive, offensive, and off-putting to a genuine relationship.

*I am a prestigious doctor; therefore, I am of superior intelligence. My intelligence exceeds your intelligence in all areas of life. If you disagree with me on any topic, you are an idiot: period, end of sentence. You are dismissed now. If you choose to argue, you'll regret it.

Interactions Lacking Respect: First, you need to ascertain if these people actually perceive your knowledge and choose to ignore it or if they have their heads so far up their asses they cannot discern or decipher if they understand your knowledge. In actuality, it may be a combination of both. Which, in my mind, equates to pure arrogance. They see themselves at the top of the pecking order and everyone else is beneath them. Any of your values or expertise are an annoyance or attack on their authority. They believe your input should be discarded or redefined to fit into their method of thinking.

*I am a great cook, and I organize my kitchen the way a great cook should. I am in control of my meals, and if you wish to serve me during

meal preparation time, I will dictate exactly what you are supposed to do. Further, when I come to your house, I will advise and override all of your decisions because you need to learn the best way to cook from me. After all, I only want the best for you.

Proper Apologies: You can forgive a child for doing something silly and lacking common sense. But when an adult exhibits the same behavior, it is no longer silly. It is impudent, showing a lack of respect for someone, and can be downright rude.

*Something bad happened, and that person thinks the situation is my fault. I cannot control what happens in life. Plus, they are demanding an apology. When I said, "I am sorry that terrible thing happened to you," they were infuriated. Apparently, they want me to own my portion of the problem, but that just doesn't make sense. Bad things happen. They must be overly emotional or crazy, and their outburst proves it. They probably just need time to calm down.

Illogical Reasoning: Ideas, thought processes and actions lack sense or clarity. Their side of the interaction is often confusing, disjointed, or incongruent. People with a low degree of common sense have difficulty with critical thinking. Basically, that means they have trouble analyzing information and drawing logical conclusions based on the given evidence. The information or situation they deem worthy is more logical than common sense and translates into them being more sensible people.

*I value a clean house. I want a puppy, although I have no experience with puppies. The puppy does not value a clean house and wants to play outside. Therefore, I need to punish the puppy until he learns to comply. The more I freak out and control the situation, the more the puppy will comply and prove me right. I do not understand why the puppy is anxious, angry, or depressed all the time. Maybe it's the breed.

Deter or Avoid Guidance: People with a low degree of common sense often refuse advice or help because they do not want to admit they do not understand. They often overestimate their capabilities and underestimate the complexity of a situation. They do not realize when they are physically or emotionally in over their heads and thus, it makes it even more difficult for them to reach out.

I am an expert on the water. I am a master's level paddler, and I want to practice for competitions during the winter season. I can take on any storm. I choose whether I live or die. I see a horrible storm approaching, but I will prove that I am an expert and stay out on the water. I am invincible.

Lacks Sound Judgment: Solutions that don't make sense or are impractical may be derived from a lack of common sense. If a child's parents or role models never let their children learn from experience, then the child never learns anything about day-to-day living. When you meet a person who seemingly should have some common sense but just doesn't, it may be because they had helicopter parents who took care of everything for them or cleaned up all the messes. There were no natural consequences or life lessons to be learned.

I am special. My parents took care of everything for me. I am successful, and I want my friends to be successful, too. I need my friends and family to cater to my every need so we can be special together. I don't understand why I don't have any friends. I am a great person.

The Bandwagon: People without much common sense tend to jump onto whatever bandwagon comes to town. They believe whatever lies, half-truths, or propaganda is being thrown at them without using any discernment. If they choose to ask questions and investigate, they find the supposed facts to back up the information they wish to follow.

Today, I want to be healthy, wealthy, and wise. This fitness guru embodies everything I desire in life. I will buy the book, deprive myself of certain quality food sources, and employ a vigorous exercise routine unsuitable for my body type or lifestyle. Hundreds of dollars later, I will be confused by the lack of progress. I guess I will find another guru because this one is obviously mistaken. I deserve it.

Jumps to Conclusions: People with low common sense usually act impulsively and jump to conclusions before considering any determining factors or potential outcomes. These emotional outbursts may or may not be accurate, but they do not consider all information. People who jump to conclusions love to take responsibility for all successes and point the finger of blame for all failures. The concept of taking responsibility for their actions doesn't make sense.

I want my daughter to graduate from high school. I will do everything in my power to control her every move because I know the right path. Oh, look, she graduated with honors and is walking across the stage. She sure does look happy. I will hug her and remind her how I finally got through to her and made her successful. I know she will be happy to hear my thoughts. This is a great moment. I am not sure why she has that grimace on her face and cringed from my hug.

Reading the Environment: People with a low degree of common sense often misinterpret the information presented to them concerning the environment. They develop unrealistic explanations for occurrences and make assumptions that are not based on reality. They may rely on superstitions or extreme belief systems to make sense of the world. There was an upsurge of this notion when the phrase "*Yolo, you only live once*" came into our daily lives. That acronym was greatly disturbing to me. In my mind, it meant doing anything your heart desires and automatically implied having no common sense.

I am young, and I love to drive fast. My parents bought me a brand new badass sports car. It is my birthday, and I will take the back roads home as a treat for myself. These roads are slippery after it rains, but I am wearing my cross. God will protect me. I know the speed limit is 25 mph, but Yolo and I will kick it into high gear. I own the road.

Reading the Room: Here is an excellent example of where common sense transforms over time. If you take a stand-up comedian from the 1970s and put them on stage in 2024, you would get a completely different response. The socially appropriate and common sense types of language and expressions used are entirely different. Instead of looking into the audience and receiving positive feedback, they would receive disgruntled faces and horrible reviews. I am sure you witness people who continue to speak every day, even when they receive negative feedback. Is it because they don't care, do not understand, or both?

I love to tell people my political views and engage in heated conversations. My views are spot on, and I will be able to entice people to take informed action. My opinions are correct, and I am simply educating people who need to understand. I presume these silent yet disgruntled faces are looking at me because they understand my plight. I am doing a great job entertaining the family on Christmas.

IQ Does Not Equal IQ: This version of common sense can go one of two ways. Either the person with a high academic IQ *Intelligence Quotient* cannot resolve a dilemma deems the situation frivolous and unworthy of their time, or says IQ, *"I Quit! I have more important things to do with my time."*

On the flip side, people with a high academic IQ often attempt to make situations seem overly complicated and esoteric, implying that the privileged information you just witnessed was only intended to be understood by a select few. They suggest you can't comprehend. They intend to frustrate you into compliance or to make you throw your hands up and say, *"I Quit! You win."* Why? I don't know. Just please stop using all those words to make yourself sound smart.

I am in a sixth-grade honors program once a week. Today, we need to solve a logic problem before going to recess. We all possess a penny, and the object is for one person to have all the pennies. We make up all the rules. We strategize, close our eyes, and raise our hands to vote. Perfect. We are down to two people. The bell for recess sounds, but there are no resolutions again and again. Impossible.

The two children remaining believe they have a very high IQ and feel they should win. The teacher sustains the process that the group created. They strategize, we close our eyes, we vote. Almost everyone wants to throw their hands up and say I Quit and go to recess anyway. But the teacher won't let us. Finally, one person simply suggests handing the penny to the person they want to win. Game over. Success. Go to recess.

This IQ versus IQ conundrum leads me to something everyone should seriously contemplate, especially if you or your children are at a juncture when they want to get married or have children. Why? Because you don't partner with a person, you participate in a relationship with someone who is part of an entire family system. One does not exist without the other, present or not.

It is important to remember that common sense is not always a given. While some people may be born with a higher capability, it can also be developed through life experience. Spotting someone lacking common sense can allow you to be more mindful and to navigate conversations, situations, and relationships. Common sense patterns, methods, and outcomes are multi-faceted and multi-generational. A lack of common sense can negatively permeate even the best of life circumstances.

Mental Superiority: *"I win"* mindset. Not everyone who has common sense is nice. They may value different things in life, and consequently, they may use their common sense to manipulate and control others. Basically, they are a wolf in sheep's clothing for their own personal gains. They are hurtful to others without realizing it, but sometimes they do know it and continue because they want to be superior, in charge, or control. They refuse to admit they may be wrong or need guidance. Being the winner is more important than being right or being nice. But, in my mind, they still lack common sense.

I love a verbal competition. It is so much fun; everyone enjoys this game as much as I do. Whenever somebody has something to say, I will one-up them, prove them wrong, or just throw out a few annoying comments to get them going. I can make up stories, drop inappropriate or ugly comments, or throw out a few facts to make myself sound superior. This game is so cathartic, and I love the control I exert over others and the situation. I don't understand why some people avoid speaking to me. This is all good fun, especially if you win. They should lighten up.

Thomas A. Edison must have had that light bulb turn on in his head, *"The three great essentials to achieve anything worthwhile are, first, hard work; second, stick-to-itiveness; third, common sense."*

False Sense of Superiority: Lack of exposure to natural consequences. We have discussed the multi-faceted world of common sense from a day-to-day relationship perspective. But ask yourself, how does this translate through the multi-generational lens of the family I am about to participate with in life? Moreover, how will my view of the world, shaped by my family and my partner's view of the world, shaped by their family, manifest in our children?

I am not asking you to methodically interview the parents of your potential future mate and run like wildfire when they freak you out. I am asking you to make a concerted effort to understand what type of situation you are getting yourself into. None of us are perfect. We are all weird in our own fantabulously fun and quirky ways. Just make sure your potential partner is just as weird as you are and you complement each other instead of tearing each other down.

If your brains do not develop properly as children, you may become stagnated. As an adult, you can't fix stupid unless you choose to fix yourself. In that case, go for it.

Children without exposure to the world don't understand basic concepts because they were never given the opportunity. They take information at face value and do not understand underlying messages. They may not understand the use of sarcasm, humor, or irony. The saying that a leopard never changes its spots may accurately describe them but may confuse them.

Hiking is a waste of time. I do not know how to hike through the woods because my parents didn't let me. The trails are dangerous, and I could get lost or injured. Wild animals are scary and could attack. I don't like being outside, it's dirty. I am not interested in the natural world. It has nothing to offer me.

Children who lack the desire to learn or have been truncated from learning by their parents choose ignorance. They are afraid to confront the truth and are intimidated by the facts. Their own set of biases highly influences them and refutes all others. Remember that old saying, ignorance is bliss? Sometimes, not knowing everything going on may make life more comfortable. But, in the long term, it becomes very uncomfortable and possibly entails living a lie.

The television in my house was always on growing up, and it filled the need for human connection. Human interaction causes problems, and the sound of television helps calm me down. I am not interested in a social life, and the television fills my head with plenty of important things to think about.

Children who are spoiled do not understand hard work and dedication. They frequently make decisions that can negatively impact them or others around them. They don't understand what causes the unfavorable results of their actions, so they persist in the same courses of action. Even if they understand, throwing money at the problem is their best solution.

I was born with a silver spoon in my mouth. I do not have to work hard. I have always gotten everything I wanted to be successful in life. I am not interested in something difficult or takes too much time. Why does everyone think I am lazy and entitled? They must be jealous of my parents' money.

Children who do not witness their parents being accountable for their actions and the reactions of others learn to deflect blame. They fail to understand the sequence of events that lead to a certain situation because they have learned to focus on one facet and ignore the others. Their interpretation of the situation is justified because it was justified throughout their parent's relationship.

My mom asks my dad to help with the chores. My dad thinks the chores are my mother's duty and fails to respond. He believes she will eventually complete the chores if he procrastinates long enough. This always happens, and we always have great dinner parties, so I don't see a problem.

Occasionally, my mom asks my dad to help, escalating the situation into an argument. He ignores her and eventually blames her for not completing her familial duties. When she reaches the tipping point, you better watch out. She is hotter than hell. My dad begrudgingly helps but makes it known she is crazy and out of control. I don't understand why she gets angry. The parties are always fun.

Children who are taught to focus on themselves lack empathy. They have a false sense of self-worth and deem anything you say an attack. They lack comfort and confidence because they do not understand how they fit into relationships and the world. These insecurities may be difficult to identify with words but may be exhibited with body language and gestures.

I am only comfortable when I am in control of a situation. When I am not in control, I puff out my chest and walk with authority. If I think you are attacking me, I will elevate my chin and gaze down at you with my eyes as if I exist above you. If you try to relinquish any of my control, I will conjure up more ways to attack you. I will take exception to everything you do and point it out to others. I don't care if you are suffering. I don't care if you are right. I don't care about anything you are going through in life. All I care about is me.

I am giving you a base of knowledge so you can build upon that base of knowledge, formulate your hypothesis, and create your theory or conclusion. Many people write books to create a theory. I am the opposite. I am enticing you to gain as much knowledge as possible, formulate your own theory, and find solutions for yourself. Embrace life as it is and seek to improve what may be causing discomfort or challenges.

Just consider if you only had two brain cells left, and they weren't getting along well. If they refused to communicate with one another, a little bit of common sense could be just the synapse you need to fire.

God, Love, Light & Energy

As you read this portion, remember that I respect all people and their versions of God. Moreover, I am attempting to explain how I view God, love, light, and energy. I am not trying to offend or discredit any religious, agnostic, or atheist perspectives. This is solely my opinion based on my life experiences. Occasionally, I may provide a frame of reference from the Bible because I grew up Catholic and attended Bible Study for many years. Following multiple traumatic life events, my spiritual perspective has broadened, heightened, and is continually evolving.

Over the years, I have been forced to rethink "Who Am I?" continuously. I've needed to reevaluate my identity, accept my limitations, and explore new possibilities at various junctures. We all do.

Without paying for an array of therapists who may or may not have been helpful, I discovered healing can be facilitated in several ways. I chose my own path and learned how to heal myself through unconventional ways. My healing methods have been used for millennia, but in the past few hundred years, we have forgotten more than we have remembered. Therefore, many may judge my actions as inappropriate or archaic.

Discovering and admitting to myself I had PTSD was threatening and difficult. In my mind, sharing that information with most people would never happen. Up until now, only a handful of people know about my suffering, and even fewer have witnessed it. I want you to know that, for the most part, I am able to process my episodes by myself or in confidence with a few people I love. The episodes have become much less frequent and intense. I doubt they will ever go away forever. However, I am still looking for answers here on Earth, and I am still looking to God.

Why am I sharing this with you? Because I believe my story serves a great purpose, and far too many people suffer from anxiety and depression alone. I want you to know you are not alone anymore.

Here is the bright side of going through adversity and suffering. There is a phenomenon called post-traumatic stress growth. Yes! Many people experience tremendous growth after tragedy has occurred.

Post-traumatic Stress Growth is a transformational process where negative experiences can lead to positive and enduring change. You may uncover and reveal areas of personal strength and fortitude.

You can explore an arena of new possibilities that may not have occurred to you before. You may be able to improve your relationship with yourself and others in more meaningful ways. Ultimately, you will have a greater appreciation for life and potentially not fear death. You may discover another reason for living and embrace the reasons you already have right in front of your face.

This type of spiritual growth constitutes a few starting points. Following is a list of how your universe can begin to expand, whether you or a loved one has endured great adversity. Together, we can grow and then pay it forward and help the next person.

Education: Intentionally rethinking ourselves, our world, and our future. We understand how assumptions or circumstances have disrupted our belief systems. We must begin by learning and understanding *the truth.* The truth can be difficult to find because many people and organizations wish to hide the truth and keep you in a constant state of dis-ease. Once you unveil the truth, the process of unlearning and relearning what you need to know can be threatening to you and those around you. Incorporating this new belief system will be difficult, and many may encourage or discourage your plight.

Emotional Regulation: Searching for, revealing, and reconciling emotional discrepancies. We must manage our negative emotions by focusing and reflecting on successes and exploring alternative possibilities. Maintaining a resilient mindset can be difficult when the pain and suffering are too much of a burden. Rather than focusing on what you have lost, focus on what you have gained and the life lessons you have learned. Then, share your wisdom.

Narrating the Story: Recounting the story from an external perspective. In the movies, did you ever notice how the voice telling the story provides the necessary context? Sometimes, the voice lets you know what just happened but then discloses pertinent information to help guide you to the next step or the moral of the story. These disclosures prompt you to pay attention and help you articulate the story and the natural consequences. Learning to reconstruct the vantage point of a story will allow the darkness to subside and the sunshine to illuminate hope to overcome the trauma.

Labors of Love, Service: Purposely finding work to help others. Whether paid, unpaid, or just being a loving companion, helping others overcome adversity is cathartic. Altruism takes you to another place and time, and your guidance will be appreciated. This was my original calling in life. I knew it from a very young age and always put myself out there, ready to serve. But, when you spend your entire life putting others first, logically, you start to question, "*When is it my turn?*" Thanks to a few helpful companions, it was my turn to receive help and ultimately help others at the same time.

I endured bereavement, natural disasters, divorce (aka war), economic stress, injuries, illness, and job loss. But somehow, my misery led to an improved mastery of life. I emerged from the darkness stronger than before, stronger than I ever imagined. I transformed myself into a *companion* filled with life's wisdom, willing to show others the way.

By the way, I used to believe some of the adverse experiences I endured were a punishment from God for leaving my marriage. I was wrong. Leaving my marriage and the subsequent tragedies were gifts from God. Now, it is my turn to share my gifts with you, my new trusted friend and companion.

> *You shall not bow down to them or serve them, for I, the Lord your God, am a jealous God, visiting the iniquity of the fathers on the children to the third and the fourth generation of those who hate me, but showing steadfast love to thousands of those who love me and keep my commandments.*
> **Exodus 20:5-6**

Iniquity and sin are somewhat interchangeable. However, iniquity implies you are violating an obligation to humankind. You are immoral or disgracefully unfair. This statement means that if you worship any other god besides Him, you are being horribly unjust to your children for multiple generations. I am sure this type of threat from such a powerful God was terrifying back then.

That passage was written by an author for those who followed this God and desired to be blessed like the stars in the heavens and the sands on the seashores. If they don't follow this particular God, they and their children to the third and fourth generations will suffer and will not possess the gates of their enemies. Ultimately, they will become the enemy.

If you take the man-made religious part out of the equation, God is acknowledging other gods or symbols of worship, and he is *jealous*. It would not make sense to be jealous if other symbols of worship did not exist. These symbols include but are not limited to polytheistic gods, glory, and gold.

The author who initiated this indoctrination (which may or may not have been necessary during that period of history) could have introduced a completely different historical perspective. If that author had stated God, also known as love, light, or energy, is genuinely omnipresent, meaning the true source of these entities in the world already existed in everything and everyone, then to worship these alternative symbols exultingly would be shortsighted.

In essence, competition between lesser gods or symbols of worship causes perpetual strife. The author of this phrase could have asked everyone to open their eyes to a broader horizon of wisdom and elevate their level of consciousness. They might have suggested that while God can be translated into an infinitesimal set of words and phrases, the origin lies within what some people call God.

I don't really care what word you call the origin, but God seems to be a universally agreed-upon word. So, when you read any words I use for God, love, light, or energy in this book, please feel free to replace them with any word or phrase that speaks to your heart. Then, we will all be heading in the same direction, and my preferred use of the vocabulary will not impede our progress.

For example, let's say you worship the spirits of the natural world, which, by the way, I do. I feel closest to God when I am immersed in nature. I love the sky and the earth, the oceans and the mountains, the plants and animals, and the lessons we learn through nature. But I need to ask myself: what is the common denominator? God, love, light, and energy are present in all creation. So, if I worshiped one of these entities above God, I would miss the bigger picture of the universe.

Next, let's say you worship the symbols of glory or fame, perhaps famous athletes, musicians, or movie stars. Maybe you desire to be the next social media guru, lead your own religious organization, or become the next politician who plans to save the world. Have you ever considered that we were all conceived in the same way and need other people and entities to help guide our way? At any point in time, any of us could vanish from the face of the earth, regardless of how famous we are. One moment in time can change everything forever.

Lastly, this is a big one: maybe you worship gold or financial success. Many believe whoever has the most money and material possessions at the end is the winner. Perhaps you worship fast cars, luxury yachts, or multi-million-dollar mansions filled with the best and the brightest. But if you are honest with yourself, it's just stuff, and when you die, you can't take it with you.

I have one more symbol of worship that significantly dictates and alters our lives: *time*. It doesn't naturally fall into any of these categories, but we need it for everything we do. Let's contemplate a few things about time before you continue:

What if you had one more year of life to live? How would you spend or invest your time?

What if you could go back to different historical periods and spend or invest your time with certain people? Let's not pick too many, maybe five. Who would they be, and why?

If you could turn back the hands of time and change one moment in your own life, what would it be and why? Be careful, though. Altering the hands of time by just one second can change everything going forward. That unknown missed courtship could have ended in marriage. That unknown unborn child could be your first beautiful baby. That unknown, missed, fatal accident could take your life

Maybe a better question would be, if you could turn back the hands of time, would you do it and why?

But now, let's move on to the constructs of God concerning religion. In my opinion, most people or groups of people need to label and identify the various aspects of God and the rules that govern those methods of existence. Why? Because it just makes sense, and the rules are teachable.

If you think back to my original statement that an author wrote in history, the first rule for governing the people was only to worship one God and to follow his rules of conduct. If you follow these Ten Commandments, you will be greater than all the stars in the heavens and multiply like the grains of sand. Awesome, that sounds like a path to success. I am going to follow his rules and neglect the others.

But, if you think about it, the common shared knowledge and wisdom to govern all religions is essentially the same. They just use different words and phrases to describe the same thing. Basically, here is how to be a good human. Now, go out and prosper.

It breaks my heart when I hear people compare and contrast why there is limited space in their version of heaven, and they know they are going because they have somehow learned to follow the rules. Therefore, if you follow any other version of religion, you obviously can't go to heaven because your version of God is lesser than mine. Hmm, it sounds like humans are jealous, not God.

Personally, I think we all have the promise of our version of heaven if we are good humans. In my mind, Paulo Coelho, Don Miguel Ruiz, Thich Nhat, Hanh, The Dalai Lama, Pope Francis, Deepak Chopra, and many others do not use the same words but have the same universal messages. Furthermore, I am sure they are all going to their version of heaven and have all learned to deliver the messages of God, love, light, and energy into *our world*.

I have often asked myself, "Why do some people endure adversity and become *a better person who wants to spread love and light into the world?*" On the flip side, I have also asked, *"Why do some people endure adversity and spread darkness?"* Possibly, that question can only be answered by the grace of God and through the eyes of a child.

Now I Lay Me Down to Sleep

Now I lay me down to sleep... is the title and first line of a bedtime prayer most of us are familiar with because it has been repeatedly invoked by authors, musicians, playwrights, and screenwriters since the 1700s. This prayer, or any modifications thereof, was a petition to God to protect the soul of a child during the night. If, for any reason, danger or death may appear in the vulnerable state of slumber, *I pray the Lord my soul to keep...* safe and secure throughout the darkness.

If I should die before I wake... is a struggle with mortality and our trust in the hands of God. *I pray the Lord my soul to take...* because alternatives to salvation entail great suffering for eternity. But think about it: Do these notions of God and mortality make sense to a child under the age of five?

I believe children under the age of five are in tune with multiple realms of existence, but they are unaware. They just exist where they are until they are taught to forget. They do not comprehend all the words or actions we take in reference to God. They are simply observers of the caretakers in their lives.

In my opinion, the only version of God a child can comprehend is the version of God their caretakers represent. Children learn by example. Each experience involving their caretaker further defines God, and unlearning these early childhood experiences is daunting.

I'm not going to use the word parent when I refer to caretakers because there is a distinct difference, and the impact of these differences can be profound. In fact, these words can incite great controversy when emotions concerning love and belonging arise.

If the caretaker was kind and gentle, the child may grow and be filled with loving grace. But on the flip side, that kind and gentle person may not have set proper limits and allowed the child to be arrogant and domineering. Unintentionally, the caretaker's personality could help create two completely different outcomes for the child they are nurturing.

If the caretaker was the protector of the home and family, the child may grow and feel comfortable and safe in their surroundings. But, if the protector was overbearing and viewed outside intrusions as a threat, the child may feel unsafe and lack trust. Unintentionally, the person who wanted to protect the child could ultimately burden them and steal their ability to live a productive and fulfilling life.

If the caretaker was responsible for enforcing rules and regulations, they may encourage the child to do the right thing, especially when others are not looking. But, if the enforcer isn't willing to follow their own rules or if the enforcement of those rules is unilateral or controlling, the caregiver (God) will be viewed as unjust. Unintentionally, great confusion arises in the child because the rules are blurry or inequitable.

If the caretaker was absent most of the time but showered the child with gifts, they may learn to equate gift-giving with love. If the child does not receive gifts, they may feel unloved. On the flip side, they may believe absence makes the heart grow fonder, but they don't realize a child can't have a genuine and loving relationship with someone who is never around. Whether or not the absence was justified (the caretaker travels extensively for work) or unjustified (the caretaker is gallivanting around town), extra care and attention need to happen for the situation to make sense and for the child to feel loved.

If the caretaker had an addictive personality, a child may learn that "enough is never enough." This can manifest as a belief that more work, exercise, drugs, alcohol, or material possessions are necessary to survive and thrive. On the other hand, the child may be repulsed by the thought of addictions and adopt a minimalistic or unkempt mindset.

Further, pertaining to which type of addiction the caregiver may be experiencing, a host of alternative circumstances may exacerbate the confusion, and the addiction may begin to feel comfortable.

If the caretaker thought everything the child did was spectacular and awesome, or on the contrary, everything the child did was wrong and reprehensible, neither one helped the child learn the natural consequences in life. The messages those children receive from God are muddled in a continuous state of bewildering disorder. If I am always right or I am always wrong, but others disagree with me, my caretaker (God) can't possibly be on my side.

I am sure you can think of more examples, but I imagine you are curious about why I am giving you all this information. Well, it's simple. I believe this is where children learn their version of God. The child may think, "*If I am good, God will reward me (maybe). If I am bad, God will punish me (maybe)...and the only version of God (comprehensible in my mind) is this person taking care of me.*"

"*If I tell this type of caretaker the truth, I am rewarded. If I tell this other type of caretaker the truth, I am punished. Hmm, this is an interesting game. I am going to play these two versions of God off each other to see how much it can benefit me.*"

"*If I ask this caretaker for more food, they get angry, make me feel guilty, but give it to me anyway. If I ask this other type of caretaker for more food, they make me understand the value of the food and ensure I eat the proper amount. This food thing is confusing. Why are adults always stressing out about it anyway?*"

"*If I cry around this caregiver, they listen and help me process the situation. I feel seen, heard, and valued. But, when I cry around this other type of caregiver, I am chastised, ignored, or told I am a baby.*"

I do not believe children can comprehend this dichotomy. They learn not to trust their instincts and emotions. You know, some of the important stuff that makes us human.

Ultimately, all this ruckus and confusion makes the world a scary and unpredictable place to exist. Some children may think, "*I am not* sure why God wants me to be sad. I was nice in the playground. I ate my vegetables and had a bath before bed. Maybe if I say my prayers and hug my teddy bear, my caretakers will love me more in the morning."

If the child within you or the child around you learned by example, what types of caretakers did they have? To me, this answers a big part of the question as to *why* some people falter, and some people fly in the face of adversity. Did this experience happen to me (punishment) or for me (reward), and why?

I do not want to add any undue burden to this discussion of a child's perception of God, but I would like to add a few things for you to consider. I believe they are important as well as controversial. If you do not agree, or if these comments make you angry or sad, I would just like you to ask yourself, "*Why?*" and then continue on. As I mentioned, these are my opinions based on my life experiences.

The process of knowing God, light, love, or energy starts in the womb. Imagine a baby who hears music and feels Mom dancing versus a baby who hears constant fighting and feels Mom struggling. Is the baby breathing clean air and absorbing proper nutrients or swimming in a pool of diet soda, processed food, cigarettes, or alcohol? If anything is physically, emotionally, or spiritually affecting your 140-pound adult body, what do you think it is doing to the 5-month-old fetus that weighs about 2 pounds?

As God, love, light, and energy illuminate life outside the womb, the baby fully depends on another human being for everything. Can the baby trust the world to love, nurture, nourish, and teach them to smile, self-soothe, and sleep? I know all babies have different personalities; some may be more difficult than others. But I am asking you to learn to listen with all your other senses and not only rely on the words of others. Huh? Listen to what your children are *not* saying.

When you learn to listen to all the other languages your children can speak, you will begin to understand who they really are and what they need to feel loved by you (God).

Another aspect I feel is of great importance and may sound somewhat obvious, but it is difficult to embrace when it happens in real life. Often, it takes an outsider to illuminate the situation and help both parties process their individual feelings as well as their feelings about the situation. That may sound confusing, but listen to my logic:

Let's say a three-year-old child experiences an unexpected trauma that alters their entire life. That same child is an adult and has learned their own version of God by attending church and religious practices. However, when adversity strikes, that adult child's brain automatically reverts to the three-year-old version of God, and they respond accordingly. From my perspective, this three-year-old was unable to process the situation, and the trauma is at their core, whether they recognize it or not. Thus, the cycle of trauma makes them angry *with* God.

Here is the second part of the story: When that adult is angry with *God*, they take out their anger and frustration on the person who exemplified God to them as a child or helped exemplify God to them as an adult. Either way, they are *taking it out on* their caregiver. In other words, some people abuse those they love, trust, and respect the most. It seems counterproductive to healing, but if caught and processed productively and lovingly, it can lead to further healing.

Lastly, an indirect adverse experience directly affects children and the adults they eventually become: What if the caregiver endures a life-altering experience and the child or adult version of God no longer aligns or manifests itself the same way in their lives? What if the protector becomes vulnerable? What if the enforcer becomes permissive? What if the emotionally distant and unavailable person decides to show love? What if your caregiver becomes disabled or passes on to the next realm? What will the child inside of you, or beside you, choose to do to continue on?

If this section makes you explore the origins of your sufferings, make a few phone calls and gather some pertinent information. People love to reminisce, especially when the stories make them laugh.

Laughter is medicine for the soul. You can take some of childhood's most embarrassing or contentious stories and make them hilarious. Then, once the conversation conjures up enough deep belly laughs, you can go in deeper and inquire about some of the other stories that may have impacted your entire life. I have had great and not-so-great results with this method. The choice is up to you.

Tonight, before you lay your head down to go to sleep, do a little research on the various ways this innocuous child's prayer has infiltrated society for hundreds of years and try to imagine the caregivers who helped to inspire the words and lyrics behind the story of the artisans that created it. Then, create your own verse or version that speaks to your soul. Pleasant dreams.

Two Old Worlds - One New World

Many of us write or tell stories about our parents. But honestly, we can only tell the stories of our parents from our point of view as their children. How many of us honestly know the whole story of their lives, *not* in relation to ourselves? We did not play with them as children, figuring out the world. We did not hang out with them in adolescence or help them transcend into adulthood over a few beers. We did not help them through school or mentor them at work. All of those things were done without our knowledge or input. Even if we hear the most in-depth stories about our parents, they are still our parents and not regular human beings, figuratively speaking.

In the last chapter, I mentioned how children view their parents as "God" when they are too young to grasp the whole concept of God. So, when did you realize your parents were just regular human beings, and when or how did you allow them to fall from grace? How did you feel when you came to this realization, and, possibly more interestingly, how did *they* feel? After all, you were just a child learning and growing as children are supposed to do.

I assume most of us realized our parents were not those awesome, heavenly deities we wanted them to be over a period of time. It's not like you woke up one morning and thought, "*Hello, ordinary human that I call Mother,*" and her reign came to a screeching end. The decline probably started in elementary school and culminated in early adolescence.

If your parents were not your parents and you happened to run into them, do you think you would like them? Would you think their life story was interesting and have compassion for them? Would you be able to hear their frustrations and offer reasonable advice? Could you form a lasting friendship and introduce them to your loved ones?

This is something we will never know. I have heard people say that they know their parents more as regular human beings after tragedy or death has struck. How sad it is that something traumatic needs to happen before we are able to open our eyes, if we are ever able to open our eyes to the truth at all.

Here is another interesting thought that may cause contradictory feelings; How much of you or your personality can be contributed to or originate from each of your parents?

If you are in a relationship or plan to be, you will need to ask your partner the same questions. Why? Because each of you is comprised of two old worlds, and whether you like it or not, you have purchased the entire package, which is non-refundable.

Then, guess what? Suppose you and your partner intend to have children. In that case, all of the attributes from you and your parents, as well as your partner and their parents, will help to create that precious little being otherwise known as your child, your fanciful and wonderfully enticing new world.

As a frame of reference, I will give a little background story for each of the old worlds that have infiltrated my life and, thus, my children's lives. These brief introductions may help you answer some of the questions, "Why in the world would somebody do that?" that may come up as you read my story.

My mom is the epitome of love, kindness, and hard work. I have rarely heard my mom speak negatively, and she always seems to find the positive aspects of a person or situation to focus on. Her wisdom is short, sweet, and to the point. She loves her family more than anything else and always encouraged us to *"Just love each other."* I still call her *Mommy*.

She grew up in a small coal mining town in Pennsylvania during The Depression. After graduating high school, she moved to Washington, DC, to pursue a new life and additional schooling. She had a strict Italian upbringing, and, in my mind, she was brave in breaking her generation's social norms. Eventually, her mother and then her father also moved into the area. She had an incredible work ethic and moved her way up in the federal government until well past retirement.

On the other hand, my father was not the same father to his four girls. I do not think it was his intention, but it just worked out that way. To me, my father was brilliant, albeit overly controlling. While he was emotionally distant, he did many things to show his love for his country and family.

He was born on a farm in Ohio during The Depression and contracted polio as an infant. He lived in a hospital for several years until returning to the farm to live with his father and brothers. In his early teens, he was left to tend the farm, go to school, and work to support himself. During high school, he moved to Washington, DC, and received a scholarship to a prestigious university for engineering.

In their mid-twenties, my mom and dad met at a dance and eventually decided to marry. They bought a home in Maryland and raised four daughters, all of whom are very different. I can honestly say my father thought my mother was the best person in the universe from the day they met until the day he passed on into the next realm. They were best friends and respected each other immensely.

The other old worlds that have impacted my life are those of the father of my children. Although I have not been around Daniel and his family in over fifteen years, their impact on my and my children's lives continues to be felt.

Daniel's father was born into an upper-class family during The Depression in another country. Since much of their wealth was in land, the Japanese occupied their properties during WWII. To my knowledge, the family was torn by political views. Many were imprisoned or killed, and the remaining members of the family prospered. Upon graduating from university, he emigrated to America to attend one of the most prestigious medical schools in the country. Eventually, he ended up near Washington, DC. He was brilliant but controlling in many ways that did not make sense to me.

Daniel's mother grew up in a small coal mining town in Pennsylvania, and upon graduating from high school, she moved to Washington, DC to pursue a career in nursing. After working for a few years, she met the man she would one day marry during one of his rotations. Eventually, the couple married and had seven children in nine years. Somewhere during the childbearing years, she stopped working outside the home and, soon after, became a breast cancer survivor.

I did not spend much time with Daniel's family, but I felt uncomfortable when I did. From the beginning, I was not accepted into the family, and we all mutually kept our distance. I thought I had a lot in common with his mother, but she did not like to open up emotionally. I suspect this was because she was treated like a servant, not a wife. Either way, I wished I had known more.

As you can see, opportunity was abundant. I think most people in that period moved to the Washington, DC area in hopes of improving their lives, and most importantly, they hoped their children would have opportunities to create a better life.

Opportunity for what, you may ask? Well, sit tight and keep reading. You will be amazed, surprised, baffled, and bewildered in so many ways. I certainly was through it all. Honestly, sometimes I have a difficult time believing it myself. I think, *"Did this really happen to me, or am I crazy?"* Well, guess what? It really did happen, and I may be a little crazy. But, if I was normal or boring, I couldn't write this book.

I have always loved the expression, *"Well-behaved women seldom make history."* Recently, I researched the origin of this quote and found it had been attributed to various figures, including Eleanor Roosevelt, Anne Boleyn, Marilyn Monroe, and I am sure a few others. However, in 1976, Laurel Thatcher Ulrich, a Pulitzer Prize-winning historian, used this quote in a tribute. She believed the course of history has been significantly transformed by *"the silent work of ordinary people."* Hmm, ironically, that sounds so familiar.

These trailblazers didn't stand on the sidelines of life, remaining unseen and unheard. They rose to the occasion and made a difference in the lives of many. Who knows, maybe your life, too.

Companions

Before we get to the juicy parts of my story, there is one more thing I would like to discuss that has significantly impacted my life. Throughout this magical, mystical, and misfortunate tale of events, you will be able to meet some of the companions who embarked on this journey with me. The reason I use the word companion is because it entails a variety of meanings.

A companion can be a person, animal, or entity with whom one spends considerable time, either personally or professionally. Perhaps you are traveling in a group, and the various members become your companions, whether you really know them or not. With that being said, all of my companions were not necessarily my friends, nor did I enjoy my time with them. However, most of the companions you will meet in this book are wonderful people, animals, or entities who have impacted my life. Whether for one minute or a lifetime, I cherish each of these relationships.

The following caveat of companion is when a pair of animate or inanimate objects are intended to complement or match each other.

For example, you can have companion pieces of artwork or musical compositions. Perhaps you are building a garden, and you might decide to plant companion crops so they can be mutually beneficial to the environment. Pairing these types of objects can help to inspire you and bring your musings to life.

When I first embarked on my writing journey, I befriended a man named David. He was in the beginning stages of becoming a great influencer on LinkedIn. His area of expertise entailed a philosophy from Japan known as Ikigai, simply defined as life purpose. I was not familiar with the word, so I did some research. I quickly realized I loved the concept as well as the history behind it. In turn, I synthesized my own ideas and formulated a modern twist on this ancient wisdom. I contemplated this notion as I walked along the sandy beaches near my house, searching for my purpose.

One day, just as high tide was beginning to recede, I stumbled upon a bunch of huge shells. And I quickly gathered them because the ocean was cold, and I did not want them to wash away. To my surprise, each new wave brought more and more of these glorious wonders, and I quickly gathered all of them. I was carrying a small blanket and used it to hold my newfound treasures. Eventually, I had too many shells and had to throw some back for the next person to discover.

I recalled my research into Ikigai and imagined these shells and all the others adorning the shoreline representing all the people I have encountered throughout life. Ikigai is a Japanese concept broken down into two symbols or characters. Iki: Life and Gai: Worth. It comes from the compound kanji variation of Kai, translating to shell.

About 1,000 years ago, shells were extremely valuable and were used for a game called Kaiawase: Shell Matching. The game was expressly played by royalty, and the shell-matching concept is still inherently valuable. It has become commonplace in society.

In Japan, it remains a multi-faceted concept that starts in youth and grows throughout life. As you grow older and wiser, you gain a more intimate understanding of the complexity of life and all it has to offer. Ikigai is not taught in schools; rather, it is a way of life.

So, what is my current twist on the old game? I created an idea called the *"Ikigai 100"*. I contemplated, *"What if we are destined to meet 100 people who will ultimately have a major impact on our purpose in life?"* How do we know when we meet these soldiers who helped us uncover, discover, or rediscover who we really are and the reason why we exist. Do we know them for a moment or a lifetime? How many of your own Ikigai Soldiers do you believe you have met? When are you going to meet the next one? What purpose do they serve in your life now or in the future?

If the word *soldier* makes you feel uncomfortable or does not match how you think, simply choose another word to replace it. I chose soldiers because they are there to serve and protect. They only fight when necessary. Maybe you prefer the words tribe, team, orchestra, or crew. Either way, these are the people you desire to have by your side.

Let's take this one step further. Magically, what if I could attend my own funeral and see those 100 soldiers in mind, body, or spirit? Who would I see and *why*? Here is another thought-provoking idea:

Which one of my Ikigai soldiers would know the most people in the room and be able to walk around, thanking each one for their contributions to the formation and transformation of Amy?

Take a look around and see if your companion's shells match yours. If you think, "*Yes, absolutely,*" then you are on the right track. If unsure, keep walking along the shorelines and explore new possibilities. If you think, "*This shell doesn't belong in my game at all,*" throw it back into the ocean, find some new shells, and move along. Tomorrow is a new day, and life is waiting for you.

You never know. The subsequent encounter could change your entire existence. But you will never know until you try. Remember, you are not alone; everyone is searching for their Ikigai 100. If someone does mean that much to you, let them know. Make sure they know you love them and that they have made an impact. That way, they would not doubt their importance if you passed away tomorrow.

Check out some intricate and beautiful hand-painted Japanese Ikigai shells online if you have time. For a deeper dive into the philosophical concept, look through some of the diagrams and see if you can answer the questions yourself. These diagrams are designed to help you discover your reason for being and understand why you get out of bed in the morning.

I must caution you: the reason you get out of bed in the morning may be as complex as your lifelong vocation and all that it entails. It could be your friends or family and the relationships you cherish. But some days, it may be as simple as taking a walk in nature or baking your favorite batch of cookies. Taking your reason for existing too seriously can overshadow the simple things in life that bring you joy. Today, I got out of bed to finish this chapter and send it to my illustrator so we may begin to create our images for you to enjoy.

I am so excited to embark on this journey with you. Bon voyage, my new companion.

CHAPTER 2

THE DREAM

Falling in Love

During my final year of college, life was progressing very quickly in the right direction. I was set to graduate with two degrees in four years and planned to apply to doctorate programs. I felt my calling in life was to help children be happy and productive. Having worked with children for eight years at a Montessori school, as a sports coach, and in a residential treatment center, I was inexplicably in my element and eager to make a difference in the world.

All of these boys and girls had multiple psychological diagnoses, and most were wards of the state. At that juncture, most of the children were victims of physical, emotional, and sexual abuse rather than the perpetrators. Upon graduation, I was offered and accepted a full-time counseling position. My motto was, *"There is no such thing as a bad child; there are only children who have endured bad circumstances."* My job was to help them work through the hardships and progress through life.

I was deeply saddened and disgusted by the forced compliance, over-medication, and abuse disguised as therapeutic intervention. For instance, when children were non-compliant with basic directions, they were physically restrained and taken to an isolation room until they could "*calm down and follow directions*," rather than being taught *the why* behind the initial request. Passionate about changing the system, I aimed to make an impact on the life of each child. I sought to create normal childhood experiences, hoping that, when faced with difficult choices in the future, they would stop and think, "*Should I really do this?*" I wanted to instill something inside their heart to encourage them to "*do the right thing.*"

Unfortunately, the children had learned to lie to survive, and I wanted to knock down that barricade by directing my focus on teaching and learning. Basically, every kid does dumb stuff without considering the consequences. I encouraged telling the truth and learning from one's experiences. If the misdeed didn't cause any harm and they were unwilling to tell the truth, they had to sit in a time-out until they confessed. Everyone knew the drill, and they had all endured it. Watching the seasoned children encourage the new children to do the right thing and tell the truth was quite amusing.

To my surprise, one of my coworkers had the same perspective. Daniel was earning his master's degree and genuinely cared about his work. Whether it was roller skating, riding bikes, hiking, camping, or reading a story at bedtime, he was always the first to step up. Even if he only had ten dollars in his pocket, he was determined to make it a great day for everyone. I thoroughly enjoyed working with Daniel, and over time, our friendship and mutual respect grew immensely.

However, Daniel had a uniquely charming way of irritating me, much like a five-year-old playing in the sandbox. He would throw handfuls of sand, then rush over to console my pain and frustration. His arrogant comments, delivered with a dismissive shrug, and his naïve tendency to overreact and blame others for his own difficulties were often grating. The biting, sarcastic, ugly, hurtful humor seemed like mere child's play. However, the good times made these unbecoming traits blur into the distance. I thought, "*I can handle this until he decides to grow up.*" No big deal. I could just sweep these irritations under the rug as if they never meant anything at all.

Several of us would go to the local sports bar some nights after work and enjoy a few beers. It was so much fun and shifted our friendship in a new direction. Trying to juggle my feelings both in and outside of work was tricky. Just before Christmas, a few coworkers were having parties on the same evening, and Daniel offered to drive us there. I was so excited and wanted to surprise him. I opted for a beautiful red cocktail dress I had been saving for a special occasion, hoping to elicit his true feelings.

Daniel couldn't take his eyes off me at the first party, and *I loved it.* A makeshift dance floor had been created in the dining room at the second party. There was mistletoe hanging from the chandelier, and he cheerfully scooped up each of the ladies and gave them a mischievous little kiss on the cheek. Everyone was giggling. But when he turned and looked at me, he paused. Both of us knew that our first embrace was going to be different, and we reluctantly turned away with smiles on our faces.

At the third party, I stood just around the kitchen corner, peering into the living room. My confident yet bashful gaze caught his eyes, and my heart smiled as I turned away. Suddenly, Daniel peeked around the corner and said, "*I just have to kiss you.*" I playfully laughed and kissed his cheek. There was no way on earth I was going to kiss him in the middle of a party filled with coworkers, even though I wanted to. This was definitely not the place for our first kiss. When he took me back to my car, it was cold and pouring rain, so we both had to hurry along and just say good night.

The following weekend, Daniel invited me to a trendy billiards room with a couple of his best friends. The lights, the magic, the fun, and the tension created a perfect combination for love. I was on top of my game and felt on top of the world. We were both playing to win. As the blissful evening ended, he walked me to my car. Just before we parted ways, he slid his hand into mine and softly kissed me goodbye. At this point, we both knew things between us would never be the same.

My emotions were running high. I thought, "*Is this what love is supposed to feel like?*" There was so much energy between us, and the following day at work, I decided to extend an invitation to Christmas dinner at my parents' house. He had to decline dinner because he was going to be with his family, but he agreed to come over and join us for dessert. He fit into my family dynamic perfectly and was emotionally overwhelmed by the love he felt from people he barely knew.

Daniel invited me to be his date for the New Year's Eve festivities at a local pub. I felt a bit conspicuous because many patrons knew us as friends, and we were obviously progressing to something more. Two of these women had asked me for advice on dating him, and I had given them some excuse about him leaving town soon and being a waste of time to pursue a relationship. I felt like I had been a bit of a liar or possibly just in self-preservation mode. Either way, I got the evil eye.

I explained that our relationship seemed to grow naturally from our friendship and that I did not intend to fall in love. We just seemed to match personally as well as professionally. As the festivities continued, a certain kind of magic permeated the air. This was not an end; it was a brand new beginning, and we both felt an irresistible connection to the past as well as the future in each other's arms.

As the ball started to drop, a man in front of us dropped to one knee, pulled out a diamond ring, and proposed marriage to his ecstatic and teary-eyed girlfriend. Everyone stepped back in awe as she accepted his undeniable gesture of love. Daniel's hand melted into mine, and the rest of the room disappeared as our hearts raced in anticipation. We kissed as if we were the only two people on earth.

Suddenly, the silence broke, and the sounds of joy permeated the room as everyone kissed and hugged their way into the beginning of the next year—the year that would change *our lives* forever.

Staying In Love

The idea of being infatuated and *falling in love* with another person is the easy part. Being physically attracted to someone makes us feel alive. Those feelings push everything else in the world into the background as we bask in the glory of testosterone and estrogen running wildfire through our bodies. The cool part is that everyone else can see your glow, especially your newfound lover. Technically, I think calling it *falling in lust* would make life seem less confusing.

Staying in love and doing the work required to build a relationship takes effort. This is where dopamine, norepinephrine, and serotonin step up to help form the *bonds of attraction*. While lust and attraction are two distinct phenomena that can exist separately, in lustful relationships, they are intricately intertwined. These chemicals make us feel energetic and euphoric, decrease our appetite, and happily keep us awake in the middle of the night.

This interwoven, magical compound we identify as love makes us high on life. But these feelings can also scare the shit out of us. Do I trust this person and stay in this relationship, or do I get myself out of here? What does it all mean? Where do I go from here? How do I maintain a sense of self and still give myself to the relationship? Many say to trust your gut.

But what if your gut tells you one thing, and yet you decide to hear something else?

Exploring the initial stages of what we identify as love can be an illustrious roller coaster ride of emotions. Love doesn't always feel great or reward us with a happy ending. Sometimes, it hurts like hell, leaving you feeling scared, insecure, and angry. But what if you want to take it a step further and create a genuine bond?

The idea of *genuine love* is a playground for oxytocin and vasopressin. These 'cuddle hormones' are released in large quantities during sexual arousal. They help to reinforce the positive feelings we already have for the one we think we love. Guess what? These same hormones also turn off regions of our brain that control critical thinking, self-awareness, and rational behavior. *Basically, love makes us stupid.* But eventually, these hormones mediate friendship and elevate emotional bonds and intimacies, thus forming a *deep attachment.*

Don't think we are finished with this little brain chemistry lesson; there is more to cover. People need to factor in the convoluted mixture of who they are and what they want in life. Twisting and turning your way through love is an everyday occurrence. You don't just find it one day and keep it forever.

Love is a verb; it requires action and must be nurtured as a state of being *every day* to remain in your life. One must learn to accept the positive traits as well as the less-than-positive traits within reason. If the idea of love is blurring or dismissing the negative attributes of a person, you may want to check your definition of love. I overlooked annoyances because I thought they would dissipate over time, and I didn't genuinely consider the origin of the playfully hurtful comments. I forgot to remember that sometimes, when people are hurting, they hurt other people to console themselves.

A major shift in our relationship occurred when those pesky little hormones were like top-of-the-line fighter jets in hot pursuit of our systems. We literally put them on a plane and flew them to a tropical paradise to attend his cousin's wedding ceremony. Can you get any more romantic than that? Look out, Hawaii, here we come!

Once we landed, rented a car, and oriented ourselves to the island, I proposed a deal for my own sense of sanity: "*If you don't irritate me, I won't get mad at you. Whoever breaks the rules is the loser, and the winner gets to choose whatever they want.*" Daniel boisterously laughed, shrugged his shoulders, and gestured with his hands as if he were purely innocent in the matter. He immediately replied, "*Deal! I'm in because I know I am going to win!*" I rolled my eyes, knowing he would not keep his promise.

As we hiked in exotic locations, ate exquisite cuisine, and immersed ourselves in the culture, it was clear this was indeed *paradise.* However, he playfully yet purposely got on my nerves as much as possible. Finally, I blew up and yelled, at which point he immediately threw his hands up and declared victory. We both enjoyed a deep belly laugh and agreed to call a truce. After all, we both had the same winning answer: *"You, forever."* Going forward, I overlooked his annoyances and enjoyed the loving spirit of the islands.

One night before his cousin's wedding, we gathered at an authentic Chinese Restaurant with his family. We sat at a large wooden round table with a rotating platform filled with various communal dishes equidistant from each guest. One by one, each succulent dish appeared in front of me, and every bite was delicious. However, the roast duck with a citrus dipping sauce was impeccable. The only thing surpassing this feast for my senses was the touch of his hand entwined with mine.

A few days later, we found ourselves at a beautiful resort resting on a white sandy beach. The bride wore an American wedding dress while the groom donned a traditional *barong tagalog* (Filipino formal shirt) made of pineapple husk. The music was perfectly timed and accentuated the experience. The smell of local flowers and international cuisine permeated the air. But in my mind, something was missing, and Daniel agreed. The spirit of joy had no voice in this room.

We quietly shared our concerns about the various marital relationships present in the room and hypothesized that such unions would never define *us*. We were different. As the sound of the ocean soothed our restless souls, we walked hand in hand, listening to the sounds of Israel Kamakawiwoʻole sing the songs of love into our awakening dreams.

Soon enough, we were back on our adventures. We swam beneath steep waterfalls at the end of ominous valleys, strolled macadamia nut farms and sugar cane fields, and refreshed ourselves with pineapple shave ice. We immersed ourselves in a Hawaiian luau, complete with hula games, fire walking, and handmade jewelry. I never wanted to leave this enchanted version of home.

After our return to Maryland, I purchased an antiquated hand-made paper scrapbook. I filled it with photographs, dried flowers, clippings from brochures, and other memorabilia I had collected along the way. This journey opened my eyes to a new world of love and opportunity. I put my heart and soul into this masterpiece and gave it to Daniel for Christmas. As he graciously accepted his gift with a deluge of tears in his eyes, he confessed, "*I had no idea how much this all meant to you.*"

As he slowly turned and touched each page, a look of amazement glistened in his eyes, one I had never seen before. It seemed as if this was *our wedding* album waiting to happen.

I love to take pictures, and making a scrapbook of *our life* became an annual tradition. Each year, I carefully crafted our experiences into a work of art, not just a piece to sit on the shelf and collect dust, but a collection that could tell a magnificent love story cherished for generations to come. I thought that as long as people spoke our names, the spirit of our love would remain alive and hopefully inspire others to live and love as we have.

In essence, I was creating my own fairy tale and fully intended to live happily ever after.

Let Love Lead the Way

Daniel had grown up in Loch Raven Reservoir and knew the trails by heart. I loved wandering through the forest for hours without feeling lost. Being with him and discovering natural wonders and new aspects of myself felt refreshingly new and different. Although I had always enjoyed being in the woods, exploring these familiar yet new territories with Daniel made me feel more confident and comfortable than ever before. I was learning how to navigate the way on my own.

Originally, the Gunpowder River ran through Baltimore County. In 1881, the first dam, Loch Raven, was built to create a reservoir to meet the growing demand for water from the expanding population and industry. As the need for water continued to increase, construction of a second dam began in 1914. However, a bustling town with multiple grist mills, churches, schools, and a post office stood in the way. Soon, the town of Warren, home to 900 inhabitants, was sold and subsequently submerged under billions of gallons of water.

I loved learning about and exploring the past. Finding buried or submerged treasures reminiscent of a time lost forever sparked my curiosity. These remnants gave me a glimpse into the past and helped me create my future. One of Daniel's favorite little excursions for lunch was situated on top of a hill overlooking the river. We would sit out on the Sander's Corner deck and enjoy being together. I always ordered the shrimp salad generously sprinkled with Old Bay Seasoning.

Between our work hours and adventures, Daniel was deciding which doctorate programs to apply to around the country. Soon after we collated all the application information for the various programs, we went for a bike ride on the NCR Trail. He always called it the Ashland Trail because we would park at the southernmost parking lot adjacent to the old red and black train station in that area. Then, we would ride north up into Pennsylvania and back again.

The NCR (*Northern Central Railroad*) historic railway, built in 1832, operated for 140 years before Hurricane Agnes destroyed many miles of track. This route, which had 46 stops, once tunneled through hardwood forests and followed the scenic Gunpowder River. President Lincoln traveled this railway to deliver the Gettysburg Address. In 1984, the first section of this flat and rocky trail opened, the beginning of the area's restoration into a quiet and shady respite to escape modern life.

I loved stopping along the trail to pick and eat the wild red raspberries and enjoy the cool breeze the river offered after a strenuous bike ride. Moments like these made discussing the various program options and subsequent relocation slightly more tolerable. The one in Hawaii was his first choice, which made us both experience a bit of euphoria. We slowed down after a long, fast stint, and his demeanor completely changed. He looked rather pale as he took a few deep breaths and asked, "*If I get accepted into any of the programs, will you come with me?*" He looked like he was going to pass out.

Joy and uncertainty rushed through my mind. Of course, I want to be with him, but I also need to get into a doctorate program. I playfully giggled, shrugged my shoulders, and replied, "*I don't know. Why don't you ask me after you get accepted? Then, let me decide.*" After all, who wants to make major life decisions based on a hypothetical situation? Let's just deal with the facts and let love lead the way.

In my mind, I really didn't have an answer. I didn't want to hold him back, but I didn't want to hold myself back, either. Sometimes, love can get complicated, especially when there are no easy answers. Either way, we both accepted the hypothetical 'maybe' as an appropriate answer at the time.

A New Hand in Ours

Since childhood, I wanted to grow up, marry the best man on earth, have the three most beautiful children, and become a doctor. Starting around the age of fifteen and continuing for the next twenty years, I experienced horrendous menstrual problems. They fluctuated between being excessive and nonexistent for extended periods of time, both creating health problems.

Around the age of sixteen, I went through a series of painful tests at the doctor's office. When the cold and distant doctor reentered the room, he abruptly explained, "*You will probably never be able to have children.*" I immediately felt insignificant and filled with shame. My life's dreams were shattered in less than ten tragic and unemotional words. I thought, "*I am broken forever.*" His mouth continued to move for a minute, but I could not hear his words. His solution to my problem was to put me on high doses of birth control pills and keep an eye out for developing cysts.

He handed me a clipboard and turned toward the desk. A part of me wanted to lash out, but I just sat quietly in shock and signed my name on a few dotted lines. Then, he quickly took the paperwork and left the room: no condolences, no explanations, nothing. 'Nothing' pretty much describes how I felt for quite some time. I guess feeling nothing was better than feeling the deep sadness within my soul.

Despite this horrible and life-altering experience, I followed through with the treatment protocols. Unfortunately, all of the birth control options exacerbated my issues and made me horribly sick. Ultimately, I was told if I ever wanted to conceive, I would need to undergo surgery or use in vitro fertilization. So, when I told Daniel I had a small lump on the right side of my abdomen about the size of a marble, I thought I had developed a cyst.

I scheduled a visit with a gynecologist. I was rather anxious because I did not want to have surgery or take more prescription medication. I promised to call Daniel as soon as I received any feedback. When the doctor entered the room and exclaimed, "Congratulations!" I obviously looked confused and thought, "For what?" She smiled and said, "You are pregnant!"

"How could I be pregnant?" The doctor and I spoke briefly as I explained the situation. On the one hand, I was relieved, but on the other hand, I was overwhelmed and excited by the unexpected news. As soon as I got home, I called Daniel at work, and they had to page him. Upon hearing his name over the loudspeaker, he automatically prepared himself for the worst and rushed to the closest phone.

I wish I could remember the words I used, but I was completely flooded with emotions, and so was he. I knew he was filled with joy, but the uncertainty of our current life situation was a defining issue. We wandered around in a daze for a couple of days and finally asked a wise and trusted advisor for counsel. She knew both of us very well and understood our personal as well as professional situations.

She explained we were two weeks away from the deadline for termination. My God, the thought had never entered my mind. I could only speak for myself as we had never discussed any available options. She encouraged us to take a week, without any outside distractions, and individually decide what each of us wanted. If we decided to keep the baby, she cautioned, *"Mothering is a tough job, and every mother needs to be mothered, and that, Daniel, is your job."*

After much thought and consideration, the time had arrived. We made plans to communicate our individual decisions over dinner at Daniel's house. He picked me up from work, and we stopped by the grocery store. It was difficult for both of us to keep our feelings inside. As we stood in the produce department, unable to decide what vegetables to buy, he stepped towards me, took my hand into both hands and leaned in close. He proudly stated, *"I want you, and I want the baby."* I could barely breathe and became lightheaded. Time ceased when I reciprocated his loving gesture, *"I want us too."*

The next six months went by rather smoothly, and I did not begin to show until the end of the second trimester. Our home was filled with joy and laughter as we prepared for our new arrival. Our dog became overly protective and did not want to leave my side. The only problem I had was some morning sickness, but it actually happened at night. I was so excited to become a mommy.

Daniel was scheduled for an in-person interview for a program in Hawaii two weeks before my due date. As soon as he purchased his flight ticket, his demeanor changed. He was torn between two important choices. He wanted to pursue his degree, but he absolutely did not want to miss the birth of our child. The morning of his scheduled departure was laden with anxiety as I watched him drive away.

As I curled up on the bed, the pangs in my stomach made me believe the baby would arrive any minute. I wondered if I could hold on until his return. Minutes seemed like hours. To my surprise, Daniel had only driven to the end of the neighborhood and stopped. He could not bring himself to go any further and returned home. As the front door opened, I ran to him, and we embraced. He was home to stay.

The day before my beautiful baby was about to arrive, I could feel the contractions doing the intended work. I drank as much fluid as I could while cleaning the house. Somewhere around 4 AM, I needed to go to the hospital. As we drove halfway up the street, I had a huge contraction, and my water broke all over the front seat as my pains echoed through the neighborhood.

Upon arriving at the hospital, I was placed in a waiting room because all the labor rooms were in use. The contractions were severe, and they administered some medications that made me hallucinate. I saw large yellow boxes above my bed. I needed to *"get to the other side of the yellow boxes,"* but the nurses insisted I lay down. I was frustrated, but Daniel said it wasn't time and I should relax.

So, I began to recite poetry inscribed on my heart: *"My love, do you know the way it feels when you first put on that rich wool sweater and walk through the crisp autumn leaves, to breathe in the earthy musk in the warm autumn glow; to just feel alive?"*

His quivering eyes and lips whispered, *"Yes."* I smiled and said, *"That's how I feel about you."*

"My love, do you know how it feels to step out onto the porch and inhale the stillness of the newly fallen snow? The way those tiny snowflakes were individually created by God as they touch our faces and warm our hearts? Do you know how it feels to hear the laughter of children playing in the snow?"

As tears slowly trailed down his cheeks, he whispered, *"Yes."* I smiled and replied, *"That is how I feel about you."*

Softly, he whispered, *"I was never sure if you actually loved me until now."*

I fell in and out of awareness until the delivery room was ready. The epidural was so strong I couldn't feel a thing. They needed to unhook me and let the anesthetic wear off. Finally, I was ready to push. I asked the doctor what the shortest labor possible was. She explained that it usually takes at least a couple of hours, especially for the first child. Thus far, her fastest labor had been one hour.

I was determined to make this as quick and easy as possible, and I insisted Daniel turn on his stopwatch. After 12 minutes and on the third contraction, my daughter was born. Within moments, they placed her on my abdomen as she reached out her tiny little hand. When she touched my skin, the most incredible feeling electrified my entire body. Love was exuberantly dancing through the air.

Our parents and siblings came to witness the most exquisite angel we had ever seen. My father offered Daniel a bit of advice: *"The best way to love your children is to love their mother the best you can."* We had chosen her name, and it was as beautiful and meaningful as she was in our life.

On the first day back home, the phone rang with many voices of congratulations. However, one voice distinctly took me by surprise, and I could not speak. I simply handed the phone to Daniel and said, *"This is for you."* The voice congratulated him on being accepted to the doctorate program in Hawaii and said he was to start classes in the fall. We quietly held each other and our baby girl.

The next couple of months were a whirlwind of joy. A few people asked Daniel if I had any postpartum depression, and he confidently replied, *"No, she has postpartum happiness. Just look at her."*

We had a difficult time finding a priest to baptize our baby girl since we were not legally married. Finally, one priest described baptism as a gift from God and believed children are entitled to receive that gift. I designed a birth announcement and invitation for the ceremony with the words: *A New Hand in Ours* on pink marbled stationery. The gathering was peaceful and sacred. It was the perfect way to say 'thank you' and 'goodbye' to everyone before we ventured to our new beginning.

This time, we planned to stay in paradise for a long time.

Living Aloha

The first expressions you learn when living on the island sound like easy translations but entail much more when you gain wisdom. These translations are watered-down versions of the spiritual significance behind them, but learning these quick versions will get you through the day.

Aloha: in common language, it is a greeting that means hello, goodbye, and love. Spiritually, *Alo* is to be in the face of, and *Ha* is the breath of life, the essence of one's being that exists in all creation. It is the way to connect and live in balance with the creative energy of life. The more you give, the more you receive. It is not something you do; it is being fully present in who you are and everything you do, which connects us to the divine. They originally called the white man ha'ole because the explorers greeted each other without exchanging breath.

Mahalo: Thank you; sincere gratitude from within.

Ohana: Family that includes your family of origin and your true friends.

Kama'aina: Local person native born to Hawaii of any origin; a person of the land.

Keiki: Child; Core of a kalo (taro root) plant, a traditional diet staple symbolizing life's origin.

Hapa: A person who is half *kama'aina* and half *ha'ole.*

Kahuna: Spiritual guide or leader, but can refer to any person or elder at the top of their vocation.

Ho'oponopono: *Pono* means being in perfect alignment with all things in life. If you live *pono,* you are living in the righteousness of the land, the ocean, and its people. Coupling *ponopono* takes it to a spiritual or universal level. When someone or something in your home or community becomes unbalanced, you have a moral obligation and a sincere desire to restore that balance. The realignment is referred to as *ho'oponopono.* All great leaders should practice this in everyday life.

Acclimating to this new way of existence brought peace and happiness to my soul. I loved working with the local people, learning their traditions, and exchanging information they needed to know in the world today.

Two expressions I learned fit beautifully into my way of communicating:

Kekuhikuhialakai'i is the guiding hand gesture in hula, which means: *Let me show you the way.* While **talkstory** is in English, it means to *sit down, relax, and let your soul speak to mine.* Both of these phrases entail genuine, loving, *reciprocal* conversation.

The pineapple and the pineapple quilt pattern are seen throughout Hawai'i and are similar to the center of this *mandala* (circle in Sanskrit, symbolizing the universe). Although the pineapple is not native to Hawai'i, it has become a symbol of hospitality and the aloha spirit, embracing the loving reciprocity of life. It lets people know they are welcome into your home.

While Daniel was attending school, I was laying the foundation for my career at the hospital and setting myself up to be a welcome addition to the doctorate program. We were very deliberate in creating our schedules, so daycare was only necessary one day per week. Each morning, I felt blessed as I drove to work and watched the sun rise over the ocean along the island's east coast.

In a store, I picked up a book of Native American poetry. The words and the images were rich and intense. I appreciated the vast similarities between traditional Polynesian and Native American cultures.

The first selection I read described a wild woman of the mountains with raven hair braided with sunlight. She had an undying passion for creating a better tomorrow for *all of our children* and realized not many would understand the true message in her heart. It spoke of the fire inside her soul and the mischief in her eyes. But clearly, she knew there would be many struggles she needed to endure. I was filled with emotions as tears poured down my face as I purchased the book *Dancing Moons* by Nancy Wood. I have kept this remarkable inspirational book handy over the years and used her words to create meaningful gifts for graduations and birthdays.

There was a huge Asian influence in the land as well. We sought out ethnic festivals to experience the culture. One of the most intriguing events was the Japanese Drum Festival. Taiko literally means *drum*, and kumi-daiko is the *art of Japanese drumming*. Centuries ago, it was predominantly used in the military, but gradually, the Buddhist and Shinto religions transformed these drums into sacred instruments. The music, images, and vibrations they co-create with the drummer seem to be an extension of their souls: it is a total mind and body experience for all.

Living life in paradise was simple but elegant. We spent as much time as possible immersed in nature, and our beautiful baby was at ease wherever we ventured. When we were on the beach, she would crawl into the ocean and only fuss when it was time to leave. On the trails, her eyes told a story I longed to hear. Her whimsical sounds spoke words yet to be learned. I intently watched and listened as my daughter retaught me how to view the world through the eyes of a child.

I was ecstatic when I was offered to be the director of a local program the hospital system was developing. My philosophy of exchanging information and developing healthy programs was being heard. Daniel had formed several attachments to people in his program, and his appearance changed. His face was soft and kind. His voice was warm and wise. His body was open and free. We were growing.

Both of us still harbored anxieties from our past, but we were able to help each other through the hardships. Breaking the unhealthy cycles we had learned in our family of origin wasn't easy, but we were definitely in this thing called life *together*. As we sat on sandy beaches with ancient volcanic mountains peering over us, we rejoiced with the sun and the moon who had come out to play with us.

We bought tickets to see a concert at the Waikiki Shell, an outdoor music venue. Our favorite artist, *Israel Kamakawiwoʻole*, was scheduled to play. 'Iz' has the most enchanting voice and sings of upholding Hawaiian voices with aloha in our modern world. He emphatically embraced life, but unfortunately, the heavens called him forth. Just before the concert, he was hospitalized and passed a few weeks later. They shut down Honolulu in his honor and buried him in the traditional Hawaiian style. Years later, his song, *"In Dis Life,"* was absolutely the most perfect choice for our wedding song.

In my mind, we had an amazing first year, and life was progressing better than expected. However, we received some horrible news. His dad was unhappy with the program and insisted we relocate, or he would not help out financially. I had no desire to leave and suggested we figure out the finances on our own. I was not privy to the conversations, but ultimately, Daniel *and his father decided we needed to leave.* I was angry and disappointed he did not stand up for himself and his family. Rather, he allowed his father to dictate our future. (*Reality #1*)

After he got accepted to a program in Atlanta, we knew our time in paradise was limited.

Fortunately, we had time to visit the Big Island, Hawaii's largest island and namesake. It is where the majestic and ancient volcanoes of Mauna Loa and Kilauea still erupt and form new earth. The steep terrains covered with vast greenery and creamy orange blossoms unfolding into black sand beaches were surreal. The short morning hike past some giant Banyan trees rewarded us with an incredible view of Rainbow Falls. Papakolea, the mysterious and glowing green sand beach was a desert oasis that few have seen. The jagged igneous rocks consuming large portions of the island, where life is scarce, is the perfect setting for the sad yet entangled love story of the wildflower Ohiʻa Lehua.

Legend says Ohi'a, a handsome warrior, was betrothed to a beautiful maiden named Lehua, and they lived happily together near the shore. One day, Ohi'a hunted high in the mountains and happened upon Pele, the Goddess of the Volcano. Pele wanted to control Ohi'a and keep him for herself. Pele became enraged when he rejected her advances and turned him into an ugly, gnarled tree upon the volcanic rock. Eventually, Lehua went searching for her lover and was devastated by his transformation. The other gods, knowing they could not undo the magic of Pele, looked upon Lehua with pity. As Lehua cried and held onto her lost love, the gods transformed her into a vibrant red flower growing in abundance upon these twisted branches. This way, these two young lovers could be together forever.

When we returned to town, we visited a few local art shops in search of the perfect souvenir. A sketch of a *kahuna* wearing an *ahi* fish hook necklace and holding an orb of healing light energy within his hands called my name. The artist explained *the light* I was seeing was in the original photograph used for the drawing. At that moment, I realized and stated, "*All children are born with healing light in their hands, and they are forced to unlearn that energy over time.*" Upon birth, my sweet baby girl had touched me with those hands, and I was going to do everything I could do to help her remember. I wanted to help all people remember, including myself.

The Wild Woman's Lullaby by Nancy Wood
Wild woman of the mountains, running barefoot through the grass
of summer, your raven hair braided with sunlight,
and a touch of mischief in your eyes, sing a song
of freedom to the dark skies of isolation:

"I am a bluebird's wing, the voice of fire rising higher
than the cloud point of summer rain. I am the
footstep you hear in darkness, leading you out of the
night. I am forgiveness and creation's daughter."

Wild woman of the mountains, swimming upriver
against the current, your body covered with leaves,
the blood of otters flowing in your strong arms,
sing a lullaby to children yet unborn:

"I am mother to the whole earth, daughter to the
falling sky, sister to dreams of rising beyond
life's ordinary claims. I am you inside of me. I ask:

"Oh, children of the coming generation, how will you live?
Oh, children of war and famine, what will you do for laughter?"

Only those who hear the voice of the mountain
can sing the wild woman's lullaby. Only those who run
barefoot through grass and swim upriver, can know
the message in her heart.

Nancy C. Wood (June 20, 1936 - March 12, 2013) was a writer and photographer who produced 28 books about the American Southwest. The region's wilderness and Native American spirituality inspired her life view and profound poetry. Aloha and mahalo for your life's work. ~Amy

Following the Dream

We had a two-month layover in Maryland between Hawaii and Georgia. Everyone was so excited to spend time with my daughter. She immediately bonded with her older niece and learned to wear shoes. Don't get me wrong, these weren't any old shoes; they were bright banana-yellow garden clogs, and it was adorable to watch her shimmy around.

The moving company claimed insufficient space in their moving van and tied several of our boxes onto the back bumper. Our boxes bounced off the truck as they entered the Harbor Tunnel on Interstate

895. Several fell into the sewer, and the remaining items blew around the toll gates. The boxes contained *all* of my photographs and all of our important documents. The toll booth ladies collected as much as possible and knew who we were the moment we pulled up to inquire. Then, they called the police, who stopped the traffic to help us pull the boxes out of the sewer. I was amazed.

Then, I did the only thing I knew how to do. I cleaned up and organized the mess and made an exquisite scrapbook of our baby's first year in paradise. One would never know damage had occurred.

For this transition, Daniel and I went to Atlanta together to make the arrangements. The best part of this move was that we got to take our dog, Ashley, with us this time. She was such an amazing part of the family and was greatly missed during our time on the islands. However, finding an apartment that accepted large dogs was an issue. But it turned out to be a blessing in disguise.

Upon our first turn into the community, I proclaimed, *"We are going to live here!"* It was absolutely perfect. We were right in the middle of the Chattahoochee National Forest, and I could literally walk out of my door and be in the woods, with miles of hiking trails to explore. Although, I could have done without the snakes and the green kudzu slime that became a regular part of my existence.

While Daniel began classes, I searched for a job. To my dismay, how the health system was set up to compensate its employees was a ginormous step backward in my profession. There was no way on earth I could support my family, or even myself, on the salary they offered. This antiquated and offensive healthcare system forced me to find a new occupation.

Fortunately, all the communication and organizational skills I learned in past jobs were highly transferable, and I quickly assimilated. I thought potentially doing alternative types of work for a few years before returning to school would prove to be a great learning experience.

Soon after we acclimated to living in Georgia, we began to plan our wedding ceremony. We both decided the wedding should take place in

Maryland and explored options. Spiritually, we chose the same priest and church that baptized our daughter because we felt connected to him and his views on gifts from God. We reserved the date within the church and picked a location for the reception.

A quaint, upscale restaurant we loved, located in Loch Raven Reservoir, seemed perfect. Next came the announcements and invitations. I found the perfect stationery to compliment the occasion, and Daniel proudly printed out the words and images I created to announce our love in holy matrimony.

Several months later, we packed up the van and headed to Maryland. We had one month to make the magic come together for our special day. I called the church to figure out the remaining logistics, but they had absolutely no record of our reservation. Apparently, the lady who took my information and deposit had been let go. *"Let go, and nobody followed up? Now, you don't have any times or dates available?"* I anxiously questioned. We were supposed to get married in a few weeks, but now I have nowhere to go. *Ugh!* Think, Amy, think, *"What other options do we have?"*

Plan B: We can have the ceremony and reception in the restaurant. It is spacious, and the atmosphere is rustic and romantic. Nope. Priests are not allowed to perform the ceremony off church grounds.

Plan C: We found a historic mansion that had a church within. The original family called it a castle, complete with a solid mahogany spiral staircase perfect enough for me to be a princess. I breathed a sigh of relief because this venue was far better than the rest. We wanted everything to be simple but elegant, and this place embodied our dreams and opened up to nature.

The Rings: We wanted something unique and visited several of the best jewelry stores in the area. Soon, we realized most of the selections looked the same. Finally, we found the magic. His ring was thick and striking to the eye. The two contrasting colors of gold accentuated an intricate tooth pattern reminiscent of antiquity. My wedding band had five matching diamonds perfectly placed to attract the most light.

The engagement ring had four of those same diamonds, with the center one setting higher and larger than the rest. There was no doubt that these rings were made for us.

Unfortunately, when we realized we could only afford to buy the wedding bands and not the engagement ring guilt consumed Daniel's soul. After a few long and arduous minutes, a glimmer of light appeared on his face as he gently took my hand into his hands. He solemnly vowed that he would buy the engagement ring for me one day, and we could have a renewal ceremony and a proper honeymoon. His romantic gesture spoke volumes of our love as we asked the salesperson for all the necessary documentation to ensure we could purchase this exact ring at some point in the future.

At the onset of the ceremony, the musician we selected played the piano. I was so nervous I could barely speak. As Vivaldi's The Four Seasons: *Spring* guided me down the aisle, I felt disoriented. Standing at the altar, I could barely breathe and was hesitant to look around. When our two souls united as *one* in the eyes of the church, we ignited two elongated match sticks with a single unity candle. Then, we individually lit our own candles and, in unison, blew out the unity candle in the center. "*Wait, was that backward?*" Hilarious! The uncertainty broke, and we kissed as husband and wife.

We were all asked to congregate outside to finish pictures. My cheeks hurt from smiling so much that I quickly scurried to the bar for a drink. I asked Daniel why he seemed so calm, and he confessed they had been drinking in the groom's quarters. We were both apprehensive about the toasts because his best man was usually abrasive. We were wholeheartedly surprised when eloquent words came pouring out of his mouth, and he ended his speech with, "*I have never seen my best friend any happier.*"

As we feasted on Maryland-inspired surf and turf, the musician serenaded each table with his voice and violin while the smell of huge white Casa Blanca lilies permeated the air. Finally, the party moved onto the dance floor, and the musician turned into the DJ and played numerous selections we had chosen from our life together. We danced with our daughter to Sebastian, the lobster from *The Little Mermaid*, singing *Kiss the Girl*. "*Sha-la-la-la-la-la, don't be scared, you got the mood prepared, go on and kiss the girl.*"

Closing Time by Semisonic let our guests know we needed to open the doors and let everyone back into the world. Nobody needed to go home, but they couldn't stay here. Most importantly, "*Every new beginning was some other beginning's end, yeah.*" Unbeknownst to me, when the musician handed me our music attache case filled with over 200 CDs, it would be the last time we would ever see it. Our life in music is gone forever. It's funny how the unity candle and the music collection foresaw the future, although the rest of the wedding guests had no idea, including myself.

Georgia

The love and power of Jesus were strong in this part of the country. The Catholic church we attended was beautiful, with a massive window behind the altar overlooking the forest. Country music was definitely the song of the South and was continuously intertwined with the power of God. It was reminiscent of Hawaiian music, and we fell in love all over again. Those small-town country music festivals with farm-to-table food and cowboy hats could really satiate the soul.

As love songs say, I believed our love was deeper than the oceans and higher than the mountains. I felt like a wildflower growing in wide open spaces, smiling with the sun shining brightly on each new day. Every March, there was an enormous field of buttercups I could not pass without joy. One glorious day, my daughter and I were lying on the ground, allowing the tiny yellow flowers to glow under our chin. Suddenly, she kissed me and smiled. "*I love you.*"

As time passed and burdens set into our marriage, life got tough, but I knew we still had each other. Every once in a while, he still looked at me with genuine love in his eyes, and the dis-ease he was trying to hide faded away. During the week, our relationship was emotionally barren, but on the weekends, we found outdoor adventures to restore our love. One fond moment is when Elton John obviously sang this song for us, *"It's a little bit funny, this feelin' inside. I'm not one of those who can easily hide. I don't have much money, but boy, if I did, I'd buy a big house where we could both live."*

I have never done anything in my life for the sole pursuit of money. But Daniel seemed to be intricately weaving financial success and happiness, which was the opposite of his philosophy in the past. In turn, I maintained my focus on people and experiences that made me happy, believing the amount of money we needed to survive would follow.

To the north, *Amicalola Falls*, tumbling white water, is the southern approach to the Appalachian Trail. It was beautiful, but many areas were difficult to access. Some of the surrounding areas were more inviting for curious travelers. One of the most picturesque areas was an offshoot called Cade's Cove. It was a naturally majestic colonial settlement with abundant resources for all. The walking trails were like stepping back into a simpler time when Jesus called forth his new inhabitants.

To the west, the Etowah Mounds were situated alongside a river with a huge V-shaped fish trap. This landscape featured a ceremonial complex, burial grounds, and a highly developed village that was home to several thousand Native Americans who controlled trade along the Etowah River. I stood atop the highest mound and imagined looking down over the land which fed and clothed the people. I tried to picture what the men, women, and children were doing as they gathered. The similarities between the Hawaiian heiau and the Etowah mound astounded me as I breathed in the fullness of life.

Both areas contained abundant life energy and felt different deep within my soul. I had difficulty reconciling the conflict and decimation between these two groups of people, as they both seemed to exist as *salt of the earth*. This phrase is derived from Jesus' Sermon on the Mount (Matthew 5:13), where he addressed commoners like fishermen, shepherds, and laborers as worthy, virtuous, and of great value.

On the flip side, depression and anxiety were a daily concern for Daniel as a full-time graduate student. The stress was taking a toll on his health and our family. I fully understood the workload and pressure of obtaining an advanced degree, but I was increasingly despondent of carrying the burden of the expenses and household chores on my own. He continued to be an integral part of our daughter's life but regularly used her as a weapon to encourage strife in our marriage.

Any boundary or limit I set was unjustified; his goal was to be her savior. Mostly, I felt like she was an innocent victim of the situation. However, one night, I asked her to clean up her toys before dinner, and she got a little fussy. In turn, she ran over to Daddy with tears in her eyes. He immediately picked her up, hugged and kissed her, and then reprimanded me. At three years old, she peeked over his shoulder and smiled with a mischievous twinkle in her eye because she had won the battle.

Whew! I was mad as hell. Daniel snidely remarked, "*Cleaning the house is your duty.*" and walked away. My brain was spinning. What happened to my husband? Where did that man go? All this time, all this money, and no progress for my own vocation in life. I was sick and tired of hoping and praying the man I loved would show up and have any type of respect for me. I could not comprehend how selfish and self-absorbed he had become. (Reality #2)

Then, the next big wake-up call came when he attempted to complete his clinical competency exam with an elderly woman. All the information he regurgitated was in no way his area of expertise. He had always worked with children, and this documentation was embarrassing, to say the least. I rewrote a portion of his paper that made absolutely no sense, and he was enraged. Ultimately, his professors only liked my contribution, making him even more angry. The committee highly encouraged him to stay in his lane and told him he needed to repeat the exam, which meant another year of living in this chaos.

To add to my level of frustration, I had been unable to conceive another child. I sought medical advice from many providers and followed all of their guidelines. However, the doctors could not comprehend anything outside the norm, and their advice and medications faltered repeatedly. I felt as broken as my heart.

The Fire

Finally, I was referred to a doctor who believed she could help me. She was an OB/GYN with a specialized interest in fertility, so she preferred to help women conceive as naturally as possible. She showed me an ultrasound of my ovaries, and there was a plethora of tiny scattered white dots. She inquired, "*Do you know what these are?*" I hesitantly shook my head and said, "*No.*"

"*They are your eggs! You will have no problem conceiving; we just need to regulate when your menstruation will begin and end.*" I explained I had conceived my daughter the day my period ended several years before, and she replied, "*Of course!*" and explained the science behind my statement. Basically, my menstruation signaled my ovaries to produce or drop the necessary egg for conception. Meanwhile, a woman's egg usually drops 10-14 days into the cycle. This was the first time someone understood and believed the explanation of what I experienced. All the other doctors and nurses thought I was crazy or naive and dismissed my statements as nonsense.

About two months later, I woke up and felt discouraged. But it was time to urinate on the stick, so I went into the bathroom and waited. "*Positive! That's impossible!*" I knew there were false positives, so I repeated the test. "*Positive, again!*" I was so excited that I ran to pick up the phone to call Daniel. But I stopped myself. This time, I wanted to tell him in person and see the look on his face.

He had a department picnic that afternoon, and his family was invited to attend. As I started to approach the gathering, he met me halfway. I opened my hand and showed him the stick. Instantly, there was love in the air, and we held each other in a long embrace. Life was optimistic again. I became thankful for the extra year we had to spend in Georgia and delighted in the gifts we had received from God.

About a week after Valentine's Day, we settled into our evening with a very long and strange movie. I was surprised I stayed awake because I was about six months into my pregnancy. We had only been asleep briefly before we heard an overly intrusive banging at our door. Daniel ran towards the front door as I ran into our daughter's room to protect her.

"*Fire! We need to get out of the house!*" I scooped up my daughter and ran back to my bedroom to put some clothes on. All I could think about was saving my babies.

As we stood by our neighbors watching fourteen condos go up in flames, everyone responded to the stressful event in their own way. The firefighters asked everyone what they wanted to salvage from their house because they were willing to put themselves at risk for us. All I wanted was my wedding ring and my photo albums. Within minutes, I was handed my most cherished possessions.

A strange sense of calmness came over me. I felt a deep sense of peace while the chaos ensued around me. I simply wanted my family to be safe by my side.

I was dumbfounded by the requests of others and the intrusiveness of the media. One woman wanted her new color television and coat. One man was plotting to sue the fire company because the water pressure to extinguish the fire was insufficient. One reporter approached people with his microphone held out in front of him. I stepped forward, placed my hand above his device, and motioned for him to lower his arm. With an intense look in my eyes and a tempered voice, I softly demanded, "*Go away.*"

Hours passed, and there was no conception of time or reality. Eventually, the Red Cross arrived and gave us coupons for household supplies and clothing. Then, we slept in a spare room above the condo office offered to us for free. The next day, we opened our apartment's front door, and my daughter's shoe floated out in front of us. The place we called home had been flooded in black, cinder-filled water, and the stench of destruction was unbearable.

Over the next few days, we purchased a few essentials to get by. I wore the same eggplant purple sweat suit and sandals for days. It was so ugly that it became ridiculous; all I could do was laugh. At least it was warm and comfortable. Buying that first new pair of shoes was a spectacular event.

The pre-kindergarten center distributed a note explaining the situation and was taking donations. There was an entire room full of stuff and an envelope of checks. I was extremely uncomfortable. I was not poor; I did not need the help of others. I could take care of myself and was always the one to lend a helping hand. When I declined the assistance, a man pulled me aside and explained that these people wanted and needed to help. Moreover, I owned *nothing*. It was my turn to accept graciously.

Learning how to receive was much more difficult than learning how to give. Apparently, humans are genetically predisposed to give, but unfortunately, our society has taught some of us to respond the opposite way and focus on the receiving part. That has never been me. The *gimmie, gimmie, gimmie* people in this world drive me crazy. But, in this particular situation, I guess the universe was looking out for me, offering my family some assistance to get back onto our feet.

As a result of the fire, we all got the flu. My daughter and I slept it off after a few days, but I watched my husband lay in bed, suffering for weeks. During that time, I salvaged items from the wreckage and took care of all the insurance people, paperwork, and relocation processes. Unfortunately, we did not have enough insurance money, but that did not stop the *bottom feeders*: those opportunistic people who seek out quick profit at the expense of others, usually during a time of great misfortune.

Even after Daniel recovered, I felt alone in my efforts. I knew I needed to take care of everything, or it would never get done. In my heart, I viewed Daniel as less of a man. He laid around whimpering and feeling sorry for himself while the entire burden was placed on me and our unborn child. He should have taken care of us and put his own emotional problems aside. (Reality #3)

Day after day, I questioned, "*Why me?*" I thought, "*Just be strong, Amy. Everything will be all right.*" I wanted to wear my wedding ring, but my hands were swollen. Sometimes, I could put it on in the morning, but by the afternoon, I needed to remove it again. One day, my ring was lying on a tissue, and I unintentionally threw it in the trash. Suddenly, I saw something sparkling, and I went to investigate.

Oh my God! I almost lost my ring in the garbage. I held it tightly in my hand and went over to lie down on the bed. I was weary and exhausted. I needed something, anything. I just wanted to feel better. I turned on the air purifier and let the sun shine brightly through the window to warm my body. I imagined what it would be like to feel safe and protected as I gently drifted off to sleep.

Eventually, Daniel showed some gratitude for my efforts and started to help me a little around the house. I think he felt remorse for his actions and intermittently offered praise for what I had accomplished. Plus, he was finishing up everything he needed to achieve in his program.

Daniel planned a simple but extraordinary dinner for my birthday and bought many of my favorite foods. As we sat in an apartment filled with old, discarded items that were new to us, I looked around the room, and all I could feel was love. It didn't look, feel, or smell like home, but it was all we had. Most importantly, we had each other. I closed my eyes and thanked God for my family and my food. We had made it through the fire. We were expecting a new baby and planning to move back to Maryland. It was a great day.

A Gift from God

I started to feel lighter on my feet and anticipated the baby would be coming any day. This morning seemed like the rest, but I had small contractions. I dropped my daughter off at prekindergarten and went to run a few errands. Occasionally, I needed to stop, rub my belly, and take a few deep, refreshing breaths. Several people around me remarked the baby was on the way.

When I picked my daughter up, we went to our usual spot on the trails alongside the Chattahoochee River as she rode her bike, and I walked along with our dog. When we got home, she asked to go outside and play with the neighbor. I could feel my contractions getting a little stronger, so I called Daniel to ask him to come home. Then, a neighbor several buildings away called me. Apparently, my little girl had walked far out of the ordinary, and they were concerned.

As I walked to get her, the contractions became stronger and closer together. By the time I got back, Daniel was home, so I decided to take a shower and told him to call the hospital. Instantly, the hot water instigated my contractions to two minutes apart. They were so intense; my toes were curling up, and I had to hold onto the wall for support. The doctor could hear me over the phone and insisted we drive ourselves to the hospital immediately, as the ambulance would take too long.

Just my luck, the air conditioning in the car had stopped working two days earlier, and we were driving through rush hour traffic with the windows down. I had one foot on the dash and the other foot out the window. I am pretty sure all of Atlanta could hear me scream. Daniel ran red lights and weaved in and out of traffic. We were near the hospital when I felt the baby's head crown as my daughter's eyes bulged in awe. I envisioned myself in a magnificent deep underwater cave. I meditated, "*I am swimming. I am swimming. I am swimming,*" as I massaged the baby's head back inside of me.

When we pulled into the emergency entrance, I had another contraction. As I took my first step through the automatic doors, another contraction hit, and staff came running from every direction. They tossed me up on a stretcher and rushed me into an emergency room. I looked a nurse in the eyes and exclaimed, "*Give me something for the pain!*"

She grabbed my shoulders and exclaimed, *"Push!"* Within seconds, my beautiful baby boy was born. They cleaned him up and laid him on my abdomen. I felt overwhelming joy as I watched my family grow. My daughter was very kind and cautious as she took hold of my hand, while Daniel proudly looked down at her and said, *"Your mommy makes this look easy."*

My doctor arrived and apologized for missing the delivery. I apologized for making him return during dinner, saying he should be home with his family. He smiled and asked what I needed. I explained I wanted the IV out of my hand and to be discharged in 24 hours instead of the recommended 48 hours. Just like the first delivery, we were both perfectly happy and healthy, so there was no reason to stay in the hospital, eat nasty food, and pay thousands of extra dollars to sleep in an uncomfortable bed. I wanted to be at home with my family. He gave me a checklist; I would be free to go the following day if I completed it. I replied, *"Great, but there is one more thing. May I please have a cup of water? I am very thirsty."*

Our time in Georgia was limited, so we intended to make memories that we would remember for a lifetime. When my son was less than one week old, we took him on his first hike up Stone Mountain. I had hiked this historic trail before, but this time, it was different. All the moments I spent with my new family were enchanting, and all sources of contention and anxiety dissipated into the distance.

On Mother's Day, I prayed for all the moms in the world to be as happy as I was and for those who wanted to have children to be able to conceive. Being a mom is the best gift anyone can receive in this world.

Some friends and family joined us for vacation on Tybee Island, and I saw glimmers of the man I loved so dearly. Late one evening, we took our daughter to chase fiddler crabs with flashlights on the beach. Hundreds of little critters scurrying around under the stars brought love and laughter into our hearts. Life was beautiful again, but now it was time to go.

On our drive back to Maryland, we tied a blue children's bed that looked like a race car on top of the van, with a life-size Pink Panther in the driver's seat. It was such a delight to see the look on the faces of those who passed by. Once we were back in Maryland, we had to stay with both sets of grandparents until we could clean up our house from the tenants who had been renting for the past five years. It was a disgusting mess and took a couple of months to complete.

Finally, we were back in our house, and I enrolled my daughter in kindergarten. When I met the other moms, I was puzzled by their very direct way of asking questions to categorize me and my family into a box. Gradually, I discovered that Baltimore still had a small-town mentality and that where you go to high school is of the utmost importance. This little game amused me, and I purposely did not offer the expected responses. Eventually, I answered their questions, and the typical response I received back from them was, "*Oh, you are a blue blood!*" which always made me want to laugh.

I was blessed to grow up in Montgomery County, just outside of Washington, DC. I attended school with people of every color, nationality, and religion. I went to their house, ate their food, and listened to them speak and sing in their native tongues. I thought that was normal, and we were all friends. As a kid, you believe everyone has what you have, and differences are fun and not frowned upon. Plus, my school was big, and we had access to so many different avenues in life. In my opinion, this arrogant, naive blue-blood nonsense was such a joke. I did my best to avoid those types of people and situations.

We had to be here for one year, after which we would find out where Daniel's final internship would be. I could not focus on settling down and creating a new life because I knew it would change again very soon. Instead, I created a happy little home, babysat a few children before and after school, and cleaned the neighbors' houses for extra money. It was enjoyable to have so many smiling faces surrounding me each day. Plus, our dog seemed to be in baby heaven. She had never had puppies, and tending to my son brought her great maternal pleasure. Sometimes, it almost felt like Ashley was human.

Part of me enjoyed being in a state of flux because I was excited about where in the world we could go next. But another part of me wanted to create a permanent home for my family. I figured everything would be fine as long as we were settled while my daughter was still in elementary school. After five years of hard work and sacrifice, I looked forward to finally getting something in return. Peace, love, and financial security were just around the corner.

CHAPTER 3

⟨✦⟩

THE NIGHTMARE

Adjusting my mindset from peace, love, and security to watching our nation become fearful and insecure was a massive blow. I felt freedom was something many of us took for granted. None of us had ever witnessed war in our land. The question was, *"Do we stand united or fall apart?"*

I thought back to a time when war ravaged our land. During the American Civil War, approximately 750,000 Americans died on American soil at the hands of Americans. Yes, we destroyed ourselves. Abraham Lincoln was president when one very important verb to describe our country changed. We went from the United States *are…* to the United States *is…* think about the connotations in our country as a whole and your personal endeavors. Contemplate the loss of innocence of our children; no matter how many wishes they blew into the wind, our existence would never be the same.

Watching the Towers Fall

I was standing in line at a home goods store on the morning of September 11, 2001, when I found out the towers had fallen in New York. A woman explained that the schools were closing, but it made no sense to me as I was in Maryland. Regardless, I headed to my daughter's school to pick her up. It was pure chaos: locked doors, frantic administrators on radios, red-faced teachers running through the halls. *"Calm down, people; you are supposed to be the leaders for our children,"* I thought, dismayed.

In the parking lot, I overheard a man explaining the situation to his son and asked him to explain it to me as well. By this time, much more devastating information had been disseminated through the various news stations concerning the attacks in America. The strangest feeling permeated every ounce of my soul. Now, I know I was in shock. But I thought, *"If I don't go home, it doesn't have to be real."*

I turned to my daughter and asked what she would like to do, "Go out to lunch!" she said, and I thought that sounded like a perfect idea. We headed to her favorite Mediterranean restaurant and ordered a combination plate of appetizers. We loved their hummus, baba ghanoush, falafel, and grape leaves. The owners loved my children and always greeted us with big smiles and extra pita bread.

They turned on the television, and pictures of men in turbans flashed before our eyes. Woefully, the men behind the counter gazed upon the hatred running rapidly through the airways as they donned their turbans and momentarily looked to the ground. When their heads arose, I looked them in the eyes and gave them a somber smile. Together, we mourned the loss of lives and the world we knew.

At this point, I did not have a cell phone. Fortunately, I got home in time to get one phone call from my mother before the lines of communication had been shut down. All you could hear was static. My mom explained Daniel was stuck between Georgia and Maryland in the mountains. Nobody knew when they would reopen the highways, and I had no idea when I would see my husband again.

For a few days, I turned the news on for a couple of minutes; it was all I could handle because the devastation made me cry, not just a typical cry, but a cry from deep within my soul. War was in our land, and it felt like we were no longer the home of the free and the brave. We were emotionally locked down, and everyone seemed to be on edge. Many seemed to view all foreigners as the enemy, even though the turmoil was coming from a select few. I felt like it was my job to keep the peace.

Finally, Daniel arrived home, and I expected to wrap my arms around him and feel safe. I expected to feel love like my family was home together. But Daniel ran around expressing anger and craving revenge. He avoided me and the children. We were an unwelcome distraction. I did not expect this, nor did I know how to handle his reactions. I felt sad, isolated, and confused. In turn, I focused all my energy on the children and thought, *"A real man would protect us from harm."* (Reality #4)

In hindsight, it felt like he was the first tower to fall, and he was signaling the next plane to crash into mine and take me down with him. On several occasions, I explained revenge would ravage the soul and the only way to *"win the war"* was to take care of your family and build a better tomorrow.

Part of the underlying frustration causing his rage was that his application for a post-doctorate in the military had been denied. I told him he should be grateful to God for *not* allowing him to enter the military and for *not* sending him to war. Just because you pray for something and it does not come to fruition doesn't mean you are a failure; it means God has another plan in mind for you.

Daniel thoroughly enjoyed working at the Veterans Affair hospital. He was helping adults regain their mental health and genuinely connected with several of the staff, especially his supervisor. I think they were good for each other in many ways and helped each other navigate personal and professional issues. Again, I saw hope and prosperity heading our way.

The following Valentine's Day, there was a massive snowstorm. For some unknown reason, his supervisor and his fancée had parked their car on the side of Interstate 95 northbound, not too far from the exit near their house. They proceeded to walk across six lanes of highway to the southbound side. Tragically, they were struck by an oncoming vehicle and died instantly. Nobody could comprehend why they chose to take this course of action.

Understandably, Daniel endured a difficult grieving period. But the narrative *he created* greatly disturbed me. In his version of the story, the entire situation was unequivocally the fiancée's fault. He had no evidence to draw his conclusion. Daniel's verdict was simply derived from the fact that *he thought she was crazy*. He could not distance himself from the situation that had compounded our lives. Further, his indecisiveness about completing the doctorate program perpetuated our state of flux.

Stepping Stones

As Daniel's emotional state continued to erode, our future looked uncertain, and the husband I knew was fading away right before my eyes. He barely paid attention to the children, and I was always an afterthought. His mind was a million miles away and consumed with anxiety and isolation.

Daniel told me he quit the doctorate program in the same spot where I learned via phone that he had been accepted into the program. The only difference was that the message had transformed from *"It's for you"* into *"I am going to leave you."* Basically, the *you* part stayed the same. I realized this entire endeavor was never about me or our family; it was about him and his desperate need to prove himself worthy as *the son of a doctor*.

I jokingly made SOD an unofficial diagnosis in the DSM Handbook. People with this diagnosis had an overwhelming desire to brag about their position in life and have an unwavering fear of success coupled with an unwavering fear of failure. Since I understood and, unfortunately, had to cohabitate with this diagnosis of a man, I continuously reminded him that the pathway to success was filled with steppingstones and completing the program was just the next step in the process.

I tried to convince Daniel to stop letting fear rewrite the past and dictate the future. Overcoming fear is an integral part of life. Courage is not living in the absence of fear; courage expands itself to conquer fears and uncover the warrior that lies within. In essence, remember who you are!

Unfortunately, I felt doctors focused on illness while I preferred to focus on health. If you spend your entire life focusing on what is *wrong* with people, you will never focus on what is *right* with them. You will never be able to see who they genuinely are and what is actually going on with their health. In turn, I wanted to create a holistic healing center that addressed the entire person and proactively sought health options to dissipate or banish the symptoms and origins of their *dis-ease*.

Without my knowledge or input, Daniel withdrew himself from the doctorate program. Yes…I mean, he secretly terminated five years of work behind my back. A whirlwind of thoughts and emotions pulsated through my mind. I was angry, sad, hurt, disgusted, and confused. I helped him every step of the way and supported *his dream* because I thought it was *our dream*. We were supposed to be a team.

Who in the fuck would waste five years of schooling and incur $100,000 in debt only to quit the doctorate program after requesting three years of extensions? The research was completed, outlined, and approved. All he needed to do was to sit down and write *one* forty-page dissertation. The title Daniel had chosen was ' *The Non-Pharmacological Approach to Treating Otherwise Healthy Adult Men Experiencing Panic Disorder.*" After all, he had been diagnosing and treating himself and others with tangible progress. Why was it such a problem for him to write this dissertation and graduate?

Further, his schooling meant my dream of a medical career had been put on hold. I worked to support and provide for our family as we moved from place to place and took whatever jobs I could get. All that fucking time, money, and effort with no reward. I could not fathom being a quitter in the final stretch of the game. No *real* man would do that to his wife and children. Rage entered my soul like a wildfire burning in a desolate forest. I thought, "*Hell hath no fury like a woman scorned.*"

After listening to his feeble-minded excuse, Daniel shared his letter of resignation from the program. I resentfully replied, "*One day, I am going to leave you,*" and walked away. I guess he was waiting for an over-exaggerated response or reprimand. I couldn't waste any more time and energy on a battle I had already lost. (Reality #5) Part of me left my marriage that day; it was never the same.

Life is an amazing teacher, and I love to learn. The marriage was filled with opportunities. I was curious: Did Daniel know what having a degree would mean even if he never decided to practice? Did he know how much validity it would afford for our business? Did he know how much I had invested in him and how he took me for granted and took away my dream? Did he know what I could have accomplished with my degree? Well, the answer to those questions was Yes. But guess what? He didn't care, and he made that perfectly clear. Easy street wasn't that easy after all.

At that point, I needed to reconstruct my thinking. Returning to school for an advanced degree while raising two children seemed daunting and expensive. Further, I wanted to raise my children and not depend on extended school hours and daycare options. In the eight years I spent supporting our household, I learned a tremendous amount of information on how to physically, emotionally, and financially support a family. Now, I was onto *my* next steppingstone.

Our new elderly neighbors quickly became family. They had raised three children and adopted three more. She loved to read books and do artwork with her grandchildren. They had a typical marriage of that generation, meaning she took care of all the household chores, food, and gatherings.

Every time my son disappeared, I could always find him in their dining room with a cookie and a glass of milk. When I asked them their secret to a happy marriage, Dick joyously slapped his hands like a circus conductor and laughed, "*Just keep moving!*" While Emily affectionately nodded her head with an "*I love you, but you are quite a handful*" type of look.

Dick taught us the basic framework to buy and sell property. He had been a professor most of his life and loved to relocate through teaching positions. He also had a side business with a house and land in each location. This created a win-win situation to help finance their travels. While this business philosophy seemed risky as a full-time career, we surmised several opportunities for improvement and a plan for success. In turn, we used *my stock* to purchase our first three properties.

The first two properties were tricky because I needed to find a lender that would allow us to purchase rental properties without prior experience. Back then, the various lenders were in the middle fold of the newspaper. So, I simply started at the top of the page and worked my way down. Around 50%, I got a little discouraged from being turned down and sometimes laughed at. Around 75%, I was discouraged but determined to call every lender before giving up. Finally, with only a few options left, I found the one. He was young, enthusiastic, and followed the current rules and regulations.

I loved revitalizing the charm and integrity of this aging community. Most of the original owners were World War II Veterans who took great pride in the neighborhood. However, since the 1980s, a stream of absentee landlords looking to make a quick buck created much turmoil and destruction. My job was to restore the health and vibrance to these heroes as well as create opportunities for first-time home buyers. Every time I finished a job, I felt a genuine and expansive sense of accomplishment.

The plan was to buy three houses and sell two every year. The ones we kept remained rental units, while the two we sold were single-family homes. Most importantly, all the units were impeccably restored. Additionally, I was highly selective with my tenants and considered many like family. Collectively, we took great pride in our little section of the world, and our street became our home.

I created a system to locate dilapidated houses and basically pay the current landlord *to go away*. I learned how to cut out the middleman in almost every step of the process to maximize profits. Plus, I created and executed all legal and contractual agreements. Every detail was clear and concise. This was a highly personalized and respectful family business; the community soon noticed.

I restored all the kitchens and bathrooms, meticulously cleaned and prepped everything for painting inside and outside the house, and landscaped according to the seasons. Each paint color and light fixture was warm and accentuated the refinished solid wood floors, giving each house its own unique glow. I did not consider my projects complete until I felt like I would rent the apartment for myself. I loved to see the enthusiasm in the eyes of the people who would one day call this home.

One adorable couple invited our family to dinner after their move-in was complete. While toasting the guests, he reverently nodded, "*Mi casa es su casa y su casa es mi casa*," and kissed my cheeks. We feasted on some Costa Rican specialties and the *incredible sopa de mondongo*. In turn, I asked her for a recipe translation and had no idea it was tripe soup. Fortunately, or should I say, unfortunately, the local grocery store carried *tripe* (stomach lining from cattle) so I bought two pounds and the remaining ingredients to prepare the soup myself.

Note to Self: Never assume you know what you are doing when boiling the stomach lining of farm animals. The overwhelmingly ridiculously horrible stench lasted for days, and I had to throw out the entire meal.

Life seemed to be moving along on an upward swing, and our business was prospering. I got to be an integral part of my children's lives and volunteered at their school for various social and athletic activities. Coaching basketball was by far the best. Teaching skills to a gym full of happy, smiling faces invigorated my mind, body, and soul. I had forgotten how much basketball meant to me. Unfortunately, a series of unfortunate events was about to cast a dark shadow over our success and happiness.

Several friends and family members passed, as did our beloved dog. Ashley did not know she was a dog until my daughter was born. Once she overcame her initial confusion, she became the perfect companion for my children. There was a human quality about her I have never seen in another dog. Often, she did things that truly amazed me. Losing her definitely changed our family. The crazy part is that she passed on my daughter's birthday, and I do not believe it was a coincidence or mistake.

The next big loss was when our neighbor, Emily, found a lump in her breast and had it surgically removed, followed by a round of chemotherapy. One morning, after a hot bath, she asked Dick to help her out of the tub. He put on tea as she sat in her soft white bath robe on the sofa. Emily called out his name for the last time as she gasped one last breath, and her heart stopped beating. Dick appeared to handle the ceremonies with composure and celebrated 68 years of a beautiful marriage and friendship. However, within a few weeks, the loss became too devastating for him, and he started to disintegrate emotionally.

He took comfort in a lady friend he had known since childhood. They grieved their recent losses together and decided to get married. It was great to see two people in the golden age of their lives run around like teenagers in love. Although many members of their families were offended by the situation, I was happy to see two people gain another chance in life. Nobody deserves to suffer alone.

These losses took a tremendous toll on Daniel, and he chose to suffer alone. I have no idea what he was thinking, as he avoided conversations unless it was to complain. Meanwhile, I felt an insatiable need to become emotionally stronger to be strong enough for everyone else, especially my children. When tragedy strikes, suffering dissipates when you are surrounded by love.

Photographs of the Soul

Most of the houses we restored had previously been owned by someone who had physically passed onto the next realm. The spirits that lingered in the houses seemed to accompany me in my work, subtly guiding me with tasks I needed to complete. These tasks were never clearly defined until I finished the work. Then, their souls revealed the spiritual reconciliation of their journey with mine, allowing them to finally ascend. These moments were not tangible, but they were distinct and powerful.

I was not the only one who sensed these souls; many others did. My children were in tune with this energy, and I was delighted to listen to their musings. Since my son was still very young, he verbalized his *intuitions as truth,* while my daughter was older and verbalized her *intuitions as potential questions.* Either way, I validated their experiences.

Once, while my daughter was in a master bedroom suite trying on some vintage jewelry, I heard her shriek. She ran out to find me, clearly startled. *"I think Hazel made me look like I was one hundred years old in the mirror!"* she exclaimed. I replied, *"Are you sure it was you, or was Hazel using you to see herself wearing her jewelry?"*

She contemplated and said, *"I'm not sure."* I suggested she return and ask Hazel for permission to look through the bedroom and see if she could keep a few items. I asked, *"Think about it. Would you want someone to look through your stuff?"* From then on, my daughter was very respectful and spoke to the lady protecting the bedroom. She had opportunities to wear the accessories she chose to keep, and a vintage hat, purse, and jewelry made her book report on Audrey Hepburn a huge success.

However, these spirits were not isolated in the houses where I worked. One little boy named Rif seemed to live on our back deck. My son would go outside to play and have conversations with him for hours. My son was a bit disgruntled a couple of days after we moved into our new house. I suggested he go out back and play with Rif.

He promptly put his hands on his hips and gave me a grumpy face. "*What?*" I asked.

Then my three-year-old informed me, "*Rif isn't outside; he lives in our other house.*" I apologized and explained I thought he had invited Rif to come and live with us here. He nodded and replied, "*Mommy, it doesn't work that way.*" Hmm. I was so curious to learn more. "*How about we make peanut butter and jelly sandwiches and talk?*" His eyes brightened, "*We have that here?*"

Conversations about parallel realms of existence intrigued my senses and often sent chills down my spine. Sometimes, I felt I might have missed my true calling. But hey, I was helping people reconcile life issues and providing safe, happy spaces while raising my children. So, *maybe* I was on the right path.

Contrary to what everyone else saw, Daniel was almost always annoyed with my attention to detail concerning the people and the houses. He wanted me just to hurry up and get the job done. His main frustrations centered around my desire to preserve or repurpose the past. Daniel wanted to focus on the end result, to make as much *easy* money as possible, which was not our original intention. This shift in operational goals caused much controversy in our relationship.

As for the spirits, Daniel desperately wanted to deny or dismiss my *crazy ghost stories,* but I felt something inside him wanted to believe. He stayed quiet and listened when I was communicating with the children, which, in my mind, was a step in the right direction.

One day, as I was dismantling wood paneling in a closet that Daniel thought was a complete waste of time, I discovered a large envelope. It contained two gorgeous sepia-toned prints of a woman from the WWII era. In excitement, I said to myself, "*This must be it! I think my task was to find this envelope.*" I ran over to a neighbor's house, and they confirmed it was Mary, the deceased wife of Jimmy, the man I bought the house from. He was one of the few remaining survivors from the Battle of Normandy in 1944. Mary was the light and love of his life. This discovery stopped Daniel in his tracks.

Everyone knew one of my favorite things in the world was to take pictures and give them as gifts. Whether I put them in an envelope, an album, or a frame, I loved seeing the joy on the faces of those receiving my gifts. I loved to walk into people's homes and see the artwork I had created from my heart. I wished I could have seen Jimmy's face when he opened the envelope I mailed with Mary's photograph inside.

Jimmy had said I was one of three angels who had saved him. The first was a figure in white who had held him back from tumbling down a set of stairs when he was about three years old, potentially saving his life. The second was a figure in black who pulled him from beneath the dirt after a bomb blast had buried him alive in France. And the third was me, the lady who saved him and helped him start to relive life.

I was saddened when my longtime companion, otherwise known as my camera, finally broke beyond repair. To my surprise, Daniel decided to purchase a digital camera. While I appreciated taking an abundance of pictures and storing them on the computer, the quality of the images and prints was not up to my standards. The film camera just produced so much more richness and depth. Further, creating albums and gifts became more cumbersome, as the digital images were stored on Daniel's computer and were not easily accessible.

In turn, I asked Santa for another camera for Christmas.

Every year, the kids and I made homemade Christmas ornaments. This year, we would make clothespin dolls with an acorn top. The tops can look like hats or hairstyles, depending on how you paint them. We painted and glued an array of characters perfectly suited for the Nutcracker Suite. As the lights on the tree glistened over their costumes, they magically came to life. We made enough to share with the extended family; each person could choose their favorite as a special gift.

That year, I made a family photo album for Daniel and a scrapbook for my daughter, which included pictures of her and her friends, certificates, awards, and selected schoolwork. She helped me pick out some stationery and decorations, but the finished work of art was to remain hidden until Christmas Day

I woke up very early that morning, cleaned the house, and made a delicious breakfast. Santa had clearly visited, as the tree was surrounded by colorfully wrapped gifts of all shapes and sizes. The shiny ribbons and bows added to the excitement of uncovering the magic in their eyes. The wrapping paper disappeared one by one, and all the joyous gifts had been given and received with love.

But there was nothing for me. *Nothing.* I sat on the sofa, watching the joy on the faces of my children and husband, but I felt overwhelmed by the emptiness. My mind felt numb, and there was a humming in my ears. My breath was shallow as I got up and asked everyone to get ready for Christmas at the next house. I told everyone I was tired and didn't feel well, so I needed to lie down for a few minutes before we left. I tried to convince myself there must be a logical explanation and that I needed to stay strong and hide my emotions. I wanted to enjoy the day.

A few weeks later, I swallowed my pride, handed Daniel an advertisement for cameras on clearance, and inquired if he was waiting for a high-quality camera to go on sale for me. He brushed the paper aside and said, "*Why would you want that? It's a complete waste of time and money*". (Reality #6)

At that moment, a part of my soul left me to escape the pain. The rest of me was torn between crying and lashing out in anger. Everything I loved was slowly being whittled away and deemed a waste of time and money. It was like I was looking at myself in the distance, wondering, "*Amy, where did you go?*"

In Native American culture, they believed permitting people to take a photograph allowed the photographer to *steal your soul*. I wondered how they would feel if they knew *not* being able to take a photograph was, in its own way, stealing my soul.

The Sound of Silence

Initially, after he quit the doctorate program and we became successful with our property investment company, Daniel seemed to be happy and productive. But soon enough, the anxiety and depression returned in full force, and the drinking compounded his issues. I had always been aware that he drank too much and too often, but he always seemed to have it under control. It didn't seem to be a huge issue until now. When I questioned him, he laughed it off with a smug reply, "I am just self-medicating." He just didn't know how to be happy, and his overwhelming desire to take away my happiness was exacerbated. Any glimmer of a smile from me immediately prompted him to tear me down.

I thought moving into an upper-class neighborhood would somehow help Daniel regain his self-confidence and improve our marriage. His mother's long-term hospitalization was casting an ominous shadow, and I tried to understand his situation. Some days, the family was hopeful, but other days, there was a dark silence. Initially, she was supposed to recover, but eventually, she was sent to hospice; her body was failing. Day after day, I watched him follow the same routine: wake up late, drink coffee, watch the news, go to work for a few hours, then come home just in time for dinner. Afterward, he watched TV or played video games and drank a six-pack of beer. Living with the ghost of a man was sad and isolating.

I watched my husband dig himself into a hole. I am not talking about a small hole where you could plant a beautiful tree. Instead, I am describing a large, gaping hole deep and dark enough to devour anyone who dared approach. He dug this hole relentlessly, and most nights, he found comfort in sleeping alone. Watching the father of your children, your husband, and your best friend sit on the couch after dinner and drink himself to sleep while incessantly clicking the remote through a barrage of B-rated movies was vulgar. I had no space in his misery besides being a weary recipient of his outbursts.

I was repulsed that his mother, whom he claimed to love, lay in a hospital bed about ten minutes from our house for over a year, and he did not make any attempt to visit her. Finally, I insisted he go and take the children to see their grandmother. It's difficult to comprehend how someone will react to the potential loss of a parent. However, complete neglect was not in any way acceptable to me.

Unfortunately, Daniel only visited his mother twice before we got the call. The machines were going to be turned off. With regret in his eyes, he mourned, "*She never got to see the house. She never got to see me be successful.*" (Reality #7)

Part of me had empathy because I could never imagine losing my mother. However, his statement about her never seeing his success enraged me. Why couldn't he see that having a wife and children and building a future together was indeed success?

Ironically, the night before that call, Daniel's mother appeared to me in a dream. She purposely kept her distance and did not speak words from this realm. She stood in a doorway with a look of solemn acceptance. Then, she reached out her hand and gazed into my eyes. I heard her say, "*I am sorry,*" as she vanished from sight. When I awoke, I felt strange, almost as if the dream was real. Curiously, that morning, both my children individually told me Grandma had entered their dreams and was sitting in her living room with them. A sharp and sudden chill went down my spine as I explained we were heading to visit Grandma one last time. I couldn't get her vision or her words out of my mind.

The family prayerfully gathered around the hospital bed to wish her safe passage. Grandpa exited the room before we received the official time of death. As the door closed behind him, her bed ascended, but the family dismissed the glorious departure and blamed the mechanics of the hospital bed. I believe he knew the moment his wife's spirit left her physical body. However, I was not allowed to speak these words into existence because I had always been considered an outsider.

The funeral and memorial services were beautiful. There were many dedications to a life well lived. She had grown up in a small town, became a distinguished nurse, raised seven children, and was involved in many artistic and youth ventures. In addition to the grief of a wife, mother, and grandmother passing, I felt deep sadness that I was never *allowed in.*

Her entire life seemed to be a fortress guarded by a pack of angry soldiers hiding in small, dark, and lonely passages. Every time I saw a glimpse of that beautiful woman, she would retreat into the fortress as I was cast out into the barren fields.

Everyone was dealing with their grief in their own way. However, at that point, Daniel crawled into that deep, dark hole of destruction, threw away the ladder, and wrapped himself in a blanket of despair. Even though I cried and prayed every day he would return, I never saw him again.

We lived in the same house, shared two children, and ran a business, but Daniel was dead inside. His thoughts were a million miles away, and he stopped speaking to me unless it was something incredibly offensive and derogatory. His skin turned a muted green, and dark black circles surrounded his eyes. His odor became harsh and acidic, like an old bar room floor, as the beer bottles lay empty.

I would burn candles each night before bed, read books, and pray for my husband to return. I did not know who this stranger was living in my house, nor did I want to know him. He never sat beside me, held my hand, or kissed me. I resented him for ignoring the children and teaching them how *not* to love. As I watched my husband metaphorically die, I was forced to listen to him call me *"fat, ugly, and disgusting"* every single day in front of our children. I felt incredibly broken.

I was spiritually weak and physically numb, even though I kept a smile on my face. I needed something to survive. My best friend then suggested I join a women's Bible study. She said, *"The best way to have a friend is to be a friend."* Reluctantly, I showed up on Wednesday morning and listened to the discussion. It was interesting and enjoyable, but I debated whether I would return.

At the end of the gathering, a song by Casting Crowns resonated with me, asking, *"Who Am I?"* Amy. Amy. Who am I that God would intentionally break the silence and call out my name? *Amy.* Why would God desire to help guide me into the light and heal my wandering heart... really *Who Am I? Amy.* I desperately needed to find the answer. I arrived every Wednesday morning for the next few years, hoping my heart would be able to hear the song of love singing my name joyfully once again.

On the second Mother's Day after Grandma's passing, I insisted we visit her grave site since we had not been there since the burial. The children were enthusiastic, and Daniel begrudgingly agreed, so I clipped flowers from my garden. I wasn't sure what they were because I had revived the plant the year before. They were big and white like a flaky snowball, and the sweet scent could fill the room.

When I got into the car, Daniel looked at me with bewilderment in his eyes. *"Why did you pick those?" he asked.* I explained they were beautiful and would probably only last a few more days. Clearing his throat, he described how those flowers used to adorn the side of his house while growing up. They were his mother's favorite and attracted hundreds of butterflies each spring.

As we entered the cemetery, he could not remember her location. I navigated our way through the winding roads and asked him to park near a large tree. As we neared her gravestone, a giant red and black ladybug landed on Daniel's shoulder. I said, *"Look! There is Grandma. She is helping us find the way."* That ladybug stayed on his shoulder throughout our visit, and the children loved the thought of their grandmother visiting us in such a playful way.

Literally, every adventure we went on for the next several years, a ladybug would join us. Coincidence? Hmm, maybe, but this one may make you think. We were headed to explore Death Valley, a desert valley in the northern Mojave Desert in Eastern California. I read it was one of the most intriguing places in the world to visit. Unintentionally, I discovered **The Sound of Silence,** which I define as the lack of noise pollution continuously infiltrating our minds and distracting us from hearing the truth.

In this magical world, you can hear a bug crawl across a pebble, a bird's wing gliding through the air, or even a lizard scurrying to the stream. As I stood with my daughter, I beckoned her to distinguish between her father's and brother's footsteps on the other side of a large sand mound where we were hiking. Suddenly, she became aware of the sounds silence can afford, and you could see a striking difference in her eyes.

As we stood upon a wooden overlook and gazed upon an ancient underwater rainbow-colored mountain, a ladybug landed on the handrail in front of us. Grandma had come for a visit. Just for a moment, try to *believe*. Better yet, look inside yourself or ask others if any signs from nature may originate from those who have passed onto the next realm and have returned to be with you. Maybe they would just like to accompany you on your journey, or perhaps they have a message for your heart. Either way, *pay attention* and learn to listen to what else is being communicated in the world.

Cookies

I had found an old 1940s radio in working condition, put it in the living room, and turned it on while writing some Christmas cards. One station featured traditional Christmas music without lyrics, perfectly accentuating our theme for that year's ornaments. We were going to make gingerbread men and women. I added glue to the cookie mixture, so the decorations were not edible.

The children were painting the first layer of clothing onto their ornaments in the kitchen when their dad walked through the front door. They immediately invited him to join in the festivities. He came in, threw his dirty stuff on the counter, and picked up a paint brush. Within a few minutes, Daniel carelessly globbed a bunch of paint on a few cookies, turned off my music, and started playing video games. *"Hey, why don't you all come and play with me!"* he exclaimed to the children.

I walked over and stood in front of the television, blocking his view. *"What is wrong with you?"* I asked. He motioned for me to move and insisted I stop ruining his fun. I was infuriated. I picked up the remote and turned the television off. "*Really, what is wrong with you?*" Daniel belted out a long, winded, confusing tirade that had absolutely nothing to do with me. I yelled, "*I did nothing to you. Why do you always take your anger and frustration with the world out on me?*

"*Well, who else am I going to take it out on!*" he boorishly shouted. I quickly replied, "*Here is a brilliant idea. How about the person you are actually mad at!*" I took this opportunity to throw a little more fuel on the fire, reminding him that it was almost Christmas. I wasn't going to allow him to ruin it again only to point the finger of blame at me for being upset.

I hadn't received a Christmas present in several years, and I sternly informed Daniel that he *would* give me a present this year. Further, he would help the children buy or make something for me. I specifically stated, "*It can cost anywhere between $1 and $1000, but it needs to come from your heart.*" I told him I was determined to enjoy Christmas as a whole family. It was critically important for him to remember who he was supposed to be in this world and allow love to come back into our marriage.

On Christmas eve, I spent hours cleaning the house and kitchen. The next morning, I woke up early and prepared a yummy breakfast. I received a small gift from each of the children, made during school activities, and I was anxious to see what Daniel had prepared.

I bought a red travel trunk with shiny brass latches for Daniel's Christmas present. I went to his high school, university, and a travel agency to acquire stickers, making the trunk appear to be around for a long time. Inside, I placed a collection of jerseys, awards, and pictures he had from before we were married. The trunk had an oddly shaped key, which I attached to a card I personally made for him. The words "*You don't know where you are going until you know where you came from*" encircled the key. Upon opening my present, Daniel cried and took a few minutes to show the kids the contents.

When all the wrapping paper was stuffed into a bag, and the children were preoccupied with playing with their new toys, I quietly sat on the sofa, feeling completely defeated. I had gone out of my way to make Christmas wonderful, and again, I received *nothing*. I was baffled. Five long years and running with no presents on Christmas for me while the entire living room was filled with gifts for everyone else. Sadly, I looked him in the eyes and softly asked, *"Did you get me anything?"*

With disgust, Daniel snidely remarked, *"You are so selfish to expect anything. What is wrong with you anyway?"* Then, he quickly left the room and headed to take a shower. I was left to clean up the mess alone. I felt completely alone, unappreciated, and unloved. I tried to hold myself together. It wasn't easy. As we drove over to the next celebration, we passed an old purple building that had been for sale, and he asked about the price. Daniel thought it was a perfect location for *"Fat Amy's Sandwiches."*

I asked, *"What do you mean by Fat Amy's Sandwiches?"* He threw his arm up, savagely laughed, and replied, *"I meant Amy's Fat Sandwiches. This place would be a great location for people to grab a quick bite."* I put my head down and tried not to cry. Daniel asked why I took everything so personally and threw out accusations, blaming me for ruining the entire day, even though it was still morning.

We arrived at our destination within an hour, and as usual, I pretended everything was normal. Technically, it *was* normal. Nobody seemed to know my normal was pure fucking shit. I never complained about my marriage outside of the marital home. I kept the pain, frustration, and anger hidden within my soul and away from the world. Besides being miserable, I was embarrassed for myself and my family.

Just before dinner, I accidentally menstruated all over my pants. I was thankful I was sitting on a wooden chair because a fabric one would have been destroyed. I grumbled to myself, *"Great, just the present I needed."* Quickly, I cleaned myself up, changed into some clothes I received, and stayed quiet. I told everyone I had cramps and didn't feel well. Daniel was intoxicated and had not spoken a word to me all day. He acted oblivious to what was really going on and pretended to have a great time.

As we started to drive home, Daniel initiated a brutal tirade. Apparently, I had ruined Christmas, and was completely disgusting. The kids were behind us and heard every word, although I did not respond. Eventually, the children fell asleep while I looked out the window in deep thought. After arriving home, we put the kids to bed, and I went into the bedroom to get ready to sleep. Initially, Daniel was watching television in the living room. But for some reason, he came into the bedroom.

By this point, I wanted to be alone. I was sad, angry, and had no desire to speak. I am not exactly sure what he said or if he spoke at all. But I distinctly looked at him and said in an ominous voice, *"Daniel, I am going to leave you"* (Reality #8); as I got into bed facing away from his glare, I pulled the blanket over me and closed my eyes. He did not reply, and I assume he went back to watching television.

A few days into the new year, I printed out divorce papers from the internet. I filled out my section and placed the documents on Daniel's computer keyboard. He never said a word. *Really, not one.* We were at a juncture in the road; he was headed left, and I was headed right. As far as I was concerned, there was no turning back. For the next year, I regularly told myself, *"Amy, this is the last holiday, birthday, special occasion, and vacation you will have with your family. Make it the best you can."*

I had control over my behavior and would be as happy as possible. I stopped waiting for him to serve dinner. I stopped asking him to go places with me and the children. Most noticeably, I stopped staying up for him to come home after drinking with his softball buddies. That move was a home run. Daniel knew I had changed, but he never mentioned a word.

I must admit I was a bit mischievous at times. I added cardamom to as many recipes as possible for the next year. These green seed pods add a spicy herbal warmth indicative of various Indian dishes. The seeds inside create that sweet, peppery aroma you can't quite identify in your chai. The kids loved adding it to my homemade oatmeal, cranberry, dark chocolate chip cookie recipe. A couple of those cookies straight out of the oven with a cup of coffee is pretty darn close to heaven.

The only problem with this scrumptious, healthy, and wonderfully aromatic spice is that Daniel hated it. Excuse me for a moment. I can't stop laughing.

Red in the Morning

Eight months had passed, and Daniel had not mentioned *one* word about the divorce papers I put on his desk. I guess he presumed I was not being serious, but he was dead wrong. Somehow, I emotionally detached myself from the situation enough to have a clear head. I knew I was leaving, and it brought me a sense of peace. I was determined not to have any ill will or negative feelings be my fault. I am unsure what he thought or felt, nor did I care. I was polite to him but safely kept my distance.

Our neighbor had a summer house in Maine, and every August, we were welcomed as family. It was near Acadia National Park, which graces the landscape on Mount Desert Island. The peaceful woodlands, rocky beaches, and glacier-cut granite peaks have been called home to a variety of civilizations for over 5,000 years. The water rarely gets above 50 degrees and is a sanctuary for abundant marine life. The highest peak is Cadillac Mountain, which we climbed near the ocean

As we approached the hike, we felt prepared. But, as we progressed, the rocky terrain grew in difficulty. We started to doubt ourselves and considered turning back because we did not want to be in a precarious situation. At one point, we crossed over some iron bars holding two rock formations together and took a break to reassess and catch our breath. Going back down seemed scary enough, but going forward was still an unknown variable.

Suddenly, a young girl and boy about ten years old came running by and politely exclaimed, "*Excuse me!*" and darted up to the next part of the path. Daniel and I just looked at each other and laughed. Apparently, the children gave us the answer we needed. The fear was in our heads, and obviously, the trail was safe and family-friendly. At the top, the children freely ran around the perimeter and checked out the 360° view, "*Can we do it again?*" they asked. I replied, "*Of course, and this time, without fear.*"

Next, we strolled through the quaint seaside town of Bar Harbor. After a long day of exploring, there were several pleasant spots to dine, and we chose a lobster house that stretched out over the water. While waiting to be seated, we were mesmerized as the entire sea wall was filled with starfish. These captivating creatures have long been associated with good fortune, regeneration, and renewal by cultures from around the world. A starfish group is called a galaxy, and I was determined to have my family reach for the stars.

For dinner, my daughter took one look at the menu, fluttered her hand, and ordered, "*I'll have the lobster, of course.*" She has always had an extensive and exquisite palate, and lobster with a tinge of melted butter made her feel like a princess. This might sound like blasphemy, but I preferred this region's sweet jumbo lump crab meat.

Oh! Don't forget the two-inch thick, flaky crust, wild blueberry pie, which was astounding. Our taste buds were extraordinarily happy with us that fine day.

As the bright red sun slowly kissed the morning dew the next morning, we boarded the ferry for Nova Scotia. My senses, as well as the scenery, were fresh, vibrant and alive. Slightly up the coast, we traversed through a golden grassy marshland where rocks extended into the ocean. The dolphins were engaged like children on the playground and delighted in our presence. The jagged rocks safely truncated our curiosity and kept all of us safe. The beach had distinctive blood-red and white sand swirls, with underground streams speckling the shoreline. I felt like a colonist taking her first few steps into an unknown land of raw beauty.

Our next excursion was to Brier Island, which is part of a set of islands that extends into the phenomenal Bay of Fundy. Some believe the bay is one of the top natural wonders in the world because it has the highest tides on earth, is home to some of the rarest whales, and has boasting rights in geological diversity, as well as fossils evidencing the evolution of life.

You need a ferry to escort you to get to every island in the chain. During your wait, local establishments serve small plates of food straight off the boat. It was the first time I had eaten a huge raw scallop doused in vinegar, and it was perfect for this notable feast for my senses. The final island had very few inhabitants and just a few roads. However, we had an all-terrain vehicle and soon found ourselves in a little piece of heaven.

Daniel and I opened a bottle of wine as the children climbed over the rocks. We nestled into a small space perfect for two people to breathe in the majesty of the sunset while toasting a good life. It was the first time Daniel had put his arm around me in years. I felt a spark of love start to rekindle. I wondered if this adventure would lead us back home, home in each other's hearts.

This picturesque moment made it look and feel like we were back on the shores of Oahu when our love was so young and pure. I missed that wonderful man I had fallen in love with so many years ago, and I hoped the feeling would stay. I could feel him looking at me as we packed up to leave. We needed to catch the last ferry back because there wasn't accommodation to slumber in this paradise.

When we returned to the hotel, the kids were exhausted and quickly fell asleep. I freshened up, slipped into bed, and yearned to feel his lips upon mine. Just one kiss would suffice. I wanted affirmation of our love. As Daniel fumbled around looking for his contact lens case, he grabbed the remote control for the television and dimmed the lights. Just as he pulled back the blanket to get into bed, the television lit up with some stupid news station, and I slowly swallowed my pride.

He lay down with an obvious gap between us as I hesitantly put my hand on his chest. Daniel grumbled and squirmed around before settling into a spot. Then, his incessant nightly ritual of clicking the remote through the channels started. It was difficult to hold back my feelings, but I knew if I said anything, it would trigger an argument about how *I was ruining* a perfect day. So, I kissed him on the cheek and rolled over. As my small, silent tears moistened the pillow, I felt defeated once again.

This vacation was a picturesque retreat from the busyness of life, but my outlook on leaving the marriage remained unchanged. This was *the last vacation* we would spend as a family. We still talk about the homemade whoopie pies from the local French bakery and the hand-made Canadian white birch oar with an inlaid black chestnut border I bought from a historic shipbuilder. These memories were intended to be a fond farewell.

The songbirds sounded the rising of the red sun for my final morning in this rural paradise. The cool and gentle breeze caressed my face as the clouds parted ways. The nectar from the flowers kissed my lips as I accepted there would never be a happily ever after.

En route back to Maryland, I put on The Dixie Chicks album, *Wide Open Spaces*. "*When You Were Mine*" spoke about waking up and crying in the middle of the night and removing all the pictures from their wedding day. Apparently, giving her husband two reasons to show him love was not blind was not enough. I reclined my seat, gazed into the vast blue sky, and sang each song word for word. I felt detached from the sadness of the songs as they whispered further acceptance in my heart. Something in my voice must have resonated with Daniel because I could feel him looking at me differently. I am unsure if he was curious or confused, but he knew I had changed.

The Honeymoon is Over

There were days when I felt very confident about my decision to leave. But there were also days when I felt scared and insecure because our children and business were doing quite well. Thoughts ran through my mind. Was I being too harsh? Could I be a better person? Could I be a better spouse? Could I be a better mom? Of course, I could; there is always room for improvement. However, I was not sure how much of my behavior was secondary to Daniel's inattention and anger towards me and the children.

If I knew I could be a better person, did that mean Daniel knew he could be a better person? Did he actually desire to drink himself to sleep every night and take three hours to wake up in the morning? Did he desire to make the bedroom smell like rancid beer shit every morning as he complained about self-imposed stomach ailments? Did he desire to abuse the person who loved him the most in this world? The answer in my mind was, "*No, I don't think so, but I am not sure.*"

How could I help extricate the poison he had been consuming for so many years and trying to shove down my throat? I couldn't consume it any longer; it was killing me. My patience was wearing thin, and I knew I needed to take action.

I purchased a small book both of us could read and discuss. It was a best-seller designed to help improve marriages and examine the differences between how men and women respond to stress. I read the first few chapters and presented the idea to him. Daniel admitted our marriage needed repair and agreed to read one chapter per week as he placed it on the bedside table. Day after day, I saw the book lying in the exact same spot, completely untouched, as the dust had no fingerprints. I knew if I overlooked this agreement, I would be enabling his behaviors.

I contemplated that romantic promise of two young lovers, financially unstable but abundantly in love. I surmised I would rather be financially stable and in love than wealthy and miserable. I took the wedding ring box out of my jewelry chest, which contained the ordering information and receipt for my engagement ring. I looked up a couple of honeymoon ideas I thought may interest Daniel. I thought, *"Let's focus on the future, and maybe the past will begin to resolve itself."* We had over $100,000 in the bank, and I felt it was time. I discerned, *"It's now or never."*

One morning over coffee, we were figuring out the logistics for the next house purchase. I prayed he would agree to take a break from *everything* and just try to rekindle our love. Or at least get to a place where we could start to love each other again. I took a deep breath and showed him the receipt for my ring and a few honeymoon destination printouts.

BAM! Daniel looked at me like he had been sucking on a lemon and was about to puke, *"Why are you so selfish? Why would you want to waste money on that?"* My stomach instantly turned to knots. Ten years earlier, my engagement ring and a honeymoon were a huge deal, and Daniel made them seem to be of the utmost importance. But now, I am a complete waste of time. Was he kidding me? I fucking hated him. The honeymoon was finally over, and I didn't want it back.

I am not sure if I said anything out loud or not. I honestly can't remember. But my heart hardened as I turned and walked into the office and threw the information on the desk. At that moment, I told myself, *"I would rather have nothing than a bad something."* (Reality #9) That's right, *nothing* is better than another moment with this disgusting excuse of a man. I was unable to calm myself down and returned to the living room to inform him of how much he sucked.

A few days before this outburst, I was standing in line at the grocery store and noticed the cover of several famous women's magazines, which read: *"120 Ways to Please Your Man!"*; *"Ladies, The Best Sex of Your Life Is In Your 30's!"*; *"Can The Scent of Vanilla Help Men Achieve Orgasm?"* I yelled, *"Strangers have sex. People who love each other have sex. People who hate each other have sex. Young. Old. Beautiful. Ugly, it doesn't matter. People even pay each other to have sex. Sex is all over the place, and we never have sex!"*

Since my son was born, we had sex about twice a year, and it was only because I initiated it. Even worse, ever since Daniel and I had met, I don't believe I had ever achieved an orgasm. The minute or so of intercourse we did have left me feeling unsatisfied, to say the least. To add insult to injury, every time Daniel had an orgasm, he would get up, take a shower, and leave me lying there alone.

I was starved for affection; the intense neglect ran deep. An agonizing thought was loud and clear: *"I am in my thirties, and if this is the best sex of my life, kill me now!"*

Over the next couple of months, my fury died down a bit, and Daniel seemed to be less of a jerk. Or, possibly, we despised each other so much that it didn't matter anymore. Halloween was just around the corner, and we prepared our costumes for the annual festivities. All of our friends would gather at one house at the beginning and one house at the end, a few blocks away. In between was the trick-or-treat portion of the evening. Every year was great, and this year was no different, except that Daniel seemed like his old self again. He was running around and having so much fun. I loved to see the smile across his face. Most importantly, there was a spark of intimacy between us.

After we got home and put the children to bed, he insinuated he would *join* me in a minute. But eventually, I fell asleep, only to startle myself awake around 2 am. I tossed and turned the rest of the night, thinking about sex. I kept looking at Daniel, hoping he would wake up and feel inspired to touch me. I rubbed his back a few times, but he didn't budge. Every ounce of me wanted to explode.

The next morning, I reached over and rubbed him until he got hard. It took a while to open his eyes and acknowledge my hand. I tried to kiss him, but he turned away and removed his underwear. I readily undressed in anticipation. After about thirty seconds of intercourse, Daniel was done and got up to go to the bathroom. I lay there and thought, *"What the hell was that?"* as he closed the door because another beer shit was about to implode. So, I got up and lit a few candles.

After he finished going to the bathroom, I asked, *"Are you coming back to bed?"* Again, he looked at me like he was sucking on a lemon and replied, *"For what?"* I told him I wasn't done yet and thought maybe he would like to get back into bed and snuggle with me. Then he rolled his eyes, turned the shower on, and said, *"Can't you just take care of that?"*

I was thoroughly disgusted on multiple levels and couldn't even bring myself to cry. As I got out of bed and put my bath robe on, I silently vowed, *"I will never touch him again."* (Reality #10)

Drinking the Poison

Remember that food pyramid you were forced to learn and abide by to be a healthy and happy person? What if I told you it was all a lie? Growing up, everyone I knew drank milk at breakfast, lunch, and dinner. It was just a way of life. Little did I know, this creamy white delectable beverage was my poison.

Early in 2006, my sister was rushed to the emergency room for horrendous cramping in her abdomen, and $6,000 later, her diagnosis was menstrual cramps. Really, you can't make this stuff up. She was a full-time student and had to pay out of pocket. Subsequently, she joined a study conducted by a prominent university to determine the effects of various foods on your bodily systems. I inquired about the direct impact on her menstrual cycle, hoping to alleviate my symptoms as well.

Dairy products were at the top of the list. In turn, I switched from regular milk to soy milk. Further, I learned that several of my cousins also had issues with dairy. It took me a while, but I concluded that this switch in milk products exacerbated my issues, prompting me to do some additional research. Both milk and soy contain high amounts of estrogen. The birth control I took many years before, which made me horribly sick, also contained high amounts of estrogen. Hmm, I was onto something.

Over the next week, I cut as many estrogen-containing products out of my diet as possible, and within *one month (yes, only one month)*, my skin, hair, and voice noticeably changed. Interestingly, my pet allergies decreased. Most importantly, my menstruation made a remarkable change and has been like clockwork ever since. What? That's right, after twenty years of suffering a multitude of injuries to my mind, body, and soul, I found out it was *the milk*. The delicious and refreshing *poison* I willfully drank every day of my life. Yum. Yum. Yum. Not.

I was so enthusiastic about my discovery; it was exhilarating to feel great. Some of the bloating had subsided, and I bought a new outfit. The pants were form-fitting and comfortable, while the linen shirt flowed below my waist. It was an indigo-blue fabric with beads of a slightly darker hue. The pattern was intricate and feminine. I felt beautiful and received many compliments.

That evening, Daniel wondered why I was glowing. I explained I had finally found a natural remedy to my problem and that everyone loved my new shirt. Then he apathetically shrugged his shoulders and, appearing to be sucking on another lemon, said, *"You are never going to just be a soccer mom, are you?"* He tried to rain on my victory parade, but this just made me more determined to shine.

Soccer mom? Daniel always proclaimed to love me because I was *different*, but now, he wanted me to be *the same*. I called that soccer mom routine *"driving in circles,"* anyway. You can't limit that nonsense of driving in circles all day to benefit everyone and expect all the children to just play soccer. I always laughed when I thought about this because I envisioned the moms being soccer balls kicked around the field and seemingly loving it. *"Yes, yes, please, kick me more! Score! You win."*

NOTE: Please do not misinterpret my rant about "soccer moms" and align it with mothers who stay home and raise their children by choice or necessity. These women should be highly respected by their families and community because they offer what most of us need and want: someone who loves us and cares unconditionally.

However, most of the moms I was surrounded by in these elite private blue-blood schools grew up in middle- to upper-middle-class families. They went to college and got a job after graduation. Somewhere along the way, they married, had children, and decided not to work outside the marital home. They did not choose to stay home to nurture their children; they chose what they considered a prestigious lifestyle and flaunted it. They spent their days obsessing about every little, tiny detail in life and described their daily routines as *"crazy busy."* The highlight of the day was getting a mani/pedi and finding a recipe in a trendy magazine or bragging about their tennis instructor. I said, *"So sorry, that is not me. It will never be me. You stupid idiot."*

I rarely used the word *"idiot"* unless I was going in for the kill. It is a major trigger word for Daniel, and this seemed like an appropriate time. I really wanted to chant the word "idiot," but I just smiled instead.

The realization that *I am not broken as a woman* prompted me to look back over what I had endured and how it affected my life. More than the typical trials and tribulations, the perception of my feminine and human existence had been shattered.

The only reason I went to that doctor's appointment after eight months of no menstruation as a teenager was because my mom took me. I was five feet, nine inches tall, and weighed one hundred pounds. I ate food all day, every day, and played on three different basketball teams year-round. I think I would have known if I was pregnant.

Unprompted by any discussion, my parents approached me in the dining room. My mother softly and hesitantly inquired, *"You haven't had your period in a long time, have you?"* I nodded, *"No."* My father put his hands together and tried to maintain composure, *"Who is the father?"*

I shrugged my shoulders, *"There is no father."* He stepped towards me and sternly asked again, *"Who is the father?"* I raised my hands in dismay, *"Come on, I have been having problems for years. There is no father."* Suddenly, my dad lunged towards me and slapped me across my face, *"You whore!"* I had never heard my father speak to *anyone* that way, let alone his daughter. Regardless, my diagnosis was *never* talked about, and my father *never* apologized.

In those frightful moments, I drank vast amounts of the poison we all know as shame. I was ashamed of my body and of my overwhelming fear of pain. I thought there was no safe place on earth for me. I felt broken, unwanted, and considered a whore.

During the same time, I started to experience panic attacks. I did not know what they were; I would simply cry incessantly while sitting on the bathroom floor, feeling like I could not breathe. I hyperventilated until the panic subsided, then wallowed in self-doubt, insisting, *"Nobody loves me."*

One evening, as I lay on the bathroom floor, my father started to freak out and yell at me. He said if I didn't stop crying, he was going to spank me until I did. I replied, *"That doesn't even make sense."* He forced his way into the bathroom and hit me several times until I stopped making noise. I wondered why a parent would punish their child for feeling sad and unloved and then blame them for their punishment as if they deserved to suffer.

Determined not to fight back, I started running away from home. I stayed at a couple of friend's houses near school to continue going to school and participating in my activities, but I was exhausted. Every time I returned home, he whipped me and promised my punishment would double each time. After my longest stint, which lasted about two weeks, I received fourteen whippings from his leather belt. I had black and blue welts all over my back and legs and vowed never to run away again. Emotionally, I felt like I was living in another person's body.

I became compliant and gave up the fight. I did everything I was supposed to and basically had a "You leave me alone and I will leave you alone" mentality. As a result of my emotional detachment, my panic attacks significantly decreased. About a year later, there was some confusion with the carpool after basketball. When we both arrived home, my dad was infuriated. He was breathing heavily on my face and blaming me for everything. He threatened to spank me when I did not take responsibility for the miscommunications.

In a soft yet ominous voice, I bravely looked him dead in the eyes and said, "*Go ahead.*" He took a step back and looked rather bewildered. I could tell he wanted to hit me, but for some reason that I will never know, he walked away. Unbeknownst to me, in that moment, the physical abuse stopped.

Over the next few years, my panic attacks became mild and relatively nonexistent. When I discovered a term for my episodes, it gave me some peace and clarity. *Panic attacks* are periods of intense fear and physical discomfort where the body reacts in a given number of uncontrollable ways. These periods of dis-ease may include heart palpitations, chest pain, and shortness of breath. Some people tremble as if being cold, feel dizzy, numb, or confused, and may sense they are losing control. This impending feeling of doom can be coupled with intense outbursts, bouts of crying, or withdrawal to find a safe place. Some people may think they are having a heart attack or feel as if they might die. The exhibiting factors may vary greatly depending on age, gender, and social norms.

Since I could assess and manage those feelings brewing inside, I was better able to help the children I worked with process their panic in productive ways. I reassured them that they could feel the fear but still recover without feeling shame or remorse. I wish somebody had explained these things to me when I was a teenager and taught me productive coping mechanisms.

The statistics in the United States report that approximately 2% to 3% of the population suffer from panic disorder, but I believe the prevalence is exorbitantly higher. Many people are too ashamed to report it or seek help, choosing to suffer in silence for fear of being seen as weak or crazy. On the other hand, some people think they are having a stroke or a heart attack and seek medical attention without proper results. Well-trained medical staff and first responders occasionally know the difference.

If you or someone you love is suffering, don't blame or chastise them. Get them the help they need. Most medical doctors will prescribe medications that may provide temporary relief, but I do not recommend long-term use. These prescriptions often mask the problem instead of helping to resolve it, and in my opinion, long-term use can be detrimental.

Instead, I recommend researching and reconciling the problem's origin and finding various natural remedies. Panic attacks often stem from deeper underlying issues and are not the actual problem. While treating these tangents can be helpful, you must address the underlying cause. If left untreated, the various forms of poison they leave behind will lead to further dis-ease within yourself and your relationships. Learning to recognize and nurture the warning signs is crucial for true healing.

Just One Kiss

Once I realized I had been ingesting the metaphorical poison while Daniel was spoon-feeding it to me like a baby and enjoying it, I gained insight into my feelings and reactions over the perpetual controversy in our marriage. Unfortunately, the only way I could imagine stopping the poison from entering my body was to leave.

I had been working on strengthening my friendships, knowing the pending transition would be difficult. In addition to my Bible Study group, I made some friendships with several of the parents from the swim team. Our kids were in the same age group and were good friends. While they practiced, we walked around the nature paths, went to the gymnasium to play ball, or used the athletic facilities.

One night, it was pouring down rain, so a few of us decided to watch the football game at a local bar. I ordered a drink, which quickly disappeared, so I ordered another in hopes of drowning out my sorrows. One swim parent who knew me quite well asked, "*Are you ok?*" I motioned for him to wait a minute and drank half my next drink. My goal was to calm down and enjoy the game.

I clenched my teeth and forced a fake smile. I replied, "*Actually, everything in my life is absolutely amazing except for the fact that my husband is a complete fucking asshole, and I am going to leave him.*"

He chuckled, "*That should probably be your last drink.*" I firmly agreed. Drinking my way through this nonsense was not the answer; I just needed to speak those words into existence. Nobody knew what went on behind closed doors, and for my own sanity, I needed somebody to hear the truth.

The following Sunday, I woke up early and decided to go to 9:00 am Mass. I took off my wedding ring and put it in my dresser drawer. It felt so uncomfortable to keep it on my finger; I needed to be free.

I had decided to leave and was looking for a sign from God. I showed up at 8:50 am, and the church was empty. Suddenly, it occurred to me that Mass started at 9:30 am. I looked up and smiled, "*Thanks, God. Is this my first sign?*" I embraced the cold and silent sanctuary as if the solitude was created to help me listen. There were no distractions, just me and God trying to figure out what I was supposed to do next. This seemed like an obvious step in the right direction.

I kneeled to pray for this dis-ease to leave my heart. Advent is when we are supposed to reflect on God's enduring love when wondrous miracles *can come true*. I rarely prayed for anything for myself, as it felt selfish. One by one, parishioners entered the sanctuary. I could sense their confusion and felt like all eyes were focused on me. Where was my family?

As the tension in my chest grew, I pleaded, "*Come on, God, send me a sign.*" The pews filled in quickly, and there came a hush over the parishioners. Initially, I felt a sense of peace, but that was disrupted when the sermon began. The priest spoke about John the Baptist, who had baptized Jesus and recognized him as the Savior. However, John, who was Jesus' cousin, still had doubts. If someone as dedicated and faithful as he was to the Lord still doubted the light, how could I be sure God was real and listening to my prayers?

When the priest said, "*Let us bow our heads and pray,*" a sense of insecurity ran through my body. I was supposed to have my eyes closed, but I kept them half open to see how or why others were feeling the power of God's love, and I just felt a strange sensation of not belonging here anymore.

During the Communion ceremony, a mysteriously bright light permeated the room through the stained glass wall, and the acoustics changed. The vibrations sent a chill down my spine, and everyone on the altar seemed to be chanting in one illuminated voice, their hands and arms moving in unison.

As Mass ended and we were to go in peace, I was deep in thought. I was contemplating what had transpired this morning as Doreen, the matriarch of my Bible Study group, stopped me. Doreen was her own unique version of a spitfire. Her kind, loving, and honorable spirit always positioned her at the front of the table and she prided herself on whipping the truth right out at you.

She inquired about my children. As I began to answer, I brushed my hair off my face. She grabbed my hand and, noticing the bareness of my fingers, she asked, "*Where is your ring?*" My voice quivered, and I meekly answered, with a lump in my throat, "*I left it at home.*"

She abruptly stated, "*We are going to breakfast.*" I attempted to get out of the invitation because I thought I would have the guilt of the world wrought down over me. She would not take *no* for an answer and touched my arm, *"Come on, you can ride with me."* Paradoxically, she was the stronghold I needed to gain understanding and movement in the light. She was willfully taking me under her wing, whether or not I wanted her help. After I got over my initial wave of annoyance, I was deeply humbled. I guess God knew I could be rather stubborn at times.

My daughter had a swim meet at The Naval Academy in Annapolis the following weekend. We carpooled with some friends because Daniel had no desire to attend. After dinner, we went to an ice cream parlor for dessert and arrived home later than expected. Daniel was beyond angry and insisted he would go the following day. I figured I could just ignore him, and hopefully, he would go away.

This was a large and highly competitive swim meet, and teams came from all over the region. Suddenly, the head coach from Virginia passed out on deck. We all thought the fainting was a result of the insane heat and humidity. Several parents in the medical community assisted as they brought in a stretcher.

During this time, one of my friends who was helping forgot to remove his daughter's pink princess crown from atop his head, and we all laughed. Instantly, Daniel barged through a handful of my friends and berated me for my insensitivity to the situation. Not only did he think my laughter was highly inappropriate, but he also made it perfectly clear that my laugh was horribly incessant, and everybody hated it. Then he darted off. I was so embarrassed as all my friends looked upon me with pity.

My friend from the bar and his wife stood beside this wretched tirade. He sadly nodded, *"I am sorry. I thought you were exaggerating the other day. I have never met Daniel before and would have never guessed it was this bad."* His wife asked if I wanted to go outside and cool off, and I gladly accepted her offer. They were a very nice couple, and so were their two boys.

Towards the end of the third day of the swim meet, my daughter swam the 200 IM (Individual Medley). She was thoroughly exhausted. Halfway through the 50-meter butterfly stroke, she started to sink. As she surfaced, the stroke and turn officials sounded whistles and blared "*DQ!*" disqualified for the next 25 meters. With each obnoxious "*DQ!, DQ!, DQ! DQ!*" my sweet baby cried and barely made it back to the wall.

One of my friends was standing on deck, and grabbed her as she came out of the pool. He wrapped her up in a towel and took her aside. He assured her everything was going to be alright. He calmed her anxiety, dried her tears, and encouraged her to breathe, "*Let's go find your mom.*"

They walked down a long corridor and exited through a door. Daniel grabbed her and yelled, "*This is embarrassing and a complete waste of time. Why are you on the swim team anyway?*" My heart sank as I heard exactly what he said. I instantly reprimanded him, "*What the hell is wrong with you? She's exhausted, and those officials were completely disrespectful. They should have never treated a little girl like that. You are the one who should be embarrassed.*" The drive home was long and quiet. Nobody spoke a word, fearing his retaliation. I was so angry, I wanted to DQ Daniel from life.

At practice, a few days later, my friend, who helped her on deck, asked me if I wanted to walk and talk. The evening was calm and brisk, and we could see the stars shimmering beyond the tree line. It was so comforting to have someone to talk to who understood the situation. His son was my daughter's best friend, and they had bought her a red swim bag for a Christmas present that evening. They knew red was her favorite color and went to several stores to find the perfect one.

As we circled back to the sports arena, my friend and I went into the gym to shoot some basketballs before the kids joined us. We usually had a pretty good size group of kids who wanted to play before their parents arrived to pick them up. It was fun to see everyone let loose and have fun.

But the energy between us had changed. We embraced in a long hug as we exited the building into the adjacent courtyard. Then, we looked at each other and leaned in for a kiss as the world spun and blurred around me. My face turned ghost white, and I could barely breathe. I was dizzy and nauseous and asked to go inside. I had never considered kissing another man but my husband. I felt confused.

The next day, the confusion subsided. This kiss convinced me my marriage was genuinely over. Yep, just one kiss. I know that is how fairy tales should begin, but this kiss determined the end. The story book of my marriage was over, and I was determined to move on. (Now, that's a new reality.)

CHAPTER 4

SCORCHED EARTH

The Big Green Monster

I mourned the loss of my marriage while I was still married. I *accepted* the divorce *was* going to happen. From my understanding, women often begin mourning the loss of the relationship while the relationship still exists, whereas men typically start mourning after the relationship has ended. How about you? Are you the type to mourn and leave, or deny the ending is near and wait for the final blow? I am not suggesting that one method is better; I am simply asking you to pay attention to the differences because time discrepancies play an important role in processing the situation appropriately. If both parties handled it the same way, I would assume it would make it slightly easier, although I am not 100% sure. I am sure many people have valid opinions.

I needed to figure out the next set of steps.

To me, the first step was to tell Daniel I was leaving, which, in hindsight, was a big mistake. One evening, he came home late after the children were asleep. I asked him not to turn the television on and sat beside him. I explained in the most simple and loving way possible,

"We do not make each other happy. You need to be a happy person, and I need to be a happy person. Our children need to have two happy parents who can love them."

Daniel tried to negotiate the situation and admitted neither of us was happy, but he was willing to change. I reminded him that all his other promises had fallen through, and it was too late. There was no going back. The only thing we could do was move forward and try to make ourselves and our children happy. Maybe if we live close together, we can be friends, and our children can walk back and forth between our houses and have two happy homes instead of one sad house.

Unfortunately, Christmas and New Year's were a barrage of negotiation and denial. Everyone on both sides of the family knew I was different, and Daniel was grasping for something, anything. For me, the decision for us to divorce was set in stone, and I wasn't going to change my mind.

On a side note, you can call me stupid right now before I divulge the next piece of information. Actually, stupid may be an understatement. Hindsight is a real bitch sometimes. Alas, I told him about the kiss. I am sure you are wondering what I was thinking. Well, I was not trying to make him angry or jealous. I simply wanted to tell the truth. If anyone knew how I felt about the sacredness of marriage and being faithful, it was Daniel. So, telling the truth validated that I was really going to leave.

Of course, Daniel exacerbated the entire situation and set out to make everyone, literally everyone, believe I was an adulterous whore. He did not take responsibility for his behavior, nor did he *ever* ask to reconcile. This became a declaration of *war*, and he was determined to win.

My life was about to become a living hell. Less than two weeks after I peacefully told him it was over, Daniel and his family had hired a prominent law firm, locked me out of all finances, and hired a private investigator to follow me everywhere. My personal belongings were tossed into the basement with no doors or curtains, and video cameras were set up throughout the house. Further, he moved our business office into the master bedroom and added an external door lock, preventing me from accessing my own business. At first, I thought this was a ridiculous and over-the-top attack and somebody in their right mind would have him stop the nonsense. But to my dismay, this was only the beginning of a long and treacherous war.

I did not know about the video cameras until the following month because my six-year-old son told me he saw his uncle fussing with "*the video monitors to keep Mommy safe.*" Apparently, his uncle had monitors set up in his house, but the reception was faulty, and they were troubleshooting in front of my curious son. This story made perfect sense because Daniel had been instigating physically aggressive arguments and then *running* to targeted locations in our house and screaming, "*Stop! Get away! Stop hurting me!*" as he pretended to tremble in fear. I thought, "*Wow, he is so desperate he will do anything to make me look bad. He is much more of a coward than I could have ever imagined.*" I needed to be extra careful because I did not know how far he would take this charade of being the victim.

I knew Daniel would be at a different stage of the grieving process. After all, I had a year to prepare. I had absolutely no idea he would nominally leap through the first two steps and plunge headfirst into anger and rage. Throughout the time I had known Daniel, envy had been his favorite companion. Now, envy was gathering an army, and I was the target of destruction as his father eagerly funded the war.

Within the next week, I was served papers to initiate the divorce. I did not have a penny to my name and thought this maneuver was over the top and would be outrageously expensive. Naively, I believed I could handle the divorce myself and confided in a couple of people I thought knew the process. Both of them unequivocally declared, "*You need a lawyer, or you will lose everything, including your children.*"

I thought to myself with disgust, "*This is fucking ridiculous.*" For the next few months, I was given an *allowance* of one hundred dollars per week to take care of the entire family, and I had to show receipts for everything. Daniel made me a prisoner in my own home. He refused to go to a mediator and insisted I was a *"tidal wave of destruction,"* so peaceful negotiations were out of the question. The green monster of envy was eating him alive and regurgitating his remains all over me. I thought my marriage was bad but relatively normal. This divorce was horrendous and not typical by any stretch of the imagination.

I was forced to attain legal services. Upon my initial consultation, I was informed there would be a $15,000 retainer fee. My law firm and every other legal entity in the area were familiar with the notorious lawyer Daniel and his family chose for legal representation. My parents, especially my father, were highly offended by the lack of respect. My dad had taken Daniel under his wing and was now facing the prospect of never seeing his grandchildren again. My dad specifically stated, *"There will be no winners,"* as he handed me a check to cover the initial expenses.

Life was ugly, but I managed to get by one day at a time. I assumed the crazy, erratic episodes Daniel exhibited would eventually dissipate. I simply wanted an amicable agreement. Every time he yelled his nonsense, I put music on from our life together and sang. Part of me was being a bit obnoxious because I picked songs that would potentially get on his nerves. The other part of me wanted to tap into *"Hey, let's remember all the good times we had and move along."*

A huge difference between us was that I felt deep compassion for him, myself, and our family. On the other hand, Daniel had gone far beyond the *tipping point* from which there was no return. He showed no compassion for anybody, including himself.

Tipping Point: This is when a series of small or seemingly insignificant incidents or changes occur, ultimately creating a major shift or change. Most importantly, this change is a critical point in a situation or relationship and there is no way to turn back. The damage is significant and cannot be undone. A common analogy is *the final straw (the one that broke the camel's back)*, which entails the final incident to make a situation completely unbearable because it has exceeded the limits.

Compassion is the act of suffering together. It can also be defined as a state of mind where one desires for others to be set free from their suffering. The effects of compassion can help restore health, while the absence of compassion can be painful or deadening. When compassion is denied, rage occurs. I did not want to be the source of any further suffering, nor did I want to experience rage. I just wanted to be free and happy. Perhaps this was an illusion, and I was off in another world. But it seems like genuinely good and kindhearted people are a threat to those who thrive on manipulation.

Weeks later, Daniel was lying on the couch in a cold sweat. His skin was clammy and green. He thought he was having a heart attack and insisted I call 911. Reluctantly, I did. In the meantime, I assumed he was having a panic attack and sat beside him. I placed my right hand upon his heart and whispered, *"Just breathe."* I put my left fingertips along the groove in his neck to feel his pulse and whispered, *"Just relax. Let's slow down your heart rate,"* as we breathed in and out together.

I kept my hands on him as we talked about a memory from when our son was a baby. He had been crying inconsolably for quite some time as I entered the room. I picked him up and absorbed his energy into mine. The comforting sway of my body and the softness of my song soothed my baby's heart as he fell asleep in my arms. Daniel remembered the feeling, and his heart rate slowed. When the paramedics arrived, they took his vital signs and determined he was going to be fine and we should get some sleep.

Daniel walked me down to my bedroom in the basement, thanked me for taking care of him, and hugged me goodnight. I would be a fool to deny that I knew Daniel was in a dark and desolate place filled with fear and anxiety. I would also be a fool to deny I had to leave. As I contemplated this experience, no matter how much I wished our marriage could have worked, there was no turning back.

Apparently, that dose of oxytocin and calming event didn't stop the green monster for long. Daniel and his entourage of envy already had a plan in place: **Operation Blackout.**

That week, a list of about twenty-five men and women who were my friends was presented to me. All the women were nice, Christian ladies with 2.3 children, a dog, and a white picket fence. Not literally; I am painting a neighborhood for you to imagine. Most men were married to my friends and participated in some type of church or sports activity with me, except two from Hawaii and Georgia. In their minds, they were *living the life*.

I had no idea what they were going to do with this list, so I thought I would beat them to the punch. I called numerous people in all aspects of my life. I asked them to write a short letter of reference about me— basically, a short description of what I offered to the community and my personality. I did not want it to be contrived for a purpose. I just wanted it to come from their heart. In turn, I received about fifteen beautiful letters to describe *Amy*.

For the next several months, the entourage developed weekly plans of attacks against me, which always resulted in the green monster calling the authorities to come to his rescue. The results were legally futile because the police understood the situation. Day by day, hour by hour, they were wearing down my capacities, traumatizing my children, and isolating all of us from the rest of the community.

Buried Treasures

I looked for a rental property for me and the children until the housing and finances could be sorted appropriately. The entourage was coercing me to live in one of our rental properties, all one-bedroom apartments. They refused to shut their mouths until I testified under oath that their legal suggestions directly violated the city housing code, in other words, against the law. I guess they hoped I was oblivious to the repercussions so they could refuse to let my children stay with me.

Finally, I found a great location within walking distance of the church and many of our friend's houses. The bad part was this house was dilapidated. The refrigerator was held together with duct tape, and the dishwasher leaked under layers of vinyl flooring. The stove had a rust smell, and only two of the burners worked. The cheap, antiquated electrical outlets shot out sparks, and the basement ceiling was soggy and molded. The house was disgusting, and I was apprehensive about how the children would feel leaving their upper-class neighborhood for this mess. So, I decided to make the repairs myself.

I worked out an agreement with the landlord. I would pay a security deposit, move items in during February, and make all necessary repairs to the house instead of paying rent. She would not agree to new appliances, so I negotiated to buy the appliances and apply the costs to the rent due in March. It was a tremendous undertaking but well worth it. Fortuitously, I had some help.

My sister gave me enough money to pay the necessary deposits, monthly bills, and moving expenses. I told her I would repay her, and she said, *"Just repay me before you die. I know where your mother lives."* Ha! Honestly, I couldn't have done this without her help. She was such a blessing in one of the worst times of my life.

As I walked through a home improvement store looking for necessary items, I recognized one of my best friends from college, Tom. We had amicably parted ways because his future wife and my future husband despised our friendship. The energy between us was immense and made them feel insecure. I hadn't seen him in years. Cheerfully, I sauntered down the aisle and said, *"Hello, Handsome."*

He excitedly responded, *"Cupcake! How are you doing?"* we talked for quite a while, catching up on life. He offered to help me relocate and expressed empathy for my situation. We hadn't skipped a beat; our friendship picked up right where we left off. Most importantly, he *treasured the real Amy.* The Amy he met in college who intended to take on the world. I really missed that woman, and I wanted her back. Thank goodness he was by my side once again.

Tom transported the larger purchases to the new house and renovated the kitchen. He bought me a red toolbox and gave me some money to buy groceries. I told him I would repay him one day, and he nodded, "*No, you don't need to repay me. Just help the next person.*"

My dad helped with the electrical issues, and some other friends assisted with necessary odds and ends. A few people brought some food over and offered money. Accepting these donations was difficult, and I promised to repay everyone somehow.

I am sure you are curious how I was able to stage this relocation without Daniel and his private investors finding out where I was heading. All I can say is that God puts people in your life when you need them. I would have never expected these people to step forward, extend their arms, and give me a helping hand up. There are so many people I cherish who have come into my life. For a moment, a month, a year, or a lifetime, each has made a difference to me and my children; I am grateful for that.

Ever since I was a child, I kept an antique wooden box filled with prayer cards of those cherished souls that had passed on from this realm and into the next. I kept it on my bedroom dresser in front of the mirror with an alabaster statue on top. The statue was an old Chinese wise man sitting with his legs folded in deep contemplation and smoking a decorative elongated water pipe.

I had a candle on each bedside table beside two more alabaster statues. On my side was a beautiful Chinese woman in a traditional kimono, leaning slightly forward with one leg stretched out. On Daniel's side was a valorous Chinese man dressed in formal regalia, bent down on one knee with respect. Both figures appeared to be listening to their *nan wu*, shaman, wizard.

I had learned how to circumvent the entourage and the private investigators. When my whereabouts remained unknown, the entourage became extremely frustrated and provoked the big green monster to go in for the kill. Daniel took my prayer box, all three statutes, and all of my photo albums.

I flew off into a blind rage, screaming and yelling profanities. I grabbed his wedding ring, sitting on a small plate, and ran outside.

With fury, I shouted into the universe, "*If you fucking call the police on me again, I will bury you.*" The big green monster laughed and made faces like I was a crazy person.

With an unwavering look of fire deep within my eyes, I exclaimed, "*I swear to God, I will use every penny on this earth to destroy you! I will take everything away from you, and you will never see your children again. I will subpoena all your loser, alcoholic, and drug addict trust fund baby friends into the courtroom and let the world see you for who you really are. Now, give me back my stuff!*"

Daniel disappeared into the house. He returned and handed my prayer box to me. With a somber look, like a dog with his tails between his legs and an outstretched hand, he said, "*I can't give you the photo albums; they are not here. But I'll let you keep my mom's prayer card. I didn't even know you had it.*"

I took the box and gritted my teeth. "Loser," I pretended to throw his wedding ring into the yard. He frantically searched through the grass but was unable to find it; it was in my pocket the entire time.

In my mind, there was no time to rest. I needed to protect myself and my belongings. The rental property was not a safe option yet for fear it would be found and ravaged. I called a friend and asked if I could move some of my boxes into her house. I promised to keep her name and location secret from everyone. I did not need or want the entourage to harass her as well.

The next day, I moved many of my belongings to her house. These buried treasures may not be of great value to anyone else, but to me, they are my world.

The Panic Returns

All these years of setting exorbitantly high standards for myself and trying to convince the world I was perfectly happy and poised were about to come to an end. Don't get me wrong. I knew I wasn't. When I figured out I could take a step back and laugh at the adversity I had endured, I knew I was healing and moving along. In my mind, every experience comes with a learning curve, and I desire to learn something new every day. I actually made up a funny little diagnosis for myself:

The Mary Poppins Complex: *a person who wants to appear practically perfect in every way.*

Remember when Mary Poppins reached into her magic carpet bag containing anything a person may need? This companion accompanied Mary on journeys to help ill-tempered children learn about themselves. Then, instead of stating her observations, she allowed her personality tape measure to do the dirty work. The boy was extremely stubborn and suspicious, while the girl was inclined to giggle and didn't put things away. When Mary measured herself, the tape obviously read practically perfect in every way.

Keeping in mind that "a spoonful of sugar helps the medicine go down" is a delightful way to remember not to take life too seriously and find the bright side in any given situation. Ha! The perfect way to ensure life will always be great, right? Well, I guess we can keep hoping for that magic to occur.

I packed my belongings in cardboard boxes but did not tape them shut. I told Daniel to look through my boxes and that if he disagreed with something, we could discuss it. After a few days, I removed the boxes from the house and put them in a safe location. The disappearing items were definitely pushing the big green monster further over the edge. He was desperate to know where I was going. My birthday was fast approaching, and the move-out day was scheduled for March 15th.

The Ides of March. Originally, *Ides* simply referred to the first new moon in any given month, usually between the 13th and the 15th. Traditionally, this day signified the new year, leading to numerous types of celebrations. Yet, when heroes in movies or literature were confronted with this phenomenon, it was usually a bad omen. Just ask Julius Caesar.

A few people were in on the escape plan. One sister spoke to me daily about my emotions. One sister volunteered to help with the move, while another sister financed it. A few of my friends would help with the children and the logistics of the days surrounding the move. The energy in the house between Daniel and me changed drastically, and neither one knew what to expect from the other.

The morning of my birthday, Daniel politely invited me to go out to dinner with the children to celebrate. He seemed very calm and almost genuine. Hesitantly, I agreed and naively considered he may be turning over a new leaf. We went to one of my favorite restaurants and sat at the table right in front of the fireplace. I ordered a clear chocolate martini, which was always made to perfection.

As a family, we talked and laughed throughout dinner. For dessert, they brought out an almond torte doused in a raspberry sauce with candles as everyone joyously sang Happy Birthday to me, *Amy*.

The rich, warm meal almost made me believe in magic once again. Then, on the drive home, I got a text message. *"Watch out. This is a setup. Can't say more. Not safe."* I knew this was too good to be true.

I frantically thought, *"What is he going to do to me now?"* I tried to look normal and kept my breath in check. I was on edge as the garage door opened, and we drove in. I was scared to open the door and enter the house. As I slowly walked through the house, I carefully tried to identify what was different. I couldn't find anything in particular, but I felt a sense of heaviness and impending evil. I made several attempts to contact my friend, who had texted me, but received no reply.

Suddenly, Daniel nefariously approached me in the narrow hallway between the bedrooms, *"What's the matter? Did your boyfriend abandon you?"* he seethed. I looked confused. *"That's right, I have all of your phone records, and I am going to destroy you. I am going to take the house, the business, and the children. Guess what? Your boyfriend doesn't want you anymore. You are going to be left to live in the gutter, all alone, forever."*

I started to freak out inside my mind while my heart felt like it was running a marathon. My escape plan was set in place. Did he know my plan? Did he think accusing me of being an adulterous whore to everyone I knew was going to stop me, or did he have another plan to debilitate me and my move further? I couldn't breathe and started to hyperventilate. Intense panic returned with a vengeance.

Brutal words lashed out of both our mouths as the children disappeared into their rooms in fear. He positioned himself directly in front of me and pointed his fingers in my face. "*I dare you to hit me, you fucking whore. Where is your boyfriend? Why isn't he here to protect you?*"

Suddenly, he ran into the foyer and awkwardly repositioned himself. Then, he shrieked loudly as he furiously threw his hands up into the air, "*Please! Stop hitting me! Get away! You are hurting me! The children are here! What are you doing? Please stop!*"

My mind was racing in a million directions, "*My God! This must be the setup! Think, Amy, think.*" I ran into the bathroom as my panic attack worsened. I had to sit down. This was the first one in years, and it was brutal. My children came to console me, and soon, there was a knock on the front door. It was the police; they wanted to talk to me. I was terrified, but I had truth on my side.

I stood by the police cars for over an hour and recounted the whole story. They highly suggested I go to a safe house for abused women and take my children with me. They said they have witnessed this type of abuse many times over, and unfortunately, "*most women stay.*" Then, I confided I had a safe place to go; I just needed a few more days to execute my plan. They were relieved and wished me success.

Knowing the police were on my side gave me some strength. I wasn't going to be one of those women who stay and love, as well as protect, their abusers. Whoever thinks being strong means accepting abuse as a part of life is *absolutely wrong*. I know it's a cycle, and cycles inherently mean the abuser was abused. But we all have choices to make in life, and he chose to be abusive, while I decided to rise above the cycle and remove myself from the extra-ordinary conditions of my suffering.

My daughter secretly disclosed the next day, "*Mommy, I know you have a plan, and I want in.*" I had been listening to my sweet baby girl sing "*Because of You*" along with Kelly Clarkson in the basement every day for months. I felt the beautiful voice of my daughter promise not to make the same mistakes that I did, mistakes that had caused her heart so much misery. She was innocently scolding me for breaking and falling so hard. She was obviously learning at a very young age to never let any relationship go that far, and all of this was because of me. I was responsible for her suffering.

My baby watched me die; she heard me cry when I didn't know anybody was listening. My God, because of me and my unhealthy marriage, she learned to stay on the safe side of the sidewalk so she could never get hurt. She learned not to trust anyone, including herself. She was literally singing at the top of her angelic voice that she was afraid and unable to cry. Apparently, crying showed weakness in my eyes, and she refused to let me take notice and point out her sadness. Every day of my life was a constant reminder that her heart couldn't possibly break because it wasn't even whole to start with.

I warned her this plan would be a huge turning point in life. I explained that once it happened, she could never take it back. I carefully asked, "*Are you absolutely sure? You know, this moment will stay with you forever.*" Years later, Reba McEntire and Kelly Clarkson did a duet with this song, which is extremely powerful from a multi-generational standpoint. I feel the depth of their emotional burdens deep down in my soul.

Both versions of this song still make me cry. Check it on YouTube and look into their eyes. Speak aloud what you see, domestic abuse stays with you for life. With sincere gratitude, Kelly, thank you. Your voice gave my daughter a voice when she was unable to speak. Fortunately, I was listening and took action. I hesitated to include her in the plan, but she insisted, and I couldn't let her down again.

To solidify my plan, the day before escaping from the marital home, I pretended to be horribly sick and asked Daniel to take care of the children. This was indeed a rare occasion, and he agreed. In false appreciation for his kindness, I returned his wedding ring and apologized for attempting to throw it away. He seemed to appreciate my gesture, which brought me some much-needed downtime.

Thus began a seemingly regular 7:00 am Saturday morning swim practice. This was the first time Daniel had ever agreed to take our daughter, and I was pleased. The schedule allowed me to get the movers in and out with all the items I wished to take and to redecorate the house with the items I chose to leave behind in a concerted effort to create two homes for my children.

This setup worked impeccably, except they arrived home just as the movers closed the truck and prepared to drive away. Daniel ran around in a frenzy and frantically called the police. The moving van and I were stopped by the police about halfway to our destination. When Daniel arrived, he was pale green, and beads of sweat rolled down his face. He erratically insisted I was crazy and should be taken to a mental hospital or arrested for stealing. His brother stood to the side with a video camera.

I remained calm and explained that I was moving out of the marital home. The police calmly told Daniel, "*Sir, if you do not have a court order in place, your wife can do whatever she wants with these possessions. They belong to her as much as they belong to you. But she has possession of them now, and you don't. I am sorry, there is nothing we can do to help you.*"

Daniel then insisted on knowing the location of my rental home. I informed the officers about the domestic abuse issues and gave the names of the officers who had responded to the calls numerous times. The most important aspect was that I did not feel safe divulging my location but assured them my children were safe from harm. Within a few minutes, the police explained to Daniel that he would need to ascertain that information from his lawyers and that he needed to leave me alone. I had the right to leave in peace and stay safe. I felt validated in my efforts.

The Entourage

I had collected my entourage of hope to help me through the divorce. Now, he was collecting his entourage of envy to help him destroy the enemy (namely me) in just **5 Easy Steps**:

Step 1: Gather the Entourage- A group of people attending to or surrounding an *important* person. I told Daniel that popularity is a state of mind and location. Furthermore, I never had the desire to be popular; *I have always had the desire just to be me.* He always felt slighted by the world. This situation was his opportunity to be the *Big Man on Campus*. The problem was that his entourage was filled with bottom feeders eager to play along in this evil game of war.

Entourage: For my story, I would like to define entourage as all of the people who proactively worked against me while helping Daniel attain his goals. Actually, many of these so-called goals were the ambitions of the entourage and may or may not have been known to Daniel. Further, there are different groups in his entourage and many of them did not know or like each other. They were from completely different walks of life, but all had the same hateful mindset. I.e., legal team, family, former friends, and new friends, especially his girlfriend and her family. As I refer to entourage in the story, know that I am referring to various people, not always the same people.

Step 2: Think Big- Daniel locked me out of my computer, so I had to handwrite my ideas on how to divide our belongings and the time with our children. I proposed a 50/50 split on everything and created a custody schedule. The only caveat was that my daughter wanted Sunday nights with me, which technically made the sleeping arrangements 60/40.

However, the entourage devised a plan to take *everything*: the business, the house, the children, and, of course, the dog. That was just the beginning. Their maniacal plan was to leave me with nothing. Absolutely nothing. They actually went out of their way trying to prove I had *Borderline Personality Disorder* and was a detriment to society as well as my children.

Since the video cameras did not collect any useful evidence, Daniel confabulated stories, worked himself into a frenzy, and called the police to his rescue. He desperately needed any type of hateful documentation. Fortunately, the officers who responded recognized this type of preconceived charade and strategically worded their reports, rendering them useless to Daniel. People who do things out of spite or hate do not realize their behavior is a worn-out pattern others can obviously see right through.

If you look up confabulate in the dictionary, you will find a term that describes what a person does when they have gaps in their memory and simply fills those gaps with details that are not true *without the intention* of deceit. Instead of calling Daniel a *liar* and engaging in *"he said, she said,"* I simply used the word *confabulate* to describe him as intentionally using part truth and part fiction to be deceitful. It worked quite well when dealing with authorities.

Step 3: Have Fun - Please wipe out whatever definition you have in your mind of *fun*. Then, take a step back and envision a person trapped in a torture chamber, surrounded by disgusting, abusive, demonic creatures engaged in dark laughter. You know, the type of laughter the devil devours for dessert. I was repulsed by the way these heathens found extreme pleasure and delight in my suffering.

Schadenfreude: a German word that describes how one person experiences the emotion of pleasure in response to another person's emotion of suffering. Schaden translates as *damage* while Freude as *joy*. The concept is common across cultures, but some languages do not have a distinct word for it.

Years ago, I developed a funny expression that I thought was the perfect antidote: *"You have to be a little insane to keep your sanity, and right now, I am very sane."* It always made everyone laugh and made light of the extenuating circumstances occurring on a daily basis. There was never a dull moment.

I guess most people at this point would seek therapy and medication. Me, *I sought nature.*

I walked six miles out and back every morning, with my turn-around point in Lake Roland. I would walk the two mile loop through the neighborhood each night after dinner with my children. On Friday nights, we often made our round over to get some Italian ice and rent a movie. The freshly made mango sorbet topped with a huge dollop of frozen vanilla custard was a must under the evening stars.

I loved to sit outside on the large stone front porch during storms. The wind, the rain, the lightning strikes, and the crash of thunder were like magic to my soul. Occasionally, a refreshing mist would blow kisses onto my face, reminding me that this dark night of the soul would soon be over.

Step 4: *Trust Your Instincts-* Here's a crazy thought. Since Daniel and I first initiated our relationship fifteen years earlier, we had only spent about three weeks away from each other in total. That may sound difficult to believe, but we had been so busy with his school, moving around, building a family, and taking care of the business, we didn't actually have time to be apart. It just felt natural.

Therefore, when the entourage set traps and tried to lure me in, Daniel instinctively knew my method of operation. Once I realized I was in a precarious situation, I had to stop and think. What would my next few steps typically be, and how can I circumvent these actions to make their plan backfire? Moreover, how can I make this stupid game blow up in their face?

Step 5: *Prepare for Multiple Falls Before The Big Break-* After being out of the marital home for several months, the entourage still had no evidence to use against me in a court of law. Desperate to frame me as a horrendous mother and person, they were trying to create new scenarios.

I was notified all of my phone records had been subpoenaed. I wasn't sure how or why that would be relevant, but since Daniel was great at projection, I asked my lawyer to subpoena his as well.

Projection: In my mind, projection is one of the most commonly used defense mechanisms. It is when a person attributes or projects their own thoughts, feelings, and actions onto another, like how a camera projects images onto a movie screen. The person who is experiencing inner conflicts places blame on another. The person's inability to take responsibility for themselves is unhealthy and maladaptive. Basically, that person attributes their own flaws or vices, bad habits, or immoral and wicked behaviors onto another. I am sure you have witnessed this your entire life.

Projection may manifest in various ways: *"I failed my test because my teacher is stupid!"* But they did not even crack open a book. *"I hate my job because everyone in the office is lazy and gossips about me!"* But they overlook that they come in late, irritate the hell out of everyone, and blame others when their work is incomplete. *"You are a liar, and you are cheating on me!"* When, in fact, that person is the one lying and stepping out of the relationship.

Basically, the crazy-ass world of deceit, lust, and revenge Daniel had created for himself was spewing out all over me. He was like a big red flag waving, *"Look at me! Look at me!"* Determined to win at all costs, he and the entourage went completely over the top this time. An unknown professional photographer was able to capture *all* of us by surprise. Two hundred pictures don't lie, especially when several of your friends and family members participated and viewed the entire show.

During the summer swim meets, I was the Clerk of Course, which meant I had to pass out all the event cards to each child. I loved to see those little smiling and sometimes nervous faces donning a swim cap and goggles. I told the little ones to make sure to *blow some extra bubbles for me* and tell me about it when they were lining up for their next event. The enthusiasm in their eyes warmed my heart.

Daniel and his drama-loving girlfriend positioned their chairs directly across the pool from where I needed to stand throughout the meet. Her cousin was married to the man I was accused of having an affair with. Daniel and these two women had been in cahoots since Christmas. During the meet, the wife kept pacing back and forth in front of me as well as behind me, shouting vulgarities, "*Cunt. Bitch. Whore. Stay away from my husband. We have your phone records.*"

All the while, Daniel and his girlfriend had cameras, and his siblings had video cameras on opposing ends of the pool. But wait, there is more. Since I did not respond to the verbal instigation, Daniel picked up a large manila envelope and waved it back and forth so everyone at the pool could see, "*We have your phone records,*" and stuck up his middle finger each time my eyes peered in his direction.

I continued to hand out cards to the children, maintaining a normal appearance as best I could. Any sign of emotion could spell danger. After the last card, I went towards the snack bar, with the wife following close behind me. "*Cunt. Bitch. Whore. Why do you keep walking away? Are you scared? I should kick your ass in front of everyone.*"

I smiled and looked her dead in the eyes, ominously whispering, "*Go ahead, I dare you.*"

She lunged to hit me, but her husband pulled her away just in time. Meanwhile, Daniel and his girlfriend were viciously laughing and videotaping the entire display. I retreated to my car, needing space to think. Going back in was not physically or emotionally safe, so I called my lawyer. She insisted I file a restraining order against the wife to protect myself.

These stupid games had turned more dark and evil than expected. The repercussions were life-altering. The most hilarious part of this entire fiasco was that the swim officials had hired a photographer, and all the photographs were displayed on the large screen television at the entrance to the pool. I asked the manager to print out all the photos containing the entourage, and he happily agreed. He had been on the receiving side of a wicked divorce and took pleasure in helping me protect myself.

Not only did their childish plan backfire, but serendipity gave me an arsenal of weapons, also known as pictures, to use against him in court. You should have seen their faces when I referred them to the swimming pool website for duplicate prints. Not only did I win the battle, but I also had the entire room stifling their laughter. They looked like complete fools.

Then came the big break: They did not plan it, but it was the most perfect opportunity they could have imagined. I was tired of the nonsense from the entourage and asked Daniel to meet me for breakfast one-on-one. I hoped he would wake up and come to his senses. I wanted to know why he was letting all of these bottom feeders control our destiny. On the way back from dropping the kids off at camp, I stopped at a red light less than a mile from my destination.

I was the second car in line as the light turned green and inched forward. Something inside whispered, *"Look behind you."* I turned my head and gazed into the rearview mirror, *CRUNCH!* A car slammed me from behind. *THUG!* I slammed into the car in front of me. *UGH!* My seat broke forward, jolting my leg up into my abdomen. I pulled over to the side of the road, placing both of my hands atop my head. I forced my eyes closed to shut out the pain. All I remember saying is, *"Oh, my head."*

I thought I opened my eyes a minute later, but unbeknownst to me, at least twenty minutes had passed, and people and paramedics were all over the place. I got out of my car and saw a woman sitting on the ground. I walked over and offered her water, noticing *she was hurt.* I had no idea I was hurt as the paramedics encouraged me to look at my car. Confused, I struggled to understand what I was looking at. Finally, a little recognition appeared as my eyes broadened, *"Oh, that's my car. It looks like an accordion."* Then, they asked me to sit down, and I complied.

The next time I opened my eyes, I was strapped to a gurney in an ambulance and saw the police officers who had responded to the domestic abuse calls. I asked them to inform Daniel to pick up the children from camp but insisted they offer no other details. They understood the circumstances all too well and went to get my phone and purse out of my car, as I would need identification at the hospital.

The next time I woke up, I found myself in a hospital hallway under intense fluorescent lighting. I needed to sign documentation, and as I was scribbling my name, I insisted *nobody* except my lawyer could access *any* of my medical documentation, even if subpoenaed by the court. The nurses provided me with a special form to protect my information.

The next time I opened my eyes, I was trapped in a freezing cold room. My hair was wet and knotted under the plastic, and I had needed to urinate for hours. They refused to unstrap me from the gurney or even make me feel comfortable. Every time I asked a nurse to help me urinate, they would shoot more drugs into my system, which made me hallucinate intense colors and patterns. I had no idea if I was going to live or die. Most importantly, I had no idea if I would ever see my children again.

Finally, I unstrapped myself, removed the IVs, and went in search of a bathroom. Then, I went to the nurses' station and asked to speak to my doctor. The nurse told me I wasn't allowed out of bed and asked me to return. I told her I would only go back if she sent the doctor in to look at my head.

The next time I woke up, I was strapped to the bed in another hallway, completely disoriented. I had no idea why I was there. Suddenly, I spotted a phone on the wall with a long cord I was able to reach. I pulled myself closer and called whatever phone numbers I could remember. I actually do not know who I called or what I said, but apparently, four of my friends were trying to figure out how to help me. Fortunately, one of my friends, a heart surgeon at a nearby hospital, came to offer assistance.

The next point of recognition was a nurse asking me if I feared being in tight spaces because I was about to enter a full-body CT scan. What seemed like a minute later, I was back in my hospital room, hooked up to more machines. The officer who responded to the call came in to check on me. He wanted to know if I had a ride home. I do not remember our conversation clearly, but then some friends arrived, and the officer left. After several more hours, the staff asked if I wanted to be discharged or stay overnight. I wanted to go home; that hospital room felt like death was upon me.

The next few weeks are lost forever. I have almost no memories from that time. Whatever my memories were back then, they were not based on reality. Comprehending what was going on was not an option. I was in a perpetual dreamlike state, which was definitely more of a nightmare. Fear, confusion, and a strange intermittent anger overwhelmed me. I genuinely did not recognize the woman in the mirror and didn't want to. She remained mysteriously incognito, unknown to herself and others. Life was safer that way; fully comprehending the trauma would have probably destroyed me.

Post Concussive Syndrome and Traumatic Brain Injury

Within weeks, I had met with a team of medical professionals led by an extremely prominent brain and spine surgeon. *"This is your new baseline. Any improvements you make from here will need to happen within the next 18 months. Beyond that, there really isn't much we can do."* I was having an extremely difficult time comprehending this new reality. In fact, nothing seemed real to me anymore.

"New baseline? Are you kidding me?" I knew nothing, and I was fully aware that I knew nothing. I didn't know my phone number or address. I had difficulty driving from point A to point B, even to everyday places like school and home. The grocery store was the worst. Even when I made a list, I would get lost and confused, rarely purchasing what I intended to buy. Inevitably, I knew I was going to have to heal myself because the medical professionals verbalized no hope for my recovery.

At the time, the research on Post Concussive Syndrome and Traumatic Brain Injury was scant and inconclusive. However, the overarching medical conclusions were grim: I was going to die at a premature age, either due to suicide or other health-related conditions. Furthermore, before my death, I would most likely suffer from depression, anxiety, dementia, and Alzheimer's. One medical journal article after another concluded I would soon be dead.

Some major athletes and military personnel had brought these issues to light and received much pushback from their constituents. I found an article about a surgeon in the military who had been ostracized for pointing out cognitive deficits he suffered after being in close proximity to a bomb explosion. Although he was not physically hurt, the sound waves jarred his head significantly. He performed surgeries with excellence but could not recall the data.

I was determined to keep my deficits a secret. I was absolutely terrified the entourage would use this weapon to destroy me and take my children away forever. I was also determined to learn as much as possible to overcome my injuries and transcend this adversity with strength and courage. Honestly, I had no choice; I was my only advocate. Most of the medical professionals brushed me aside.

The biggest dilemma at this time was I had no short-term memory. I could tell you things that happened twenty-five years ago but not five minutes ago. I could fake my way through conversations, and most people didn't notice a difference unless I said something totally stupid. So, I learned to be quiet. I empathized with Alzheimer's patients and was curious to know if they knew about their deficits. The literature specifically stated brain injuries had an astronomical correlation with developing Alzheimer's at an early age. My resolve to heal myself heightened and expanded. I wanted my brain back, forever.

The doctors confirmed my findings but offered no solutions. Consequently, I took a part-time job that entailed simple data entry for electronic medical records. It took me several times to read each word on the paper forms and transfer it into the computer. Then, I would go back and check for mistakes. Fortunately, over time, my speed and accuracy improved.

One devastating result of the accident was I developed severe and debilitating migraines. The back right side of my head was soft, and the slightest touch caused severe pain. Bright lights, loud noises, elevators, and emotions were major triggers. I had to force close my brain like a computer reset before I could continue on. The potential for onset was relentless and required me to pay constant attention. If the pain shot up over my eye and down my nose, it was too late; the migraine was in control.

The doctors prescribed a bunch of pills that felt like a burning pit in my stomach and did not alleviate my symptoms. These episodes would shut me down for days. In response, I learned how to take a nap or meditate proactively. Basically, quieting the noise in my brain and detaching from reality for twenty minutes at a time either stopped or postponed the migraine episode. Then, I would drink plenty of water and eat a light, healthy snack: no caffeine or alcohol.

My vertigo was whacked, and my depth perception diminished. I went from hiking 30 miles a week and playing basketball to barely being able to walk from the house to the car. I fell off curbs and plummeted down steps because my brain did not understand how or where to go next. If I did not pay attention, I walked to the right and bumped into people or objects. It was so embarrassing.

The medical professionals explained my brain was like a car out of alignment. If I took my hands off the wheel, I would surely crash. So, they sent me to vestibular therapy, where I got to pass a basketball and dribble down the hallway while the therapist watched me. Hmm, quite ordinary and not helpful. However, an interesting phenomenon occurred when I was doing some basic stretches. Shining through the blinds, the sunlight created an imbalance of flickering light patterns on the wall. I became extremely dizzy and nauseous. This confusion prompted me to report my findings. Years later, I discovered this condition is called flicker vertigo.

The surgeon referred me to a therapeutic treatment I actually thought was helpful. I sat in a chair that was supposed to suspend my perceptions of the outside world. I wore light-blocking goggles and sound-blocking headphones. The therapist shot sparks of light, sound, and air from all directions. Initially, I felt very uncomfortable, as though I were on a full-blown roller-coaster ride. Eventually, the whirlwind of confusion subsided, and the experience felt more like a merry-go-round. Apparently, that was a one-time deal because the intervention was supposed to fix my problem instantly.

Mostly, I was left to my own devices and resorted to creating my own protocol for healing. I accessed every staircase I could find and practiced walking up and down while holding onto the handrail so I wouldn't fall. Initially, I could only step with my right foot first, but eventually, I taught myself to use alternating feet. Next, I went to the reservoir, where they blockaded the road every weekend for pedestrians. I practiced standing still on the double yellow lines, then closed my eyes and took 30 steps, forcing myself to *think straight* and, hopefully, walk straight.

The sunlight twinkling off the water confused my brain, making it difficult to think straight and not get distracted. Walking in the shade was easier. Eventually, my slow and steady pace increased to a moderate walk through the park. I had to stay on the road because the trails were filled with rocks and roots, further confusing my brain. I planned to tackle those obstacles another time.

I stopped menstruating and experienced night sweats and hot flashes. The research on this topic concluded I was more prone to die by the age of fifty if my menstrual cycle ceased in my thirties. "*What the hell! One more reason I am going to die!*" Fortunately, I found a blog by some women who had suffered from Traumatic Brain Injury, and they highlighted the gap in feminine hormones that regulate a woman's body. Apparently, over time, my hormones *may* be able to return to normal. That was definitely some much-needed good news.

I envisioned myself as an Olympic athlete, understanding they do not menstruate under extreme training programs. This allowed me to view myself in a different light. If I am in an extreme training program,

I will return to normal when my training is complete, hopefully in the next eighteen months. These thoughts brought forth some comfort.

I lost hearing in my left ear and often heard loud pitch noises. Therefore, learning how to position myself in a crowd was important to comprehend the conversation. However, background noise and people looking away while speaking remained an issue. Additionally, I had no idea how loud I was communicating in return. Eventually, I learned hearing loss isn't stigmatizing and asking people to look at me while speaking isn't difficult to deal with. When I don't want to listen or pay attention, I have the perfect excuse—hilarious, selective hearing at its finest.

Throughout this ordeal, my emotions were like a roller coaster. There were days when all I wanted to do was sleep and other days when my determination was through the roof. In the end, my children are what motivated me to keep going. I needed and wanted to rise above any challenge and achieve the seemingly impossible task of full recovery. Failure was not an option, and more issues were lurking.

My vision was sporadically blurred, and black squiggly floaters were a constant in my line of sight. I found it amusing to lay on a park bench and control the floaters as the clouds passed by. The blue sky, white clouds, and black floaters seemed to calm my brain from fear. I was told these eye floaters would subside.

Despite my fatigue, I could not sleep for more than two hours at a time. The doctors explained my brain was like an old-fashioned Jello mold: after shaking it up, it took a long time to settle down. It was difficult to tell the difference between being awake and being asleep. I was never quite sure if something really happened or if I imagined it. Was it real? Was it a dream? I had no clue.

When I was overly tired or anxious, I would stutter. I taught myself to think, "*Stop speaking now.*" Then, I would relax my shoulders, take a deep breath, and allow my chest to sink in momentarily. Then, I expanded my torso and thought, "*You can speak now,*" and the words came out clearly. Eventually, the time I needed to pause and restart decreased and became less apparent.

I resumed reading books every night and decided to read aloud. My goal was to improve the correlation between what I was thinking and what I was saying. Each sentence was a struggle, and I usually had to practice three times before I was correct. Eventually, I worked my way up to a paragraph and then a page. I was so excited that I joined a women's book club in my neighborhood. Ironically, the first book was "Eat, Pray, Love" by Elizabeth Gilbert. I thought it was highly relevant.

In the book, Liz is "living the life" and thinks she has everything she wants. When she looked around and realized this was not the life she wanted to live, she got a divorce and left it all behind. Then, she sets out on a journey of self-discovery and ends up in Italy, India, and Indonesia. At one point in the book, she envisions speaking to her former husband and shares what is in her heart. At that moment, I sat up in bed, started to cry, and spoke aloud, "Daniel, I know you can hear me! I don't care that it is 2:00 AM; you need to listen! I am sorry for everything that has happened between us. Please stop the nonsense and get yourself some help. Our children deserve it!" Speaking those words out into the universe was amazingly cathartic, and I finally got some rest.

However, when the book club got together, most women thought the author was selfish, short-sighted, and arrogant. Their main concerns were what type of diapers didn't leak and where their husbands threw their dirty socks. They were still building "the life" everyone thought they desired to live and reported being very happy with the process. I was torn between sad and angry with their comments. Sad? Because I knew many of their marriages would end in divorce, and they were judging each other for wanting to attain happiness. Angry? Because they were judging me.

So, I sipped on some wine, kept my comments to myself, and thought, "Ha! Check back with me in about ten years, and let me know how you feel. In the meantime, I am going to create my own journey of self-discovery right here and now.

Obviously, I could not pick up my life and head to three different countries to relearn my method of existence. So, I decided to relive my existence from home. I imagined I was a new person in a new town. Where could I go for new experiences? What could I do to meet new and interesting people? How will I choose to live my life? How am I going to do this with no money? It's time to get creative.

I wanted to create as many new neural pathways as possible to compensate for my lost ones. I wanted to re-experience where I lived as a brand new person to compensate for the life I had lost. This endeavor seemed to be a win-win situation. Whew, count me in.

Tactile stimulation became increasingly important and helped me understand what I saw. I developed better comprehension and memory by touching objects or images on paper. I felt funny asking to touch things constantly, but oh well. It was better than not being able to understand and look stupid.

My sense of smell intensified. Good or bad, my nose knew the way. The scent of familiar flowers created gloriously new fragrant pathways, while the aroma of familiar foods made me salivate in anticipation of an incredible meal. But hey, don't get too far ahead of yourself and be jealous. The smell of day-old trash could keep me awake at night, and that dog poop at the end of the road made me want to vomit.

Even though my ability to use my eyes and ears had greatly diminished, I felt like I could see and hear in ways unlike before. Facial expressions and bodily movements stepped into the forefront. Voice tone and eye movements were exacerbated, and minor hesitations, breaths, and posture bolstered the conversations. Basically, my intuition was expanding, and my experience of conversations drastically changed.

Essentially, my *Super Spidey Senses* were quick-witted and fun and were an integral part of my pathway back to success. Every time I updated my medical team, they reciprocated with a blank stare, did *not* document my findings, and sent me on my way. On one visit, I inquired about my prognosis. The doctor swiftly replied, "*You are going to have to give up this dream. You are never going to be able to return to your old self. Just accept that now, and life will get easier.*"

I know for a fact that most, if not all, survivors contemplate death and dying. After all, dying seems so much less painful than living, so why not take it into consideration? Do you know what else I was thinking? "*Fuckers like you contribute to life sucking ass a little bit more each day. So, I don't give a damn if your degree is from Harvard; you are an idiot. I am going to go out and prove you wrong.*" What I actually said was, "*Ok, thanks,*" and I smiled as he handed me my next appointment slip.

Beyond the diagnosis and subsequent prognosis, the fierce battle within my soul was far worse.

"*Why me, God?*" I thoroughly believed this accident was punitive for my actions. I believed I was being punished for not saving my husband from the depths of hell. "*Guess what, God? I don't care what you throw at me; I am never going back.*" Do you want to know one of the many reasons why I never considered returning to my marriage?

Listen to this one. It was a major turning point: Hours after the police informed Daniel of my car accident, he took the children to the Friday Night Outdoor Family Concert Series in our neighborhood, just three miles away from the hospital where I lay, not knowing whether I was going to live or die. He was extremely intoxicated and loud. He laughed hysterically, made strange guttural noises, and told everyone I exacerbated a fender bender and opted to go to the emergency room. He proceeded to make jokes about my accident and encouraged all the children at the concert to join in on the laughter. Within a couple of days, several people from that concert called to check on me, and all recounted the same disgusting version of the story. When I told them the truth, they were appalled.

That day is when, and most definitely why, I stopped loving my husband FOREVER.

Note: The current medical research suggests that worldwide, between 1.5 and 2 million people annually suffer Traumatic Brain Injury, and it is one of the leading causes of death and/or disability. Those who suffer may be twice as likely to attempt suicide or self-harm. Just to let you know, there is help and there is hope. You need to act fast and get people the help they deserve. Time is of the essence, and there are multiple modalities. TBI is a lifelong struggle you cannot ignore. The signs and symptoms may dissipate over time, but they can return at any time or cause an array of difficulties in the future. Please contact medical professionals for guidance and treatment. God bless.

The Art of War

While I was focused on healing and getting my life back to some degree of normalcy, Daniel and his entourage were not only perpetuating the discourse, but they were also purposely exacerbating it by using all aspects of a paradigm known to instill FEAR, WAR, and REVENGE.

The legal language and process of marriage is easy. You show up with a valid photo identification, fill out the form, and pay $35. Then, there is a 48-hour waiting period until the license is valid; you have six months before it expires. No witnesses or appointments are required.

The legal language of divorce can be intimidating, overwhelming, and confusing, but it doesn't have to be. At the time, a legal document declaring divorce cost $115 and took 365 days. The couple simply needed to live separately, not engage in sexual intercourse, and have one witness to testify on their behalf in court. If both parties come to an amicable agreement, an absolute divorce is granted.

Serious problems arise when one party is distinctly at a disadvantage and unwilling to accept change. When that change is going to leave them lost and vulnerable or is going to make them face their own mortality, serious problems arise. Most importantly, in my case, Daniel knew it was his fault.

He physically, emotionally, and spiritually left our marriage years before the final tipping point and subsequent blowup. Now, I simply wanted to terminate the legal aspect of our agreement. I *never* expected this magnitude of revenge. What Daniel and his entourage did to me should never be done to another human being, especially the mother of your children and grandchildren.

Brace yourself. I can't make this shit up, and I would never wish it upon any human. Not only was I in the midst of trying to recover from a car accident where several paramedics and doctors told me, "*You shouldn't be alive.*" I was in the midst of *asymmetrical warfare* where the enemy wanted me to die, figuratively, and I thoroughly believe, literally as well.

I had no desire to fight a war; I simply wanted my freedom. However, freedom isn't free, and it comes with great cost. That financial or psychological debt may stay with you for a lifetime.

Asymmetrical Warfare: Unconventional strategies employed when the military capabilities of the belligerent force of power are so significantly different than their opposition they cannot employ the same types of attacks. Fortunately for me, history has shown *that victory* does not always go to the superior military force. Oftentimes, war's outcome is contingent upon the valor of the people fighting.

When the overwhelming desire to torture me, knowing full well I was entitled to half of *everything,* did not produce the desired results, their unilateral decision-making processes exacerbated. All outcomes were intended to benefit Daniel and destroy me.

Up to this point, every skirmish or plan of attack had failed. The Supreme Commanding General in *The War Against Amy* was defeated in court several times. I am not talking about Daniel; I am referring to his legal representation. I actually testified that this incredibly notorious lawyer was *The Devil* and did not get reprimanded by the judge. He always employed multiple forms of deception, and I brought it to the court's attention. He was infuriated, and his reputation was on the line while this young truth-telling woman was kicking his ass in the courtroom. Although my testimonies took a considerable toll on my soul, I was proud I could access the energy reserves within myself and stay in my own power.

Lying by Omission: When one *passively* omits relevant information.

Lying by Commission: When one *actively* uses false statements.

Paltering: When one actively uses truthful statements to create a false impression and mislead others. People engaging in this type of negotiation focus on the veracity of their truth-telling statements. Think of veracity as verifying or conforming to facts and using those facts to prove a lie.

The Devil enthusiastically employed the use of all three types of lies, especially paltering, to enable a self-serving assessment of his morality: I want to be rich and powerful. I want to win the war. I need to destroy her to win the war. The more I destroy her, the richer and more powerful I am.

When Daniel had to assess his own morality, he was willing to put his reputation on the line to coerce people onto his side. Unfortunately, the deceptions took him further down into the depths of darkness and destruction. When he set out to win the war, he had no idea he would destroy himself, his family, and his business. However, once he was in hell, there was no turning back. Unfortunately, Daniel embraced the notion that compassion was for the weak at heart.

His legal representation slammed me with every type of legal document and incessantly churned fees. Every word and allegation followed the same line of paltering and created an illusionary version of the truth. I firmly believe Daniel learned to believe the version of the truth they were creating was valid. My job wasn't to confirm or deny the lies; my job was to tell my version of the truth. My words and actions were highly frustrating to Daniel's lawyer because he was used to being in control and getting his way in the legal system. Apparently, lies and deceit are acceptable in his realm.

However, at times, my Traumatic Brain Injury and Post Concussive Syndrome made the truth seem overly difficult and out of reach.

I could no longer remember or distinguish between reality and non-reality. I kept hoping I would wake up and this nightmare would be over. I thought maybe I had actually died in that car accident, and I was living in hell. My existence resembled what I used to call my life, but instead of appearing vibrant and alive, it was cold and dead.

Besides creating the language of war, the Supreme Commanding General, also known as the Devil, and Grandpa (Daniel's father), who financed the war, rallied support. The entourage sought further avenues of mass destruction.

Attrition Warfare: This usually defines law-abiding military combatants. Their missions represent an attempt to grind down an opponent's ability to participate in war by destroying their resources by any means necessary. Any battle apart from the decisive battle is a belligerent attempt to win the war by wearing down the enemy to the point of complete exhaustion.

Guerrilla Warfare: Usually defines irregular combatant forces comprised of civilians. Individuals or small groups of insurgents purposely employ tactics such as ambush, sabotage, deception, and espionage. The intent is to undermine an authority figure through long, intense confrontations. In Spanish, *Guerra* means war, and *Illa* denotes small, but the word's connotation is considered *violent action* within the normally accepted rules and regulations of war.

Terrorism: Depicts *violent action* directed at civilian targets, and the terrorist's goal is public attention. Terrorism is designed to destroy any sense of safety and security in all people and places familiar to the victim. Further, terrorists wish to publicize their strength and threaten to impose sanctions on those who do not abide by their wishes. Basically, if you are not with me, you are against me, and you will suffer.

Attenuation: A battle of will, personal determination. The most important task for the entourage was to prove they had more time, money, and resources than I did. They made it perfectly clear that I would be penniless, alone, and in the gutter if I did not back down and succumb to their requests. The greater the costs, the more powerful the outcome. Remember the list of my friends in the community who provided love and hope for my future? Well, Daniel showed up in most of their living rooms and pleaded for mercy. Could they in any way help him and save his children? Then, his legal team personally called them to gather information and issued subpoenas for them to appear in court.

Most of my friends were horrified by the disturbing display of emotional threats. They expressed sympathy but asked to be removed from the situation. Technically, they asked to be removed from my life. Regrettably, I understood and agreed. At the time, I didn't understand they were *friends of the road*, and each one took little pieces of my soul with them when they disappeared.

Friends of the road are situational friends we encounter along the road of life. They are companions or acquaintances due to time, place, or circumstance and naturally change over time. *Genuine friends* love you and want the best for you. The strong bonds never dissipate whether you see them once a week or once a year. Unfortunately, my friendships were growing weaker or had already terminated.

Intimidation: The next important task was to block all of my financial resources. Daniel had already shut down all the joint bank accounts and credit cards and reopened his own personal accounts. Then, he refused to pay the court-ordered alimony pendente lite, which was alimony pending litigation.

Next, they unlawfully voided all twenty-two of my legal rental lease agreements with my tenants and mandated them to pay Daniel solely and to render all payments to a post office box to which I did not have access. The notice specifically stated I was not permitted on my rental properties, and that if they engaged in any communication or financial exchanges with me, their leases would immediately terminate.

I had a great relationship with all my tenants, who came from all walks of life: single, married, young, and old, with various religions, nationalities, and sexual preferences. What did they all have in common besides me? They were all awesome people, and I wanted them to live in my apartments as much as they wanted to live there. When they broke this news to me, I simply said I would stay away until the divorce case was over and insisted, "*Keep yourself safe. Don't worry about me. I'll be back soon.*" It felt like a knife had just been thrust into my gut as I walked away and cried in my car.

Provocation: Metaphorically means to ignite the fuse. The entourage needed to persuade my children: *Your Mother* is mean, crazy, and unworthy of love. *Your Mother* must be vigorously resisted if you want to have access to money and be happy. After years of ignoring my children, his family suddenly desired to purchase expensive clothes and shoes. They took them to nice dinners and bought them presents. They invited their friends on day trips and to the movies. Life without *Your Mother* is better. Trust the entourage, and abundant wealth will be at your fingertips. Daniel and his family were emotionally manipulating my children. In my mind, these grotesque manipulations of the truth have left a permanent scar.

I have *Your Mother* italicized because the entourage used this title for me when speaking to the children. They aggressively accentuated the words and made them sound demeaning and disgraceful. Whenever the children heard the words "*Your Mother*" spoken, they felt ashamed, and their shoulders slumped as if they had been defeated and punished. It was painful to hear and watch.

Further, they convinced my children that normal childhood chores and responsibilities were *Your Mother's* duty in life. They did not need to clean their room, wash the dishes, complete their homework, or go to bed on time. They did not have to go to school or be respectful to teachers, coaches, or classmates. Basically, everything *Your Mother* has taught you is bad and wrong, and the entourage was determined to save them from their evil *Mother.*

Initially, I was safe, and my babies loved their *Mommy* with all their hearts. But the *reiteration effect* was in full force, and it was definitely taking a major toll on both my children, especially my preadolescent daughter. She was trying to find her way in the world, and the desire for money was being thrust at her in all directions. She was in an expensive private school, and materialism was a distinct way of life. I encouraged her to accept the gifts but to be careful not to get brainwashed.

Reiteration Effect: Also known as the illusory truth effect, which means that after being repeatedly exposed to false information, there is a tendency to believe it, and it feels familiar or comfortable. Ultimately, my children were examining an incorrect version of the truth, and it caused great discomfort. But they may or may not have known why. Either way, it was detrimental to their well-being.

Every time my children returned from their scheduled custody time with their father, they were exhausted and took turns having meltdowns. These cathartic releases each took about an hour and required all my attention. I helped them process their emotions and taught them to self-soothe before bed. On the flip side, I wanted to have meltdowns, process my emotions, and self-soothe. But instead, I crawled into bed thoroughly exhausted and felt the weight of the world upon my shoulders. I sincerely thought I had failed to protect my children and keep them from harm.

Spoiling: Means to purposely sabotage the peace. Initially, both children were doing well at school, but the emotional exhaustion of dealing with their life situation wore them down. Obviously, the schools were aware of the marital separation as our individual contact information was provided. The schools were not used to communicating with Daniel, as all prior communications were with me. Thus, they were receiving mixed messages from us, which caused much confusion.

Beyond the initial confusion, the entourage was on a mission to get the schools to turn against me. Since Daniel had been nonexistent in the school systems for a couple of years, he needed to make up for lost time. He continuously sent a barrage of emails to the teachers and administrators to make me look like a detriment to my children. Subsequently, in-person meetings and general assemblies became severely uncomfortable for everyone because he was incredibly anxious and acted like a fool. Honestly, it was utterly embarrassing for the entire family.

Fortunately, the school officials saw through this charade and made great efforts to help keep the peace. As the entourage increased their efforts, school officials grew weary. They did not want to be a part of a huge escapade of lies and deceit; they had their own reputations to uphold. My daughter's school did a great job and held on as long as possible. My son's school, however, not so much. They couldn't get rid of my son fast enough, although they pretended to care about his well-being.

Outbidding: The overzealous combatant force the entourage did not expect to work with or contend against was a young, crazy, low-class piece of white trash looking to move up in the world. Within one month after I told Daniel I was leaving him, his new lustful love interest had been strategizing a secret *coup d'etat*, a seizure of power. Daniel was so insanely desperate that he did not recognize the elephant in the room. This bitch took pleasure in devising plans to torture me and wanted to be in control of the entire situation. Moreover, she wanted to control Daniel and, of course, the money. She was willing to do anything to get her greedy hands all over it and believed she could outsmart all of us.

This twenty-eight-year-old acted like an adolescent, pretending to care for my children and buying them gifts. Lucy was her code name, as she was apparently Daniel's long-lost cousin. She lived at the marital home when the children were not around, but her presence was obvious, especially with the laundry situation. My children were disgusted when her undergarments were piled up on the dresser beside theirs. My daughter gasped when she accidentally picked up Lucy's underwear as they both ran out of the bedroom. As their romance was in full force, they intentionally and sometimes unintentionally got sloppy in hiding their relationship. The text messages they sent to each other were often graphic and sexual. My children knew the truth and complained.

One morning, I received an automated text message: *school was canceled due to a snowstorm*, and I had to drop the kids off at Daniel's house before I went to work. Upon arrival, Lucy's car was in the driveway. The children started to cry and refused to go inside. I called him several times, but he refused to pick up the phone. So, I knocked on the front door. He peered out the window and made loud, strange, undulating noises while contorting his face and arms.

Impatiently, I raised my voice and talked through the glass, *"Daniel, the kids are crying and don't want to come inside. I have to go to work; it's your day to be with them."* Daniel began to make barking noises and pretended to shoo me away like a stray dog. Then he grunted back at me, *"That's your problem. I am not supposed to have them until this afternoon."* I explained this situation was ridiculous and that his girlfriend needed to leave so the kids could come inside.

Just then, Lucy started chanting, *"Thanks for the money, bitch! How does it feel to be poor? Thanks for the money, bitch! How does it feel to be poor? Thanks for the money, bitch!"*

I rolled my eyes in disgust and tightly clenched my jaw, feeling darkness overwhelm my soul. I put my face near the window so only Daniel could see and hear my rage, *"I am going to drive away and come back in ten minutes. If that stupid fucking cunt isn't out of the fucking house when I get back, I am going to subpoena her and her entire fucking family into court and make them testify. I can absolutely guarantee YOU will lose everything."* Fortunately for everyone, within ten minutes, she was gone.

Don't get too excited; Lucy's shenanigans lasted two and a half years. She stayed until she found out Daniel was out of money and had nowhere to live. Honestly, I am surprised the rest of the entourage tolerated her drama during their expensive dinners, excursions, and vacations. After all, he charged all their expenses on credit cards and left a massive paper trail of their relationship that I could use against him in court. Brilliant, right?

Espionage: The entourage had various methods of spying on me to gain truthful information and sufficient information to help them palter more lies.

They installed tracking applications on the cell phones in the family plan and monitored my cellular calls and text messages. When they could not obtain any usable evidence from my phone, they disconnected my service, and I had to get my own plan. However, the entourage always knew our location when the children were with me. Individually, Daniel, his girlfriend, and his brother would regularly drive by me or sit in parking lots, observing my actions. It was obvious they were videotaping my activity. Sometimes, I would wave and acknowledge them like they were my friends, but at other times, I would do whatever I could to get away from their insane bullshit. I mean, don't they have anything better to do with their time? It was beyond creepy.

They went through a series of private investigators to follow me and document my every move. I contacted my lawyer each time I caught the private investigators in action, who subpoenaed their information. This legally prevented that particular company from tracking me but did not deter or prevent the next one. With each new hire, the private investigators became harsher and more ruthless. The last company I am aware of willfully documented lies after spending $10,000 in their pursuits and asking for $5,000 more before they could continue to report their findings.

This continuous invasion of privacy left me extremely paranoid. In every ounce of my body, I could *feel* I was being pursued by unknown men, in unknown cars, into unknown places every day for nine months *after* leaving the marital home. I was being whipped into compliance by unknown shadows of men, although I would not label them as real men. I could not fathom what type of human would do this work and document things like: "She went to the grocery store and bought two bags of food," "She went to church and put boxes in the trunk of her car," "She is sitting on her front porch listening to music." And yet, somehow, they managed to find and report extraordinary faults in my ordinary life. I hope karma was paying attention to these cowardly shadows.

My code name for these shadows was Bill, like "dollar bill," because I knew how much money these low-life scumbags were making to follow me around. Each time I confronted them face-to-face, I said, *"Excuse me, you look familiar. Is your name Bill?"* The looks on their faces were always priceless.

I was desperate to feel safe and developed strange behaviors to protect myself. I parked in obscure places and cut through wooded areas, streets, and buildings. Instead of driving down main roads, I would zigzag through back streets and circle around an area before entering. I rotated the lighting options in my house to create confusion about whether I was home or not. When I left the house, I exited through the back door and cut through the neighbors' yards. I felt insane, yet I knew it was for survival.

The only reason I knew *I was sane* was because I caught them at their own game, and they documented my actions. My lawyer was astounded and inquired, *"How do you always know?"* The only response I could conjure was, *"I don't really know. I just decide, 'Who doesn't belong here?"* Then, most of the time, I ask others the same question, and oddly enough, we always pick the same person.

Even with all my safety precautions, sometimes I was still followed. One day, I was headed for a hike and felt Bill. I pulled into Starbucks and purchased a cup of coffee. I hit the gas as I drove onto the highway, swerving through traffic at eighty miles an hour. I jolted to the right and exited near a university parking lot that I knew was a dead end. I quickly parked and ran to Bill's car as he jumped into the back seat to conceal himself. I pounded on his window and screamed, *"You better leave me the fuck alone! Why don't you get a real job? You are such a coward! You won't even show your face!"* You would have thought we were filming a scene in an action thriller movie!

I was trying to live a normal life. Yet, another time, I was playing billiards in one of my favorite little dive bars. Pappa's Restaurant & Sports Bar has the best crab cakes in Baltimore. I have frequented that place since I was in college. Suddenly, I got the *Bill vibe* from the guy at the pool table beside mine. I asked the bartender, "*Who doesn't belong here?*" to verify my gut feeling. He motioned towards the stocky guy with a biker convention t-shirt from Marina del Rey, California. Curiously, I inquired about his shirt and asked if I could put quarters on his table to play against him. He said he preferred to play alone and consumed at least five or six beers quickly.

At this point, I thought these idiots had traumatized me long enough, so I decided to make it a fun game. I went over to the jukebox and flirted with *Bill*. I playfully giggled, tossed my hair around, and asked him to select a song for me. He looked both aroused and confused. Then, he inquired who my male friend at the table was. I said, "*Oh, that's my brother. His girlfriend will be here soon if you want to play doubles,*" as I looked at him with a gleam in my eyes.

Soon after, he disappeared out the back door, and the bartender warned me, "*He's on his phone, and he's not leaving. Be careful out there.*" By this time, the fun had worn off, and I wanted to irritate him a little more. I got into my car and circled the neighborhood multiple times before stopping at the track field at the local high school. I parked in an obscure spot and ran around the perimeter. If he was going to follow me, he had better have his running shoes on! I thought the entire thing was hilarious, so I cut through the woods, returned to my car, and went home. Unbelievably, he tracked my every move.

I contacted my lawyer the next day, and we had to issue a court document demanding he stop following me. Apparently, the private investigators had installed a tracking device under my car and could watch me on the monitor screens and talk to each other via cell phones to try and guess my next move. They were so desperate for any type of information to use against me.

The breaking point was hacking into my email and obtaining all my personal and legal documentation. I am not sure how long they had access, but it definitely gave them some insider information they could use to perpetuate the war. In case you are wondering, this is illegal.

I think Daniel instinctively knew that chaos wouldn't take me down. I can thrive in chaos and create a sense of organization in the situation. The only thing that would take me down was my inability to control my response to certain situations. Unfortunately, he knew that as well. They were going to use OUR CHILDREN as weapons of mass destruction.

Psychological Warfare was the only way to capture *Amy* as a prisoner of war, a prisoner he never intended to release even when the decisive battle was over. I can still see Daniel's curdled face, hear his wicked voice, and smell the stench of evil as he proclaimed, *"I promise you one thing: I am going to torture you every day until the day I die."* This evil commitment will be etched in my memory forever.

Just Disappear

The financial burden I incurred and Daniel's complete disrespect for the law was increasingly difficult. He kept all of the income from our business and did not pay *any* of the mortgages or utility bills for our rental properties or marital home. He was not paying the $2400 per month in alimony, as dictated by law. All of his personal and professional expenditures were being charged on credit cards, which, by the end of the divorce, totaled $180,000. Daniel naively thought these charges would be divided in half. To top it off, his father gave him $5,000 per month and paid his legal fees.

One of my biggest dilemmas was locating the magical disappearing income streams because Daniel insisted he was dead broke and could not afford to pay me alimony. I was paying for my rent and utilities with a monetary gift from my sister and living off $100 weekly for food and gas. The church allowed me to take food from the food pantry after Sunday mass. I was embarrassed and uncomfortable, so I asked to do some additional volunteer work to compensate.

Daniel asked to take the children to the Adirondack for two weeks just before an important court date. I assumed that all people who proclaim to be penniless decide to take their children on expensive excursions in New York and create the necessary legal documentation. However, Daniel refused to provide the required itinerary and just *disappeared*. The real kick in the ass is that I had asked to vacation in the Adirondack for many years, and he always ignored me or grumbled at my request.

In line with the emotional abuse I was enduring, he took away the children's cell phones and did not permit them to call me for the entire vacation. With each passing day, I became increasingly anxious as I was not able to get in touch with them. One night, I received a phone call from my daughter. She was terrified and had snuck into the back bedroom of the house where they were staying to call me. We only talked for a minute because she did not want to get caught. She just wanted me to know she loved me and wanted to hear my voice. I assured her everything was alright, that I loved her and would see her soon.

Ironically, some of that disappearing money magically appeared. At the church, I was assigned to collate the checks and total the monetary donations after the masses. Flip, flip, flip, my hands started to shake. In a room filled with people, I was handed a starter check, and the signature was absolutely Daniel's handwriting. He donated $15 from a bank account he failed to mention in his *interrogatories*. I covertly copied down the account numbers. I felt lightheaded and nauseous and continued to shake. This behavior caused some strange looks from those around me, so I excused myself to the bathroom.

Interrogatories are a limited set of inquiries you must answer *under oath* as a preliminary fact-finding mission for the legal teams on both sides. They are supposed to include a financial summary, a child custody summary, and an asset summary. Legally, one party is only supposed to be able to ask 60 questions, but his entourage slammed me with 125 different questions with subcategories. The funny part was that their line of questioning actually provided further evidence on my behalf. So, I agreed to answer all the questions even though I could have legally declined.

The most ridiculous part of the interrogatories was that the entourage included a three-page dissertation on borderline personality disorder and attempted to create multiple illusions to use against me. Apparently, I had stolen guns from my father, bought promiscuous lingerie for twelve different lovers, and was an alcoholic and a drug addict. Moreover, I was a danger to the children and society. Hilarious, I wonder how I found the time to do all those things and raise my children while running a business.

My lawyer suggested we ignore the circus show they were trying to create and just stick to the facts. *"Exactly! I was doing what I was supposed to be doing in life and was demonized for it."* I told her to consider this for a moment: If my business is worth $3.5 million and I was out getting drunk and high with twelve different lovers while my husband just sucked ass, wouldn't I stay married and reap the benefits? She paused randomly, "Oh! I never thought about it that way!" we both laughed.

The next day, my lawyer subpoenaed all records from that bank and found he had opened three different accounts and deposited over 96 checks containing my name but not my signature. The entourage accused me of entering the marital home and stealing his mail. Oops, sorry. Nope. Nope. Nope. God was on my side for this one.

Finally, my children were back from vacation, and I waited and waited. Several hours passed without any communication. I called Daniel to find out where the children were, and he was enraged. He exclaimed that I was emotionally unstable and a danger to our children. If I came near his house, he would call the police and have me arrested. I told him we had a signed legal agreement for his vacation and that it was over. I was on my way over to pick them up.

Upon arrival, the police were waiting for me, and his lawyer was on the phone. Apparently, *the signed legal agreement* I created was not notarized, and his lawyer insisted it should be disregarded. Daniel was running around the yard and freaking out as the children watched from the bay window. The officers suggested I go home and pick the children up in the morning. It had been a long day, and everyone was exhausted. I spoke to the officers on the side and asked them to document the erratic behaviors and failure to uphold a written contract. Then, I went home.

I called my father-in-law, hoping he would help to alleviate the situation. I began by asking him to tell Daniel to follow the legal agreement. Then, there was a pause and a click. I said, *"Oh, I guess I am being recorded."* Then, there was another click, and Grandpa burst into a robust, evil laugh, *"Well, you are the one who asked for the divorce, and now, you are getting it. You should be careful what you ask for. Never call me again,"* he said as he hung up the phone. Wow, this man was more evil and involved than I thought. The apple doesn't fall far from the tree.

The following week, I made another appearance in court. The bombs and lethal gases from Daniel's lawyers permeated the courtroom. I could not stop crying at one point, and the judge called for a short recess. I walked over to a small window that used to adorn a beautiful courtroom chamber made of mahogany and marble. I peered between the wrought iron bars and saw a woman walking down the street. I wondered what it was like to live in the real world. I wondered what it was like to be free.

That afternoon, I returned home, closed all the blinds, and lay in darkness. A migraine overwhelmed my brain as I suffered in silence. Technically, the court case decision was in my favor, but I did not feel victorious. I still felt like a prisoner of war who had received a short letter from home. Unfortunately, the enemy confiscated my letter and threw it into a fiery pit in hell.

The only way to keep myself safe was just to disappear. Disappear into my own world.

The next day, my best friend from college called to check up on me. I was still lying on the couch and had no intention of moving. Tom arrived at my house about twenty minutes later and told me to shower and put on some nice clothes to go to dinner. When I was getting ready, he cleaned my living room and kitchen. Tom was one of the few people I allowed into my world. When I was with him, the rest of the world would magically disappear, and we were safe together.

Small Victories

I knew my counterterrorism efforts were starting to pay off when I could laugh at the adversity. I never instigate or perpetuate a fight. I have no desire to control, manipulate, or hurt anyone, but I also have no desire to lose. I can affirm, "*If you back me into a corner, I will fight and win.*"

It was disgusting to watch the entourage destroy my business, my credit, and my reputation. Since they could not find fault with my past, they focused on creating fault in my present-day life and attempting to ensure my future would be dismal.

In turn, I had to hire a business lawyer. He was a very nice and down-to-earth family man with two children. He was on a path to become a judge in the city and was highly regarded in his vocation. He suggested we file a lawsuit to restore ownership of my business and try to salvage what remained.

I had no documentation to present because Daniel had jointly filed our taxes for eight years, and unbeknownst to me, I was labeled "*Homemaker*" with zero income. Beyond that, he confiscated all of our electronic and paper business documentation. Fortunately, I was extremely meticulous with all contractual applications, leases, addendums, and termination agreements. I created and executed all the legal documents for our business, and upon leaving the marital home, all paperwork was up to date and collated in the corresponding property folders. But this evidence was nowhere to be found.

Fortunately, the judge was an elder in the legal community, bringing a strong sense of calmness and curiosity to the courtroom. He mentioned his grandson played soccer in Europe, and we struck up a wonderful conversation about some friendship leagues between religious adversaries.

The judge asked Daniel and me a series of questions about our company. Daniel's knowledge skirted around the maintenance of the properties while I extrapolated on various legal, financial, and philosophical topics. I had facts and figures I could easily convey and a basis for how and why I used my methodologies. In ordinary people's words, I knew what I was talking about because I created it. It was mine, and I testified that Daniel's position in the business was hireable.

Did I need him to run the business? No. However, hiring someone to do the maintenance work does cost additional money. However, I planned to cover those expenses and keep half of the properties. The judge was attentive to my business plan and asked several pertinent questions. He seemed impressed with my verbal knowledge, as that was all he had to base his decisions on. I still do not understand why Daniel refused to submit any documentation. He made himself out to be a fool.

The judge did not allow the lawyers to say much; I believe he was familiar with The Devil and his games. The judge called a short recess, and upon returning to the courtroom, he and I continued our delightful conversation about soccer and a few other things. My lawyer informed me I wasn't supposed to have outside discussions with the judge, and I replied, "*Oh, I didn't know. He is the one who initiated it.*" When the judge read his verdict, The Devil's hands gripped the desk and turned white.

Victory! I was overwhelmed with joy but maintained my composure. This verdict awarded me 50% of my business and mandated that I be included in all business decisions until the final divorce and business proceedings concluded. Nothing is like spending $5,000 to make your husband play nicely in the sandbox. When we were dismissed, I promptly headed to The Devil, extended my hand to gesture a handshake, and mischievously smiled, "*It's been a pleasure doing business with you, Sir.*" But for some odd reason, he did not shake my hand in return. Hilarious! Any real man would have graciously accepted the inevitable defeat.

In addition to the court case, we had to deal with personal property, including our truck, which Daniel drove and was legally in my name. We purchased all of our automobiles under my name because I had better credit and a better driving record, so the insurance was much cheaper. However, he refused to make the truck payments, and the bank threatened to repossess the vehicle. I did not find out about this for several months, and to save my credit and the truck, I had to pay in full, which was very expensive on my limited budget. I had no money to buy groceries or pay my utility bills. In turn, some friends offered me money, but I said I would only accept their money if I could do something for them in return. I did some painting, yard work, reorganizing storage areas, and house cleaning.

Legally, I asked to be reimbursed. Yet, two more months passed when I had to pay for the truck he was driving. Finally, I went to the police station to file a report. The people at the desk said they could not help me with the situation and found humor in my complaint. So, I asked to speak to their supervisor and sat on the bench.

Almost three hours later, a man came out of the door to speak to me. He explained they do not get involved in marital disputes. I explained I owned the truck and my soon-to-be ex-husband was keeping it hostage. I simply wanted possession of the truck that I paid for. As he half-heartedly contemplated my request, I burst into tears.

Out of pure mental and emotional exhaustion, I said, "*Sir, I am a law-abiding citizen. I go out of my way to help others and do volunteer work. I own my own business and support my two children. I have never even had a parking ticket, and you are telling me you refuse to help me against a man who is stealing all of my money and getting away with it? I am simply asking you to do the right thing and help me get my truck back*". Surprisingly, he replied, "*Gimmie a minute.*"

He walked into the back room and returned with one piece of paper on a clipboard. "*Just sign this, and we will get your truck back.*" I wiped away the rest of my tears and thanked him for his kindness.

Within a few hours, I received a phone call from my father. Apparently, Daniel had taken the children to Washington, DC, for the day, and unbeknownst to me, the truck had an anti-theft device installed on it. Federal marshals ambushed the truck. That's right, several armed marshals charged at Daniel until they saw the children and lowered their guns. Then, they confiscated the truck and left the three of them on the side of the road.

Whew, when I said, "*Do the right thing,*" I didn't mean that. This entire fiasco was a complete disaster, and retrieving the truck took forever and was very expensive. Ultimately, this issue ended up in court, and I looked like a fool. But how on earth did I know that was going to happen? Either way, Daniel agreed to make the payments, and I agreed to let him keep the truck until the final divorce proceedings.

One more little victory came out of this disaster. When we got the truck out of the compound, I thoroughly investigated every tiny thing I could find. Fortunately for me, he was very messy and discarded his trash in the back seat. I found brochures for hotels and travel amenities, to-go menus, bank printouts, homemade music compact discs, and jewelry. Most disgustingly, I found used condoms and lubrication jelly in a fast-food bag with some stale French fries.

I called all the establishments and phone numbers I could find and asked for "*a copy of my receipt.*" I explained to each customer service representative that I was on a business trip, had lost all my receipts and statements, and needed to turn them into work for reimbursement. "*Could you please help me?*" They happily assisted and faxed all the information directly to my lawyer's office. Again, my lawyer was baffled by how I retrieved this information and why people were so willing to send it. I was unsure how to explain that the universe was helping me in mysterious ways. The next example tied together a few missing pieces to the puzzle.

On one of my fact-finding missions, I pulled into the parking lot of a hotel/restaurant Daniel frequented with his girlfriend and saw a payphone. It was about a mile from her house, where she lived with her parents. I am not sure what made me get out of my car and call my house, but I did. When I got home, I researched the number in my notes and realized it perfectly matched the number that was prank-calling me during intense private investigator maneuvers. Bam! "*How stupid!*" They called me from their sleazy hotel room to try and prove I was having an affair. I couldn't stop laughing.

Go away, Go away, Go away!

All of the chaos in my life left me feeling disjointed and spiritually empty. In turn, I joined a new non-denominational bible study for women, and we met every Thursday evening. I was the only woman in the midst of getting a divorce in the group. I often didn't talk much; I just found comfort in being a part of something I thought was bigger than myself. It helped sometimes.

However, the night before my birthday, I felt disheartened. It had been a year since I decided to leave, and I felt lost and alone. The discussion was about strong women in the bible who stayed with their husbands through arduous trials. A few ladies seemed to be judging me and inquired about how I dealt with such circumstances. My stomach turned to knots as tears welled up in my eyes.

After all, didn't these women understand God counts our tears? There weren't enough tissues in the world to catch all the tears I had cried trying to save my marriage.

After the study group ended, I got a glass of wine. It was all I could afford on my tiny budget, and I wanted to relax and unwind. There was a nice place down the road that was great for conversing with friends and strangers. Everyone there seemed to enjoy a friend to talk to before returning home after a long day at work. It reminded me of the sitcom "Cheers," and I did need a break from all my worries.

I sat on a bar stool where I could be alone but still partake in conversations around me. There was an attractive yet austere-looking man quietly sitting in the corner. He had been fussing with his phone for quite some time. Every so often, he looked over and pleasantly smiled. I knew he wanted to talk.

Initially, I pretended not to notice. Eventually, I reciprocated with a bashful smile and a reverent nod. After the area cleared out a bit, he moved to the stool beside me and began to speak. I am unsure what he was saying because I could only think, "Go *away, go away, go away.*"

When he asked about my occupation, I said I was returning to school to become a nurse. "*What kind?*" he inquired. I deliberately tried to create something very intelligent sounding to scare him away. "*Palliative care for oncology*" had scared off a few other men interested in speaking, so I tried it. Unfortunately, he knew exactly what I was talking about and decided to offer free job consultation advice. Awesome, right?

Begrudgingly, I listened. Within a few minutes, we were engaged in a great discussion about where I was in life and where I needed to be. He was open, kind, and knowledgeable. I had met a true gentleman. He gave me his phone number and email address. He explained I could peruse job listings and send them to him for feedback. He also offered to review my resume, which I still needed to write.

Over the next few months, he provided much-needed advice to calm my weary soul. He insisted any money I get from my divorce should be considered "*bonus money.*" I should not depend on it in any way. With less than three months to go, I did not have a plan for financial security and needed to be self-sufficient. I had been working for myself for eight years, and returning to the workforce seemed anticlimactic but necessary. His advice couldn't have been more accurate.

Once the divorce was final, he wanted to introduce me to the woman who runs three of his programs in addition to her regular job. His description of her was extremely flattering yet intimidating. I graciously accepted the offer but had no idea what to expect.

The only thing I knew for sure was that my ultimate job description was to protect My Boss and the three innovative programs they had developed into one amazing endeavor to help save and protect mommies and babies. I was intrigued and humbled. Having a permanent job meant I could support my own babies without depending on any of the money from the divorce settlement. A tremendous burden had been lifted off my shoulders, and the gift of a new life was upon me.

Hope Springs Eternal means having hope and remaining optimistic even under the worst circumstances. I used this phrase because The Devil used to refer to me and use this expression. However, he meant I was the adverse circumstance, and hopefully, I would come to my senses and allow them to win. Oops. Nope, not this time. It's my turn.

Part of my brain was thoroughly confused because I felt as though I knew nothing. I had come a long way in my treatment for my brain injuries, but I felt inadequate. When I told my new friend/mentor my feelings, he nodded and gave me half a smile, *"You should really give yourself more credit. You know far more now than you are willing to believe."* I sighed in relief and smiled. *"Thank you".*

He reminded me, *"Just keep your head down and do your work. You will be fine."*

Freedom Is Not Free

Pending the final divorce litigation, I had to engage with more lawyers. I know, really! The word "lawyer" still disgusts me. Some good lawyers are out there, but the bad ones are incredibly easy to find. It baffles me that people who study the law and swear to uphold truth and justice can sometimes be the most dishonorable out there. The people who work alongside them in the legal system know who they are, and they should be held accountable for their actions. But they are not. Most often, they are financially rewarded. Guess what? Many of these villains live a life full of dis-ease.

The first one was the lawyer assigned to the children so they could have an unbiased opinion in the eyes of the court. She was pleasant but very timid. She asked me many questions and suggested we send the children to therapy for a while, which I agreed to. Of course, half of the fee for these services would be automatically withdrawn from my portion of the proceeds following the divorce.

I was invited to a two-hour meeting set up by Daniel's legal team that encompassed five different lawyers with divergent opinions that were supposed to benefit me. Unfortunately, their goal was to subjugate me into compliance. I listened to the fifteen-minute bloviated introduction and interjected several direct questions. They wanted me to sign the entire business and marital home over to Daniel and withdraw any and all of my authority because it was *in my best interest.* Did they genuinely believe I would be so naïve and agree to any of their bullshit?

Somewhat bewildered, I stood up and assertively put my hand on the table. I clenched my teeth and growled, *"I am having an extremely difficult time believing I need to pay you all $2500 per hour to hear you tell me I need to walk away from my house and my business for my own good. You all disgust me. I am done here."* I picked up my belongings and walked out. The entourage had grown, and the absurdity and greed had escalated. Every one of those lawyers just wanted a piece of the pie.

Minutes before the final divorce hearing, the children's lawyer approached me for a brief discussion. She looked at the ground and said she was sorry. The 50/50 custody schedule was to remain intact, and none of Daniel's indiscretions or direct law violations would be considered. Apparently, mortgage fraud, tax fraud, bank fraud, and over a hundred accounts of contempt of court in no way portray a person's character.

I lost my mind, and horrific words blurted out of my mouth. I exclaimed that she was disgusting and was not protecting my children as a lawyer, a woman, or a mother should. She was a complete sell-out and opted for the side of *Daniel's father's money.* I don't think the other lawyers gave her a choice. Either way, I demanded she never stand near me or look at me ever again. When we entered the courtroom, she stood at a distance and nodded respectfully. Eventually, the judge asked her to move into her proper position next to me, and we both felt each other's sadness.

Years later, I saw her at a local restaurant. She was a nice lady who had been put in the middle of a horrible situation. I approached her and identified myself. She knew exactly who I was. I apologized for my prior outburst and explained I understood her position. She looked at me with deep sadness in her eyes and said it was the worst divorce case she had ever known, and it still bothered her. She frequently prayed I had been able to find peace.

When Daniel was called to testify, he answered the first few logistical questions and then pleaded, "The 5th" for almost every other question imaginable. I couldn't believe it! Fourteen months of hard-core lies, allegations, accusations, interrogatories, stealing, and defamation of character slammed down on me, and he is allowed to respond "The 5th" for hours. "What the hell! This is a complete mockery of the court system." I cannot believe the judge let him get away with that. Who pays over $300,000 to destroy his wife only to be a spineless fucking idiot and reply "The 5th" seemingly a million times?

The divorce decree was final, and the custody schedule remained intact. However, I did not understand that the business trial had not yet been delineated. Daniel had not paid one penny of child support or alimony as dictated by the court system, and I needed to wait an undetermined amount of time before any monetary discussions took place.

My brain was buzzing at that moment, and I just wanted to be alone. I helped my lawyer get her belongings together, and we spoke for a few minutes in the hallway. Voices echoed through my head; the commotion in the hallway blurred my sight. My heart accelerated, and my lungs collapsed. I couldn't breathe, and I needed to escape. I exited the courthouse, and to my dismay, the real world still existed.

Still disoriented, I noticed a massive crowd standing at the crosswalk. There were too many people for me to comprehend movement, so I stepped to the side. I put my head down, and hot tears poured from my eyes. Suddenly, a deep voice of wisdom burst through the crowd, *"Hold your head up high!"* It wasn't a nudge; it was a command from the heavens. I raised my head, and my eyes immediately connected with a stranger. But was he really a stranger? He held his head high and motioned for me to do the same. When the pedestrian signal lit up to proceed across the street, he nodded for me to cross into a world where I was free. When I turned back to look at him, he was gone.

But freedom is not free. Finally, I returned home after an exhausting day and fell into a deep sleep. My dreams were filled with colors and intensity, but the content was confusing. The chaos was more like microscopic flash photos falling out of a scrapbook into a supernova blasting through the universe. I was supposed to go to a celebratory dinner with a new friend, but I had absolutely no desire to go. I needed time to recover.

CHAPTER 5

PHOENIX RISING

Scorched earth is a war term many military forces have imposed, and that is the way my mind, body, and soul felt after the initial war had finally come to an end. Have you ever seen movies where that war-torn soldier is traveling back home but home and its surroundings are nowhere to be found? Home is merely flattened gray earth smoldering as far as the eye can see. Over time, something astonishing rises from the ashes and symbolizes hope. That feeling is like a phoenix rising high into the sky and watching over the land, allowing the soldier to be human once again. Unbeknownst to me, hope was preparing me for an enormous undertaking.

Survival of the Species Sex

A few months before my divorce proceedings, I stopped in a place for a hot bowl of soup. A man sat on the stool beside me and started a conversation. Ted reminded me of a more attractive and athletic version of Mr. Rogers asking me if I wanted to be his neighbor. The sweater was included!

Our conversation evolved into an ethereal interplay of words I desired to hear. My current situation in life seemed to dissipate, and a world of emotions unfolded before my eyes. Philosophically, we were on the same level of existence, and I felt alive. If sapiosexual had a picture and description in the dictionary, Ted would be it. Yum! Awesome. He asked to see me again.

Sapiosexual is when a person is sexually attractive due to their high level of intelligence. We both felt the same amount of physical attraction, but it was compounded because we were also overwhelmingly attracted to each other's intelligence, knowledge, and wisdom.

Ugh, back to reality. I explained I was in the midst of a horrible divorce, and I couldn't possibly invite him into my world. He inquired about the dates of my Final Divorce Proceedings. Then Ted replied, *"If you don't mind me asking, why three days? It usually only takes one or two at the most"*. I told him I was being dragged through the gutter, and he nodded in understanding.

In turn, Ted took out his phone and added my name to his calendar for the last day of the trial. This would be our first date. My brain was racing, *"Wow. This man is telling me he will wait over three months to go out on a date with me. Ha! We will see."* Regardless, we agreed to keep in touch via talk and text until our first date. After all, he seemed genuine and respectful.

Like clockwork, the invitation arrived. Unfortunately, I asked to delay our date for a day as I was exhausted from court. I was so nervous that I ran into the bathroom and dry-heaved over the toilet. I had not been on a date in over fifteen years. Am I still sexy and sophisticated? I had no idea! How was I supposed to convince myself I was still attractive to the opposite sex? What was I going to wear? How was I supposed to act? I never, ever expected to be in this situation.

The next morning, I went on a hike with one of my friends, who was like a sister to me. Kathy and I look like sisters; we met when our boys took their first swim lessons. Our friendship grew as we watched cute little three-year-old children blow bubbles and splash around the pool. Her daughter was about the same age as my daughter, and they also became friends. Over the years, we walked miles, ate amazing food, and enjoyed raising our children.

Kathy was the only friend I met while I was married who stuck with me through the divorce. I trusted her opinion and felt comfortable telling her everything. When I was done rambling about the chaos, she replied, "*Well, you know, you can't fix stupid.*" Simply brilliant and accurate. It made me laugh and decreased the tension in my brain. She didn't care about all the nonsense; she cared about me. I was so happy and grateful she was in my life.

As we approached the end of the hike, she asked me what type of underwear I would wear on my date. I replied, "*The same ones I always wear, they are comfortable. Why?*" She exclaimed, "*Throw out those granny panties and put something on that makes you feel sexy on the inside!*"

I laughed and replied, "*Oh my God, I am not going to have sex with him; we are going on a date.*" Apparently, that didn't matter, and Kathy insisted we go buy some new lingerie, her treat. Simply brilliant and accurate once again. We went to a posh lingerie boutique in a small shopping area nearby. I felt awkward trying on bras and underwear that could pay my electric bill, but we continued. I found something very sexy but also comfortable. I thought it was a good compromise.

I asked her what she thought, and she replied, "*You look great! Don't worry; he is going to love you.*" That was wonderful yet difficult to hear. I was still very nervous and went home to get ready. Finally, whew! I was emotionally prepared for my first date, maybe. I looked into the mirror and felt dizzy, "*Breathe, Amy. Breathe. Look normal.*" I texted Kathy, and she replied, "*Breathe.*" I smiled and thought to myself, "*She definitely knows me. I guess I should breathe now.*"

Ted came to pick me up, and we went for a short drive before dinner. He had a really cool hat sitting on the back seat, so I picked it up and put it on. He smiled because he could feel me beginning to relax. Dinner was excellent, but most importantly, my company was too. I had been starved for emotional intimacy. On the way back to my house, he stopped in a parking area near a lake, and we got out to look at the stars. They were beautiful that night. We kissed for a few minutes before leaving. My feelings were definitely intense, but I was having difficulty deciphering my emotions.

Over the next couple of months, our conversations were as intriguing as our passion and energy. The sexual tension between us was powerful, and we finally decided to make love. I explained it had been years, and I was scared to trust again. Ted's strong hands gently caressed my body while his soft lips passionately inhaled my breasts. His fingers penetrated areas I forgot existed. My body was trembling in sheer delight. I couldn't wait any longer. Something playfully and mysteriously erotic lying dormant inside my body suddenly awakened, and I emphatically pulled him into my pulsating thighs.

Initially, he was slow and smooth. But as my body trusted his touch, I *opened up*, and he thrust in with a desire I had never felt before. Sweat glistened and dripped from his body onto mine as I flipped over, and he penetrated me from behind. Stroking and throbbing, he pulled out and satisfied me with his tongue. My body was vibrating as he again penetrated, and I screamed in ecstasy.

Our breaths were in unison, and I saw colorful orbs of light. At first, I saw yellow and orange, but as our energy shifted, I saw purple and blue. Pure, calm, peaceful, and erotic ecstasy. Something I didn't know existed in myself or literature. Absolute pleasure. As exhaustion overtook our bodies, we lay wrapped in each other's arms. The bed was soaked, and we pulled a dry blanket over us and slept. As we awoke, I could feel him throbbing. So, I lifted my leg over his shoulder, and he entered me again. I jokingly blamed him for soaking the bed as he smiled, *"It's all you."* Although I did not understand.

Later, he explained I was completely in the moment, and the resulting climatic experience was called squirting or female ejaculation. I was the one having orgasms from multiple erogenous zones on my body. Again, I was amazed, *"Could this be true?"* For the next several months, we explored each other's bodies in new and wondrous ways. I experienced such a variety of orgasms and coined a term:

Survival of the Species Sex: The insanely intense sexual pleasure you attain from the first physically erotic love interest one has after experiencing a divorce or separation. When our sense of familial foundation has faltered, a piece of our soul must die. This emotional death makes us believe we are going to die, and we need to sustain our survival as an animal species proactively.

Unfortunately, many of these relationships fizzle out when you return to reality, and the physicality of the relationship can't withstand the transition into the real world. With that being said, I researched erogenous zones and the subsequent types of female orgasms, which are very different than the male orgasm. Further, the female orgasm is relatively individualistic, can change over time, and is influenced by your emotional health, age, and personality. If you are unsure if you have reached a climax or a series of climatic events, don't worry; you still have time!

The various erogenous zones that can stimulate orgasm in a woman include but are not limited to the clitoris, which is made up of millions of tiny nerve endings and the area surrounding the clitoris. This is probably the most common erogenous zone that reaches its climax. Next would be the G-Spot and the A-Spot, which are located on the walls of the vagina. These areas stimulate a climatic event, which may be felt deeper inside a woman's body because they contain ligaments as well as nerves. Two areas that may or may not be apparent to attain orgasm are the nipples and breast region. Some women can orgasm by nipple stimulation without having their genitals touched potentially because both areas stimulate the same portions of your brain. But guess what? Any area a woman finds erotic can stimulate an orgasm or multiple orgasms, and we do not necessarily need time to recover in between climaxes.

Now, back to the story. We were at the height of our instinctual behaviors when Ted told me he needed to relocate to another state for work. He was scheduled to leave in the fall but left much earlier emotionally. It was probably easier that way. When I inquired about the distance, he said I had to stay in Maryland with my children. There was no way Daniel would let us move. I knew he was correct.

It was a painful truth to accept. This was a great relationship, but now, he would disappear. His kids were adults, and he had nothing to hold him back. Our *social timelines* didn't match. We were at a completely different point in life, and there was nothing either one of us could do about it. The last month before his departure was almost silent. Solemn acceptance was my goal.

To me, a **Social Timeline** indicates significant life events and how old you are socially when they occur. The easiest example of a direct correlation between me and Ted was the ages of our children. My kids were in elementary school and his were attaining advanced degrees. Socially, he was a much older parent than I was, and his priorities concerning his children were vastly different from mine.

A second easy example of defining my *social timeline* concept was that he had been divorced for several years, and I was in my first year post-divorce. Again, his social timeline and his emotional health concerning the divorce far exceeded mine. I think it takes a minimum of one year to come back to yourself, even in the best divorce situations. Logically, it just takes time for the dust to settle.

When you look at yourself and a potential partner, jot down some timeline indicators and discuss the impact they may or may not have on your life. Communication and understanding will significantly decrease the frustration of being different and may even improve your level of physical and emotional intimacy with your partner. Other examples may include but are not limited to the age you got married, the age of your parents, if and when you graduated from college, the age you became financially independent, and the age you reconciled your own mortality. Huh? At this age, you realize you are not invincible, and your actions directly impact the quality of your life and those around you.

After he had acclimated to his new location. he contacted me occasionally. Eventually, he visited me a few times, which was always enjoyable. Further, he invited me to go to dinner and spend the evening with him before his mother's funeral. She sacrificed her entire life to guide and support him, and I understood the significance of her death. I was deeply humbled by the gesture, and the dinner was exquisite. Although he was disappointed, I did not stay the night in his hotel room. Despair glistened deep within in his eyes when I drove away. I felt so guilty. I know he needed me. But I could not return and make love to him once again.

After several years, I finally took him up on his offer to visit his home. He had a big, beautiful house on a lake with a pier. His swimming pool and hot tub were refreshing, and his dogs were great companions. He wanted to re-establish our relationship and attempt to rekindle our passion. I did have love for him in my heart, and I was grateful for our relationship, but one big thing was in the way.

Ted traveled extensively for business and worked seven days a week. He was absolutely brilliant and had several hobbies outside of work. He only had a couple of friends who were contingent upon his goals in life. I felt like I was at the bottom of the *To-Do List*. I had brought this topic up a few times before, and his response was always the same, "*Well, I need to work.*"

That response broke my heart several times, and although I knew we had a decent relationship, it was not what I wanted in my life. With regret, I looked into his eyes and said, "*I need a best friend. I don't think you will ever be my best friend. You are married to work, and work always comes first. Then you have all of your other priorities, which are great, and I don't want to take that away from you. But I feel everything you have will always be more important than I am, and I deserve better. I am sure you understand. Our priorities don't really match. I hope you know I do love you.*"

We remained friends and understood our intentions at this point in life were not the same. About a year or so later, he got married, and I was happy he had a new life companion. Their timelines and their outlook on relationships aligned quite well. Bravo, my dear friend.

The Pomegranate

Starting to work in a large organization after working for myself for so long evoked various emotions. I was disappointed, yet excited. I was confident, yet intimidated. I loved the adventure, but missed the freedom of being my own boss. I did not have a choice, and honestly, this choice was perfect.

My Boss was kind, patient, and never arrogant about her knowledge. She had two Master's degrees from two Ivy League colleges and was in line to receive her doctorate. Further, she was beautiful, down to earth, and bilingual. Her husband grew up a few miles from where I grew up in Maryland. She thought we had grown up in a bubble because of our love and appreciation for different cultures.

She explained my job responsibilities step by step and beautifully illustrated an accurate picture of what she had in mind. Once, she had me read two medical journal articles for feedback. They both contained one name from an influential person in the field. I responded, *"Both articles are extremely well-written and organized, but why isn't your name included?"*

She was quietly surprised, *"Is it that obvious?"* I boldly replied, *"Well, it is to me, and I am so sorry you didn't receive any credit for your work."* She and I had a mutual understanding of the world and the way many people chose to live in it.

She was the reason I was able to raise my children and successfully maintain a full-time job. I worked on my schedule and always got all my work done, so there was never an issue. She said I was like water cascading down a mountain. *"Completely unstoppable."*

We stood strong and united for doing the right thing in the world. Professionally, we went above and beyond the limits for our programs and our people. Personally, we cared about each other and our families. I had the optimal work environment and was genuinely making a difference in the world.

This program is where I learned how to create badass spreadsheets and training slides. It was amazing to have a computer system that could be my pen and paper for what I was creating. These abilities are essential for innovation and growth now and in the future.

I delivered babies from various manikins. I developed techniques to be the non-medical person in the feedback loop. I specialized in high-risk birthing procedures and made body parts, bones, and moulage. I was available to every department and thoroughly enjoyed learning and making a tangible impact.

Moulage: the art of applying elements of realism such as wax, blood, latex, vomit, wounds, hair, and make-up. These cosmetic alterations allow the use of assessment and critical thinking.

A downfall of using simulators and moulage is that the materials are expensive and time-consuming. An integral part of my job for proper and effective training was creating cost-effective products myself. I told everyone, *"If you can paint the picture inside my head, I can make it happen in real life."*

Once, she took an entire day to develop a simulation program for pre-eclampsia, but the following day, it would not run. So, she asked me to be the patient. I put on headphones and strapped on the birthing simulator. The moment she said, *"Seize!"* Whew! I almost flew off the bed. Two doctors restrained my ankles, and another one grabbed my shoulders. The fourth one attempted to lift my shirt to assess my heartbeat. My arm covered my chest, and with one eye open, I whispered, *"Simulation."* Suddenly, he opted to shove the stethoscope down the top of my shirt instead.

Within minutes, the simulation was an invigorating medical success. Simulations like these expounded upon my idea of letting go of my ego and absorbing the experience of the patient. Such simulations often drained emotions I didn't know I was harboring. Further, these trainings gave medical professionals an experience unlike anything they had ever experienced before.

Afterward, My Boss inquired, *"Is there anything you would prefer to change?"* I told her it was absolutely perfect except for one thing, *"Can I pick the doctor who is going to feel me up next time?"* We broke out in laughter and agreed some of these young men were quite attractive, and the doctor mindset hadn't destroyed their personalities yet. It was a shame to see both men and women change so drastically between the beginning and the end of their advanced education.

The easiest way to categorize these personality changes is to describe "the gray zone," an existential area that exists between light and dark, between living and dying. The longer people live in that area, the more their souls are transformed. With each passing year in a medical program, many doctors go deeper and deeper into this area and are unable to return. However, some doctors who have been lost in the abyss get jolted with a wake-up call and feel the need to return to the light.

I witnessed people who lived in the gray zone and watched them *"eat their young."* The medical community frequently uses this term about how senior members devour the newcomer's time, energy, and resources. They are inundated with emotional indifference and always enjoy hunting down their prey and feasting on their misery. It's a disgusting cycle of abuse some view as a rite of passage.

Some doctors develop a God complex because they believe they *are* the light and are entitled to live beyond the ordinary human experience. They create their own rules and view people as servants or followers to their end goal. However, their dark arrogance overwhelms me, and their lifestyle choices are counterintuitive to their perceived calling. Their presence is gray and insular. They are only interested in their own experiences and agendas. Unwelcome intrusions are immediately dismissed.

Other doctors learn to detach from their emotions and walk through life needing genuine human connection. Unfortunately, they are too afraid to feel what it would be like to live in the light again. To experience the pain and suffering is too much for their soul to bare.

They turn gray as a means of survival. Occasionally, someone or something may spark a light in them, and the feelings may be intense but confusing. Ultimately, the good feelings become a distraction, and they walk away.

Miraculously, there are some doctors and people in other professions who can navigate the secret passageways to and from the gray zone without experiencing an existential death. These professionals are the ones you want to find who make a difference in the world. It is like they got a glimpse into the abyss and figured out how not to get caught. Potentially, they taught themselves to appreciate the totality of life and have learned to accept what little time we actually have to live a happy and prosperous life here on earth. Their will is strong, and their knowledge is powerful.

The mythological image that comes to mind is the Goddess Persephone. She was the daughter of Zeus and Demeter, who collectively ruled the Heavens. Later, she was infamously abducted by Hades, the Leader of the Underworld, and became his Queen. This Goddess of the Dead yearly sojourns back to the world and embodies Spring. She is a symbol of agricultural functions, vegetation, and crops.

Metaphorically, Persephone is aligned with a pomegranate with diverse cultural and spiritual significance. Intrinsically, this fruit is a magical womb of juicy little seeds representing life and fertility. It is one of the oldest known edible fruits, and valued across many cultures, it has been smashed in bridal chambers to invoke fertility and encourage the birth of children. The etymology of two words we are familiar with today comes from this mystical fruit.

First, garnet is a gemstone that revitalizes, purifies, and balances energy. It comes in various colors. The vibrant red garnet is the most common and widespread gemstone found on every continent. It is metamorphic, which means it was altered by heat and pressure. It inspires love and devotion as well as the instinct to survive.

On the contrary, the grenade is a small explosive that resembles the pomegranate fruit's size and shape. Technically, this spherical-shaped bomb is a receptacle filled with chemicals or gases and is used at short range. They can be launched out by hand or projected by a special launcher. Once the transport safety pin is removed, these missiles are used to target death and destruction.

My Boss was being groomed for a prestigious position, and I would not abandon her to explore the pomegranate orchard alone. As each one of the trees matures, the yields can become extremely high, but there is always a price to pay. My job was to love and protect her and our programs from all the people who wanted to use her and her resources for their own personal gain.

She used to say, *"My dear, if we could figure out how to bottle your intuition, we'd all be rich."*

My Guardian Angel

Another person I met in this time period helped to transform my life. It was like the phoenix was purposely calling others to rise up from the ashes to help me regain my sense of mortality and prosperity. Sometimes, I had a difficult time accepting these people who loved and accepted me for my intelligence because I still felt like I had some cognitive deficits from the accident.

As the winter holiday season approached, I stopped by a local restaurant to have a drink. The place was dimly lit with a variety of patrons. Families were in the back, young adults to the left, and a large square bar filled with mature business people to my right. As I searched for a place to sit, I noticed one vacant seat, and it called my name. Suddenly, WHACK, I tripped over a strip of wood on the floor and landed directly on top of a very distinguished-looking man. I was mortified, and my face turned bright red.

He smiled, *"Hi, I'm Ben."* I could barely speak, *"Hello, I'm Amy. I am so sorry. Please forgive me."* His eyes smiled more than his mouth as he offered me a seat and a glass of wine. I graciously accepted. He was so endearing and respectful. We spoke for a couple of hours, and

I learned he was formally the President and CEO of a large clothing manufacturing conglomerate. I assumed he was trying to impress me with his fancy resume. In turn, I touched his shoulder, donning an impeccably made pin-striped business suit, and said, "*Well, I guess that explains the suit,*" and we both laughed.

At the end of the evening, he offered his business card. I flipped the card over, wrote my number down, handed it back to him, smiled, and said, "*My mom told me not to call boys.*" Hilarious, whatever I did must have intrigued him. He asked to escort me to my car and politely reached for my coat, which he held for me to put on. When walking to my car, he asked to hold my arm as he put his elbow close to mine. Then, he opened my car door, hugged me, and walked towards the streetlight, illuminating the crystalline sprinkles on the back of his long wool coat.

I knew Ben was too old for me, but I decided to go out on a few dates with him anyway. I found out we were both looking for companionship, and it felt so comfortable to be around him. I didn't necessarily care about his age anymore. I invited him to Christmas dinner because his daughters lived out of town, and I didn't want him to be alone. Miraculously, he passed *my dad's "boyfriend test"* with glowing colors. It was cute to watch Ben transform into a loving grandpa persona around all the children. He always started by putting his huge hands together finger by finger when he was about to recount tall tales of adventure to entertain their curious minds.

Our emotional relationship progressed rapidly, but physically, it just wasn't there. I was not ready to put myself out there again, and the age gap remained an issue. Moreover, I loved to be immersed in nature, and Ben's idea of hiking was to park in the farthest spot away from the restaurant where we were dining. Don't get me wrong, I absolutely loved getting dressed up and going to fancy restaurants with him, but I needed more from a significant other in the long term. I was very honest with him.

However, he set his mind on changing my mind. He created the perfect vision for a future together with my children. There was a huge new house on some old farmland named Sugar Hill, and his plan was definitely as sweet as the name. I seriously contemplated what my life would be like if I agreed to marry him. I considered finding friends to enjoy the great outdoors with instead of him.

That Spring, he experienced significant health issues related to a prior back surgery. He couldn't recover, and the antibiotics severely upset his stomach. His personal flora oscillated between a sweet, charismatic cologne and a strange, unexplainable bitterness. We were supposed to meet for dinner one night, but he called to say he was running behind. He was *never* late. I knew something was wrong.

He was pale as a ghost. The bitter smell wafted out of his Hummer, and he passed out on the steering wheel. I pushed him into the passenger's seat and drove his H2 tank down the middle of the highway. He was on the board of a local hospital system, and I decided to drive him there myself. I called ahead to ensure medics were waiting for him at the emergency entrance. The operator said, *"We don't do patient intakes like that,"* I yelled, *"Well, you do now, and I will be there in less than ten minutes!"*

Once there, he was rushed into the emergency bay. I calmly answered questions as best as possible and called his best friend. My serene demeanor confused Saul. Regardless, he arrived within the hour to help me. The doctor explained Ben's organs had shut down and he would have died if I arrived five minutes later. The reason for his lethargy and subsequent near-death episode was because MRSA had entered his body during a routine surgery and remained undetected for almost a year. A strange sense of gratitude, fear, and bewilderment overwhelmed my thought processes. I walked the hallways of the hospital in a dreamlike state. Saul was a God-send and brought me back to reality.

MRSA is a superbug that surrounds infections in your body like a medieval fortress. So, when your white blood cells come to conquer the invaders, they are rejected. Regular antibiotics are futile and Ben had to take a course of super-antibiotics that cost $10,000. He was bedridden and could barely eat five bites of food without wanting to regurgitate. In his house, I nursed him while watching his mind and body completely deteriorate. Within a couple of months, he went from a very handsome and debonair gentleman to a frail senior citizen. The bitter smell was a constant reminder of death.

By this point, we were mutually dependent on each other every day. My business case and his health were both pending annihilation. We decided it was safer to stick together as companions on a journey through the darkness and hopefully back to the light. We made a great team.

When I first met this ostentatious and austere man, my hand could barely grasp half his bicep; now, I needed to help him perform everyday tasks. He always proclaimed he was my guardian angel sent to help me through *"all the bad stuff,"* which was collectively everything I had endured in my lifetime, especially my divorce and the pending litigation. He insisted I was *his* guardian angel sent to save his soul. Although his body was weak and fading, his smiling eyes stayed strong.

In the next section, I will explain how Ben and Saul insurmountably helped me through much of the bad stuff. I am eternally grateful for all their help and can't imagine the alternatives.

We stayed as a platonic couple for about another year. We were always kind and respectful to each other, and neither one of us ever stepped out of the relationship. Genuine companionship was key to our success. We arrived at a turning point once my business case was resolved and his health was restored. We knew a long-term commitment would never lead to our happiness.

Our final night as a couple ended in the exact spot where we met. We had an intimate candlelit dinner, and he held my arm as we walked towards my car. He placed big, bold hands gently upon my moist cheeks and said, *"You have the most beautiful face I have ever seen, and you will be my best friend forever."*

We embraced and cried as the sky showered us with tiny droplets from heaven. We didn't want to let go. Finally, he opened my car door; I got in and drove away. We both thought, *"Goodbye, my beautiful guardian angel; thank you for saving my life."*

We stayed friends and spoke frequently on the phone. Life was progressing until he suffered a devastating car accident. During a hurricane, a large green highway sign detached from the post and crushed his Hummer in half. Again, the MRSA kicked in, and along with diabetes, he was unable to recover. Saul and I took turns taking him to medical appointments and kept track of his progress. Ultimately, he was deteriorating quickly, and there was very little we could do about it.

A few days before his passing, I had an overwhelming feeling something was wrong, and he did not respond to my phone calls or texts for the first time ever. So, I sent Saul a message.

The next day, Saul called and informed me Ben had died. I guess I was in shock because I felt as though I was outside my body looking at the rest of the world. Life was in motion, and I was merely an observer. I waited for him to appear in my dreams with a sign or a message. But he never did. I thought about this for a while because most of my loved ones bring a message to me through my dreams or in nature within days before or after their passing.

I believe he did not send me a message because he is still here and watching over me. Occasionally, I feel his presence and thank him for his help. One day, when I am ready, I will figure out how to allow him to return to the light and find rest. Peace and love to you, my guardian angel. One day our souls shall meet again, I promise.

All The Bad Stuff

Unfortunately, the entourage and I could not come to an amicable agreement for the business. In turn, the judge mandated the sale of all the properties and appointed another set of lawyers as the trustees. However, this law group merely informed me of what they were doing *after the fact*. I know they constantly communicated with the entourage and thus disregarded my input. They spoke in code as if I were the enemy and gave each other curious glances when it was my turn to speak.

Further, the car accident and subsequent treatments required extensive medical attention, and the woman who hit me was deemed responsible for my medical bills. However, she did not have a sufficient car insurance policy. In fact, she didn't even have enough coverage to be driving in Maryland. In turn, I had to procure another lawyer to oversee my healthcare negotiations and reimbursements with the insurance company, doctors, and physical therapists.

Keeping the car accident lawsuit a secret was of the utmost importance. Otherwise, Daniel could potentially have access to half of my settlement money before my medical bills were paid, totaling over $70,000. I had no idea what the lawsuit's outcome would be, but I hoped it would be in my favor. After all, I was in compliance with the medical treatment regimes.

From the onset of our relationship, Ben took it upon himself to be my business consultant. Even when his health was failing, he didn't skip a beat. He had a doctorate in law and was a forensic accountant, which is like a certified professional accountant on steroids. He had worked for and represented two Fortune 50 companies in their business affairs throughout his life. He knew the language, the law, and the art of intimidation by heart. His instincts were as valuable as his wisdom.

We went to a meeting where the trustees and the entourage were going to bury me alive and proclaim victory. I felt anxious as we sat down at an exceptionally long and perfectly polished boardroom table inside an exquisitely decorated law office. Ben motioned for me not to speak and whispered, "*The walls have ears. Just relax.*" The meeting started with the trustees presenting a barrage of information as if it was a done deal and I would get what they offered. Period. End of sentence.

Ben's eyes gloriously smiled as he took a business card from his Armani suit pocket. This wasn't a typical business card. It was thick, embossed with gold, and curiously vague. Then, he meticulously laid out a series of documents across the table. He lowered his hands for a moment and paused. His persona transformed into a ravenous lion silently waiting to pounce. Then, he stretched out his huge fingers on the edge of the table, looked everyone in the eyes, and declared, "*Gentlemen, we have a few details we need to discuss.*" It was difficult to hold back my enthusiasm as I sat silently and smiled in my heart.

Ben confidently presented information and delineated over a hundred accounts of where I had been legally and financially raped, pillaged, and plundered. Every single person at that table turned ghostly white except Daniel. He was pasty green and sweating as usual. An ominous cloud of fear permeated the room as these men prepared for the accurate and brutal assault of their ill-perceived victory. After Ben's brilliant presentation, the Trustee of this legal proceeding called a brief recess.

Ben and I spoke in private. He explained we couldn't get any of my money back because it had disappeared, and there was no way to find or recover any of the funds unless we wanted to pursue the criminal aspects of the situation and send Daniel to federal prison. We both agreed sending my children's father to prison was a horrible idea. When we returned, Ben made our intentions perfectly clear and highly suggested the lawyers "*do the right thing*" so there would be no future consequences. Have you ever seen arrogant assholes cower and tremble in fear? I have, and it is a beautiful thing.

Coincidence? I think not. When Ben and I went to the car accident lawyer's office to discuss the final financial agreements, he greeted us with a faxed memo in his hand. The fax had just arrived and was sent to the local legal community. The Supreme Commanding General on the War Against Amy, AKA The Devil, had died. Daniel's lawyer had lost his battle with cancer. Apparently, the onset had come quickly and took him just as fast.

A moral conundrum shot through my soul. The Devil had died. I know I am supposed to feel sympathy, but I just couldn't bring myself to feel sad. I felt emotionally validated.

During our discussion with the car accident lawyer, Ben realized he had not represented me properly and confronted him with pertinent questions. By the end of the discussion, the lawyer agreed to redevelop his plan of action, promised to renegotiate with the insurance company, doctors, and physical therapists, and apologized for his oversights in my case. Was he being malicious? No, I think he was lazy and just looking for a quick buck.

In the meantime, the entourage had a newly appointed leader. I thought he was a nice guy, and I would converse with him before the various meetings. At one point, he said he enjoyed speaking with me, but it was a conflict of interest under the circumstances. I nodded my head in agreement and said, *"I'm sorry. It must be difficult representing a client you have no respect for."*

Ultimately, I was awarded 60% of the business, while Daniel was awarded 40%. Plus, he needed to pay all the outlying bills and his credit card debt. Basically, the judge was allowing me to walk away and give me a small amount of money to start over. But my business had been completely destroyed, and every bottom feeder got their piece. In my opinion, 60% of shit is still shit.

The marital home, which he had resided in for free for two and a half years, finally went into foreclosure, and Daniel had to move in with his sister. The entourage dispersed, and his girlfriend dumped him. I thought the war was finally over. I had a job and was prospering in life while he remained anxious, depressed, and alone. Unfortunately, he still had his two biggest weapons to use against me—my children.

I planned a vacation with my children and Alexa. She was my daughter's best friend and had been a part of our family since first grade. She was the youngest of five children, and her mom had Parkinson's Disease and Alzheimer's for several years and was predominantly unavailable. In turn, I always included her in our family plans and loved her like a daughter. Alexa was intelligent, athletic, and beautiful. We had a mutual respect for each other, and Daniel's behavior deeply saddened her.

When Daniel discovered my plan for all three birthdays, it set off all his emotional triggers. Instead of self-imploding, he thrust all those triggers onto us. Both of my children were emotionally filled with versions of "*Their Mother*" trying to control the universe, and his verbal as well as written tirades were firing at me from all vantage points. I was weak and wounded. Panic mode set in hard.

My daughter and I had a huge argument, and she packed up her orange runaway bag. That bag was the final trigger my brain could withstand, and there was a massive blowout. She called her daddy to come save her from her "*Mother*," and he rushed right over. That evening, Ben and Daniel spoke on the phone and agreed she could come home the following morning, and I thought all was well. Three days later, the entourage was back and slammed me with a restraining order.

"*Why three days?*" Because this was a preconceived attack, and all complaints appear in court on Wednesdays. If they had filed their complaint on Monday or Tuesday, I wouldn't have my children for a few days. Since they filed the complaint on Wednesday morning, I couldn't have "*any form of communication*" with either one of my children for a week, or I would go to jail.

Think about it: months earlier, I neglected to pursue legal action against Daniel, which would have ultimately landed him in prison, and he knew it. All I was trying to do was plan a birthday weekend, and the first idea he had was to throw me in jail and take my children away from me forever. Thank God I had Ben and Saul by my side. Their love and support were my beacon of hope to stand strong.

Here's another thought for you to ponder. If I was such a danger, why would Daniel return my daughter to me and wait three days to cry out and plead for her safety? Ben knew this attack was bullshit and assured me everything was going to be all right. Since Ben had not taken the Bar Exam, he was not formally a lawyer in Maryland. Fortunately, Saul volunteered to take my case. Since my children were not allowed to testify in court, Alexa's parents volunteered for her to appear on my behalf.

When I entered the courtroom, the entourage was lined up on the far right wall, looking quite smug and casually holding their briefcases. When they saw me looking at them, they rubbed elbows and covered their mouths to laugh. However, when the entourage saw their opposing team and a young, opinionated girl and her parents walk into the courtroom, they panicked. I loved watching them squirm in and out of the courtroom and making calls in the outside corridor.

Daniel's testimony simply reiterated a series of events that matched his version of the truth. He had nothing new to say and seemed confused and desperate. He demanded the judge award him full custody of both children because *"Their Mother"* was crazy and abusive.

My testimony recounted the various trigger-stacking events that occurred over the past few months and how he had thrust his lies and insecurities upon me and my children. Next, I explained that I had a prestigious full-time job and had moved on with my life. Further, he did not have a job, and his only hobby in the world was to harass me. He was using my children as a weapon, and I was disgusted.

Trigger Stacking is when a person experiences multiple stressful or scary situations within a short time span. In turn, the person may feel completely overwhelmed and overreact to an otherwise minor event. Since Daniel had lost the court case, moved in with his sister, and had no girlfriend, he obviously had nothing to do but obsess over every little thing I was doing and find fault.

Then, he became a **Trigger Stacker** and projected his anxiety and depression onto others. First, he instigated the children. Then, he sent me daily emails, text messages, and phone calls, which I collectively labeled as *"Hate Mail."* I'm sure his sister wasn't feeling the love either. Basically, all of his words and actions were intended to ignite a huge fire.

The judge dismissed the case but not without some final thoughts:

"Sir, you want me to overturn the work of multiple people in the court system over the past two years based on the fact you think your ex-wife is crazy?" He responded, *"Yes."*

"Ma'am, what would you like?" I replied, *"I just want him to leave me alone."*

Then the judge moved a few pieces of paper around and prepared to end the session, *"Well, ma'am, I suggest you stop cutting your children's father off at the knees and continue on with your life."*

The judge turned towards Daniel and indistinctly nodded, almost in confusion, *"Sir, you really need to seek therapy and get yourself healthy and productive."*

Suspending Disbelief

Daniel took every opportunity to threaten me with legal attacks, which left me feeling uncomfortable on so many levels. In the back of my mind, I was always vigilant and prepared for an attack. On the flip side, work was going well, and the depth of my empathy and teaching abilities was ever-expanding. Every time I began a medical simulation as an expectant mom, I reached deep into my soul and drew upon the well of divine love, thus transforming myself into the patient.

I envisioned how the doctors gently placed my beautiful baby girl upon my chest, and her tiny hand reached out to touch my laden skin. How the most incredible electric shock permeated my entire existence, and without a doubt, I knew I had created a miracle. The energy in her delicate little hand astounded me and allowed a glimpse of eternity to penetrate my soul.

I remembered how the energy stayed in her hands for several months. The radiance reminded me of a sketch I had bought years earlier on the Big Island of Hawaii. The artist captured a photograph of a kahuna during a healing ceremony. His hands were positioned in front of his chest and were slightly concave. The emanating glow from his hands was challenging to recreate on canvas, but you could see the power in proper lighting.

I reminisced about how long it took to conceive my son and the way I felt like less of a woman because of how those doctors chose to deliver the bad news. I remembered how he was in such a rush to pop out of the birth canal as I envisioned the deep blue tide pool of water that helped to keep him safe. I recollected the sights, sounds, and people running around after I arrived at the hospital, how the nurses rolled me over and insisted I *"Push!"* and how I was disappointed they did not immediately place him on my belly. But, after a few minutes, I felt heaven in my arms.

I embraced the overwhelming joy I felt every time I nursed my babies for the first year of their lives and how lucky I was to be the mother of the most beautiful babies in the universe. I recalled the horrible devastation I felt when I received a five-sentence form letter stating my son may have a genetic defect and the overwhelming sense of relief I felt when I found out the test they used was outdated and simply needed to be re-administrated to be in compliance.

Then, to properly prepare myself for the training scenario, I imagined all those memories being ripped away. Yes, that is right. I imagined my life without my children, and it brought great despair into my heart. Sometimes, it was difficult not to cry. But I needed to save those tears for teaching. Then, I researched the high-risk patient I portrayed in the scenario and what her life may have encompassed. I believed my job was to be the patient, not act like one.

Sometimes, I was a poor 15-year-old heroin addict and other times, I was a wealthy 40-year-old alcoholic and everything in between. Leaving my ego behind was the first step in creating a scenario that allowed us to suspend disbelief. In these precious minutes, it was my job to create an opportunity for genuine empathy or permit them to stay in medical mode. I could feel the difference and allowed my body to respond appropriately. I let go of the social etiquette I had learned throughout my life and instinctively allowed my body to experience emotions as if I had never been taught to sit still.

Some participants were thirsty for more than medical knowledge. They can get that all day, every day. They wanted to draw upon water from the well of divine love. This is where genuine communication creates opportunities for long-term learning. These individuals desired wisdom.

My initiative was to care for the caregivers and give them the best possible opportunities to quench their thirst. When the scenario terminated, we engaged in genuine conversations with me as the patient and then with me as the trainer.

I had no prior experience in immersive training. It came to me naturally. Most importantly, I could see, hear, and feel when those transitional moments occurred, and our experience became *real*. *We suspended disbelief together*. It was such a fantastic phenomenon, and I was so grateful to be involved.

Suspend Disbelief: In simulation training, participants cognitively agree that the situation is real and that they are functioning in a clinical encounter. Theoretically, it is a poetic philosophy concerned with appreciating beauty and appearance. It describes a set of principles underlying a work of art where a semblance of truth is woven into the fabric of a fantastic tale, suspending judgment and making the story feel *divinely real*.

Although my vision was poor and often blurred from the accident, I could see people more clearly than ever before. The power of divine sight was blossoming beneath my eyes. Even though my hearing was poor and often confusing, I could hear in new ways that gave meaning to spoken and unspoken words. The power of divine perception was vibrating between my ears.

My hands were weak and fragile, but I could feel the energy in people and situations stronger than ever before. The power of divine touch emanated from my warm hands and contained wisdom. When a provider touched me with their hands or their heart, tears welled up in my eyes. If their empathy continued, I cried. Yes, these real tears were pouring down my cheek and seemingly suspended time for a few brief and fleeting moments. However, the impact always remained.

Everything she touches and changes evokes an image of a tree. I was that tree with deep roots and long branches. I bore sweet fruit in the spring and colorful foliage in the fall. I nurtured the young and was a sanctuary for the old. I provided a shady respite for conversations between souls.

A light arises between us when my soul sits down and speaks to your soul. This is wisdom.

Ironically, I always knew I had these abilities. But I was never allowed to express them. Intuition can neither be proven nor disproven; it just exists. When the brave wish to share insights, they are often mocked or chastised. In turn, I learned to keep quiet, and sometimes, I learned to forget who I am. My goal was to allow people to hear and to teach myself to remember.

The best way to get as many people to hear as possible is simple: Be the best listener, then choose the best words to respond. Remembering who you are will uncover the veiled layers that have accumulated over time. When the veils have been removed, there is no turning back. You cannot unsee, unhear, or unfeel anything you have intrinsically learned. Accepting a new version of the truth is undeniable.

As we grow, we are taught to hide our visceral reactions and not allow our bodies to experience emotions fully. But what if our bodies could express emotions without words? Just let loose and be free?

In simulation, I allowed anger to tighten and arch my back, anxiety to quiver my knees and rub my hands, depression to slump my shoulders and dim the light in my eyes. In turn, I allowed the doctors and nurses to have insight into their words and actions with and without my verbal response.

These experiences gave me great insight and understanding into the real world of people who seemingly live extraordinary lives. Celebrities literally go from "*Hey, I am trying to pay my bills just like everybody else*" to "*Hey, I am on the cover of every magazine, and everyone wants my money to pay their bills.*" When these celebrities come down off their high and purposely or inadvertently ruin their life, it may just be a function of perceived reality.

I learned personally and professionally that returning to reality can be overwhelming, confusing, and exhausting. As intense as those exchanges may have been, I would probably never see them again. It was my job; they were here for medical instruction and research.

One major curiosity remained: Why was I steadfastly successful in intuitive and emotional exchanges at work and still having major difficulties at home? I was thirsty to draw more water from the well of divine love. I was thirsty for wisdom.

Super Full Moon

When I was married, my father had a great relationship with my husband, and it broke both their hearts when we got a divorce. They finally had the father-and-son relationship they hoped for all their lives. Initially, they kept in touch via phone calls and emails but kept it hidden from the rest of us. Technically, I wouldn't have been overly bothered except that Daniel had been using the information he gained from my father to use against me. When I inquired about the communication, my father indignantly replied, *"It's none of your damn business."*

Instantly, I felt rage and sternly said, *"Well, maybe it is my business when everything you say to him ends up on a court document and costs me hundreds of dollars every time you two speak."* That news shocked my father, and you could tell he felt completely betrayed by the man he loved like a son. Unfortunately, my father chose to take his anger and frustration out on me, the messenger, instead of the person who obviously manipulated him for an extended period of time.

This discovery prompted a massive blow-up in the entire family, and of course, I was to blame.

In this same time period, my father asked everyone to make a list of everything they wanted from the house so he could put it in his Last Will and Testament. I thought about it and finally wrote on a small paper: *"Dad: Your vintage train set. Mom: Some of your jewelry. Plus, I would like the first choice to have anything I gave you in my life back."* I have no idea what anybody else wrote, nor did I ask. It was none of my business.

The next time I went to my parent's house, my father was seated at the dining room table. I sat on the sofa, and he turned to look at me. Without a hello or any pleasantries, he firmly stated, *"Just so you know, you have already spent all of your inheritance, and the remaining money will go to all of your sisters and the grandchildren."* The only thing I could think was, *"Hey, Dad, great to see you too. Thanks for the feedback."*

Without showing any emotion, I nodded and replied, *"Ok."* He looked a little annoyed and repositioned himself, *"Maybe you didn't hear me correctly. You have already spent all of your inheritance, and the remaining money will go to your sisters and the grandchildren."*

Again, without any emotion, I lifted my shoulders and said, *"Ok, Dad, it's your money. I have no say over it."* He shifted his seat to the side and appeared quite agitated, *"Did you hear me? I said you aren't getting any more of my money."*

"Yes, Dad, I heard you. I didn't earn your money, and I didn't save your money. I have no say over what you do with your money. It's yours." I responded and picked up a magazine to make myself look occupied. The situation remained subtly intense. As I pretended to read the magazine, I thought, *"If he is going to die, can't he just be nice about it? I wonder what I did this time?"*

The next time I visited, I brought along a book I had been reading. One of the tasks from the book was to find words that *do not describe you.* Huh? Everyone is always willing to tell you what they think about you. But how many people go around and tell you what you are *not*? So, I decided to ask various people, including my family. It was usually an entertaining conversation piece and led to much laughter. Not today! I described the self-help book to my father and told him I was completing the tasks. In turn, I wanted to know what adjective did not describe me. He looked over and grumbled, *"Nice."*

"No, Dad, I need to know what adjective does not describe me." He assuredly repeated, *"Nice. I have never seen you be nice."* he returned

to reading the newspaper. I could feel the rage stirring inside me, so I went into the kitchen to chill out. My mom and sister were there, and they had overheard the conversation. They asked, *"What word would you use that doesn't describe your father?"* I guess they thought I would have a rude comment to match his, but I did not want to give them that satisfaction. So, I thought for a moment and calmly replied, *"Refined."*

Somehow, this supposedly fun task from my book perpetuated the huge blowup we had a short while back concerning my father and his communication with Daniel. The conflict got ugly and intense. Panic overwhelmed my soul. Everyone accused me of instigating the fight, which exacerbated my rage. Finally, I picked up my coat and yelled, *"If anyone wants to see me, you know where I live. I am never coming back to this house."* I didn't speak to anybody in my family for three months.

To my surprise, my father called me a few days before my birthday to ask if I was going to visit. I told him I could visit the following weekend and bring the children. Upon arrival, he looked like a ghost, and his physical and cognitive functioning had significantly declined.

My oldest sister and her husband came to move a bed into the living room as my father could no longer get himself upstairs at night. I encouraged the children to ask him questions to inspire conversation as we felt the end drawing near. It was sad to see such a brilliant man unable to perform basic math or recount history, which I knew he had explained multiple times.

When it was time to leave, I gazed upon his weary body lying on the couch. He did not appear to be the man I knew as my father. Moreover, he was a man trying to resist letting go. *Something* inside me knew I would never see my father again. I rummaged through the desk drawer and found his old brown memo pad from work. Upon it, I wrote, *"Bye Daddy, I love you."* and put it within his reach.

As we left the home my dad built with his two hands, we paused at the bottom of the hill to see the stunning beauty of the full moon. This low-hanging and amplified view of the moonlight created a strange and mystical effect. The children leaped into the front seat, almost expecting to be able to reach out and touch it. They asked why the moon was so big and bright. With tears in my eyes, I said, "*The moon was sent to enlighten Grandpa's pathway to heaven. I think it's time for him to go.*"

The backdrop of the celestial light through the blackened trees peacefully swaying in the wind over a narrow rocky stream comforted our sadness as I explained we would probably never see Grandpa again. The next morning, my dad awoke briefly and spoke his final words to his wife. His saving grace was that he loved my mother more than anything else in the universe.

He quietly whispered, "*It's been a long time.*" as he closed his eyes and let go of his final breath.

At the viewing ceremony, I declared it was going to take something spectacular to take the life of my father, and God had sent the super full moon to alter the hands of time. We were filled with sadness but felt a strong sense of relief because he had been sick for five years, and now the suffering was over.

Within weeks, a huge burden had been lifted from behind my mother's eyes, and her fragile shoulders were held high. Faith and hope illuminated her face as she proudly reminisced about the man who had been her lifelong companion and husband. His blue chair remained occupied by his spirit for quite some time as his grandchildren opted for other seats without hesitation.

My mom and dad coexist in different realms in the same house, and sometimes he unwittingly makes himself known. Sometimes, my mom can see his shadow or hear his bellowing cough. Occasionally, she hears the floor creek and expects to hear him call her name. I explained she should reply to him by speaking inside her mind. Think of everything she wants him to hear, and he will respond. Pay attention to the signs; he is still with you.

I knew my father loved God, his country, and his family more than most people could comprehend. Further, throughout my lifetime, he always remarked that he had the most beautiful wife, four daughters, and grandchildren. I have always given him full credit for his statements.

However, I have always doubted that my father loved me, *the real Amy*—*the little girl* filled with curiosity. *The teenager* determined not to conform. *The woman* who desired her own path. *The mom* who cherished her children. *The wife* who wanted to be loved. From the simple to the life-altering, *Amy* did not exist in his mind.

Why did I always get a vanilla birthday cake with peach ice cream for my birthday when my favorite was chocolate with mint chocolate chip?

Why did he take credit for all my accomplishments and blame me for all my failures?

Why did he insist I be independent and self-sufficient and then proclaim I needed to conform and abide by his unrelenting rules?

Why did he beat me into silence when I was screaming out for love?

The contradictory messages left me confused and continuously on edge. No matter what I did, it was wrong or not good enough. I rarely received any praise for my accomplishments. I built walls to protect myself, which still exist today and need to be dismantled. I learned to keep myself perpetually occupied outside the house because my activities and my social connections were highly rewarding. The moment I stepped into my parent's house, everything became punitive.

Don't get me wrong, I am not blaming my father for all of the chaos, confusion, and abuse. That would not be fair or accurate. There were six people in our household, and everyone was uniquely different. That said, there were six interpretations of every situation, six different responses to those interpretations, and the various interplay between people. These differences inherently created frustration because we did not understand or sometimes respect each other. My two older sisters always considered themselves to be in control of me and caused confrontations. Plus, they are polar opposites and do not get along either. My younger sister remained silent. I guess that seemed optimal.

In every family, frustrations are exhibited in different ways. I firmly believe the varying sets of circumstances and subsequent reactions to those circumstances compound and create more frustration. Thus, the cycle of abuse may look very different to each member of the family. Further, some people feel obligated or attached to the abusers or may dismiss the abuse altogether. So, I am sure you are wondering what I did that contributed to the chaos. Well, I made observations and pointed out what seemed obvious to me. Being the voice in a family who kept secrets wasn't safe.

I was nice about it when I was young but always ignored, chastised, and blamed. Eventually, I yelled because that was the only time anybody would listen to me. I simply wanted to be heard and respected. That stopped working because they just brushed my yelling off as Amy being Amy once again. I would get a positive response for a few days, but everyone returned to their old ways.

I reached a tipping point during my teenage years, and there was no turning back. My main goal was to get the hell out of that house, and the more my father yelled at me, the further away I went. Yelling was relatively pointless and ended with me crying out in physical or emotional pain.

As an adult, I rarely yell, but I still reach a tipping point every once in a while, and I am not nice. Although I may be loud and overbearing, I feel my words are accurate. One of my main goals is to state my words calmly, even under extremely stressful or traumatic circumstances.

I contemplated his last phone call before he passed for a long time. I surmised the call was his way of saying he was sorry or in some way had regret. Our relationship was always contentious, even under the best circumstances. I would have loved to hear, "*Amy, I am sorry I hurt you.*" I never did. This burden saddens me, and I am working towards reconciliation within myself.

Years later, I was collecting rocks from that narrow rocky stream I stopped to look at during the super full moon. I wanted to relocate them into my beautiful Zen garden that was green 365 days a year.

The bold white and tawny rocks curved around what appeared to be the water's edge and separated my low-lying shrubs and my delightful rosette batches of chicks and hens.

As I selected a large rock, I distinctly felt my father's presence lingering a few feet behind me. I hesitated in silence so his spirit would not drift away. I slowly turned around and asked with a heavy heart, *"Why can't you love me the way I am? I have always been Amy, pretty much the same Amy for my whole life. What did I do that was so wrong?"*

There was silence once again. I looked around for some type of message from nature. I longed to feel something, anything, to ease my weary mind. But I still felt the emptiness inside. I closed my eyes, put my hands over my heart, and whispered, *"Dad, I want to forgive you, but I don't know how."*

Darkness

Tough love is beyond tough when you let go of the fight and watch your beautiful baby girl fall into the hands of Darkness, collectively defined as all of the internal as well as external pressures that are not conducive to a healthy way of life. The daily conflict was too much for any of us to withstand. I told her, *"If you want to leave me and go live with your father, go ahead. When you are ready to come back and be a respectful part of my family, I am here. If you cannot be respectful, you need to stay away."*

One of the worst moments of my life culminated in a series of events. As I look back, much of it is a blur. I was dealing with memory loss and personality changes from the head trauma. I was still unable to sleep through the night, and my daughter was stuck in the Darkness and continuously pulling me down into misery with her. I have some images in my mind that may or may not be real. Between the brain injury, the extraordinarily high levels of stress, and the physicality of my body, I may never remember the truth. Honestly, that may be better than truly knowing.

My daughter was at an important juncture in her life, and those teenage years were already difficult enough. Somewhere between her braces being removed, going through puberty, and entering high school, she was becoming a woman. Moreover, she was entering this rite of passage during a tumultuous time in her parents' life. The struggle to choose which path to follow was more than exhausting; it was destructive. The laborious task of becoming an adult was difficult, and she surrendered to the Darkness. I assume it was easier for her to give up and stay in bed than to overcome the fear.

I woke up two hours early every day to get her out of bed and, hopefully, to school. It was physically and emotionally exhausting for both of us and always included an intense argument. Regularly, she would call her father to complain. All he needed to hear was, "*Mom's crazy*," and he would run to the rescue. Then, she would pack up her orange runaway bag and disappear. I hated that orange bag.

I worked with her school for ideas and incentives, but she and her father sabotaged all efforts. The conflicts between us became increasingly worse and ultimately aggressive. One morning, as I was trying to pull her out of bed, she kicked my knee with the full thrust of her leg. Excruciating pain shot through my leg, and I wasn't sure if I could walk. As she was struggling to return to bed, she punched me off of her, and I snapped. I twisted her around and put her on the floor with a passive supportive restraint technique I had learned at work. It is supposed to protect and not hurt the attacker.

Instead of de-escalating the situation, it heightened the intensity, and in the struggle, I drew my right hand back in a fist, ready to strike. Instantly, I stopped and thought, "*What in the world am I doing? I don't want to hit my daughter.*" I was thoroughly disgusted with myself and got up to walk away. Physically and emotionally exhausted, I thought, "*I am done with this fight.*"

I walked downstairs and sat on the front porch to calm down and think logically. Daniel had been drowning my baby in lighter fluid and anxiously waiting for the torch to ignite. My only option was to let go of the various power struggles, those I could see and those I could not see. Ultimately, you cannot save somebody who does not want to be saved.

Tough love sucks when it means setting proper boundaries and allowing the natural consequence to unfold. Instead of her running away, I made her go. I made it extremely clear she had to leave the house, and I set three rules for how she could return. First, she needed to go to school every day. Second, she needed to be in an activity or have a job. Last, she needed to be a respectful member of the family. This decision was torture. My baby is gone. I loved her, and I loved myself. There was no easy answer.

There wasn't a moment I didn't wish God would just take me from this world because death seemed so much easier than life. I didn't want to kill myself. Moreover, I wanted to feel alive. Having my daughter gone ripped open a huge gaping hole in my soul, and I had absolutely no idea how to fill it.

Every day, I questioned myself and accepted much of the blame. I should have been stronger. But being strong doesn't mean accepting abuse and hoping it will go away; and being strong means standing up and doing the right thing for everyone involved. Seemingly, short-term losses will eventually lead to long-term success. But, my God, when you are immersed in the Darkness, how can you be sure you are heading for the light? Moreover, how much pain and suffering can any of us endure? When hope diminishes, sadness permeates your existence.

One night, my son cuddled up with me on the couch when he knew I was sad. He kindly said, *"Mommy, she just needs some more time."* I smiled and kissed him on the cheek, *"I know honey, she will figure it out. We are in this together. I just really miss her."* Then he innocently explained, *"Dad could barely handle losing you, and now he wants to make sure he never loses her."*

I knew he was right as chills ran down my spine and my entire body quivered. It's incredible how smart children can be. My beautiful baby girl was trapped in the Darkness and needed time before she was able to escape. Time, the word haunted me; how much more time would be wasted? Each day I spent without her was precious time lost, and I could never get back again. I tried to live a joyful life, but the Darkness was always present and perpetually lingered in the background of my existence.

When you are filled with Love, Time ceases to exist. When you are filled with Darkness, each moment in Time feels like an eternity. I could not find joy no matter how happy I appeared. I wanted my daughter back, but I had to let her go and uncover her own path without me. Letting go of the power struggle is the only action to take if you want to experience freedom.

Power Struggle is a term used in crisis prevention. It is a situation in which two or more people compete for power and control in a particular sphere of influence or situation. I had to choose. Do I fall and bring my daughter down with me, or do I let her fall into the Darkness with her father until she chooses to see the light?

In my mind, the only way she would be able to see the light was if I walked the path first and showed her the way. I needed to show her the way back to health and prosperity and the path back to loving herself. Ultimately, I needed to help her uncover her pathway back *home*.

When she was a little girl, she would squeeze her way into the middle of hugs between Mommy and Daddy and lovingly insist, "*Room for me.*" When we picked her up, and she nuzzled in, we kissed each other's cheeks back and forth. We all giggled and called it the *triangle kiss*. Whoever got the most kisses always rejoiced in laughter, and in case you couldn't guess, she was always the winner. Now, I just wanted one kiss. I wanted to feel *home* in each other's arms.

During this time of Darkness, I have no idea what my daughter or her father did daily, but I can assure you it was not happy, healthy, or productive. Further, he used my health insurance coverage to devise treatment for my daughter that was not clear and accurate. Most importantly, he was making unilateral decisions and blaming me for all the problems in his household. When it became time for me to stand up for my daughter against her father's ill-advised and life-altering decisions, I scorned the professionals who took his version of the story as absolute truth and never even contacted me for my version of the story. I advised them of their unethical behavior and warned them to stop. Fortunately, I never heard from any of them again.

Rocky Trail

Several months after all of my legal drama finally ended and Ben and I had gone our separate ways, I met a guy on a twelve-mile group hike who seemed pretty cool. He explained he would be moving to Europe towards the end of the year and would probably stay for three to five years. We got along quite well and decided to date casually until his departure.

One day, we were riding our bikes on the Ashland Trail, and he had an idea. Obviously, we would stop dating but would remain friends. Instead of rushing to sell his house before the big move, he suggested I rent his house as it was in a nice neighborhood near the high school. Then, when my kids graduated, I could purchase a house. I helped him pack up the belongings he wanted to keep and put them into storage. Next, I helped him plan, organize, and execute a yard sale for the remaining items. The situation was going to be mutually beneficial.

It was a great idea until his plans faltered. After three months, he returned from Europe with no job, was angry, and defeated. Whew, going from casually dating to living together with two children was *not awesome*. We made the best of it while he continued to search for a job in Europe. We both enjoyed hiking, camping, and riding mountain bikes. Oddly enough, his name translates as *rocky trail*.

One day, Rocky Trail suggested attending My Lady's Manor Steeplechase Race. It is one of Maryland's oldest and most competitive days of timber racing. Since 1909, this day has marked the beginning of Spring in the equestrian countryside. The buzz of *Horse Country* brings out the men in colorful cotton shorts with loafers and women prancing around in high society hats and sundresses.

We packed a picnic lunch and got two bottles of wine. He picked out a spot quite a distance from any other group. I mentioned some friends were there and asked if he wanted to walk around with me. Rocky Trail suggested we eat first. I prepped the food as he poured the wine. I had half a glass of the first bottle and half a glass of the second bottle.

As we walked around and talked, he was distant and preoccupied. It made me and my friends uncomfortable, so we returned to the blanket. After the finale, we went to a local pub where many traditionally gather post-race. We stood at the outside bar and waited for a table. A friend of mine joined us and purchased several rounds of drinks. For some reason, my drink kept disappearing.

Suddenly, Rocky Trail spoke in a thick, traditional Irish accent and aggressively flirted with all the women. A few people asked if I was with him, and I nodded in disappointment. The weird part is that he is Italian and has never been to Ireland.

Then, Rocky Trail disappeared for about an hour. Suddenly, the manager informed me they had escorted him out of the establishment. He was backing out of a parking space and beckoning me into the car. I begged him to let me drive because I did not know how much alcohol he had consumed. Fortunately, the roads were empty, and his driving seemed tolerable.

Suddenly, Rocky Trail ignited a long and vicious tirade about his failure in Europe. Everyone hated him; the teachers and the students were all idiots! His life was ruined, and apparently, it was all my fault! During his outburst, I calmly interjected, *No, everyone hates you because you are an asshole, and that has nothing to do with me.* Then he shrieked out in anger, "*You are a fucking bitch, and everything is your fault! You did this to me! You are the one who ruined my life!*"

At that moment, a faint streetlight lit up a sharp curve in the road. The breaks screeched and rumbled while the sound of agitated gravel permeated the air. I grasped the door handle. In those brief yet eternal moments before striking the telephone pole, I had an intense and one-sided argument with God. *"Why did you keep me alive for five more years only to let me die like this? Why did I have to suffer? What have I done that is so wrong? Why do you keep punishing me?"*

Finally, I closed my eyes and accepted it was time for me to die. CRUNCH! When I opened my eyes, I exclaimed to God, *"Why am I still alive? Why didn't you let me die!"* I took a deep breath and looked around. My side of the car was occluded in close to the console. My body was trapped. There was no way out. Pain. Oh my God, searing pain! My body was enduring the most excruciating pain, and I was fully coherent. *"Think, Amy, think."* I kept telling myself. The car was so compacted I was afraid it might catch on fire. *"Think faster, Amy."*

Rocky Trail repeatedly whined about how his life was ruined, and now he was going to lose his driver's license. Surprisingly, he was not injured and had no sense of urgency for the situation. All he cared about was himself and his stupid driver's license. He wouldn't stop complaining and blaming me. He was so self-absorbed he didn't even notice or care that my side of the car was destroyed.

I looked him dead in the eyes and said in a deep voice, *"Shut the fuck up and get out of the car right now."* Then, he got out and walked away. I crawled out of my seat belt and over the console. Maneuvering my way out of the tangled mess of steel and vinyl was difficult. To this day, I am not sure how I had the strength or agility to get out. It was by some miracle I did not black out from the pain.

The neighbors came out of their houses as the police and ambulance arrived. I held a woman's forearm, *"Look, lady, I don't know who you are, but please don't leave me. This is the worst pain I have ever experienced in my entire life. I am sorry, I need you to stay with me. Please, please don't leave me alone. I don't want to die all by myself. I am sorry to burden you."*

The police questioned Rocky Trail and me separately. They said they had no desire to *"ruin this guy's life"* by taking his license. But then they explained that if I got into that ambulance and went to the hospital, they wouldn't have a choice but to file the paperwork and see what happens in court. Ambulance. Hospital. Court. No, absolutely not. I was not going to subject myself to more excruciating legal drama. That was the last thing I wanted in my life.

I feebly convinced the officers I was okay and just wanted to go home. Rocky Trail refused to call his friends or family for pick up. He tried to keep this insane mess a secret. He offered me no physical or emotional comfort and insisted I make some phone calls to find a ride for us. I called Ben, and although he lived 45 minutes away, he instantly agreed to come to my rescue.

Upon return, Rocky Trail went into the house and passed out. I stayed in the car to talk with Ben. He understood why I refused to get into the ambulance but insisted I get medical attention in the morning. The next day, Rocky Trail said he had no recollection of events and took me to the hospital. He apologized once, but I believe it was a ploy to manipulate my feelings and protect himself.

My body was bright green and purple with splotches of black and brown. My breathing was inhibited and painful. Hiccups and coughs were torturous. My neck was sprained and stuck in the forward position, and I had to tell myself to swallow. My spine and ribs were sprained, twisted, and swollen. My intestines and organs shifted out of place, which caused intense bursts of pain.

My right arm shook for months, and I couldn't use my hand or fingers for about a year. The accident totally distorted my body and left my pelvic bone several inches out of alignment, and my left foot was contorted and hung sideways. I was unable to have bowel movements without physical therapy, and many internal as well as external triggers caused severe anxiety and panic attacks. Driving was an intimidating task. Dead animals, loud noises, and sirens were causes for high alert mode.

My friendship with Rocky Trail and unintentional living arrangements were over. I needed to figure out how to relocate and fast. Oddly enough, I was relocating my entire training center at work at the exact same time I was relocating my house. My whole life was literally in boxes. I worked day and night organizing, packing, and moving boxes from one place to the next. Looking back, I am not sure how I functioned through this period in my life. I guess I had no choice. It was necessary to find my inner strength and move on. Staying in either location was definitely not an option.

Unfortunately, neither Rocky Trail nor his insurance company were willing to pay for any of my suffering. The county received $30,000 for a new telephone pole. Rocky Trail received $20,000 for a replacement car, and upon returning to court, I received $7,000 to put my body back together. How is that for justice? His insurance company figured out a way to keep most of the evidence out of court because he had already pleaded guilty in a different lawsuit against him from the county. That evidence was my primary course of action. The only thing I had left was my testimony and some medical bills that did not follow the standard medical protocol in such cases.

Making the best possible choices for my healthcare and keeping my expenses as low as possible is not advisable in the courtroom. These slimy accident lawyers have learned how to use sound judgment against you. I guess if I had run around screaming to save me, save me, save me to all the doctors, and shoved a bunch of addictive painkillers down my throat, I would have received more compensation. The only course of action I would have changed was that I should have gotten into that ambulance and let Rocky Trail suffer the consequences he had coming to him.

As I courageously stood in the middle of a vast wasteland, the shadows seemed taller than my soul. I could smell the smoldering buildings in the distance and hear the faint echoes of the fallen trees. Were they laughing in jest or sending me a message? I reached down, picked up a handful of ashes, and blew them into the wind. Just then, a large birdlike figure emerged from the destruction and twisted back and forth as if trying to break free. It was the phoenix, and the fiery commotion uncovered two paths I could follow. The choice was mine and mine alone. I chose the path home.

Our Home

Concurrent with moving, I knew I did not want to move into another rental house. However, the divorce affected my credit score, and I needed to clean it up a bit to qualify for a loan. It was much easier than I anticipated because Daniel had left an incredibly noticeable trail directly linked to his personal bank accounts, not mine. I think credit companies were slightly more lenient considering many people had been affected by the 2008 Global Financial Crisis and needed to rebuild their lives. After a few phone calls and conversations, I was good to go.

I intended to live in the county near the local high school because my daughter had opted out of her private school attendance, and eventually, I wanted her to return and live with me. However, the housing choices were less than desirable. Against my better judgment, I asked a real estate agent to help me, and it ended after one long, frustrating day. So, I took matters into my own hands and started driving around areas that seemed suitable. It remained frustrating because I felt the houses were highly overpriced and poorly maintained.

After an appointment to view a house I was interested in, I walked around the neighborhood because it was in the city instead of the county. Out of the corner of my eye, I saw a small red *For Sale By Owner* sign peeking at me through the window of a charming house built in 1924. I knocked on the front door, and an eccentric woman came to greet me. I explained who I was and that I was interested in looking through her house. She said, *"Sweetie, come around to the behind door. I am from Texas, and we don't call it a back door down there. I'll let you in."* I giggled and agreed.

As I opened the gate, I saw a beautiful English garden, and upon entering the house, I fell in love. *"This is where I am going to live. Try* to look normal, Amy. Don't look too excited." I tried to convince myself several times. It was an open kitchen with exposed brick. Solid wood French doors divided the area between the dining room, which was embellished with antique lighting fixtures. The original wood floors had an exquisite mahogany inlay, and the staircase was a masterpiece.

The man who lived there was a steelworker and created a handmade wrought iron staircase with a recurrent bird of paradise and leaves. His wife had antiqued the wrought iron with greenish and gold paint. Nearby, she had painted a marble faux finish on some pillars separating the living spaces repurposed from an old church. The front window was stained glass, which created a rainbow of colors during sunset. After the display descended, the room remained golden from the additional stained glass adorning the house. The prophetic golden hour was indeed a majestic site.

The elevated ceilings had crown molding, and two built-in curio cabinets adorned the dining room, perfect for a lifetime of little treasures I had saved. Amazingly, this house had two large bedrooms upstairs and an efficiency apartment in the basement that would be the perfect respite for dynamic and tireless teenagers.

I explained I could take care of everything and save them the real estate commission. In turn, I asked to move some of my stuff in early to help expedite the process. My only ask was to be able to walk my friend through first to make sure I wasn't missing anything. They were more than willing to agree because the house was immaculate. I planned to come the following day.

Tom, my best friend from college, who also happens to be a general contractor, and I walked through the house. He evaluated all the parts and pieces properly, and after we finished the tour, we engaged in some idle chit-chat with the couple. The moment we exited the gate, he enthusiastically said, "Amy, you have to get this house. It's perfect for you." That was music to my ears! The next step was to walk around the neighborhood to ensure it would be safe for my children. We wandered around the streets and stopped at the shopping center. Then, we walked down to the main strip, where all the local foodie establishments were located.

We had drinks in a couple of places and decided to eat in the third. What a great adventure. At the end of the evening, we strolled back to the house where we had left our cars. I called the couple on Monday morning to say I intended to buy their house and hoped to move in within the next month. I just needed to get my financing and all the other paperwork processed.

It was a perfect situation for them because most of their belongings were in storage in Texas, where they planned to retire. They had been the second owner and resided there for twenty-five years. They had put their heart and soul into this house. She was overwhelmed with joy when she noticed all my possessions matched the house perfectly! I told her the instant I entered her home, I knew I had found *my home*. It was like she had created it for me. Everything seemed perfect.

Two days before closing, I received a horrible phone call. The lender declined my loan because I could not prove I signed over all financial and legal rights to the marital home that had gone into foreclosure. I immediately picked up my belongings and left work. Nobody questioned me because I had never left work like that before and was obviously on a mission.

I went to my house, collected two huge boxes full of court documentation, and drove directly to the lending bank office. I asked to speak to the person in charge. I was told my arrival was completely out of the ordinary and everyone was busy. I said I would wait as long as necessary. They seated me in a large conference room, and soon, a very nice and professional-looking woman walked through the door. She explained the problem with my documentation, and I presented the boxes to her.

I explained my confusion and told her she could keep every piece of documentation to prove my innocence. I did not know how to locate that information and briefly described the tragedy I had endured. I asked her, as a woman, to believe in me and have faith in me to do the *right thing*. I literally cried a river of tears on the boardroom table, and she brought me some tissues.

After a short hiatus, she returned with an approval letter and wished me the best of luck in my new home. Then, she quietly nodded and walked away. As the door closed behind her, I continued to shed a few tears. This time, they were tears of joy. That woman I only knew for a few short minutes of my life changed the course of my life forever. I am eternally grateful for her trust and understanding.

On schedule, closing occurred, and I was handed the keys to *my home*. I couldn't wait to pick the kids up from school and walk through the door for the first time together. When the previous owners and I said our goodbyes, the woman hugged me and cried. The Star of Texas was finally heading back to her home. For years, this house had meant the world to her, and then, it meant the world to me. *My world. My children. Our home.*

The Golden Hour remained my favorite time of the day in our house. Those shimmering moments illuminated our living room with awe-inspired golden pixie dust. In photography, it refers to the hour immediately after sunrise and the hour before sunset. The sunlight is redder and softer than at other times of the day and has a healthier glow. Ironically, when I was researching the Golden Hour in trauma management, it hit home. This Golden Hour is the hour between life and death. If you are critically injured, you have less than sixty minutes to survive. You may not die immediately, but over forty years of research has shown that something irreparable has happened to your body. I believe that pixie dust was sent to aid my spiritual repairs.

The Way

Somewhere in between the different Bible Study groups, I left the Catholic Church, or as I prefer to say, I was ex-communicated, and I joined another Christian-based church. This place didn't pretend to have a pristine face and welcomed those who had metaphorically fallen from grace in their former places of worship or in real life. It was much larger and more diverse than any church I ever attended.

The sermons were well thought out and executed. These speakers were extremely knowledgeable and charismatic. The musical selections were beautifully orchestrated and a feast for the senses. There was one woman in particular I loved to watch. She chose songs that spoke to me, and her presentation seemed to evoke a natural and mystical beauty from a different place and time.

In church, I sat with a lovely older couple who welcomed me into their home several times and made my children feel like part of the family. They introduced me to several of their multi-generational friends within the church. I was asked to help lead activities but declined to keep my boundaries safe.

I joined House Church, a tangent of the same church comprised of various age groups of women and men. Some were married, some single, and encompassed several ethnic backgrounds. Our time was an intellectual study of the words and their origins, as well as fellowship between participants. One elderly couple from Egypt knew how to translate the words we read into several languages. They were a wealth of knowledge and had such a kind, loving, and generous spirit.

The groups were enjoyable, but we were not allowed to speak about other belief systems because they were considered dark. People intrigued by or following alternate paths would never be regarded as believers or permitted to enter the gates of Heaven. Apparently, they believe there are limited seats in Heaven and the elders believed they already held a space. *Hmm. Interesting.*

Strangely, people regularly asked me if I was "*a believer.*" Moreover, they would begin and end their sentences with the same self-glorifying phrase. I learned to answer "*Yes.*" Why? Because they never asked me what I believed in. They just asked *if I believed.*

Either way, it was a nice respite from the world, and I appreciated being in such an intellectual and spiritually-based community. I was invited to gatherings, parties, and other activities outside the study group. I was pleased to learn that a few women loved to hike, just like me.

I was still recovering from everything I had endured throughout my life. A form of numbness enclosed my sense of being, masking the pain and emotional discourse. I needed a paradigm shift. The universe was calling, but I was unable to hear or find *the way*. The desire for God to take me from this earth still existed every single day, even though I was desperately trying to feel alive. Acupuncture was helping to process my pain, but my aloneness seemed eternal.

When my perceptions wavered, I was asked to run the Communion Ceremony with a lady I got along with quite well. Roz was married with four children and lived less than a mile from my house. Her daughter and my son were like two peas in a pod. Our friendship grew in actual *communion,* an exchange of intimate thoughts and feelings, especially on a mental or spiritual level. We naturally connected on many levels, and she quickly became an integral part of my family.

When she moved thirty minutes away, I was worried I would lose my friend. However, it actually strengthened our bond. She told me her friends of the road had faded into the distance and I was the only one to make the journey to see her. We loved many of the same things in life, and our parenting styles complimented each other nicely. I couldn't imagine life without her.

When she told me she and her husband were separating, I was sad with her. When asked if she was making the proper decision, I replied, "*Well, I like both of you, but you don't exactly match.*

She asked for more feedback, and I could tell she was sensitive. So, I decided on an analogy to lighten the mood: "*Roz, you are like a glass of fine aged red wine, and Bob is a can of Budweiser. Both are good depending on the situation, but they don't match.*" as we both laughed hysterically.

One night, we were heading out to listen to some live music. She had an attractive outfit on and picked out a matching scarf. It was a beautiful scarf, but it screamed, "*I am unavailable!*" I laughed, "*Roz, you need to take that mom scarf off! I am not going dancing with you looking like that!*" Yes, clothes speak volumes about who you are. They can be a reflection of the inner self. The right clothing may be waiting for you physically, emotionally, and spiritually.

Let's think about it for a few minutes. First, please do not think about the price tag or the name of the brand of your clothes; that is not important. How you feel and want others to feel about you when you show up is important. We danced the night away that night, and she looked and felt great. Seeing my friend start to feel like herself again was wonderful.

Over the next few months, we performed the Communion Ceremony for our House Church, and it was relatively pleasurable. Increasingly, we both felt the need to move on but kept it between ourselves. This group wasn't what we thought it would be or what we needed in our life. Sometimes, I felt like they just wanted us to drink the orange Kool-Aid like we were lost sheep looking to be brainwashed into salvation. I thought these self-proclaimed shepherds were greatly misguided.

My decision to leave came after a life-altering event. I was driving up the Jones Falls Expressway, a ten-mile bridge built above the water to connect the city to the suburbs. The roadway curves through the valleys like a snake, and the skid marks on the concrete traffic barriers are prolific. At the approach of a curve, you cannot see ahead, and any accident is cause for duress.

One evening, I left work and headed to House Church. My speed was around 60, and suddenly, all I could see were red brake lights. I grasped the steering wheel and pumped my brakes as I came to a barreling STOP! The jolt hurt a little, but I did not crash into anything or anyone.

Crunch! Crunch! Crunch! The highly distinguishable noise of steel crunching steal penetrated my soul as I held onto life. At least forty cars and numerous passengers piled up all over the highway. Finally, the noises stopped. *I was safe.* I looked at the man in the car beside me and rolled down my window.

"*Do you want to get out of here?*" I asked. He released the steering wheel, "*Yes! Tell me what to do!*"

"*Gimmie a minute*". I said as I exited the car and checked with the passengers in vehicles near mine. Everyone was startled but motioned for me to move on. That man and I shimmied our way out of the multitude of collisions. I am not sure how or why we were spared. A million thoughts were running through my head. Were these warning signs, wake-up calls, or something else?

I took the next exit, pulled into a gas station parking lot, and a deluge of hot tears poured from my eyes. I closed my eyes and prayed out loud, "*Please, God, I know you can hear me. I promise to stop praying for you to take me away from this earth. I want to live! I want to live my life fully. Please help me. I feel lost and confused, and I am not sure which way to go.*"

My tears subsided, and I continued on to House Church. During the group prayer request time, I recounted what happened to me and asked for prayers. Everyone fell dead silent. The older man from Egypt looked at his wife and took her hand. He quoted scripture from the Bible to acknowledge my fortitude. Together, they honored my courage in pain and adversity as if they were feeling my burden with me. I felt a sudden sigh of relief and smiled.

Suddenly, the House Church leader truncated the message, stood up, and gloriously applauded the man from Egypt. He asked everyone for a round of applause for the wise messenger and his words. All the while, the leader chose to ignore me. He did not look at me or acknowledge my suffering. Instantly, I felt a tinge of anger and resentment, but most importantly, I felt that my time here was over. This box was too limiting for me and was holding me back from finding my true purpose in life.

That night, as we were all finishing our snacks and preparing to leave, I thought, "*Farewell, my friends of the road. I wish you well. I believe in God, but I don't think your version matches mine. There is a space in Heaven for all of us.*"

I thought about the leader's oversight of my feelings for quite some time. I found it difficult to believe he was doing it intentionally and trying to hurt my feelings. That just seemed inaccurate. But really, what was his motivation? I am not the only person who noticed, as some people commented to me later. Either way, I believe I received the intended message, *"I don't belong here."* The question remained, *"Where do I belong?"* Maybe a better way to phrase this message would be, *"Where does Amy belong in this world?"*

CHAPTER 6

AWARENESS BEGINS

Throughout our lives, we may have experiences that are pivotal to our survival and bring us to another level of understanding of why we are here. For me, there has been an inner drive and desire to discover who I am, and in mysterious ways, the most arduous challenges helped me achieve incredible results. The car accidents that nearly killed me led me to a trip to Peru. The knowledge and subsequent awakening freed me in ways I could have never imagined.

Instruments of Light

My neck had been stuck in the forward position for weeks, and I was experiencing excruciating pain. I could actually feel where my neck and spine were protruding out of place. Waiting any longer for a physical therapy appointment was out of the question A friend of mine suggested I see a manual physical therapist she had used for her hip injury, and he was able to get me in right away.

Manual Physical Therapy is a specialty within the field of physical therapy that utilizes specific hands-on techniques without the assistance of devices or machines. Traditional PT *treats the symptoms* *of the disease* process. At the same time, Manual PT addresses the person as a whole and harnesses the knowledge of anatomy *to identify and treat the origins of the disease.* It sounded perfect to me.

Upon arrival for my first visit, we went through a questionnaire, and the therapist physically assessed my body. As I lay down on the table, he rested his hands and fingers on the base of my skull. The pressure *opened up* my spine and nervous system. It felt as though his hands were melting into my body. This portion of his technique is known as cranial sacral therapy.

Cranial Sacral Therapy is a gentle and non-invasive form of manual therapy that works with cranial nerves and the spinal column through the sacrum to relieve stress in the body and balance the flow of cranial sacral fluid. This technique is excellent for migraines, chronic neck and back pain, coordination impairments, and brain and spinal cord injuries. It is significant in the treatment of PTSD, Post Traumatic Stress Disorder.

He slowly helped the tendons, nerves, and muscles relax, taking some pressure off my neck. His hands and fingers performed a magical little dance as all the bones in my neck popped back into place. Surprisingly, my jaw was out of place as well. As he worked his way around the extremities of my body, he slowly made his way into the core of my pain. My intuition went into overdrive as I could sense his intentions and followed his moves as he tried to put my body back together again.

When the PT session was complete, I released more liquid than I knew my body could hold. I was so embarrassed because I was certain he could hear what seemed to be the most extended mid-stream release ever. We had a short discussion before I left, and he encouraged me to hydrate and rest for the best results post-session. Apparently, my body would process this treatment for the next few days.

I was determined to heal with every fiber of my body. My PT moved energy through my body every Wednesday for over a year. First, he brought it to the surface and then released it. He was so kind, respectful, and knowledgeable that I never felt uncomfortable. It looked strange to see his hands appear as though they were inside my abdomen. I certainly could feel my organs and intestines returning to their proper locations. Consequently, every Thursday I was able to have a bowel movement.

When healing started, I closed my eyes. Spherical streams of yellow and orange haze appeared inside my mind's eye. They were beautiful and peaceful waves of color; sometimes, a little pink would swirl into consciousness. A huge part of me knew we were making progress.

Over time, the healing process went deeper. Purple and blue orbs of light created a mysterious sense of calmness while my physical body was experiencing pain. I had to work through and remove this pain to restore my body. When tears filled my eyes, I always encouraged him to continue; pushing beyond my limits was the only way I could overcome the trauma.

Without any verbal feedback from me, my PT experienced moments of completion. Unbeknownst to him, I knew when these moments occurred because they were unlike the others. Genuine healing occurred when an intense flash of white light permeated my internal world.

Sometimes, during each session, I opened my eyes and watched him motion his hands in such a way as to throw away the energy he had removed from my body. I inquired about what he was doing. He replied that if he did not discard this energy, it would manifest itself within him, and he would suffer, or it would return to a different location in my body, and I would continue to have pain.

He knew my emotional as well as physical pain was deep and explained that they are intricately woven together. Eventually, we got to a point in therapy where he explained he had done almost everything he could do for me physically. He did not know how to treat the emotional aspects of my pain, as this was not his area of expertise. However, he shared a suite with an acupuncturist and asked if I was open to this technique. I trusted him, so I agreed.

At the end of the following session, my PT brought Radianthawk, the acupuncturist, into the room where I was laying on the therapy table. They had a clinical debrief over my body, and she took a few notes. Then, she put her index finger on a point on the left side of my abdomen. That small and gentle touch induced intense pain. Initially, I thought, *"Ouch, what just happened!"* But my thought quickly transformed into, *"Ha! I knew I would like her!"*

My PT and Radianthawk created an integrative treatment plan for me. The intent was to transition me away from my PT and allow Radianthawk to process the emotional side of my physical pain. My PT is a true healer because his hands are instruments of light for me.

Not to my surprise, his practice was alive and thriving. So, he had no immediate openings when I needed impromptu visits to restore my physical body. In turn, he referred me to one of his cohorts. Coach was also kind, respectful, and knowledgeable but had difficulty accepting the situation's emotional aspect. The moment my emotions came into play, he would back down.

Don't get me wrong, he was always able to process my pain and restore my body to health, but I rarely experienced the healing colors, and I never experienced the healing light. I am not discounting his abilities; I just say they are different.

For example, I injured my knee on a kayaking trip. The impact of the rock slamming into my knee caused my hip to move four inches out of alignment. Any movement caused excruciating pain. Driving to his office was difficult, and walking up the steps to the therapy room took forever. As his eyes widened with concern, he asked, *"What in the world did you do to yourself?"*

It took Coach about an hour and a half to put my hip back in place. My body was weak and vibrating in shock. My mind was fuzzy, and I felt strange. At the end of this session, the healing was complete, and it took the next couple of days to process fully. I genuinely appreciated and needed the physical healing. But now, I needed to figure out the emotional healing on my own.

The kayaking incident set me back even though the pain was alleviated. The emotional experience of the pain triggered my anxiety and PTSD, leaving my entire bodily system on high alert. That evening, I opted for a hot Epson salt bath by candlelight, mystical music without any words, and a glass of semisweet red wine. I had to convince myself that the adverse situation had ended and that I was safe. This process soothed my soul and helped to restore my mindset and get a good night's sleep.

Healing Energy

From the beginning, Radianthawk was different. She had a quality about her that made determining her age difficult. On one hand, she was a mature woman with grandchildren. On the other, she had a youthful mystic within the natural world along with the words and needles of a powerful elder with healing energy. However, she was careful not to share too much wisdom. The research was *my work*.

After my first acupuncture session was complete, I expected to feel different. Surprisingly, I felt nothing except a little more rested than before. I put on my clothes and prepared to go home. Everything drastically changed as I took that first step out of the building. I grabbed the handrail because my legs could not support me, and I could not take another step. I was suspended on the landing for about fifteen minutes before I willed myself over to my car.

The experience is difficult to describe, but it was like a musical Rhapsody had taken control of my body. This masterpiece embodied an extraordinarily intense and highly personalized movement of energy, reconstructing my mind, body, and soul into existence. The episodic responses surfaced in my suffering as well as my euphoria. It was confusing and overwhelming, as well as blissful and peaceful. Either way, this incredible session left me unable to drive.

I called a few people to come and get me. Fortunately, I found someone who was available. We went to dinner, and I decided only to drink water to keep the healing process alive. After a couple of hours, I could finally drive and allow the intense feelings to transcend. Over time, Rhapsody found covert ways of continuing to process the immense energy running rapidly through my body. My job was to listen to music and discover the lessons being brought to my awareness.

Lesson One: In Chinese philosophy, Qi is the vital life force or energy contained in everything and everyone. We intrinsically possess it from the nascent stages of birth. This life force is the essence of existence that unites mind, body, and spirit. Qi flows through meridian channels in the body. Key points along the meridian lines are used for acupressure and acupuncture.

Traditional acupuncture began over 3,000 years ago and is used to cultivate and balance Qi. The literal translation of Qi is vapor, air, or breath. Hmm, sounds like Ha, the breath of life in Hawaiian. Further, I know the Asian culture has had a significant impact on Polynesian culture.

Lesson Two: We see Qi manifest clearly in the change of the seasons. This can help to discover and treat the root cause of a person's illness. It is based upon the principles of the Five Elements of continual health and flow of nature. They work interdependently in an elegant and systematic balance. Each one sustains and supports the next one in the cycle:

1. **Wood:** Corresponds to the birth and growth of plants and trees in the spring.
2. **Fire:** The growth of spring comes to maturity under the heat and vitality of fire in the summer.
3. **Earth:** The warmth of fire creates an abundance of harvests on the earth in late summer.
4. **Metal:** After the harvest comes the decay of autumn. This is when the leaves fall from the trees, nourish the soil, and produce metal mineral resources.

5. **Water:** The mountains and mineral rocks create and bind the flowing streams of water. Water moving quietly under the winter ice is the source of germinating the wood seed.

Lesson Three: I asked Radianthawk what element I was, and without hesitation, *"Fire, of course!"*

I asked how she knew, *"It's your laugh!"* as she mischievously smiled over her shoulder and left the room. I went home to research and discover, *"Why am I fire?"*

Pros: Energetic. Exuberant. Creative. Believe in the power of charisma and desire. Highly intuitive and passionate about life. Fire signs are known for their confidence, especially when the going gets tough. They think fast on their feet, do not mind pressure, and are brave and independent. Fire is filled with optimism and the courage that ignites action. People who are of the element of fire exhibit unprecedented strength to fight through difficulties in life. They are always aware.

I thought, *"Cool. I can deal with those attributes. Who wouldn't like to be described like that."*

Cons: Competitive. Bossy. Arrogant. Combative and Aggressive when they feel stressed or betrayed. Can cause team members to burn out. Desire to take control. May lack collaboration skills.

I got slightly bothered and thought, *"Hey, wait, these cons don't sound like me. Sure, I can get crazy mad at times when I feel trapped in the corner or betrayed, but I am not bossy, arrogant, or controlling. I desire to control myself and my work, but I think that is an asset."*

Also, fire is usually Aries, Leo, and Sagittarius, and it is to be the weakest against water and earth.

I am a Pisces, and that is a water sign. Loving and compassionate. Tolerant with a keen understanding. Pisces channel their emotions into an art form to feel more centered and enlightened. Intensely empathic and sensitive to their surroundings. Calculated and slow moving. Vulnerable to criticism. Worry about how their actions may affect others—influenced by their surroundings.

Water can actually be more powerful than Fire or Wind because it can be a tidal wave of destruction or a single drop. Drop by drop over time can wear the strongest of rock formations.

"Ugh. I am so confused. Most of these attributes can be stated about most people sometimes. How is this going to help me? I need a course of direction." I pondered in frustration.

So, the next day, I went to work and asked My Boss if she knew about the Five Elements. If yes, which one am I? *"Ha! Fire, of course!"* I replied, *"What is this a conspiracy? Did you and Radianthawk exchange emails about me or something?"* With a huge smile, she explained, *"No, it's your laugh. It is highly infectious and can fill a room. It makes people desire to be around you. But don't let people get too close, or you'll burn them."*

I thought for a moment and agreed with her, *"Well, that is true. I love to laugh, and I don't really trust anyone anymore. Although I used to trust almost everyone."* In turn, she asked what changed. I replied, *"Well, when the people you love the most overwhelmingly betray you, it's difficult to trust anyone. I used to trust most people most of the time without thinking about it. But now, I don't trust anybody until I find a reason to trust them. Sad but true. It seems rather pessimistic, but it's safer."*

Lesson Four: Every morning, I woke up at 2:00 am. According to Chinese medicine, this is the time of the liver. It is a time when the body should be asleep, toxins are released, and fresh new blood is made. Waking up at this time every day interfered with my detoxification pathways. I was filled with physical as well as emotional poison and had no way to release it.

Did you know if Qi energy stagnates in your liver, it affects the body's ability to digest food and leads to bloating, constipation, and abdominal pain? It also causes emotional reactions such as depression, anxiety, and irritability. The liver also holds onto anger. Apparently, walking and dancing can reduce angry reactions. I assumed figuring out all this new knowledge would help to guide me in my healing journey or at least give me an alternative perspective of choices.

Funny thing… I noticed every time I got angry and was trying to conceal my emotions; I experienced a sharp pain in my liver area. So, I questioned, *"If I love people with my heart, do I hate them with my liver?"* Ha! That really amused me. From then on, every time I felt that tinge in my side, I laughed and thought, *"Oh, I didn't know you bothered me that much! Be gone."*

Lesson Five: Maybe if I fix my Qi, I can rid myself of the negative aspects of Fire and keep the good ones. I am not sure if it works like that, but I will try it.

Qi Sources: Sleep. Breath. Nutrition. Digestion.

Qi Deficiency: Irregular sleep patterns. Improper breathing patterns. Poor digestion, which leads to nutritional deficiencies. Fright and fear disperse and confuse Qi like a frightened animal that doesn't know which way to run. Obviously, I was filled with poison and not enough Qi. At this point, I realized I needed to adjust my thinking, reactions, and the way I was living life.

"So much information to sort through! How do I learn to understand and fix myself!" I decided not to focus on the words and turn my attention to the experience. Outside of my acupuncture session, I did all the work I was supposed to do to restore my health. Fortunately, during acupuncture, I let go of my ego and let the energy flow. This was very therapeutic and healing on very deep levels.

Strong Qi

1. Trust your feelings and intuition.
2. Feel connected to people and situations.
3. Let life flow.
4. Find your inner strength and feel empowered and peaceful.
5. Understand your life has a purpose.

Acupuncture created orbs, streaks of light and color in my mind's eye, just like in physical therapy. The beginning usually entailed yellows, oranges, and pinks. Midway, my mind would travel through some indistinguishable shadows of light, and sometimes, I felt like I was sleeping but was still aware. Then, some of the blues and purples would surface. I found this fascinating and just went with the flow, enjoying the newfound connection to whatever was happening, which was greater than me.

Often, I could distinguish the route the needles moved the energy through my body and describe them to Radianthawk. Amazed, she replied, "*You feel more than anyone I have ever met.*" This confirmed that I have a unique relationship with the universe and myself. It was important for me to honor who I was becoming without all the constrictions and external influences placed upon me.

Sometimes, the energy would get stuck in my feet and hands. They felt large and hot when the rest of my body was cold. After treatment, I verbalized my physical feelings, and Radianthawk released any lingering energy. A few times, I returned the next day because the truncated energy was very uncomfortable and distracting.

Occasionally, she used moxibustion on my fingers, toes, and forehead. The dark sticky paste used is called moxa. She kept the ignited resin on my body until I said, "*Hot.*" At this point, the moxa should have removed excess cold and dampness from my body to relieve the pain. Thus, restoring balance. At each point where she used the moxa, I counted for my own reference. Amazingly, the hand with the most damage could withstand much longer periods than my other hand. Further, the two fingers that experienced the most damage never reached the "Hot" point.

Radianthawk never fully answered my questions but always gave me some information to go on in search of myself. Sometimes, it frustrated me because I really wanted a hint or a nudge in a certain direction. Ultimately, my own research was mine, and I found it for a reason. I just needed to trust the process. She always reminded me, "*You know your power.*"

Spirit of The Dance

I met one of my best friends, Daniela, because we were both intrigued by the idea of sex on the beach. I am sorry to disappoint you; I am actually referring to ancient ocean creatures that still exist today. Horseshoe crabs date back over 400 million years and love to spawn with multiple partners within three days of the full moon in May and June on the coast of Maryland. Then, they leave their tiny little blue-green eggs all over the beach to start the cycle of life all over again.

At dusk, literally hundreds of thousands of these creatures find their way to potential mates along the sandy shores and partake in these rituals. If they accidentally get stranded ashore, they can bury themselves in the sand or fold themselves in half for up to four days. Amazingly, each time a female digs a nest, she can bury a cluster of about 4,000 eggs and can do this up to twenty times a year.

After a group hike, several of us watched the sites. I was invited to dinner with my new friend, her former husband, and their son. I thought the ability to be friends with your ex-husband and spend time together as a family was incredible. I thoroughly enjoyed all of them.

They were born in Romania and emigrated to America after the fall of Communism. Subsequently, they got a divorce, and she had to find her own way. Her incredible work ethic and overwhelming desire to live life impressed me. The best part is that we both love many of the same things, such as hiking, camping, eating, drinking, and dancing.

When she first invited me to go dancing at a club, I felt hesitant and insecure. I had not danced since college. It was like my body had forgotten how to feel free and move to the rhythm of the music. But soon enough, with the help of a bit of tequila, I fell in love with dancing all over again. Our international adventures in and around Washington, DC were always a delight. The sights, the sounds, the energy, I felt so carefree and alive.

Dance is where movement becomes our medicine. Physically, it improves our mobility and coordination while reducing muscle tension. It strengthens our immune systems through muscular action and physiological processes. Therefore, it promotes healing benefits in prevention as well as recovery from illness, especially stress.

Spiritually, dancing was a way to communicate on a different level with myself and others. Connecting with the divine self through bodily movement speaks louder than words. We are guided to embrace the movement's beauty, passion, and grace. Then, we feel sensual, intelligent, and free.

Indigenous peoples believe you need to know how to dance if you are going to help heal others. The **Spirit of the Dance** allows you to hear the music deep within and builds bridges over unknowable gaps among our communities. The movements begin to unveil the mystery of our existence in the universe.

When you find a dance partner who understands this unique connection, your bodies become instruments of the song. The interchange of movement is free-flowing and seductive, in a spiritual way, not a raunchy display of vulgar movements. It always irritates me when people insinuate or accuse women who desire to dance are just craving attention or desire to hook up with a man. The freedom to express your energy creatively is immeasurable and should not be tainted with judgment.

Daniela's soul was satiated with the Spirit of the Dance, and her exhilarated movements can take your breath away. I loved to watch her on the dance floor within the community who wanted to experience her freedom. During the day, our hikes embodied the beauty of nature, while at night, our dancing embodied the spirit of a higher power.

But it is apparent that the Spirit of Dance and the Spirit of Alcohol can also embody the dark. Hedonism is the pursuit of pleasure and sensual self-indulgence. It is also the Devil's playground.

Distilled Spirits: These are variations of alcohol that have independently existed since the dawn of humanity in every culture and civilization. The process of making liquor was more complicated than other fermented beverages and was primarily used for religious and medicinal purposes.

The term spirit dates back to 14th-century alchemists. Originally, they believed alcohol had mystical properties that could turn metals into gold. This *magical essence* was thought to be able to fill one's soul with the *vital life force energy*. Spirits were used for festivals and ceremonial purposes.

Beer and Wine: They were made for everyday consumption and served to purify the drinking water by preventing bacterial growth. Traditionally, they were ranked very low in alcohol content. Beer was around 1%, while wine was and still is around 13%. They were considered a necessity for normal, everyday life.

It wasn't until the science of the fermentation process expanded that all these products were used to intoxicate the mind, body, and soul. Philosophers and scientists noticed an excess of alcohol had a dark side and preached for moderation. They publicized warnings against its improper usage. It may keep your sailor alive during a long voyage across the sea in search of treasure, but he may return home a ravaged pirate ready to steal your gold.

Even during the musings of Plato, humans were perplexed about the consumption and subsequent effects of alcohol. Classical Greek philosophers believed that if a man drank in moderation, he might become a more intimate lover of wisdom. However, if one wanted to unveil the various weaknesses or wrong doings which may lurk behind a man's facade, one simply needed to get him drunk. While intoxicated, a man would ultimately exhibit his moral vulnerabilities. In turn, he may not be rewarded prestigiously.

So, the next time you partake in spirited festivities, understand who you share your time, space, and movements with and ensure they are of your desired caliber. People often lower their standards, morals, and values when they want to go out and just have fun, insisting it doesn't matter. As I so eloquently express, *"If you hang out with trash, you will eventually start to stink."*

For a couple of years, I spent every other weekend at Daniela's house and referred to this sanctuary as *Chateau Ashburn*. It was my home away from home and provided a respite from the world's busyness. I was again learning to be a single adult in a bountiful world, and further, spending time with her son filled some of the gaps in the mommy portion of my soul. He was sweet, handsome, artistic, and always had a smile on his face.

When her parents visited from Romania, we did not understand each other. But they loved to listen to my stories and always laughed at the right moments. Her father said my stories were animated, and my gestures told much of the story. I guess he just filled in his own words. Her mother loved to cook traditional food, and more importantly, she loved to feed me.

The language of love spoke beyond words. As long as we were together, our indulgences were always in the spirit of fun. We appreciated each other's quirks and laughed our way through our happy and sad moments. Experience was our best friend. I always cherish my time with such a loving family. Instead of looking for ways to exclude me, they brought me closer.

Reality Crossing

The reality of my situation in life versus the reality of who I was was a twisted tale I needed to unwind. If I was going to rewrite my story, I wanted to start my story positively. I didn't want a knight in shining armor to come and save a damsel in distress. I wanted to be an equal partner capable of a reciprocal relationship. I wanted a best friend with whom I desired to make love every day.

I needed real-life experiences with *real men* to ascertain what aspects of Amy were beneficial to healthy relationships and which were detrimental. I needed a plan because I was not choosing my potential partners correctly. My best friend from high school often remarked, "*Amy, there is nothing wrong with you except your (man) picker is broken.*" I guess the real problem is how do I fix my picker? I wish there were some lemon law against receiving a broken one, to begin with.

Real Men: There is an array of attributes you can offer to define a real man. Confident but not arrogant. Adventurous but not reckless. Intelligent but not pompous. Attractive but not vain. You get the gist of it. But how do you know if that man is based in reality?

Moreover, how do you know if that man compliments you? Remember the shell-matching game? Just because he looks or feels good doesn't mean we match in the long run.

I came up with the concept of *practice dates*. I coined the term to describe a date with the intent to have the most enjoyable time possible. I would go out with men I thought were interesting, adventurous, knowledgeable, and pleasant to be around. But it was not my intent to kiss them. If you do not kiss them, it is not a *real date*. I did not want to mislead them or misconstrue any feelings.

If, by chance, we happened to kiss, I identified it as an actual date. I explained that I was not interested in a boyfriend if we desired to get past the second date. But I was willing to hang out and be friends. Further, I was very clear we were not going to have sex. Basically, you live your life, and I live mine. Then, we just enjoy each other's company. Live in the moment, and don't ask too many questions.

However, those friends only existed in my own little world. I rarely spoke about them to others; when I did, I called them by nickname. Our relationships were wonderfully private and emotionally intimate. I could know who they truly were without the pretense of the rest of the world to interfere. I had love in my heart for them, but I was not in love with them. I did not desire any type of relationship beyond what we already had. I put a Z in front of their names on my phone so they would all be kept private at the end of my contact list.

The Z List was not real life. It was like a perpetual romantic comedy where you get to fall in love repeatedly. Work problems were easily tempered. Personal issues were quickly met with empathy. All we focused on was being in the moment together. Being fully present was the best gift I could offer, and we all learned some fantastic lessons about life, love, and laughter. I was usually happy when I went home, but I was not fulfilled. Something important was missing.

One day, I stopped to grab a bite before going home. A handsome man who looked a million miles away was sitting near me. I asked, "Did you lose your smile somewhere?" He replied, "Is it that obvious?" I politely nodded yes. He had a demanding job that required most of his time. He was only in the Maryland area for business a few days out of each month. We had a delightful, charming conversation until we both finished our meals.

In turn, he invited me to walk through the harbor. As we crossed the intersection, he held my hand. The lights on the water danced while faint music played in the background. The city had built an interactive playground, and we tested the new stainless steel slide, which was perfectly built for two. We felt like children on the playground of life awaiting their first kiss. He leaned in as our lips gently touched, and we slowly descended to the bottom of the slide. It was adorable and romantic.

For over a year, we met when he was in town. When I presented my thoughts about not having sex, he agreed because we both had issues in need of a resolution. His story was a beautiful testimony to the love he kept in his heart. Further, I had some love in my heart that I had been unable to resolve. We found sanctuary in each other, even if it was just one evening a month. It was a different kind of love.

The sad part was that I knew the next day he would be gone again, and I had to leave the reality of Amy and return to the reality of my life. I tried not to overthink it. I tried to appreciate our relationship for what it was. It was real. Unfortunately, we lived distinctly separate lives in different parts of the country and there was no way to resolve that issue anytime soon. I actually never inquired, as I did not want to spoil our short time together in any way.

The confusing part I needed to resolve in my heart was that I felt that same kind of reality crossing with Tom. For years, I insisted he was not my type, and I did not have *those types of feelings* for him. I was content being his friend. But remember, the only constant thing is change, and our relationship was constantly there. Regardless of the circumstances, he was always my friend, and I thoroughly enjoyed my time with him. He knew the real Amy and loved her.

The worst part was admitting to myself I had profound feelings for Tom and I was purposely creating emotional distractions. I was waiting for him to be free. I did not foresee that happening and concluded I was wasting my life waiting for a man who would never be mine. Besides needing to heal from my divorce and accidents physically and emotionally, I needed to mend my broken heart.

The friends, food, hiking, drinking, dancing, and social gatherings were great, and I was enjoying my life, but I felt I was on the wrong trajectory. These things helped create happiness on the surface, but I was still hurting inside. The solutions I found were temporary fixes for larger issues. When the opportunity to go to Peru and work with a shaman presented itself, I was humbled.

When I returned from Peru, I knew I needed my heart to be free and open for genuine love. These safe, comfortable and private relationships were blocking me from a *real* relationship I could love and nurture *every day*. Don't worry; I am not skipping over my adventure to Peru. Hang on for a while, and I will tell you about this wonderfully mystical and magical adventure.

When I heard the song "*Colder Weather*" by the Zac Brown Band, it brought me to tears. The lyrics say, "*She would trade Colorado if her love would take her with him.*" She wondered if her love was strong enough to make him stay and give up his gypsy soul that was made for leaving. Even though her voice is the voice of love that calls him back again and again, "*he ain't never gonna change.*" I felt myself in the same life cycle, always leaving with a fear of staying.

Saying goodbye to Colorado was heartbreaking, but saying goodbye to Tom was life-altering. All of the conversations I had were beautiful endings to beautiful friendships. Initially, those conversations drained me, but after some deep and much-needed rest, I didn't feel empty; I felt full. I was alone but not lonely. I was ready to be the love I wanted to see in the world. I was determined to find the description of a man Hemingway eloquently describes in a movie I watched. I made a copy of the quote and put it on the front page of my Month at a Glance calendar.

Even though I genuinely missed my best friend, I refused to speak to Tom. I needed to stop loving him. Then, within a few months, I got a call from him, *"Amy, I know you don't want to talk to me, but I need you. I trust you more than anybody else in the world. I want my friend back."*

I listened to his story, and he was finally free. Surprisingly, I was in shock and ran into the bathroom to dry heave over the toilet for the second time in my life. Six years earlier, he helped me through my divorce, and his only ask was for me to help the next person. I would have never guessed he would be the next person, and technically, he was not free yet. He had moved into a dark man cave and invited all his demons to join him. His man cave already existed, but this series of events was like an avalanche of rocks and debris toppled over him as he posted a sign to the rest of the world, *"Keep Out."*

I vowed to be the best friend and best person I could be. I promised to stand by his side and wrestle the demons with him. It was not easy. In fact, it was miserable, and I felt inadequate. I had traveled down that treacherous road he was walking, and lovingly, I was there to extend my hand. I hoped to be his companion and help guide him through the darkness.

The bottom line is that most people equate or confuse their life situation with the reality of who they are and their life purpose. Think about it if you ask people, *"Who are you?"* What is the typical type of response? Many state their occupation or their marital status. They may list their hobbies or activities, but how many people acknowledge who they are on the inside? Then, when something in their life changes, they have difficulty with the reality of self because they never had a clear definition of self to begin with. Uncovering this magic alone is a beautiful melody, but sharing this magic with a loving companion helps you compose your new life song.

In my situation, my most important attributes were being a wife, mother, business owner, and athletic coach. Within two years after my divorce, I was no longer a wife, and I only had my children fifty percent of the time. I did not own my business anymore, and I was unable to coach. The removal of these attributes ripped away the Amy I wanted, and going to Peru would hopefully unveil the real Amy.

Independence Day

Music has always been of the utmost importance to me. Beyond entertaining, I find it highly therapeutic, and it helps me reminisce about the past, peruse the present, and contemplate the future. I love most genres of music and find certain lyrics speak to me more than others. When my mind is racing, I can put on music without lyrics, filling a space in my mind and allowing me to concentrate better and feel more at ease. Basically, it drowns out the noise.

Depending on my mood, I choose male or female singers ranging in style and age. One female singer who seems to explore my moods across many years of my life is Martina McBride. I believe she is labeled as a country music artist, but she could perform in most categories. Her voice is powerful and accurately portrays what it feels like to be fully alive. When I hear the song Independence Day, it takes me back to this very important juncture in my life.

It was a chilly morning when we left for my son's baseball game. I had long pants and three layers, including my bright orange Gore-Tex hiking jacket. I called it my *Safety Cone Coat* because you could see me coming from a mile away. The field we were stationed to play on was just over a grassy hill and took direct hits from the wind. I put my hat and gloves on to stay warm.

I always stood for the entire game behind first or third bases, depending on which dugout we were assigned. I kept to myself mainly because I had been a player and coach for many years. Other coaches would join me, and you could tell who we were by our stance. It's a sign of respect for the game and the players. Today, I was behind third.

The opposing team, their parents, and their coaches were so loud and obnoxious that it was far beyond unsportsmanlike conduct. The commotion they created was pure harassment and directed at my eleven-year-old son. A man leaned over and said, "*Don't wake up mama bear when her cub is out to play.*" He couldn't have been more accurate.

My son was the starting pitcher and was generally tolerant of distractions on and off the field. However, the opposing coach positioned himself between third base and home. He flagrantly ran back and forth while dipping up and down and pointing his finger at the baseline, yelling, "*Right here! Right here! Right here!*" even though the bases were empty.

From the beginning of the game, the horrendous donkey chants from the opposing side were highly distasteful. After the first three innings of *three batters up and three batters down from strikes*, the chanting became so intolerable that my son appeared shaken and had tears in his eyes.

I stepped forward and yelled at the coach, "*Come on, these are children!*" He ran towards me, shoved his finger in front of my face, and shrieked, "*Back off, or I'll have you kicked out of the game!*"

I looked him dead in the eyes, "*Leave my son alone.*" He continued to run his mouth, hoping to intimidate me. I pulled my hat off, stepped forward, and threatened, "*If you want to fight me, game on!*" The umpire came over, told the coach to simmer down, and issued him a warning. Further, he announced to the crowd the donkey chanting needed to stop immediately.

By inning four, my son's momentum was floundering. A couple of boys made it on base, and by the time we got to two outs, the chanting had resumed. The coach was going crazy and flagrantly ran up and down the baseline. I aggressively stepped forward and motioned to the umpire. He gave the coach his final warning and told the crowd to quiet down. Finally, the inning was over, and my son looked defeated. The second pitcher started the next inning.

Unfortunately, they lost the game by one run, and my son felt responsible for it. I explained to him that those men were small-minded and insecure. They needed to emotionally defeat a child to win. I insisted he hold his head high and be proud. Then, I insisted he go up to each coach to shake hands, look them dead in the eyes, and say, "*Good game, sir.*" I wanted him to be genuine with his words.

"*Wait, you want me to do what?*" he asked. I held my head high and proudly responded, "*Baby, I want you to be the bigger man. Now smile and go show them what a real man looks like.*"

Miraculously, my son came running over and told me three of the four coaches refused to shake his hand! Instantly, I replied, "*You just won the game.*" He reminded me they had lost, but I told him he proved he was more of a man than they could ever hope to be. "*My love, you won the real game.*"

At the end of every game, my son had a ritual of going up to the plate and, with self-pitching, would knock three balls way into the out-field. Then he would retrieve them, and we would go home. Today, he got his bat and balls, turned to me, said, "*Why don't you show them how it's done?*" and handed me the bat. I knocked three balls into the outfield, and we both laughed. Now, it was his turn.

As I approached the mound, the opposing coach confronted us. He halfheartedly apologized for "*the enthusiasm*" his team had issued and agreed it got out of hand. Further, he highly praised my son for his pitching and hitting abilities. Next, he explained his team was headed to Cooperstown for the Little League World Series. They seriously needed another player and invited my son to join the team. My son was overwhelmed with joy and absolutely wanted to participate. Cooperstown, New York, and The Baseball Hall of Fame, can you believe it? My son could not stop smiling.

Over the next few weeks, I spoke to the coaches multiple times about sportsmanship. Unless they cleaned themselves up, my son would not be participating. They assured me Cooperstown did not allow such behavior anyway. So, my son practiced with the boys and befriended the obnoxious head coach. Eventually, the coach apologized and admitted he was rather embarrassed.

There was a strategy to get to the playoffs. My son pitched the final practice game for the win, and we were ranked mid-stream. However, his batting in that game was a little off. His favorite bat had died. The perfect ting had turned into a billowing thug. We went to town to buy a new bat, but considering our location, everything was overpriced. The man in the store adored my son's knowledge of bats and his respect and enthusiasm for the game. In turn, he gave us a nice discount.

But what happened the next day was worth every penny. First inning, three up, three on. Bases loaded. No outs. The coach put my son back on the mound. There was a limit on the number of innings each boy could pitch, so the coaches had to be selective. My son was fully focused on the game, so he threw three more up and three more down. Three opposing men left on base. The boys on his team went crazy!

The heat was on! My son was at the plate for the first time with his brand-new, shiny white bat. He let the first one go by. "*Strike!*" He repositioned himself and knocked the second one over the fence. "*Home run!*" He enthusiastically ran around the bases and gave everyone a high-five. He picked up his bat and ran to the parent's dugout. He held his bat out with two arms in front of his chest, rolled the blue ink Cooperstown tattoo from the ball around in my direction, and said, "*Mommy, this is for you.*" My heart was overwhelmingly filled with joy, and I felt validated in my efforts to give my son what he needed to thrive and be respectful and respected in baseball and life.

My son received a gold Cooperstown ring and a vast array of trading medallions from boys around the United States and Canada. The closing ceremony was filled with flags and patriotism. Baseball had brought us all together as one team who loved the game. As we left the stadium, with deep sincerity and a tinge of sadness, he said, "Now, I understand why you and Dad had to get a divorce."

He clearly explained that everything happens for a reason, and one thing leads to another. My decision to leave gave him the opportunity to live the life he was supposed to be living. That week was perfect in so many ways. The next day was July 4th, and we planned to watch the fireworks at a nearby lake.

Hesitantly, my son asked to return to Maryland to go to the festivities with his father. I was extremely disappointed but understood and valued his thought processes and agreed. Surprisingly, this Independence Day did afford me some unexpected freedom.

From this juncture on, I stopped receiving his father's daily tirades and hate mail. I am not in any way stating they disappeared. I am simply saying they were less frequent. When the hate mail arrived, my favorite reply was, "I am in receipt of your message, and I respectfully disagree."

Sit tight if you are curious about how or why this baseball tournament fits into my story. I will explain in the following few sections. There was more than one way I received some unexpected freedom. The question in my head is how on Earth did one small decision to hike lead to a lifelong altering journey.

The Alux

While my son was practicing in the skills clinics at Cooperstown, the parents were not welcome to attend. So, I had an opportunity to hike and explore the area. I located a small lake on the map about forty-five minutes from the rental house. The rolling hills and sunshine were stunning that day. I turned down a gravel road leading to a small parking lot near the water. I meandered down a short path and saw hundreds of lily pads peacefully floating atop the pond. Suddenly, an extremely unusual-looking small young man donning a red and black scarf came out of the woods to greet me. He seemed pleasant, and we conversed while watching the frogs and turtles swimming around.

I asked him where the hiking paths were located. He explained that all the trails in the area were on private property, and you couldn't access them very easily. In turn, I asked him about local attractions that may interest me. He quickly steered the conversation in the direction of spirituality. He had just returned from a retreat in Indonesia and boasted about ayahuasca being a medicinal plant that had significantly altered his life. I had never heard of this plant, but it sounded rather interesting.

We returned to the parking lot, and he asked to hug me good-bye. He felt as though we had met for a reason. Although extremely eccentric, he was very nice, so I hugged him and patted his back. He got upset because he said I gave him *a mom hug* and asked for a real one instead. I laughed and apologized because he was correct. I gave him an adult hug before I got into my car and drove away. The entire experience seemed out of the ordinary.

When I returned to town, I went into some stores and realized I had lost my phone. I remembered that guy lived within minutes of the pond and asked the woman behind the counter if she had a phone book. I looked up his last name and found three choices. I called each one of them and finally got an answer. Awesome! I had his brother on the phone and explained the situation. He assured me his brother would help and told me to return to the pond.

We found my phone in an awkward spot near a tree with a hand-written note, *"I hope you find your phone."* I found the location of the phone and the note quite odd because it was not obvious and not near the parking lot. By this time, I was starving, and I invited him to join me for a late lunch to thank him for his help. We talked more in-depth about ayahuasca, and I was intrigued.

After returning to Maryland, I went to acupuncture and told Radianthawk about my experiences at the pond that day. She exclaimed, *"Oh, you met an alux!"* I replied, *"Hmm, ok. What is that, and what does it mean?"* Sometimes, things happen, and we must open our minds to accept them as real.

Radianthawk explained the alux (pronounced aloosh) was a mischievous woodland creature sent to give me a message. These mythological spirits love to play tricks on people. If you are respectful, you will receive good luck. If not, they may cause havoc or spread illness. She said he was leading me to my power. I was confused, so I asked, *"Power? What is my power?"* She replied, *"Oh, you know your power."* My head was spinning, trying to make sense of it all. This talk of mythology and little men in the woods enabling my power was a bit much to comprehend.

Obviously, I did not know my inner power because I was still going to physical therapy and acupuncture every week and was incapable of healing. I was in constant pain and only had one bowel movement per week after my treatments. I was *literally* full of poison, and it was slowly killing me.

Radianthawk was taking a group to Peru to participate in a life-healing journey, which included ayahuasca, the Vine of Life. The locals call it La Medicina. She had not mentioned it because she thought I was straight-laced and would run away screaming. I interrupted before she could finish her explanation, "*I'm in! I definitely want to go. Just tell me what I need to do.*" I was desperate; I had tried every type of remedy to heal, and this plant seemed to be a gift from God. What are the chances? I had just learned about ayahuasca, and now, I was being given the opportunity to experience it in its country of origin. I was going to heal in Peru.

It was summer, and I needed to do many things to "*prepare my garden*" before properly planting the seeds of change. Radianthawk advised me we would be working with a Shaman. I read several books, learned the science behind La Medicina, and studied the philosophy of Shamanism. I was so excited to meet my Shaman and learn how this perspective embraces and directs his methods of existence and healing in today's world.

This philosophy of life has existed for thousands of years and used to be a common practice in society. I was very disappointed to learn that something so powerful and beneficial for humanity has been purposely neglected in modern society. We have much to relearn about nature, spirituality, and healing. In fact, we owe it to ourselves and our future.

The old world meets new world methodologies to heal my mind, body, and soul. I was convinced this would be the transformational experience I needed to finally heal. I had very high standards and expectations for myself. Ironically, I studied words and phrases that streamed my inner thought processes. **The Five Agreements** is common sense eloquently expressed as a way to live your life

Be impeccable with my words: I create my own story. I need to choose the proper words for myself as well as others. Speak with integrity and use the power of my words to spread love, light, and truth.

Do not take things personally: The actions of others have nothing to do with me. What others say about me is a projection of their own reality. What people think about me is none of my business.

Do not make assumptions: Find the courage within myself to ask questions. Learn to be curious and express what you desire. Communicate as clearly and concisely as possible to bolster understanding.

Always do your best: Defining my best in each moment is mine and will change over time. This is not a competition. This is an agreement to put forth my best effort under given circumstances.

Be skeptical, but learn to listen: Listen to the words as well as the intent behind the words being spoken. Use the power of doubt to question everything you hear from others as well as yourself.

Don Miguel Ruiz created these agreements through his knowledge of ancient Toltec wisdom from Mexico. The first four focus on agreements we make with ourselves, and the last focuses on agreements with others. The one word from his literature that resonated with me the most was the Mitote, which is created by contagious gossip, otherwise known as poison.

The Mitote: The chaos of 1,000 voices all trying to talk at once inside my mind. If I could learn to quiet these chaotic voices, I would be able to listen to the one true voice. I would be able to understand I am worthy of real love. Love the way I define it.

Growing up, I trusted everyone until that trust was stolen away. Then, I rarely trusted anyone until I had a reason to trust them. I felt pessimistic but was trying to protect myself from suffering. Sometimes, it seemed like those voices showed up with antique quill pens, trying to rewrite my history or predetermine my future.

In turn, I was brilliant at finding men who were emotionally distant and unavailable. Most were attractive, intelligent, athletic, successful, and adventurous. But those attributes only grabbed my attention. As soon as I focused on who they were on the inside or set boundaries within the relationship, they would distance themselves and eventually disappear.

Then, I realized it was me! I was emotionally distant and unavailable, and the men I was attracting were a self-fulfilling prophecy. I had created a fortress around my heart and did not allow anyone to enter.

If they broke through the fortress by chance, the relationship significantly changed.

Years later, I told a friend, about my favorite quote from the movie *The Kite Runner*. Baba said, *"There is only one sin, only one. And that is theft. Every other sin is a variation of theft. When you kill a man, you steal a life. You steal his wife's right to a husband and rob his children of a father. When you tell a lie, you steal someone's right to the truth. When you cheat, you steal the right to fairness."* While discussing the deeper meaning of this quote, an amazing and life-resonating realization hit me over the head like a ton of rocks. I couldn't believe I had never unveiled this thought process before.

The problem with all these men I dated was that I had stolen their facade. My ability to genuinely see people and love them for who they are on the inside skewed perceptions they showed others and threatened their existence. The death of their ego, which took a lifetime to create, was devastating and diminished their self-worth. In turn, I was destined to suffer the consequences for my intentional yet unintentional sin of theft.

The Garden

I needed to purify my body so La Medicina could process the origin of my suffering instead of dealing with my everyday consumption of poison. This daily consumption may be a choice or just a way of life. We may be cognizant of it, or we may be oblivious. Either way, it keeps us away from the truth and the light. It allows us to live a long, slow death. Each day, as you think, pray, meditate, walk, or run, contemplate, *"Am I slowly living or slowly dying?"*

Poison: Anything in excess of what you need to live a happy, healthy, and productive life.

Food: The food pyramid is not for everyone. Accepting that we do not all have the same body types, adversity and life choices may have altered our genetic predisposition. Accepting that you need to cater to a healthy diet to meet the specific needs of your body type and consuming food and beverages in moderation is vital. Anything in excess leads to discomfort and opens your body to dis-ease.

Work: Accepting you need to work forty hours a week to sustain your life may be advantageous. Or accepting that you will never fit into an organizational box and finding a new vocation may be a better choice. Either way, working eighty hours a week to sustain a particular lifestyle or level of prestige can ultimately lead to burnout and put your body into a state of dis-ease.

Exercise: Physical assertion allows us to accept the proper amount of motion to sustain a healthy body and mind. It is excellent for your physical as well as spiritual well-being. Incessantly exercising to the point of complete exhaustion and causing long-term physiological problems is detrimental and can keep your body in a state of dis-ease.

Fear: Experiencing fear is a normal reaction to identifying a threat. It is how we evolved as humans. Fight, flight, or freeze until we can accept how to find safety. Fear may also be the companion of uncertainty. If we learn to accept a moderate amount of uncertainty in our lives, our companion will be allowed to experience adventure and grow. Otherwise, we stagnate and live in a state of dis-ease.

Anger: Becoming angry is a normal reaction to occurrences that may be outside of our control. We become tolerant if we learn to accept anger as a part of life. If our state of being is tolerance of people who choose to live a life of intolerance, our anger will transform. Then, we can choose to be silent with our anger or express it. If we accept our reaction as a healthy and productive option, then we are genuinely tolerant. If not, our feelings will fester and create a state of dis-ease.

Hate: Expressing hatred or disgust towards an atrocity is a normal response, and you may find those emotions difficult to process. In time, you may learn to be completely indifferent to the person or situation because indifference is the opposite of hate. However, complete indifference is also the opposite of love. Do you want to experience apathy about everything in the world, or do you want to experience unconditional love? Through unconditional love, we get to feel our feelings and accept every emotion as a lesson to be learned. If not, hate infiltrates our soul and creates a state of dis-ease.

The list continues, so create your own. See what you come up with for yourself as well as others.

This work hard, play hard in your face type of attitude so many people succumb to in order to achieve success is counterproductive to genuine long-term success. You may think you are incredibly awesome in the short term, but in the long run, you are not.

Stop. Think. Look through your list of contacts on your phone and social media. Are they life giving or life-sucking? Then the choice is up to you, "*Would you rather have nothing or a bad something?*"

I try my best to choose *nothing* because I get to start at *zero* and build my way up. If I choose something bad, I am starting in the negative and need to work up to zero before I can progress. It is a basic mathematical fact in a world filled with equations. Once you no longer function in the negative, you will start to experience the life you were meant to live. Now that I had a more robust understanding of poison, I had to reassess each aspect of my life.

The understanding helped me purify my existence and figure out how to reallocate all expenditures. Then, in my mind, I had to justify and approve my choices.

For one month before my journey to Peru and my initial plant healing experience, I needed to purify myself according to their guidelines:

I should eat a vegetarian diet and refrain from any caffeine or alcohol. I should read several books on the topic of science and spirituality and refrain from any sexual activity.

I should moderately exercise and get plenty of sleep.

Last, I should meditate. Basically, I need to go back to the basics of living with pure thoughts, intentions, and actions.

The vegetarian diet and meditation were a burden. I have already refrained from dairy and avoided gluten, and this additional aspect made enjoying a meal rather difficult. My sitting still and meditating for periods of time does not come easily. I naturally run around all day, every day. Relaxing usually meant falling asleep or ridding myself of migraines, not focusing on enlightened realizations.

Over time, I developed the notion that my body is The Garden of Life and each time you enter into ceremony, you should *prepare the garden* for abundant growth. When my children were young, I loved singing a song from one of their books: "*Inch by inch, row by row, going to make this garden grow…*" Now, I was the curious child preparing my own garden.

I needed to remove the weeds and debris, which I deem poison. Then, transform the dirt into soil.

Dirt originates from the Old Norse word *drit*, which means *excrement*. It does not contain any of the necessary ingredients for life and is not an organized ecosystem. Plant life is weak and truncated.

Soil consists of organic matter and living organisms. It provides a stable structural base and sources water, oxygen, nutrients, and air. It allows deep roots, robust plants, and fruit.

Praise the light of day and darkness of night. Both are necessary for life. (God, Love, Light, Energy)

Select the proper variety of seeds or seedlings. (Knowledge, Wisdom, Medicine, People)

Embrace fungi, worms, birds, insects, butterflies, and bees to perpetuate the cycle of life. (Connection)

Experience the air and wind with all the wisdom it carries. Breathe deeply. (Holy Spirit, Qi, Ha)

The purpose of the garden comes to fruition through *the work*. Then, you can share the fruits of your labor and propagate wisdom. Remember, you are the light and the medicine. Our breath connects us. I felt like I was ready to go on my journey to Peru. I had prepared my garden, done the work, and was ready to transform and heal.

The Next Realm

The plane flight down to Lima, Peru, was uneventful, but the anticipation of the adventure made it seem almost magical. We had to wait a couple of hours for our next flight to a smaller airport closer to our destination, and I found a wonderful book with pictures and descriptions of the region. It was helpful to write important words down because some people had very thick accents or called things by various names unfamiliar to me. From the onset, I felt very connected to the land and its people.

From the moment I met the Shaman, I felt as though I already knew him, possibly for a lifetime. After a van ride through the countryside, we entered the hacienda, which was like stepping back into a forgotten time. I felt my modern attire and demeanor to be out of place. The Shaman walked around and spiritually bathed our hands with Agua de Florida. We clapped in front of our chest to awaken, cleanse, and restore our spirit. Then, we pulled the fragrance up and into our breath as we closed our eyes while absorbing the energy.

Agua de Florida: begins and ends all of our ceremonial experiences. This aromatic citrus water is made with essential oils from exotic flowers and tropical citrus fruit. Metaphorically, it has been referred to as the fountain of youth. It clears the mind, supports emotions, and invigorates the soul.

Our Shaman grew up in a traditionally mixed culture encompassing the old and new worlds. His family had been integral to the land and the society for many generations. He began his Shamanic training at age 12, and the practice became his way of life. He had multiple advanced degrees, including a doctorate in archaeology. Almost 60 years later, he appeared to be like any other person except that his energy felt different, and he had a really cool hat.

We stayed at his hacienda, the main house of a large estate in a Spanish-speaking country. This two-level ranch house had multiple guest rooms, spaces for dining and entertainment, and a ceremonial structure with wood-planked vaulted ceilings. Its rustic charm mystically merges the European Spanish and Native Quechua details into life.

The central garden had magnificent floral displays and was home to the largest hummingbirds I have ever seen. The cactus donned large white flowers and stood tall beside the benches for quiet contemplation. The eucalyptus trees provided shade from the sun's heat, and its leaves and branches accompanied our steam bath in the healing sauna.

On our first day, we received a welcoming ceremony from an elderly Native Quechua Indian-speaking man dressed in traditional attire who chewed coca leaves and stored them beneath his bottom lip. I did not understand his words, but he made a pyramid of grains, seeds, and tobacco smoke to signify welcome. His message offered growth, prosperity, and peace, all of which I was desperately seeking.

The use of coca leaves concerned us because we were only familiar with the illicit American uses of the coca plant. The unprocessed coca leaf looks like a mint leaf and is an integral part of the lives of Andean peoples from countries such as Peru, Bolivia, Chile, and Argentina. The leaves are on reception tables at hotels and restaurants. They are served as an after-dinner tea to soothe the stomach or help with altitude sickness. They are a natural multivitamin and can sustain life for several weeks along with water. It can be used as a mild stimulant and is known to suppress pain and sickness.

Now that we had been introduced to a new way of living, it was time to understand how the energy of the land is strong here. The sacred and isolated district of Machu Picchu was extraordinary and is often referred to as the *Lost City of the Incas* because it was unknown during the Spanish Conquest. It lay beneath a vast jungle untouched and was not discovered by the outside world until 1911. My only point of contention was the tens of thousands of tourists who pass through each year, which mutates the energy.

As we stood in Machu Picchu, the Andes Mountains range was a glorious backdrop and the epicenter to which the *Huaca* markers point. We walked a series of trails and located various size huacas that mimic the size and shape of the Andes Mountain top from your current vantage point. The size and temperature difference of the huaca stone was dependent on your distance to the epicenter, thus creating a map that points you to the origin of human existence. In modern words, we call it an *energy vortex*. Each point on this ancient mapping system had significance. These sacred sites are ancient trail markers for those to sojourn during their quest.

At the end of one of our paths was a large cylindrical stone-walled structure with an entranceway. Inside this structure were several openings cut into the wall and shaped like a trapezoid. These shapes appeared where windows may exist, but they had impenetrable stone backings. Our Shaman asked us to stand and face the openings. Then, he instructed us to lean our heads in, take a deep breath, and hold OM as long as possible.

OM: A mystic syllable considered the most sacred mantra in Hinduism and Tibetan Buddhism. It appears at the beginning and the end of most Sanskrit recitations, prayers, and texts. It is said to be the essence of supreme consciousness.

We practiced this sacred formula several times. My mind, body, and soul vibrated in unison with the group, the stones, and the land. It significantly altered my perception. Our OM could be heard miles away. This ancient system allowed communication between people near and far.

We walked along an ancient Inca agricultural science center. *Moray* looks like a massive amphitheater, but it actually tested various crops in micro-climates afforded by the terraced mountainsides. Along with the soil the Incas transported from various regions, the amount of rainfall, and the underground irrigation system, they could mimic climates and grow as many crops as possible. This ancient irrigation channeling system is so advanced that Moray has never flooded.

The ancient experimental research lab developed hybridization and modification methods, allowing them to adapt crops and make them edible. The orientation of each section accounts for depth and design, along with the wind and sun. There is a 15-degree Celsius temperature difference between the lowest and highest points. Peru is famous for potatoes, and this place has contributed to the development of over 6,000 varieties in the region. It is close to the ancient Maras Salt Mines, which are still operating today and use the same cultivation methods.

We visited a textile village where I watched a lady with a baby on her back harvest tiny white cochineal bugs from prickly pear cacti and created an intense red dye. This extract has been used to color food, textiles, and cosmetics for thousands of years. After the Spaniards arrived, this vibrant pigment spread like wildfire across Europe and was responsible for dying religious garments and painting artistic masterpieces. These tiny little bugs, about the size of a *Tic Tac* mint, were once a commodity valued as high as silver and gold.

Eventually, we got to an ancient rural archaeological climb up the side of a mountain that tourists could not access. The stunning beauty was all my heart could tolerate. I was supposed to be there with my family. I was supposed to have my husband by my side with my two children and our dog running around and experiencing life together. As we got to the first plateau of spiritual existence, I burst into tears and sat down. I deeply mourned the loss of my family and yearned to feel their touch.

Most importantly, I mourned the fact that my definition of family was gone forever.

As we got to the second plateau of existence, our Shaman spoke for a while and invited us to eat lunch before we descended back down. I was not hungry and asked to continue up the path. After I crossed over a series of rock piles, the path disappeared, but I was called to continue. Suddenly, I saw an opening to a cave covered by the surrounding plant growth. As I drew near, I felt fear as well as curiosity. I turned around, and although I could no longer see the group, I could hear them calling me. So, I decided to head back. I located the path near the rock pile, but a horse blocked it. I asked, *"Can you move, please?"*

The horse stomped his foot at me. I motioned, "*Can you please move out of my path?*" The horse stomped and neighed. I whirled my hand around some more and spoke louder, "*Can you please move out of my path? My friends are waiting for me?*"

The horse stomped a few times, neighed and vigorously motioned his head to the right of the large stone structure. I said rather loudly, "*Are you trying to tell me something or just being stubborn?*" The horse just looked at me as if I had no choice in the matter. I replied, "*Seriously. Fine. I'll go this way,*" the horse turned away and resumed eating his grass. You must be thinking, "*Really, she talks to wild horses?*" But, honestly, I didn't have a choice.

As I walked around the structure, I saw hieroglyphs that looked much larger and older than anything I had seen thus far. The stone was lighter in hue and had a different texture. These symbols and their method of creation were intriguing. They were distinctly different. When I returned to the group, I mentioned I had gone off the beaten path and described the cave and the large symbols I found. I was very excited, and the group went to take a look at my discoveries.

When I asked my Shaman what I had found, he simply replied, "*The next realm of existence.*" I was intrigued and wondered what that meant and why I had found it alone. I asked, "*If you knew all this stuff was up here, why did you keep the group down there?*" As usual, he smiled, readjusted his hat, and told me I already knew the answer. I instinctively knew I could never turn back and live the life I thought I was supposed to live; this was my new calling. I just wished someone would give me some clues on which direction I was headed. At least I had some hope.

Qué Rico

A couple of days later, we drank a ceremonial cup of San Pedro and left the hacienda under the guidance of our Shaman. Pachamama reverently stood on the side of the mountains as she comforted and guided our journey—Pachamama, commonly known as Mother Earth, is a fertility goddess worshiped by the indigenous peoples. After the explorers entered, Pachamama's depictions correlated with Mary, the Mother of Jesus, except that her persona and attire embody earth and mountain.

San Pedro or Huachuma (*Echinopsis pachanoi*) is known as the Forgotten Grandfather healing plant. It is a Ceremonial tea brewed from cactus for almost 4,000 years. It is milder on the body than ayahuasca and was named after Saint Peter because its effects are said to hold *"The key to the gates of Heaven."* This medicinal teacher can catalyze deep healing by opening the mind to profound introspection. It's a feel-good, loving compound and can be great for people who suffer from PTSD.

Further, Pachamama's divine feminine energy is responsible for the elements of the earth that create earthquakes, and in my mind, it symbolizes the power and wisdom of the Holy Spirit. She is married to the divine masculine energy Inti, the Sun god. *Together, they are necessary for life.*

By the time we got to the approach of *Sacsayhuaman*, I was in my realm. I contemplated my focus and decided to absorb the shadows being cast by the light. I was called to take alternate trails to the same destinations as the group, and I communicated my intentions. It just felt right.

Sacsayhuaman: the locals love to call it Sexy Woman because the pronunciations are relatively close, and everyone giggles. It is a formidable Inca complex constructed of boulders that fit tightly together without using mortar. The architectural design allows for movement, which makes the area capable of withstanding earthquakes. It is located just outside the city limits. It is constructed at the highest point in Cusco and appears to have been used for military and ceremonial purposes.

We ended up on some terraced hills, and I focused on three small rocks. One rock was an illusion, depending on how you looked at it.

One variation was an older woman with a scarf, and the other was a beautiful young woman with long hair who reminded me of my daughter. The next rock was a monkey hanging with one arm from a branch with the curiosity of my son. The last rock had the face of a yellow lab that had been my faithful companion for so long. I felt immense joy.

The group approached a spot where our Shaman wanted us to meditate. He spoke in the native Quechua language and Radianthawk instructed us to cleanse our Chakras. I asked for guidance because I did not understand what to do. I followed directions. I guess I felt emotionally lighter, but I really wasn't sure. Next, we were instructed to sit atop some mounds that contained an ancient underground stream dedicated to the divine feminine.

I closed my eyes, and San Pedro helped guide me into a meditative state. I could feel the subtlety of the earth quaking below me, and the deeper I went inside myself, the stronger the quakes moved me. Suddenly, the darkness behind my eyes opened up into a vast, colorful external landscape. Land formations dissipated as I surged beyond the landscape, and I entered an expansive universe. The energy I felt was beyond erotic. I wanted to make love to the entire universe and felt the possibility.

As my most primitive and instinctual yearnings penetrated unknown boundaries, a lady in my group touched my shoulder, "*Are you ready to go? The group is heading down the hill.*" I opened my eyes and thought, "*Ugh! This is the kind of stuff you see in movies and now I have to get myself up and go!*"

At the end of the path was a local man selling necklaces made from native polished stones woven together with twine. His dark, wrinkled hands contained ancient knowledge. I wanted a necklace made with moonstone. I could hear my voice in my head but could not formulate the words. I mumbled a few words to a group member, and he helped me communicate as if he could hear my thoughts.

We had reservations at a restaurant nearby. I sat down beside my Shaman and remained relatively quiet. However, I could feel a conversation going on between us. I can't describe the words because we were speaking between our souls, and I had not learned his native tongues. Suddenly, my cheeks turned red, and I turned to ask, *"Can you hear me?"*

His aged appearance turned youthful as he put on his hat and laughed, *"My hat is going to protect now!"* I thought as loudly as possible, *"Qué rico! San Pedro, you are a feisty little spirit."*

At the end of our celebration feast, I was peacefully enjoying some anise liquor. Traditionally, it is served to aid in the digestion process. The group had difficulty calculating the bill, and anxiety filled the air. In response, I swiftly collected and collated the various currencies. One member was not feeling well but managed to perk up with half a smile while watching my brain go to work.

When we returned to the passenger van, I put on lip balm and situated myself as usual. Suddenly, the same man poked his head through the seat and inquired, *"Are you always this OCD?"* I smiled and replied, *"All successful people are a little OCD; it's actually mandatory."*

His comment took me back a few years to when my daughter inquired, *"What does OCD mean?"*

O is Obsessive, which is when I continuously think about things repeatedly before I do them.

C is Compulsive, which is when your brother does things over and over again.

D is Disorder, which is when these behaviors get in the way of your life and cause problems.

Instantly, her little brother fell on the floor and started laughing and pointing. My daughter was irritated, *"What are you laughing at?"* He replied, *"Mommy is the O. I am the C. But you are the D!"*

My daughter retaliated, *"You are stupid and ugly!"* Her brother laughed even harder, *"That's hilarious because we all look exactly the same!"* It was so funny that we all laughed and jumped on the bed. That acronym still brings a smile to my face.

The joy transformed. I missed my children tremendously, and I felt deep sadness. I rolled myself into my jacket, leaned against the window, and absorbed the beauty I longed to share with my family. I contemplated how to fix the brokenness I felt in myself, my family, and my world.

I noticed the seemingly impoverished people living off the land, most likely earning pennies a day to sustain life. I observed their tattered clothes and one-room houses with children running around or being carried on their mother's back. I appreciated how they walked everywhere and greeted us with as many words as they knew how to speak in English. I learned how that land would be ripped from their existence to build an airport for curious travelers and missionaries wanting to create progress.

Most importantly, I noticed how these people of the land had genuine smiles and probably did not comprehend the interpretation of their life being *"poor."* Their existence was full of love, connection, spirituality, and acceptance of life.

The next day, many discussed how everyone could or should help impoverished people in this country and in ours. I contemplated the difference between people who were impoverished and suffering and those who have very little but are genuinely happy.

I interjected some of my thoughts and concluded, *"I am not sure what you all witnessed yesterday, but in my eyes, those people in the countryside are rich."*

Let Go

Even though my soul was enticed by all the knowledge and wisdom I had gained through the various Ceremonies and excursions, I still felt like I was missing something. Something important.

One morning, the group was horseback riding through the Sacred Valley, and we had to turn back because the ground was wet and dangerous for our level of expertise. On the way back, we took an alternate route and stopped to explore a cave dedicated to the Goddess of the Moon.

Initially, I could see, but as we drew closer to the end of the cave, it was cold, dark, and wet. Fortunately, at the end of the path, an opening allowed some light to enter. I climbed up on top of a rock and sat down. Miraculously, pellets of clear bluish hail showered me as I felt immense joy penetrate my heart. The frozen droplets looked like the moonstone from my necklace made by the man with wisdom in his hands. I thought maybe I am not missing the point after all.

The final Ceremony in Peru was upon us. As I drank from the cup and situated myself in a comfortable position, I put my hand on the floor, and a spider bit the palm of my hand. It was slightly painful and irritated me throughout the evening. More importantly, I felt the Ceremony emulated death. It was not a horrible, frightful death, more like a moratorium of life where people were entwined in gray cocoons.

After returning to my room, I was confused and angry. Not only was I angry with the universe, I was enraged with myself. I am obviously not worthy of healing. I felt my anxiety escalate, and I ran to the bathroom. I know this sounds disgusting, but the only thing the plant did for me was clear my bowels. At least I could be thankful for that one. I could take the plane ride home in comfort.

Over the next few months, I tried to remember. The plant does not create the change. It opens pathways into the next realm of existence. There, you find resolutions. The relationship with Ceremony is not one-sided; it is reciprocal. The plant offers access to wisdom, and I need to accept the wisdom into my method of existence and then do the work.

The phrase "*Do the work*" irritated me because I felt like I was doing the work, but it did not provide any tangible results. I was determined to get that agonizing ball of PTSD out of my stomach. Besides hampering my ability to perform routine daily activities, it was trapping poison in my system that exacerbated multiple forms of dis-ease.

Further, I thought the next realm was my own personal experience. My realm lived within the confines of my imagination, and outside influences could change my perceptions. I created what I needed to heal myself and recreate my story. I was in charge of my journey.

When I learned my Shaman was coming to Maryland, I thought I should give Ceremony another chance. Maybe I just wasn't accepting La Medicina as I should have been, and maybe *my work* was not addressing the core issue.

I believe the origin of my PTSD was created and compounded by perpetual fear due to the circumstances in my life. I believed my fear stemmed from my father and was exacerbated by my former husband and included any other person in my life that caused fear, pain, anxiety, and rage. So, all I had to do was rectify the situation in my mind and a resolution would present itself.

I vaguely remembered a movie I watched in college, *Jacob's Ladder*. The name is an allegory from the Bible in Genesis. While sleeping, Jacob receives a dream from God that changes his life. He sees a ladder or staircase that reaches up from earth to heaven. God is letting Jacob know this world should not shape him. He should change his way of thinking from within and then be able to discern what God genuinely wants from you. God will lead the slave to freedom.

In this movie, they reference the allegory and this modern-day Jacob, a soldier who has returned from war. He suffers from PTSD and just like so many veterans, his purgatory is an agonizing metaphor for the reality of life after war. It focuses on the aftermath of war and how it affects those long after the fighting is finally over. The movie was confusing because it bounced around between reality, nightmares, and flashbacks so often that it made you forget which one you were experiencing.

Jacob's Ladder is also the namesake of a plant. Its Latin name is *Polemonium reptans,* which means *creeping plant* and refers to its unique ladder-like foliage. Just like Ayahuasca, it has been metaphorically called the *Stairway to Heaven.*

Ayahuasca is known as the Vine of Life and La Medicina. (*Liana, Banisteriopsis caapi*) The presence of large Liana vines provides an excellent indicator of older, more mature strands of forest.

If you drank a tonic made with Liana vine, your chemical journey of DMT would last about four to five minutes because that is how fast our systems take to process the chemical. However, for centuries, indigenous peoples have used other plants that contain an alkaloid which naturally inhibits the breakdown of DMT in the digestive system. The experience lasts four to five hours. Our bodies naturally create DMT, but its origin and purpose have yet to be scientifically validated. Although many believe endogenous DMT is responsible for our dreamlike states.

As the golden hour let go into darkness, we purified our space and bodies. We lit the candle and drank from the cup. *"Heal me. Teach me. Show me."* Our Shaman called forth the spirits with a mesmerizing chant. Within the hour, the external journey of Ceremony was vibrant and alive. But today, my journey was internal. I kept my eyes closed and breathed in unison with the plant.

Initially, orbs of color and gusts of light sparkled like prisms before my eyes. The visions were relatively chaotic until the light created shadows of people walking near a bridge in the distance. I could see myself standing in the middle of the bridge. The shadows transformed into stacks of dark squares resembling photographs. The photographs sorted and lifted to my left and to my right. As I motioned forward, the photographs contained images of people I had known in my lifetime.

As I gently pushed each one of the photographs out of the way, I wondered what they all had in common. I realized the photographs were images of people who had caused fear in my life and I needed to discern their level of importance to my end goal.

At first my movements were slow. *"Not you. Not you. No, not you."* These fears were small and insignificant. Then, the images came at me faster and my movements became rapid, *"No, not you. Or you. Or you. Wow, will this ever stop."* Then there was a vast array of images that quickly passed by my line of vision and then suddenly, it all stopped. In total amazement I asked, *"It's you?"*

I was filled with intense emotion and reached out my hand, *"Grandma, it's you? I have missed you everyday of my life. I love you."* My Grandmother whispered, *"Don't be afraid any longer."* As she slightly bowed her head and faded back into the abyss.

I gasped for air and thought as loudly as possible, *"Grandma, please come back!"* as I extended my hand in her direction. I wanted to talk to her more, but she did not return.

Finally, I opened my eyes and looked around the room. I had to go to the bathroom but it appeared as though Radianthawk had switched seats and was blocking the entrance and I did not want to disturb her. She looked so peaceful wrapped up in her shawl with her left hand extended out onto the floor.

I noticed a shadow in the corner which appeared to be a valiant man donning a large headdress and sitting up tall with his back straight and hands on his knees. I was amused by how my mind played tricks with the shadows and made it appear like our group had visitors.

The beginning of my personal healing with the Shaman proceeded as expected. Then, he stood up and walked in front of me. He leaned forward and whispered, *"Tell me about your Grandmother."*

Again, I gasped for air. Breathing was difficult. My chest was tight and my stomach ached. Our souls spoke as I painted this picture in his mind. Words were not necessary.

When I was born, my parents worked full time and my older sisters were in elementary school. My younger sister didn't come until four years later. My grandmother raised me. She held my hand as we went for walks and collected rocks. Each morning she made breakfast for me as we sat by the kitchen window and watched the red cardinals singing and dancing on the lilac bushes and blackberry vines. My favorite was a peanut butter and jelly sandwich with chocolate milk.

When I was five, she took care of me after a dog attacked me and I had to go to the hospital. I had twenty-six stitches on the inside of my ankle and a few more on the outside. I loved the authentic Italian Ice flavored with anise or lemon we could buy at the small grocery near her house.

I loved the little pink soaps she kept in her bathroom that looked and smelled like roses. Sometimes, I can still smell them while walking through department stores. Oddly enough, I smelled them when no soap was found. Her living room carpet had swirls I could drive my toys through like a highway. I remembered she had to move into our house, but I did not know why.

When I was six, I made a small ornament wreath for her as a Christmas present. A week before Christmas, on my mother's birthday, almost to the minute she was born, my grandmother passed away. I remember sitting beside the bed and crying. I told her about the present and told her I would give it to Mommy for her birthday instead.

Months and years passed. I do not remember anyone processing my emotions with me. Maybe they did but, I was only a little girl who had lost her best friend and her grandmother. For many years, we would visit her grave site on Easter and bring daffodils, one of the first signs of Spring in our yard.

A few years ago, I arrived at the tree trimming dinner a little late, and my younger sister approached me. She handed me the small wreath and said, "*Here, I knew you really liked this one for some reason, and I saved it for you.*" Tears entered my eyes as I took it from her hand and placed it on the tree.

But now, through Ceremony, my grandma has told me, "*Don't be afraid any longer.*" Suddenly, my legs felt weak. My Shaman breathed light and love into my solar plexus, put his hand on the big ball of PTSD in my stomach, and softly whispered into my ear, "*Let go.*" My legs could not support me as I knelt on the ground. I thought I was going to throw up because the commotion in my stomach was intense. Radianthawk put a trash can in front of me and beckoned me to "*Let go.*"

I desperately wanted to *let go of the PTSD*, but I could not regurgitate. So, I just spit a little bit and hoped that would suffice. I felt something leave me. At least, I thought I did, although I was unsure.

The next day, the group gathered to discuss Ceremony. I stayed quiet because it was a lot to process, and I was not ready to speak. Five group members described the shadows of my imagination precisely how I saw them. I thought, "*Wait, this is my imagination. Keep out.*" But one description after another, I thought, "*This can't be my imagination if everyone else sees what I see. It must be real.*"

A week later, I returned to acupuncture, explained my observations to Radianthawk, and asked if she was the lady with the shawl in front of the bathroom. She pleasantly smiled and replied, "*No, that was the Shaman's grandmother. He called her into Ceremony. She was also a Shaman and taught him many things. Unfortunately, she passed away when he was a little boy.*"

It took me a few days for my brain to grasp the idea. Basically, I used to think there were multiple realms, like heaven and earth, and somewhere in between. You can call it the gray zone, purgatory, or the subconscious, or whatever term you prefer to use. Occasionally, these realms may overlap, but you can get a brief look into the unknown.

Love, Light, Faith, and Hope were asking me to believe these realms, along with a few others, where creatures and spirits exist, were real. We are not separate. We are together. We coexist.

We were born with an innate ability to communicate across realms, and through words and socialization, we learned how to forget. Ayahuasca was the pathway that helped me begin to remember. I could not unlearn, unhear, or unsee any of my experiences. Now, I was aware.

About a month later, it was a bright sunny day, and I was cruising down a major interstate highway. This portion of the road is fun because you can see for miles into nature, and the speed limit is relatively high. Then, I hit some traffic congestion and slowly crept into the passable lanes.

I looked over and saw a car identical to the car I drove when I got my Traumatic Brain Injury. Usually, this type of event would have triggered my PTSD and caused a panic attack. However, I just kept driving and made my way through the congestion. That car was over the guard rail and crunched on its side. I thought, "*Thank goodness they were driving a Volvo. My Volvo saved my life, and it will probably save theirs. But, man, that sucks; it is going to be a long process."*

Suddenly, I screamed, *"Wait! Oh my God, wait! I didn't freak out. I am ok!"* I was ecstatic. I wanted to call someone and tell them the good news. But who do I call first and wait? What do I say? How do I explain the Ceremony and the healing? Hmm, I decided to keep the joy to myself. My drive through the countryside was more beautiful than ever before. As the sunlight warmed the side of my face and the rolling hills sang sweet songs of freedom, I spoke out loud, *"Grandma, thank you for helping me let go. I love you. Please come back again."*

CHAPTER 7

⋘☙✦☙⋙

PARADIGM SHIFT

I was doing well at work and with my friends while proactively healing. I was learning many lessons, both intentionally and unintentionally, through my daily experiences. A higher level of awareness became my foundation to explore various methods to restore my health further. Unbeknownst to me, mystical spirits were escorting me down an unknown path that would ultimately catapult me through a life-altering paradigm shift. One from which I would never return.

Leave Me Alone!

My relationship with Tom fluctuated tremendously. Some days were incredible, and some days were like crickets. He was never mean; he just liked to disappear. The door on his man cave still had a huge *Keep Out* sign and was meant for everyone, not just me. So, I attempted not to take it personally. As friends, it is normal when you don't speak for a few days or weeks. But, when you are in a relationship, and you are not even sure if they are dead or alive, it causes tremendous anxiety.

One thing that always baffled me is he chose to disappear when we were at our best. For example, we went to my friend's wedding on a beautiful horse farm. The golden sunlight lit fields of grass donned with a massive, beautiful white tent for all the guests. We feasted on an array of international food, conversed with many other couples, and danced the night away. Ironically, his version of what heaven will look like emulated this ceremony. Within days, he disappeared.

Initially, I tried to be understanding and reached out gently. But when I received zero responses, it infuriated me, and I got nasty. I knew him better than anyone else, and bringing his personal issues to the forefront of the problems most likely felt like a knife in the gut. I may have been accurate, but who wants to hear the cold-hearted, nasty truth about themselves when they are already down? Time passed, I forgave him, and we were good again. Tom can take responsibility for his actions and properly apologize to my heart. Which is one of the main reasons I kept going back.

Another instance was at a college rugby reunion; we were on top of the world. Many of his cohorts inquired if we were still just friends or if our relationship had progressed into something more. Suddenly, I overheard Tom telling a man I did not know we were just friends, and I had been his roommate in college. "*Really. Is that who I am?*" I sternly thought to myself.

Note to self: Never drink Red Bull and Vodka when you are mad at your boyfriend.

The man who had inquired about our dating status was physically attractive and was definitely flirting with me. So, I decided to reciprocate. Tom pretended not to be jealous, but I knew better. He has always loved the competition for my affection, and this little charade sparked his ego. I never liked the game, but I was determined to play along tonight.

When we got back to his truck, he unbuckled his pants, and I dove down to please him. Neither one of us could get enough. He had never been so boisterous in his pleasure. Suddenly, a bunch of young guys came walking towards us and flashing pictures with their cell phones. Hilarious. We better get out of here, and we dashed out of the parking lot.

We barely made it inside the house before he threw me over the dining room table. The juices ran down my leg as he thrust himself inside me like never before. Deeper and deeper until he exploded and yearned for more. The living room became a swirling sea of passion that drenched our bodies and enlightened our souls. Each time we exploded, we came up for a breath of air before returning to the deep mystical waters. Our breaths became *one* as we explored this world of ecstasy.

Within a few days, he was gone again. I played his stupid game, and we both won. But now, I was the loser once again. He said he wanted me to go out with that guy because he was not interested in commitment. I was infuriated, and the next few months completely sucked because we couldn't stand to be around each other, and we also couldn't stand to be apart. How could our love be indispensable in one moment and sabotaged in the next?

As time passed, we both decided to give *the relationship* another try. However, I told him I was done with the disappearing act, and the next time it happened, "*I was done.*" I insisted there must be a better way to rejuvenate the soul than hibernating in the man cave and destroying our friendship.

Our relationship progressed nicely, and he began to attend friend, family, and work functions as my boyfriend. I felt like his crazy divorce had started to work out, and he was ready to move along. However, his soon-to-be ex-wife's onslaughts were random and swift. She could easily knock him down to his knees and absolutely loved to see him suffer. Sadly, her greatest weapons were his children. I understood his pain and wanted to love him through it. We were best friends but fragile partners.

Then came another wedding—a beautiful woodland ceremony with a magical feast for the senses. The merriment lasted for several hours, but the heat and humidity took their toll on many of the elders who left early. The rest of us remained until dusk. At one point, Tom and I wandered far back into the woods and found a stream. We slowly undressed each other and made love. Suddenly, the tiny fish nipping on my bottom reminded me that the forest has eyes, and we should probably get dressed.

The next day, we went for a long hike through some historic ruins and had dinner. We were both exhausted, so I decided to sleep at my own house because I had an early meeting at work the next day. Yet again, he disappeared. This time, *I was done.* I sent a few nasty grams and blocked him from communicating. I needed to stop loving him. This was one of my most difficult decisions, and it cut me to the core. My relationship with my best friend had failed.

I kept repeating to myself, "*Love isn't supposed to suck.*"

He continuously entered my dreams. No matter where I was or what I was doing. Poof! He was trying to get my attention. The day before my birthday, I dreamed Tom was trying to communicate with me by walking through a train car. I could see his mischievous smile and his hands slowly touching the top of each seat while stepping closer and closer. I insisted, "*Go away, leave me alone.*"

He playfully jested and took small steps towards me, "*We are the only two people on this moving train, and I am coming up to talk to you.*" Instantly, I opened the sliding door on the train and threw him out onto the side of the mountain. I yelled, "*Leave me alone!*"

In reality, I threw myself off my bed and barely caught myself before crashing to the floor. My heart was racing, my arms were strained, and my hands were tensed. The dream seemed real, and I said aloud, "*Well, I did warn you!*" Eventually, I fell asleep, and he stopped contacting me in my dreams for quite some time. You probably think this is my imagination. However, I believe life has its unique way of revealing truths. Pay attention to where your mind wanders and the interconnectedness of people, places, and things.

Years after our breakup, we rekindled our friendship, and I was telling him about my dream. Apparently, he had spent my birthday that year in a hospital bed. "*Hospital bed?*" I inquired.

Tom is an excellent athlete with a passion for skiing. On the same day as my dream, he was casually skiing on top of a mountain and was inexplicably catapulted over the side of the mountain. There was no apparent danger. He was badly hurt and had to be medevacked to the hospital.

"*But now I understand! The danger was you! It was all your fault!*" as he pointed his finger at me and laughed exuberantly. This highly unusual mishap was so hilarious we could not stop laughing.

"*Well, I did warn you, but you refused to listen.*" I mischievously smiled, ordered another drink, and took a big bite of food, "*Mmm, these crab cakes are delicious.*"

Paradigm Shift

Speaking of people refusing to listen, I never felt like I belonged in my family of origin. I knew how to show up and fit in, but the moment I spoke my truth, I was wrong in four different ways all day, every day. Further, I was encouraged just to *love* everyone anyway. Our definitions of love were vastly different, and this divergence always made me feel sad and uncomfortable.

I tried to express myself and be as true to myself as possible. Unfortunately, my truth was undervalued, disregarded, or dismissed. I was not being heard. Therefore, my sadness turned to anger and eventually, rage. This cycle of dis-ease nourished my panic and fear as well as disgust.

My panic and fear were not necessarily incessant or uncontrollable. The precursors or manifestations of my rage were more like living in a constant state of hyperarousal. I learned how to control my reactions until I was safe and could allow a *cathartic release*.

Basically, after a perceived threat, I learned how to alter my mind-set and make a healthy adaptation to the situation. Most of the time, the adjustments I made led to the panic being able to dissipate on its own. However, if there were multiple triggers or the magnitude of a specific trigger was too intense, I isolated myself and occasionally experienced a panic attack.

Hyperarousal: When the mind and body unintentionally relive the trauma. Your amygdala, located in the primitive part of your brain, triggers the fight, flight or freeze response. Then, anything that reminds you of the trauma leaves you hyper-responsive. IE: Anxious, angry, overwhelmed, or out of control.

Hypoarousal: This is also when your body unintentionally relives the trauma. But instead of having an outburst, your body wants to shut down. IE: Numb, spacey, zoned out, depressed.

Window Of Tolerance: Describes an optimal zone of arousal. When operating within this zone, a person can effectively label, manage, and cope with their emotions. Thus, their window can shrink to decrease tolerance or expand to improve tolerance of perceived stimuli.

How do you identify the perceived stimuli? Images, sights, lights, sounds, vibrations, smells, words, expressions, music, anger, aggression, betrayals, anxiety, pain, and the list continues. Further, how do you know when you are about to go *over the edge or have reached the tipping point?*

The Mirror: Pretend you are holding a large mirror and seeing a distinct reflection of yourself. Now, allow the mirror to fall from your hands, land on the ground, and fracture.

There are large pieces, small pieces, and fragments. The large pieces are easily recognizable as you piece yourself back together. The smaller pieces may be a little more difficult to decipher, but you will eventually figure it out. Some of the fragments may be too difficult or indistinguishable. Moreover, you may not see tiny shards of glass, which could lead to potential danger.

Tell yourself: *"I am letting you break apart or disassemble so we can rebuild and reconcile together."* The opposite of this mindset would be to view the breakdown as a mechanical failure.

Finally, when you look into the reconstructed mirror, do you see yourself as happy and whole? If not, what pieces are missing, and how do you find them?

Eventually, I got to the point where I wanted and needed someone to *listen*. The myriad of emotions I pushed deep down inside me needed to be released. My short-lived verbal tirades cut to the origin of the issue and, in my mind, were dead on. However, my rage was a burden that left me feeling physically and emotionally drained.

I found this quote in high school, which has always resonated with me. Honestly, I consider this quote to be an art form. Being a creative person helped me to refine and release my anger appropriately.

"Anybody can become angry – that is easy. But to be angry with the right person and to the right degree and at the right time and for the right purpose and in the right way – that is not within everybody's power and is not easy."
Aristotle

As I grew up and moved on with my life, I thought I knew what to do and what not to do to create the family I desired to live with and love for the rest of my life. As you have discovered in the unfolding of my life journey thus far, I believed I had failed miserably.

When I closed my eyes, all I could see was my dream. My dream was to marry the best man on earth and have the three most beautiful children and a dog. I wanted to be a doctor and help children be happy and healthy. I wanted a house with a huge kitchen and the entire back wall as a window. I wanted to look out and see my family and friends playing football in the backyard before Thanksgiving dinner. My dream was simple but elegant and full of love.

Losing the dream of this kind of family I coveted my entire life was devastating beyond words. Besides the feelings of deprivation permeating my existence, the traumatic experiences I endured shattered my spirit. When I looked at myself in the mirror, I was not happy. I was not whole. I did not recognize myself, nor did I know how to reconcile the discrepancies.

When people said, "*Well, you just need to love yourself,*" it made my skin crawl. I thought, "*You have basically known five minutes of my life story. I opened my heart up to you, and your entire response blames me for my suffering because you somehow think I don't love myself. Ugh! I want to scream. I have always been and will always be my own best friend.*"

After repeatedly being condemned after making myself vulnerable, I learned not to confide. I withdrew trust and kept to myself. It was safe and I enjoyed my solitude much better than the insensitive or naive nature of others. Sometimes, I was alone, and at other times I was lonely. However, I wanted to reconcile the lonely part. I wanted to feel valued and to belong to someone or something. I wanted to create the opportunity for reciprocal unconditional love.

There is a circle of belonging:
Belonging to Yourself
Belonging to Others
Belonging to Nature
Belonging to Society
Belonging to God.
The circle begins and ends with you.

> "*You only are free when you realize you belong no place – you belong every place – no place at all. The price is high. The reward is great.*"
> **Maya Angelou**

Long-term learning and change are key to living in this world but not being of this world. To genuinely belong everywhere and nowhere is not an easy task. For me, it took a paradigm shift. A major shift I did not know had already begun.

I am sharing some thoughts about belonging I have learned along the way. Hopefully, these observations can help you to navigate the negative experiences, dark energy, and toxic relationships you may have encountered when you feel uncomfortable or at dis-ease. Maybe by clarifying emotions and situations, you can reconcile your journey and your quest to belong.

Situational Belonging (*Concerning Your Location or Surroundings*) Where you feel a sense of security and support within the confines of the group. IE: Schools, neighborhoods, places of worship, places of employment, athletic and leisure organizations. Once you leave the situation, you will eventually lose your sense of belonging, even if you maintain friendships with a select few.

Imposed Situational Belonging (*Concerning Your Set of External Circumstances*) Where you feel a sense of obligation, compassion, or enthusiasm for a group experiencing the same set of circumstances. IE: Natural disasters, disasters because of human negligence, a massive outdoor music concert or stadium event, or a highly publicized historical event. Once the situation has concluded, you will eventually lose your sense of belonging, even if you still feel the impact.

Ambiguous Belonging (Uncertain About Your Internal Truth Concerning Circumstances) You inadvertently find yourself in a situation open to more than one interpretation. Your choice between alternatives is unclear or inexact. You are not sure if you belong. IE: Being in a cohort for a disease or disability, attending family or high school reunions, or being the outsider to anticipated gatherings or holidays. You may be enchanted or disenchanted if you surmise your sense of belonging.

False Belonging (*Connecting on a Superficial Level*) Connection appears real until further examination. The relationship only has surface-level value and lacks depth, IE: Appealing to the masses. Social media ploys. Propaganda schemes. Crowd control rallies and calls to action. Sales pitch outreach.

Fitting Into The Crowd (*Quieting Your Truth*) Where you feel welcome and included to a point. People know your name and support some of your values. However, you cannot freely speak or engage in certain behaviors. Therefore, if you stay quiet or reserved and only express yourself within the written and unwritten confines of the group, you can feel a certain sense of belonging. *IE:* Controversial situations, political or religious discussions, personal choices concerning health and lifestyle.

Standing Out in the Crowd (*Speaking Your Truth*) There are various ways to speak your truth. Depending on the situation and your audience, there are various methods that may be beneficial or detrimental.

Verbal Onslaught (*Aggressive conversations with a hidden or overt agenda*) These types of exchanges may seem reciprocal but are usually one-sided. Often, the method of expression lacks a filter and disregards the experiences of another person or group. The conversations or confrontations usually intend to control or manipulate a person or situation.

Candidly Speak Your Truth: (*Straightforward, open, and honest conversations*) Mastering the art of having candid yet compassionate conversations takes skill. Even though you are speaking your truth, you refrain from sharing certain aspects of the dialogue because you want to be respectful and not create an uncomfortable situation. Through purposeful practice and the constant pursuit of knowledge, candidly speaking your truth will plant the seeds of genuine belonging.

I had an existential death during my time in Peru, a death to the mindset of my dream of family. Over the years, I realized my true friends are my family. I purposely and intentionally find people I can connect with and be my genuine self. Trying to depend on the family I was born into or the family I married into left me feeling slighted, especially when obstacles arose.

Learning the definition of *family* is in your heart and soul, not on a piece of paper detailing your genealogy, is a tremendous undertaking. It sounds logical but requires so much purging of the old paradigm to allow space for the new paradigm to grow and manifest its way productively in your life.

Soon after my return from Peru I was relearning the huge paradigm shift Jesus had created in the Jewish faith. Like a giant movie with a bright golden filter, I watched him break bread, drink wine, and discuss how this shift would change the world forever. Some members of his family would stay loyal, while other members of his family would betray him. All the while, his enemies would have more ammunition to destroy him.

Passions would fly and faith tested, but in the end, this newfound family would remain by his side and fight to the death and rebirth of *Love*—a total paradigm shift.

I am amazed and disappointed by how humans and the constructs they have created could take vast amounts of wisdom and convert them into self-serving doctrines. Humans love to create boxes of knowledge and define them as superior. Therefore, if you exist in another box, you are obviously inferior. They use these boxes as weapons to convert and control how and why other people think, feel, and act.

It's time to blow up your box! The universe is believed to be at least 10 billion light years in diameter and is continuously expanding. We are one tiny insignificant spec in time. However, I believe we are highly significant in our time together.

I choose to live in the light and avoid the darkness. I choose to stop eating poison every day. I choose to shift my focus away from the paradigm of the sick and focus on the paradigm of the healthy. I choose to detach from those constantly searching for and living in constant despair.

I suggest you figure out what makes you genuinely happy and do it! If you do not know what will make you happy, go find some new experiences. Immerse yourself in life, and Wisdom will come in search of you. Once you are ready, Wisdom will teach you how to fly.

The Tree of Life

My birthday was quickly approaching, and I wanted my celebration to be special. I was not in a relationship, nor did I desire to be in one, so all my options were open. I considered throwing a party for myself, which might be weird, but then I thought, *"Who cares! I am going to do it anyway."* I had been staring at the dining room wall for quite some time and could not decide what type of finish I desired. All my other houses had some of my artwork I painted on the walls, and now, it was also time to help celebrate this festive occasion.

The Tree of Life is typically planted at the center of the world and often in a sacred garden or forest. Some believe the Tree of Life bears the fruit of immortality. In Buddhism, the Bodhi Tree, or *tree of awakening* with its heart-shaped leaves, produces the sacred fig. These large shade-bearing trees are great for contemplation and a great source of nutrition and traditional medicine. They are believed to help guide the way to mix life experience with the potential for enlightened perfection.

The Tree of Life was about to explode all over my dining room wall. This was my house, and I had purchased it all by myself. I was so proud of the beauty, and now, I was going to create this detail that was impeccably mine. However, you could not sit at the dining room table and look at the *tree of awakening* in the distance. Moreover, the mural was painted from the viewer's vantage point, sitting within the tree and gazing out into the world, thinking, *"Where am I going next?"*

I was about to turn 46, and it had been years since I desired to create a faux finish on my walls. I purchased three paint colors, all with a golden hue and a transparent finish. I gathered brushes, rags, sticks, and sponges to create various textures. A deep, rich perspective emerged within each of the six painted layers, and the images seemed to move within your eyes and breath. I bought a large antique Chinese foil painting to enhance the scene.

This wall was my birthday present to myself and would be the party's centerpiece. The foil painting depicted a knotted dogwood tree intertwined with various rose bushes, all in bloom. I created the illusion of the branches from the painting extending out onto the walls. The exotic birds in flight and the muted green earth perfectly complemented the birds of paradise in my wrought iron staircase. At the same time, the flowers on my antique brass chandelier accentuated the frame.

Creating this mural to signify my new Tree of Life was the easy part. Creating a party to nourish fifty people took some time. Inviting people I considered my friends who did not know each other provoked anxiety. Everyone knew some of Amy, and all those boxes were about to collide. People from all over the area and from many different cultural backgrounds were coming to my home.

Besides the anxiety of all these people converging into one place, I contemplated how to get them all to engage. I invited a friend who owned a unique, handmade artisan pizza truck to cook in the back alley. I had a variety of local beers and a seating area on the patio. The kitchen was filled with homemade beef and chicken fajitas and tacos. The living room had a wine selection with comfortable seating by candlelight. Last, the dining room table was filled with appetizers and birthday cake in front of the Tree of Life.

Essentially, you had to socialize if you wanted to feast. I arranged the food, beverages, and ambiance to encourage conversation so everyone could bond with the experience. Seeing the people I cared for caring for each other in such a festive atmosphere was such a joy. I watched everyone's eyes brighten as they ventured through the different sections of my party and find out the names of strangers were often familiar in my line of storytelling.

I invited a relatively new friend, and I was happy she accepted the invitation as she lived far away. She was strong-willed, feisty, and full of life. Her vibe was slightly different because she grew up in India under Jainism. Like Buddhists and Hindus, Jains believe in reincarnation. One's karma determines the cycle of birth, death, and rebirth. When she was young, her family moved to America, and she created her own path. We had a mutual understanding and appreciation for each other.

As the party ended, she invited me to a late-night concert downtown and promised to get me back home. This concert was very different from what I expected because I had never experienced this type of crowd and their music. I decided I would absorb the experience and walked in like I owned the place. The dance floor was huge, and the energy was intense. The vibe became mine for the night.

When we took a break to get something to drink, a group of guys was trying to look tough and take pictures. I laughed and reached for their phone, *"Let me take some pictures for you!"* Again, the tough guy poses came out on display. So, I playfully coerced them to smile, *"What is the matter with you guys? It's my birthday, and you need to smile! Come on, show me those dimples!"*

Finally, the tough guys broke their badass routine and started to laugh. *"Girl, you two are crazy."* We were laughing so hard and having so much fun our stomachs were hurting. Eventually, we returned to the dance floor and the beat of the music satiated our souls.

Afterward, she drove me home, and we sat at my dining room table, peering out from the Tree of Life. We had a few bites of my cake and recounted the events of the evening. We had good karma, even if we were a little bit crazy. I thought, *"I need to paint some more trees."*

The Offering

As the spirits revealed pathways and corridors in my new paradigm of awareness, my healing uncovered a beacon of hope for my future. The arduous process of letting go in order to rebuild was apparent. I needed to restore and nurture my soul for purposeful living. But as I always say at the beginning of a journey, "*I don't know what I don't know.*" But I had every intention of finding out.

It was time for our group ceremony in Maryland, and a new woman was asked to join. Outwardly, she appeared like any other person, but on the inside, *she was broken*. She had been trapped on the third floor of a burning building, and as first responders held the life safety net beneath her, she plummeted to the ground and suffered devastating injuries. Although the surgeons had been able to reconstruct her body, she did not feel safe and whole.

As dusk settled over the land, Ceremony began to unveil herself. The air was satiated with the sweet and sensual scents of Sage and Agua de Florida to cleanse and restore our energy. As the curtains to the outside world closed, a single candle of light showed us *the way*. One by one, we drank *La Medicina* from the ceremonial cup and prayed, "*Heal me. Teach me. Show me.*"

When it was time for the new woman to heal, spirits unlike any I had seen before crowded the room to assist in a mystical surgery. The taller spirits guarded the perimeter as the smaller ones brought forth supernatural instruments. My Shaman picked up a smoky gray needle and assuredly threaded the opening with a piece of white pearl twine that appeared to be woven by angels. Red sparks of light flickered and dispersed throughout the room. Time ceased to exist.

My Shaman picked up a blade of white light and cut open her chest. By then, the room was so crowded with creatures, that I could barely see what was happening. I believe he extracted her fear and pain and proceeded to stitch the fabric of her body back together again. Within moments, the spirits vanished.

When it was time for my healing, I approached the center of the room. I felt exceptionally tall, and my body was on fire. It felt uneasy to speak my name and walk back and forth through my life. My Shaman devoutly approached me, stood at arm's length, and asked a few questions,

"Am I a man or a woman?"

I answered, "A man." as he looked through me.

"What is my name?"

I replied, "I don't know." as he repositioned himself.

"Am I young or old?"

I sadly replied, "I don't know." I felt inadequate to answer questions.

Next, he beckoned my feminine energy with a small musical instrument. I could feel the percussion reverberate through my entire body and entice my spirit to awaken passionately. His staunch face and fiery eyes penetrated my soul. As our human forms blurred, his spirit walked through mine, and I felt as though my body had dispersed for a few moments before becoming whole again.

Then, he wound me up into my own mystical strings holding onto the past. They glowed white and glistened behind me as if flowing into the wind. He wielded a curved blade of thick white light and swiftly cut the strings that bound me. He breathed my soul back into the present through my solar plexus and thanked me for my trust. He softly whispered prayers as my healing was coming to an end. I expected to feel some type of catharsis. But all I felt was energy being churned inside me with no way to escape. It was existentially stuck. I anticipated the release would manifest itself in another way.

My consternation grew over the next few months without any forms of release, and I was disheartened. I witnessed so many beautiful healings that mystical night, but mine didn't seem to work. The next ceremony was anti-climactic, and I pulled my Shaman aside to express my frustrations. He respectfully explained he had severed the ties and "the only way they still existed was if I was the one still holding on." He asked what purpose those bindings serve. Sadly, I still did not have an answer.

I understood that Ceremony was only part of my healing and that I needed to *do the work* in between. I was at a loss and felt I needed some additional guidance. I didn't want to let go a little bit; I wanted to let go all the way, forever. The pull of anxiety and depression deep in my chest affected me every day. Hiding the pain or pretending it didn't exist was not the answer. I needed to release it from my body. My Shaman gave me a task of offering as a way to fully disconnect, reconnect, and heal. I modified it a bit to fulfill the cycle, knowing this was a necessary step. I had no idea it would be such a life-altering day.

The power of our will can force us to hold on to our past or catapult us into the future. It can cure illness or create dis-ease. Strengthening our will is a crucial component to attaining spiritual growth. Focusing our will radically expands the limits of what we believe we can accomplish. Exerting our will exponentially expands our self-discipline, not just in one aspect but across all areas of life.

I did not consider my focal point as part of the dis-ease and thus created my own saboteur. I had been focused on the spirits who were attempting to steal my light when, in fact, I should have been focused on the spirits who were protecting my light and providing hope for my future.

I purchased a dozen lavish red roses, a bottle of semisweet red wine, and three fragrant rosemary plants to initiate the offering. I gathered my work gloves and a garden shovel with the intent to find the location of my second car accident. I had to start at the restaurant and retrace my steps down that curvy back country road to find the location of the accident and a location for my offering.

First, I dug a small hole and embedded the rosemary. Then, I poured myself a glass of wine and separated the petals from one rose. I allowed each petal to fall to the ground as my tears fell alongside them. I felt deep gratitude and thanked the spirits for *"allowing me to live."* I took a few sips of the wine and used the remaining to consecrate the hallowed ground. Before departing, I sat in my car and looked at the offering in the rear-view mirror. As the tears started to subside, I continued.

In horse country, the traffic is scarce, and the scenery is abundant. As I approached the main road, I could see an extensive procession of cars with funeral tags in the front windows. The thought of Death passing me by seemed surreal. As I watched car after car drive by, I could sense *Time* was moving in slow motion. I couldn't help but think this procession was meant for me or possibly a part of me.

As I rounded the bend near Loch Raven Reservoir, a volt of vultures devoured a huge buck in the middle of the road. I came to a complete stop. They refused to flee and simply glared at me while continuing to feast. I inched closer and closer. These ominous flesh eaters have the ability to focus each eye in two directions—one on their current prey and one on *me*. I felt like they were anxiously awaiting to pry in on my soul. Finally, I tapped my horn, and they flew away but left a dark shadow behind.

The drive to the location of my first car accident seemed exceptionally long. Again, I repeated the rosemary, red wine, and roses ritual. This time, my emotions were a little more intact. I was in a neighborhood close to my house, and I didn't want to look foolish in case someone I knew drove by. There was one last step to complete the series of unfortunate events.

I drove to the parking lot where I had asked my former husband to meet to reach an amicable agreement before our divorce proceedings. Even though I know he did not intend to meet me, I wanted to imagine that conversation taking place. I spoke aloud. *"Daniel, I hope to God you are listening! I am not sure what I can say to make the pain go away. We did try, and we have two beautiful children to show for it. I am sorry our love was not meant to last forever. But now, it is time to let go."*

By this point, I was emotionally drained, and my eyes were so puffy I could barely see. I went home, drew a hot Epsom salt bath, added fresh rose water, and finished my bottle of wine while bathing by candlelight. The pain and grief of the experience started to leave my body. The spirits of the light knew I was alive and well, and the spirits of the dark were most likely disgruntled. I curled up on the back porch with a blanket and watched the stars twinkle in the sky. I spoke aloud, *"Tom, I know you can hear me; you always do! Thank you for helping me through the darkness. I wish you peace, happiness, and love. Your friendship helped to make me a better person. But now, it is time to let go."*

As I watched a few stars twinkling in the sky, I pondered, *"I wonder where love goes when it dies?"*

The city was oddly silent that night as the moon fell behind the tree line. A few streams of clouds had crept in over my house as soft music began to cradle me to sleep. My day had come to an end, and I thanked God I was still alive. I went inside, put my *(po jammies)* pajamas on, and hopped onto my bed.

SLAM! The front left side of my bed frame broke, and I crashed down. I looked up and complained, *"Seriously! That is not funny. I guess this whole thing isn't over yet."* I took a deep breath and went to the other side of the bed. I peacefully crawled in and pulled the covers over me. I know the energy of unfinished business doesn't disappear into the universe. It manifests itself in mischievous ways. I spoke, *"Thanks, God, but not tonight. I had a great day. I am not going to let this little mishap ruin it."*

Kindred Souls

Years ago, my children encouraged me to join Facebook and insisted I have at least one hundred friends. I thought that was ridiculous because I could not come up with one hundred people from my past I wanted to converse with. I finally surrendered and quickly added friends to my page. It was a pleasant surprise to connect with people I used to be friends with and have brief exchanges about our past as well as our present. These connections were tapping into something wonderful inside of me.

I contemplated the exchanges and decided it would be nice to occasionally post something to let friends and family know I was alive. Also, I wanted to show my connection with my two beautiful children through our hikes and outdoor activities. This amount of sharing seemed to be sufficient.

I felt inclined to post something the first Christmas after my father passed. Many of my childhood friends knew my father because he was always willing to carpool after school and on the weekends. He did a lot of volunteer work at the school and the church to impact our community.

A guy, Vince, whom I was good friends with from my youth reached out to me. His father had passed away at a very young age from an autoimmune disease; therefore, he had grown up with his mother and grandmother. Unfortunately, his grandmother passed around the same time as my father, so he understood how I felt in this season of my life. These conversations led to us reuniting our friendship.

I enjoyed being friends with Vince because he connected me to my past. A past I had almost pushed out of my memory. He had remained in touch with most of our childhood friends and was always up for an adventure, a person who highly valued the meaning of life. Unbeknownst to most of us, he had inherited the same autoimmune disease as his father and had intermittently battled it since he was a teenager. He desired to live the best life because he knew it would not last forever.

One night, Vince invited me to dinner with another old friend. This friend had wanted to be a pilot since elementary school. We went to the same school, church, and swimming pool, and our parents were friends. The Pilot and I were always engaged in friendly competition and playful mischief. We held many responsibilities in our endeavors and always made our duties fun and memorable. Both of us were called to serve.

Thankfully, our friendship had not skipped a beat. We picked up right where we had left off so many years ago. Sharing our life stories felt natural. It was so comfortable and exciting to be around someone who knew the real *Amy*, the little girl who wanted to take on the world. He did not judge me for my life experiences. He listened with love, empathy, and compassion in his heart. I was so proud to call this honorable officer and gentleman my friend.

One night, The Pilot called me with consternation in his voice. He asked if I was alone, and I went outside to listen fully. He wanted to be the one who told me, "*Vince had been sick for a few months and finally passed last night.*" Our strong, intelligent, and handsome football coach and friend had become sick and frail for the last time. Finally, he was no longer in pain. We would all be gathering in his memory and arrangements were being made.

I planned to attend the funeral, as I wanted to pay my respects to him and his family. As I entered the church parking lot, a strange and uncanny feeling of deep sadness and uncertainty permeated my body.

Walking into his service was like stepping back in time. I was in high school again and wasn't sure if I belonged. I had not spoken to most of these people since we graduated. As I approached the pew, I looked to my right and saw my best friend from elementary school. When Tia smiled that overwhelmingly amazing smile she always had and mouthed my name, "*Amy*," tears welled up in my eyes. I could hear her insatiable laugh and longed to give her a huge hug. Later, I found out we both still cherish some photos we have kept of each other from our youth. It genuinely warms my heart.

One by one, distant memories of faces from my past turned and smiled. A younger version of myself emerged from the perceived void inside my heart. Joy and sadness intricately wove patterns of light and love into my heart. Old wounds and insecurities dissipated. The voices inside my head telling me I wasn't good enough and didn't belong here were silenced by the outpouring of emotions that filled the room.

I've learned that nostalgia produces dopamine in the brain. Besides making you feel good, it is a learning chemical. In this case, it was a relearning chemical because I was experiencing positive emotions as though they were etched into my brain. We had all gathered to mourn the loss of our dear friend and to partake in a celebration of a life well lived. However, it distinctly felt like he had just stepped out of the room momentarily and was about to run back in and yell, "*Surprise! I have been trying to get you all back together again.*"

Throughout the day, the gatherings traveled to four different destinations, each with its unique personality. So many people approached me and joyfully called me by name as if I had seen them yesterday, even though it had been twenty-eight years.

Apparently, I was the smart, pretty, nice and tall girl everyone liked but was unwilling to talk to for fear of rejection or whatever our immature teenage brains were thinking at the time. These conversations gave my inner self an entirely new perception of the world my teenage self experienced.

The following evening, I had a vivid dream. I was in a serene place surrounded by non-descriptive images, all appearing bright white in contrast to his smooth, dark skin. Vince looked healthy and peaceful as he slowly walked towards me. He put his hands together and reverently bowed his head before fading into the background. He bestowed a majestic gift of rekindled friendships upon my soul.

Weeks after Vince's passing, another classmate I had seen at the funeral invited me to a Pachamanca. Everyone at this traditional feast had work, although it felt like play. The men and the women cook and tend to the children's participation. It was such a joy to see a thriving familial environment. Watching my newly found old friend, Rene, eat evoked pure bliss. When he pulled the hot meat out of the earthen oven and dipped it into the homemade *aji verde*, everyone could feel his overwhelming affinity for the food.

This party was reminiscent of the multicultural community I grew up in. The love and respect we have for each other, our similarities, and our differences felt like home to me. I recalled feeling this same sense of home while living in Hawaii. But I knew it was severely lacking in the location where I was currently living. My son told me he could finally understand what I longed for all these years.

Pachamanca originated in the Incan Empire in Peru and is translated into the Quechua language as Pacha *earth* and manka *pot or "Banquet of Mother Earth."* It is an offering to the earth after the harvest. These stone ovens dug into the earth symbolized cooking in the womb of Pachamama.

The earthen oven we used in the backyard was several feet deep and wide. The stones had been heating for hours by the time I arrived. The layers of pork, beef, chicken, potatoes, roots, plantains, and vegetables were covered with a marinade of spices and banana leaves. Then, they used a brown cloth to cover the layers before adding more rocks and dirt. After several hours of festivities, the earthen oven known as huatia was unveiled for a succulent feast for the senses. Everyone was mesmerized.

Aji Verde is a spicy Peruvian green sauce made with aji peppers, cilantro, green onion, garlic, and lime. It is a traditional sauce, and when compared to salsa made with jalapenos, it can be up to ten times hotter.

An unexpected and intriguing aspect of this gathering was that all our children were around the same age and instantly connected as if they already knew each other. I was amazed that we were friends as children, and now, our children can reap the benefits of our bonds. I could feel a different version of love I did not know was lacking in my heart.

For years, Rene invited me to various gatherings, and I was able to rekindle old friendships and make a few new ones as well. He never seemed to be going out of his way to make me feel special. Another aspect of these relationships I found intriguing was meeting people I *almost* knew growing up.

Almost knew? Yes, people who grew up in the same environment with many of the same cohorts, but I never met them for whatever reason. Then, when we got to know each other, the feeling inside us almost mimicked knowing each other for a lifetime. It was almost like an innate attraction, a different form of indistinguishable belonging until you can distinguish the *Why*.

Almost everywhere I have gone in the world, I have met someone from Maryland, especially Montgomery County. Within minutes, we discover our connection and *why we are who we are*. We are kindred souls.

Zona Nudista

I encouraged my daughter to make new friends and travel to gain experience outside the box created for her. Initially, she fumbled around a few ideas that didn't seem advantageous. Then, she discovered her school offered a variety of internships in foreign countries. She wanted to be an *au pair* in Spain and asked if I would help. *Absolutely!* It was a great idea and a safe option to travel alone.

Au pair: Nannies and au pairs help with childcare in a family home. However, a nanny is a standard employee with a paid salary, while an au pair is integrated into family life and receives spending money. Although temporary, Au pairs have their own space in the family home and share meals and activities with the family members.

There was an application and interview process. She had four video conferencing interviews and obtained three offers. Her eyes lit up the room as she enthusiastically recounted the various options. She smiled in amazement, *"I can't believe so many people want me."*

She chose a family with two adorable little girls an hour north of Barcelona. They lived less than a mile from the beach, where people *on holiday* and au pairs were integral to the scenery.

On Holiday: In the United States, people use the word *holiday* to mean time off of work due to a law or custom like Thanksgiving. However, in Europe, being *on holiday* simply refers to taking a break from daily life to rest, travel, or partake in recreational or leisure activities. Being on holiday in this community wasn't an obligation but a way of life.

She took online classes, worked five hours a day with the girls, and had weekends free. She called me almost every day and we had the most wonderful conversations. I especially loved the moments when she recounted my parenting skills as accurate and effective.

One of the little girls was fussy in the morning, and she noticed they kept her up a little too late watching television. When she exclaimed, *"They need to put that baby to bed!"* That was music to my ears because both my kids loved to stay up past their bedtime and now, I wasn't the bad guy any longer.

Further, my daughter was emotionally filled by the raw beauty of the beachfront known as Zona Nudista. Everyone there was completely exposed, but not in a sexual way. The romantic lure of the landscape reminded her of inner beauty and prompted her to reminisce about growing up in Maryland.

People of all shapes and sizes walked the coast, lay in the sand, and terraced the rocks simply being beautiful. When she discarded her clothes, she knew she would not be judged on the material value of her appearance. Instead, she would be judged on her strength, love, and light.

Immersed, she let go of burdens that had stifled her growth. The food, wine, people, mystery, and passion were waiting to be discovered. Everyone had a light breakfast and an early lunch while looking forward to *siesta*. Each night, people drank wine, spent quality time together, and made love. Making love is not defined as a sexual act of pleasure. Moreover, it is experiencing others on an intimate level through the pleasures life has to offer while the rest of the world disappears.

Siesta: Most people associate a 15-30 minute afternoon nap with Spain because they take their siestas seriously. Many businesses shut down so people can eat, relax, and escape the heat. Siesta, which literally means *the sixth hour*, is common around the Mediterranean and many Latin American countries. However, the practice originated in ancient Rome as *the art of riposo*, rest or repose.

One thing that intrigued her was the exuberance of the Catalan people who wanted to be independent from Spain. They were very proud people who relished in their culture. Music was an integral part of their heritage and spoke to the soul of the nation. When the previous president was extradited to an island, he sang a *native song* atop a sacred mountain to give his people hope.

"*Moon On The Water*" was a song that symbolized the people's struggle and the struggle in my daughter's heart. The lyrics beckoned freedom to dance swiftly in the moonlight. They called forth the heartbeat of the rebel to allow freedom to be real and not a figment of our imagination. The song boasts of torches burning and passages screaming. Turn up the music and let the freedom fires burn!

Even though independence was a wonderful thing, she realized it caused a lot of problems and was kind of crazy. After all, Spain had protected Catalan many times, and the outbreaks left many rioters injured or dead. She interjected; everyone rolled their own cigarettes, and it looked so badass even though smoking isn't healthy. In her mind, she contemplated the necessary path of resistance.

She loved the *allioli* they put on everything. It literally means *garlic and oil*. Plus, they add a pinch of salt. It is made by emulsifying all the ingredients together and resembles mayonnaise. People in other parts of the world add eggs, lemon juice, or other seasonings. But in Spain, purists keep it simple.

In her mind, allioli symbolized *the savory parts of life* created for all to enjoy. If you were meant to be on holiday, then allioli was your faithful and scrumptious companion.

The sense of community was a metaphor for the origins of *paella*. In eastern Spain, Valencia is one of the largest natural ports in the Mediterranean and is one of the most important rice-producing areas since the Moors introduced the grain over 1200 years ago. The dish's humble beginnings were when rice farmers and workers added what was available during meal preparation. When the magical mixture was ready, everyone had their own wooden spoon and ate directly from the pan.

Over the years, rice from Valencia was abundant, and many adaptations of the famous dish became widespread. The word paella or, to be more precise, *la paella* is actually the name of the pan used to create the blend of vegetables, meats, snails, herbs, beans, and seafood. Try it and *Disfruta!* Enjoy.

One cool afternoon, my daughter was sunbathing on some rocks by the ocean, warmed by the heat of the sun. She noticed a white bird on a rock all alone. Suddenly, she realized she was alone. As she pondered the moment, a sense of beauty filled her because they were alone together. She drifted off to sleep as the ocean sang a sweet and gentle lullaby. When she awoke, she envisioned flying as high as the bird and felt the refreshing wind beneath her wings.

My daughter called me at midnight on the first hour of her 21st birthday. My beautiful baby was now an adult sitting on a beach drinking wine in Spain. The images she sent me were modest yet erotic and filled with a sense of joy and wonder. She felt no shame in her natural beauty and desire to live life. Our bond was strengthened through understanding and empathy. I fell in love with her all over again.

The notions she explained to me based on her experiences resonated with my own experiences concerning my sense of ego. As I have mentioned, I believed my self-confidence was high, and my ego was low. But, when it came to my divorce and my injuries, I felt like less of a person. My ego had been crushed to hell, and it was taking a long time to recover. Sometimes, feeling naturally beautiful and full of life was a struggle.

Every day, in some way, I felt less than. You know, like that little math symbol **Amy < N**. Basically, N felt like everything I was before my adversities, and accepting my new limitations was not something I wanted to do. Feeling invincible was way more desirable than feeling defeated. I wanted to fall asleep, wake up on that rock, and fall in love with Amy all over again.

When I discovered Amy < N was saturated in shame, it led me to learn more about overcoming the nature of the beast. Shame is gloriously alive and waiting to be unleashed if you let it. Even though I had a reason to get out of bed every day and impeccably execute any number of personal or professional endeavors, that little beast inside my head was a constant reminder, "*I was not good enough. I did not deserve to be loved.*" The only way to silence that beast was to accept the new version of Amy. Then, hopefully, cherish everything I used to have and everything I have now and in the future.

You can't really talk about shame unless you include the work of Brene Brown:

> "*I define shame as the intensely painful feeling or experience of believing that we are flawed and therefore unworthy of love and belonging - something we've experienced, done, or failed to do makes us unworthy of connection.*"

She believes guilt is adaptive and helpful. It means we are holding something we've done or failed to do up to our values and feeling psychological discomfort.

She does not believe shame is helpful or productive. Shame is much more likely to be the source of destructive or hurtful behavior than the solution or cure. Our fear of disconnection can make us dangerous:

> "*If you put shame in a Petri dish, it needs three things to grow: secrecy, silence, and judgment. If you take that same Petri dish and douse it with empathy, it can't survive.*"

Sick and Tired

As I spent my life enduring painful experiences and yet incredible healing opportunities, my ability to continue to get up each day with grit and determination allowed me to succeed personally and professionally.

I completed four major multi-million-dollar projects on time and under budget at work. But I was physically and emotionally drained and desperately needed a break. So, I was delighted when I was asked to complete a short project before I began my next major endeavor. It was something near and dear to my heart: a medical simulation center at the local school. It was partially funded, but I would need to enlist numerous volunteers to complete the task.

Without going into great detail, I can say I was thoroughly disgusted with the system, its people, and its processes. The physical structure and all of its contents were absolutely horrendous. However, I was able to complete it on time, although far beyond the allotted budget, thanks to many donations of people's time, money, and efforts. Collectively, we created something great for the children and the community.

There was a ribbon-cutting ceremony two days before school was in session. To my dismay, the 105 volunteers who helped to make the project successful were not invited and received no credit for their work. In fact, the credit I afforded them was swiftly removed and discarded.

I listened to a few strangers stand at the podium and take credit for all the hard work and dedication put into this innovative learning center. Whew! I was hot, but I kept my mouth shut. I was so thankful to complete that project and escape that hell hole. Although I knew I had helped to create something great, I was enraged by the audacity of those who had *refused* to help but devoured all the glory.

But hey, it was only three months of my life, right?

Shortly after the project started, I developed a cough. I thought it was my allergies because there was an excessive amount of mouse poop and five different types of mold all over everything in the building where I was working. It was summer, so the temperature and humidity were out of control. The air conditioning was not in service, and the roof leaked in multiple areas, so everything was wet or moist.

However, after the project ended, my cough did not go away. In fact, it got worse. Most days, I felt like I had pneumonia, and when I coughed or sneezed, my tissue was filled with blood. I was thoroughly exhausted and had a difficult time focusing on work. At home, I went to bed early and struggled to wake up. I thought my body would eventually process this crap, and I would feel better.

A couple of months passed, and unfortunately, it was time for the mandatory flu vaccine. So, I asked for an extension. I was sick and did not want to compound my illness. They told me I had one more month before it would become an issue. The month passed, and I was still sick. My throat and lungs were on fire, and my coughing was incessant. I tried numerous prescriptions, over-the-counter, and natural remedies. Nothing seemed to alleviate my suffering.

Then, I got an email. I had until the end of the week to get the mandatory flu vaccine, or else I would be suspended from work without pay. It was abundantly clear that I could not use any of my 425 hours of accrued sick leave because that would be out of compliance with hospital standards.

I waited until the last moment possible and got the required vaccine. For the next 10 days, I was as close to death as I thought possible. I slept 22 out of 24 hours daily and isolated myself from the world. I did not eat any food and attempted to drink as much water as possible when coherent. I did not urinate or have any bowel movements. I literally thought I was going to die.

Individually, each one of my children quietly asked, *"Are you going to die?"* I solemnly replied, *"I don't know. But I know I love you."*

Returning to work was difficult due to the exhaustion and respiratory dysfunction. After a couple of days, my symptoms started to exacerbate. I gave up and went to the emergency room. After a long, drawn-out series of medical appointments, invasive tests, and methodical interviews, the medical system concluded I needed help.

The laundry list of medications I was prescribed made me dizzy and nauseous. I was unable to concentrate and stayed in a perpetual brain fog. When I returned for guidance and support, I was given additional medications, one of which was an inhaler.

The first time I inhaled the vapor from this cartridge, my heart rate immediately escalated, and I fell back in my chair. My chest was pumping so intensely it caused severe pain to shoot through my heart. I believed I was having a massive heart attack. I frantically took some aspirin and attempted to control my breathing. I called one of my friends, who was a doctor and asked for guidance. After several queries, we determined it was the inhaler and I should not take it again.

When I returned for a follow-up visit, the physician's assistant initiated the usual interrogation of my physical symptoms and medical compliance. I explained the inhaler issue and was swiftly reprimanded, "*Who do you think you are? You are not a doctor. Why would you make a decision like that? If you do not follow protocol, I am going to have to document this in your chart. Then, your appointments will not be covered.*" Then, she jotted down some notes, and her face looked like she was sucking on a lemon.

Employee health, my ass! I was enraged. I couldn't believe I was reprimanded for having common sense. She had absolutely no empathy; she was simply making me follow some unhealthy and undesirable protocol that was not benefiting my health. In fact, the protocol was severely detrimental. I thought, "*Well, guess what? You are not a real doctor; I am in charge of my health. So, when I think I am having a heart attack, I am going to stop the source. Thanks.*"

From then on, I stopped taking all of my medications except one. It was a mild decongestant and helped a little bit. However, to stay compliant with the *dictated course of action*, I reported complete medication compliance. Otherwise, they would not continue to support the issues directly caused by my employment. They should call it an Unhealth System; it would make more sense.

After several more hours of intrusive inquiries that were recorded on videotape, a doctor concluded my respiratory illness was the responsibility of the medical system. Instead of feeling vindicated, I felt violated, unsafe, and insecure. Their dismissive attitude made me feel my health was not important, nor was I. I was having a difficult time believing I had dedicated 14 years of my life to this stupid place, and I was being treated like a criminal under investigation.

Through the illness, I still went to work every day and completed all my projects on time and under budget, but my heart was no longer in it. I was sick and tired of being sick and tired!

After eighteen long months of battling my respiratory illness and *not* asking for any compensation, The Manager, who was privy to all my health information, called me into an office and closed the door.

After a strange and relatively obscure conversation, I was told I was *"rude, arrogant, and lazy."*

I inquired, *"Huh? Is there a problem with my work? Were there any complaints or discrepancies?"* Apparently not. Nobody had issued any complaints, and my financial statements were perfect.

Apparently, The Manager didn't appreciate being bypassed in the chain of command concerning my projects and wanted to kick me while I was down. The adjectives The Manager used against me more appropriately described the management style of our department. The few people I confided in were blown away by the complete lack of respect being thrust upon me.

The moment I walked out of that office, I returned to my desk and opened LinkedIn. One month later, I turned in my resignation to The Manager and thanked everyone for allowing me the pleasure of serving this organization. Oops, sorry, I meant displeasure; that must be a typo.

Before my last day of employment, I made sure absolutely everything was completed and everyone I had worked with was notified. I wanted to ensure no blame would be placed upon me for any unfinished business. The last several people who left that department had left behind a huge mess nobody wanted to clean up, and I believe they felt justified because they had also been slighted. I did not care about The Manager. I cared about my projects and my people. I knew I would never return to this organization, and I desired to leave on a positive note. Overall, it was a great learning experience in many personal and professional ways. Undoubtedly, it strengthened my sense of self and the boundaries I am willing and able to create and accept.

Falling Into Place

Like all teenagers, my son struggled with normal adolescent dilemmas and the plethora of voices and tasks needed to apply, be accepted, and enroll in his university of choice.

One huge voice shouted *"D1 D1 D1"* in his face all day, every day. It wasn't just one voice; it was a collective mindset in the highly competitive world of high school baseball. D1 refers to Division One college sports and baseball, which currently includes just over 300 ranked higher education institutions.

Playing D1 ball sounds enticing, but it is a full-time job. Once on the team, they *own* you. Baseball is your life, and anything outside of baseball is a distraction. This concept wore on my son because he loved many things in life, and his varsity coaches did not value the humans beneath the jerseys. In turn, I put him in a high-profile clinic so he could get a feel for the D1 community and decide for himself.

Many other voices attempted to dictate the burden of the college application process. In my opinion, the business of college applications was genuinely a money-making endeavor and consumed months of your life. I did not have the desire for my time, energy, and money to be thrown in ten different directions. Nor did I feel these processes were beneficial for the children involved.

I told my son to do some research to pick his three favorite schools. His criteria were baseball and engineering. Upon selection, we visited the first school, and he thoroughly enjoyed the baseball team, but there was no engineering department. The campus was beautiful but remote, and it had a great cafeteria and numerous outdoor adventure opportunities.

The next visit was in the middle of the mountains alongside a river. They had three levels of baseball, which appealed to my son. He could participate on the intermediate level and then decide if he wanted to move up to the D1 level of competition. Either way, he would be an integral part of the team.

Further, this university had an exceptional engineering department. When we toured the automotive department, the award-winning, highly competitive formula yellow race car made his eyes glow. He engaged in long conversations with the project manager and design engineers. The words they were speaking were not in my realm of knowledge. So, I stepped back and observed my son in his element.

Hearing his voice create images in exceptional minds and ask intriguing questions instilled great pride in my heart. He asked to go to the school store to buy a sweatshirt or jacket. This was his first school of choice, and had been for a couple of years. He looked exceptionally handsome in his blue jacket as he held his head high. Everything was falling into place.

When we returned home, he completed the early application process and was as happy as he was relieved. All the voices of burden returned one by one while he navigated this milestone in life. An onslaught of *"You need to"* permeated every move he made. Apparently, receiving early acceptance to your number one school of choice wasn't good enough. He was advised to obtain a new game plan.

I told him if anybody had a problem with our method of finding the right school, they needed to call me and leave him alone. Unfortunately, some people who had a vested interest in his future endeavors did not agree and caused tremendous anxiety and uncertainty in my son. Suddenly, I found myself surrounded by all the voices in his head, but they were coming out of his mouth and directed at me.

The *"You need to"* voices were trying to dictate my time, money, and resources, and they did not sound like my son at all. I did not recognize the young man standing in front of me. I was not angry. I was actually very sad because I knew what he was experiencing. Moreover, I knew how to alleviate the problem, but it was going to be a disgusting lesson for him to learn.

I attempted to tolerate and dissipate the problem and hoped the situation would work itself out. But eventually, I had no choice. The worst part was that I was going to be the messenger for a lesson I did not want him to learn at this point in time. I gave him extremely distinct instructions on what to say and how to say it. I insisted he sounded genuine and encouraged him to practice his wording beforehand.

Fortunately or unfortunately, depending on how you view fate, the outcome of the situation went exactly as I imagined it would. The devastation of learning the truth was unbearable, and ultimately, the messenger needed to suffer almost as much as my son. I remember the look in his eyes when all the pieces fell into place. Any amount of childhood innocence left in his body had vanished.

Finally, he went to university, and one of his best friends from high school was his roommate. Life was going to be grand. But things didn't fall into place as he had planned, and he felt confused and isolated. Just as things were looking up and he was beginning to acclimate to his new way of life, tragedy occurred. He was riding his skateboard down a steep hill and hit a small bump in the road. He knew how to fall correctly, but his right elbow hit the ground at the most perfect little point and shattered.

He got himself up, held his arm in place, and walked back to his dorm. He eventually went to the emergency room and had an eight-hour wait. Then, I got "the" phone call. He was scheduled for emergency surgery at 7:00 am the following day. I felt horrible I could not make it up there to console him, but he assured me everything would be all right.

The eleven-inch scar and twenty-two surgical staples looked like they belonged to Frankenstein. He had his arm in a cast for several months, and the worst part was no more baseball. It was difficult to get around, and he lost thirty pounds of muscle mass throughout his entire body.

As my son was working his way back to physical and emotional health, Covid decided to shut down the world. The university shut down, and all students had to evacuate. As the online class structure was coming to fruition, he fell back into a strange type of depression. The dreams of his childhood had come to an abrupt end, and now the world was filled with uncertainty.

How do you recreate your life when most of the life we had all learned to live was nonexistent?

He took one full-time and one part-time job and saved most of his money. He was determined to do something productive with his life, but something seemed different inside of him. His skin coloring was muted, and his smile was less intense. This young man who one year earlier had been on top of the world had fallen from grace. It was devastating to watch the change.

When my daughter was returning to Oahu, he decided to go for a few weeks and help her move and see a few sights. He had always loved the thought of Hawaii and often recalled how paradise had been where his mom and dad had been the happiest. It was beautiful to see and hear how the spirit of aloha was starting to replenish his soul. Three weeks later, he stated, *"I'm staying here."*

Within a couple of months, he had a job, an apartment, a small SUV, and a surfboard. He basically taught himself how to surf, and by learning how to fall properly, he learned how to get back up and try again. He sent a picture of himself surfing in front of the iconic Diamond Head at Waikiki Beach and wrote, *"When I am on top of the wave, it's like looking down from Heaven."*

I was so proud of him, so I did some additional research. Everything in Polynesian culture has such deep meaning and richness. I wanted to share it with you as well.

Hawaiians are credited for inventing surfing or *he'e nalu,* wave sliding. Original wooden surfboards, *papahe'e nalu,* made surfing more than a sport. They are sacred objects alive with symbolism and history, connecting souls to the ocean. Additionally, natives believe ancestors take on life forms found in nature and act as spiritual counselors.

He'e, octopus, has many meanings. They are multi-faceted masters of disguise and extremely flexible. They are highly intelligent as well as mystical beings. Their arms are master problem solvers with multiple sensory perceptions, including taste. To avoid danger, he'e creates a blast of water to propel and ink to camouflage itself. Its skin can change form and color. All he'e are deaf, have keen eyesight, and possess three hearts and nine brains. They are highly adaptable blue-blooded creatures that can crawl and swim.

Technically, **Nalu** means "surging waves," but combining the two words transforms the meaning into a form of ocean literacy by connecting them to the rhythms of the tides and currents and helping them navigate history. Additionally, Nalu means to "reflect or meditate" and comes from the root na, "peace, calm," and alu, "to cooperate and act together."

Papa literally means something flat for sliding on waves, and the individual creation of one's board is sacred. Before chopping down a tree, a surfboard maker places a kūmū, ritualistic fish, in a hole near the roots and prays. Then, they follow ancient rituals using plants, tools,

306 White Heron: A Creation Story

and fire to bring this board to life. The length and type of wood differentiated the classes.

Ali'i, royalty, boards referred to as *olo* were 14–16 feet long, made from wiliwili trees, and could weigh up to 175 pounds. While the *Makaainanas'* commoners, boards referred to as *alaia* were 10–12 feet long and made from denser koa wood. Before its first use, it was dedicated to the gods.

Hawaiians believed talking about your knowledge wasn't enough. You had to prove yourself through a demonstration. This is why the sacred traditions that entail surfing and the creation of one's own surfboard were used to keep powerful leaders in top physical, mental, and spiritual health.

In the 1770s, Lieutenant King, Captain Cook's successor, was the first to document a description of the great art of surfing in a journal entry noting *"the most astonishing velocity of the participants."* In the 1800s, missionaries abolished *Kapu*, a strict set of laws for society. This act dwindled the number of surf, hula, music, and cultural activities. Fortunately, by the 19th century, King Kalakaua, the Merry Monarch, revived many ancient practices, and before he died in 1891, he said, *"Tell my people I tried."* I wonder if he felt validated for his efforts or passed onto the next realm feeling empty.

By 1905, a teenager named Duke Kahanamoku frequented Waikiki Beach to ride waves with Diamond Head in the backdrop. By 1912, Duke became a 6-time Olympic swimmer and water polo medalist, eventually introducing the surfing tradition worldwide. Also known as The Big Kahuna, Duke is the father of modern-day surfing and served as ambassador to visitors and dignitaries visiting the islands until he died in 1968.

Over 100 years later, my son has been living in Waikiki and was captured on film with the famous Diamond Head in the background. He'e nalu has transformed his life, deepened his connection to the ocean, and reminded him he is a powerful leader. Thank you, King Kalakaua and Duke, for keeping the spirit of Aloha alive for all generations. The Hawaii state motto is, "*Ua mau ke ea o ka aina i ka pono*, " meaning "*The life of the land is perpetuated in righteousness.*" If you ever step foot on sacred ground or watch the surfers ride 40-foot waves, you will feel the intense energy in the life and love of the land. Then, you can bow your head and thank he'e, the octopus.

Curious, who helps keep your spirit alive and well? What sacred objects remind you of who you genuinely are on the inside? What animals speak to you with wisdom or guide you through the day? I would love to sit down and talk story with you—just my soul to your soul in perfect harmony. We can let our loving light of aloha shine through to each other and ultimately brighten the world.

Talk Story

Sometimes, I wonder why bad things happen to good people. My story is loaded with bad things, yet there is a gut feeling that I would not be who I am today if they were not a part of my life journey. Despite all the trauma my mind and body had endured, I instinctively knew there was much more for me to experience. I had to learn to stop asking, "why me," and begin to look deeper for understanding.

One Tuesday, I left work early because the coughing from my respiratory illness had taken a brief hiatus, and I was excited to get outside. A friend agreed to join me, and we met at the intersection near our houses. As we cut through the park, it started to sprinkle, and the temperature dropped. We were losing daylight because the clouds had thickened.

We cut up a side street to head back home, which was relatively inconvenient because of the numerous crosswalks. The sprinkles increased but were still manageable. There was no need to stop, but I put my hat on to stay warm and dry.

As the crosswalk lit up for us to proceed, he stepped onto the road, and I was about two steps behind. Out of the corner of my eye, I noticed a car zipping around a parked car and heading straight for me.

Instantly, I jumped forward and landed firmly on my left foot while my right foot was elevated behind me at a 90-degree angle. The car brakes squealed as the car bumper nailed my right inner foot. BAM!

I was thrown out of the crosswalk and fortunately, landed on both my feet with my hiking boots intact. I was dazed and confused, unsure of where I was or what just happened. I cautiously turned around.

The driver of the car jumped out and berated me for not paying attention to the traffic. I slowly pointed to the white crosswalk signal permitting me to walk. He looked thoroughly disgusted and scolded me with his finger, *"Well, did I hit you?"* Confused, I replied, *"I think so."* My friend stepped towards me and looked concerned, *"Did he hit you?"* Again, I replied, *"I think so."*

Then the man jumped back into his car and drove away. We were about two miles from my house and continued to walk. The street-lights, coupled with the car lights and the rain, perplexed my mind. I asked to hold my friend's arm because I felt lost. He walked me to my gate because I was not sure how to get home. I went into my living room and sat down on my couch. The soundless room seemed loud.

"Ouch" was all I could muster up to say as the pain slowly crept in. My sister called and wondered why I sounded so strange. I simply said, *"The car hit me."* She politely responded, *"I know, honey, it's been a long time. I'm sorry you are still in so much pain."*

"No, I mean the car just hit me when I was walking home tonight," I said regretfully. She encouraged me to seek medical attention. I refused. I wanted to be left alone, in my pain, all by myself. I needed shelter from the storm; my home was my sanctuary.

As the night progressed, my body tightened as rage emerged in my soul, *"God! I know you can hear me! What do you want from me? Why are you punishing me?"* After several hours, my body gave up, and I fell asleep. The next morning, I awoke unrested and struggled to get to work for the next few days. I prayed my coughing would subside because every movement caused severe pain.

I went out to dinner with some friends on Saturday and got home early. Exhausted, I went to bed. Around the stroke of midnight, I was awakened by an insanely sharp shooting pain running down my spine and into my thighs. I was completely paralyzed except for my arms. I wanted to call someone or 911, but my cell phone was about six inches out of reach. For several hours, I cried and contemplated, "*Will my children come home and find me? Will I ever walk again? Please, God, can you help me?*"

Around 5:00 am, I wiggled sideways and could barely pick up my phone. I called 911 and told the operator the situation. She explained she could send assistance. I would need to be able to open the door and let them in. Apparently, they are not allowed to break into your house unless it's burning down or something. The operator encouraged me to take deep breaths and open the door.

Finally, around 6:00 am, I heard the paramedics knocking. With a sudden burst of energy, I went downstairs, opened the front door, and fell onto one of the paramedics. They carried me to the couch and gave me an ice pack. I explained what happened. Much to my dismay, they could not do anything but give me a ride to the hospital. The ambulance transport was going to be a very expensive out-of-pocket copay, and since I was not paralyzed, I opted to stay home. So, they carried me back to my bed and left.

I scheduled a visit with an orthopedic surgeon. The x-ray showed I had three fractures in my spine, and my pelvic bone was several inches out of place. He gave me a laundry list of medications and told me to take them for six months and then return to see him. "*If these medications do not fix the problem, we will have to operate.*" I was frustrated and thought, "*Seriously, that's your only solution! Here, shove these pills down your throat; they will fix the problem. No, that is absolutely ridiculous!*"

Instead, I politely thanked him for his time and handed the list of prescriptions back to him. He jolted his head to the side and asked, "*Why?*" I replied, "*I am not interested in putting band-aids on my injuries and potentially creating more damage. I am willing to work through the pain. Do you have any other recommendations?"*

This slender, physically fit hiking enthusiast and an award-winning orthopedic surgeon smirked and jested, *"Oh, you are one of those. What would you recommend?"* as he removed the images of my fractured spine from the light source. I quietly thought to myself, *"Oh yes, I am one of those... Do I really need to recommend the physical therapy associates you share space with down the hallway and the acupuncture group you have working on the third floor, all of which are in your medical department? Seems rather obvious to me."*

I replied, *"How about a prescription for physical therapy and acupuncture so I have a lower co-pay?"* He politely agreed but warned I would still need surgery *if* I wanted to walk again. *"Oh, and may I please have a doctor's note to park in the garage adjacent to my building? My space is quite far away."* Again, he smiled and politely agreed, saying he would see me in six months.

As I was leaving his office, I thought to myself, *"Hmm, third time's a charm."* Furthermore, I would find a way to make these cars stop hurting me. It was like I was a magnet or something.

Paulo Coelho in The Alchemist wrote:

> *"Everything that happens once can never happen*
> *again. But everything that happens twice will*
> *surely happen a third time."*

I had lived through the prophecy and was determined to leave it behind. I remember being young and thinking a car accident would be the best way to die. Quick and easy, no long-term suffering for me or my loved ones. I no longer wished that ending upon myself. I was over it.

I wished to recreate my story and ending, which would not involve a car or an accident. My new affirmation: *I want to be old and sit on the porch in a rocking chair with the sun warming me while watching my grandchildren run up to hear my stories. I want to share my magical wisdom and talk story with people I love. Maybe one day, when it is my time to move onto the next realm, I will just quietly fall asleep and let nature take its course.*

Down Under

There is an old saying, *"Where there is an ending, there is another beginning."* Ending does not necessarily mean physical death; instead, it is a metaphysical end to what has run its course and something more beautiful is waiting to be born. My accident symbolized an ending for me while my daughter was finding a new beginning. We were miles apart, yet there was a bright umbilical cord of light connecting us in an alternative dimension that brought us closer to ourselves and each other.

Now that my baby had become a woman, she could experience the sights and sounds of a rich and vibrant life in the world. She was about to discover the vastness of wealth and abundance of her world, the universe within her bright and beautiful soul.

She went to Australia to work on an avocado farm. This delicious fruit has been revered for centuries as a symbol of love and fertility. These nutrient-rich delicacies grow in pairs and have influenced many cultures through art and stories. This delicious source of energy was the theme of the fourteenth month of the Mayan calendar and still holds spiritual significance in contemporary cultures. Avocados are widely used in traditional medicine and are commonplace at important milestones such as baptisms, confirmations, and weddings.

While the avocado farm enticed my daughter to venture to Australia, the avocado farmer was a bearer of false fruit and promises. Less than seven days in the land down under, the farmer showed his true colors and turned out to be a creeper. As soon as she told me about his unwanted and unprovoked sexual innuendo, I told her to get all of her belongings together and *"Leave now! We will figure it out."*

That day, my daughter left the farm and went to the city. Alone. All alone on the east coast of a wild and wonderful remote paradise. Most importantly, she wanted to figure out the isolation part of her life independently. She got a job cleaning at a hostel, which gave her a place to stay and allowed her to maintain her online class schedule. The first few weeks for her were emotionally brutal. Failure after failure was running through her head like wildfire.

As she watched the real wildfires blazing across the continent and causing mass destruction, she asked the universe, "*Why me? What was I made for?*" With an inner strength to survive, she learned to enjoy being alone. She learned how to meditate on a deeper level and wrote her musings in a journal. Shortly after being on her own, my daughter befriended a beautiful young girl with long flowing brown hair and mystical brown eyes who reminded me of a younger version of my daughter at the innocent age of seven. They cherished each other in so many ways.

The number seven is spiritually significant in most major religions in the world. It is a symbol of perfection and eternal life. It is seen as a spiritual pursuit when the higher beings ask you to shift your mind to prayer and gratitude as part of your spiritual practice. It promotes independence and isolation.

I thought back to when my daughter was seven as we were preparing for her First Communion. We were trying on dresses in the store, and she picked out her two favorites. Before showing me her selections, she asked, "*Do I look more like Audrey Hepburn or Judy Garland?*"

The first selection was simple but elegant, befitting the sophisticated and stylish flare reminiscent of Audrey. The white sleeveless silhouette dress perfectly complimented my daughter's tall and slender physique while a sheer white scarf hung halfway down her back. She wore my gold and pearl nuptial crown and my mother's white gloves during the ceremony. Watching my daughter eloquently receive this sacrament was a precious gift from God.

A month later, her school choir sang at a senior citizen center. During intermission, an older man was playing the piano, and she went up to request the song, Moon River. Audrey Hepburn originally performed the composition in the movie Breakfast at Tiffany's and won an Academy Award for Best Original Song.

Everyone in the room paused, and the energy changed when this bright, beautiful child requested such a simple but elegant song published forty-five years earlier. You could hear many enchanted voices singing along with memories from their past—the golden memories of a time gone by but not forgotten filled the room.

The song is a metaphor as it describes the wide river as a dream maker and a heartbreaker, all in the same line. It contemplates the delightful and disastrous outcomes of relationships throughout life. But whatever the outcome may be, the romantic sway of the moonlight glistening on the river still beckons the singer of life to follow their heart.

I remembered my daughter's enticing dance with the moon in Spain to serenade her fiery quest to overcome imposed societal shame and purposely choose a life of richness and beauty. But now, her alluring dance with the moon in Australia was a quiet and contemplative way to experience and love the world within.

The next time you crave a little guacamole or avocado toast, may you thank the ancient Aztec and Mayan deities for their quest to connect us with the world and ourselves in a powerful way. Then enjoy it, and make sure you don't forget the lime.

Here is a funny little prophecy to help you remember you can find your destiny in unexpected places: When I was pregnant with my daughter, I used to nonchalantly tell people I would deliver the baby in Australia. Of course, I got several different looks of curiosity and occasionally a *Why?*

I smiled and replied, "*Well, you know, she's going to be born down under, in the bush.*" Cheers, Mate!

Water Seeks Its Own Level

I had no idea I was suffering from empty nest syndrome. Analyzing my emotional state didn't seem appropriate since we didn't have a traditional family life. All I knew was that a voice was screaming in my head to change my life. So, as I was creating new long-distance relationships with my children and searching for a new career path, I met a guy who seemed to fill in some of the gaps for a few months. When he found out I had refused to date for two years, understandably, he inquired, "*Why?*"

I explained the gap was to give myself time to recover from the physical and emotional pain from my injuries as well as my extensional pain of terminating a relationship with my best friend. Basically, I wanted to feel free of those burdens before initiating a new relationship.

He assumed I was still in love with Tom and was somehow waiting to rekindle the relationship. I honestly couldn't give an *absolute* answer because we had not spoken a word to each other in over two years. In my mind, I knew our relationship was over. But inherently, I knew my heart needed proof.

One night, I met the guy at a local crab house. It was rush hour, so my trip took much longer than expected. Upon arrival, the only seat in the restaurant was the one he had saved for me. As I walked in his direction, I saw Tom in the mirror in the seat adjacent to mine! I scurried back into the corridor and felt a little dizzy. I frantically thought, "*Really! Which way do I go?*"

Just then, a lady asked me if I was all right. I briefly explained the situation, and we both laughed hysterically. She wished me luck as I gulped a shallow breath of air. I thought, "*I got this,*" and returned to my seat. I nervously sat down and put my entire backside towards Tom and turned white. As the guy put a glass of water in front of me, he asked what was wrong. I simply replied, "*The traffic made me anxious. I'll explain more later.*"

Minutes seemed like an eternity. Tom ordered a fresh beer and a shot of Jamison. I knew Tom would see me with the slightest turn of my body. I squeamishly leaned over to take a sip of water, and instantly, *"You're kidding me."* came barreling out of his mouth. He took a bunch of cash out of his pocket, threw it on the bar, and walked out. A few people commented, *"What's up with that guy?"* I shrugged my shoulders as if I had no clue in the world.

After a refreshing Long Island Iced Tea, I confessed the truth about the stranger who had abruptly left the bar. It all seemed to make sense. Feeling the truth that had eluded me for so long was invigorating. I no longer desired to be in an intimate relationship with Tom.

Within a couple of weeks, Tom called and asked if we could be friends again. He confided I was a part of his soul. Apart from his children, I was the *one person* he trusted the most in the world. We mutually agreed we did not want to date ever again. But we both desired to have our best friend back and experience the family we had chosen.

During the last few months before I escaped from Maryland during the Covid shutdown, Tom and I went to dinner a couple of times a week. He had just completed several rounds of surgery, so physically, he was not able to help me much with the house. Emotionally, though, he was perfect. He was so proud of me for making this huge move and commended me on regaining my health. He admitted being jealous and wished he could escape with me. He loves to say, *"I am your number one fan."*

So, the conundrum was how to properly engage in a ceremony befitting our shift. It was not an end; it was a new beginning. What was the best way to celebrate thirty-one years of genuine friendship and create new pathways for our *love* to grow? We decided to eat psilocybin mushrooms and hike through his favorite area of Gunpowder State Park.

The Gunpowder River was named for its abundance and subsequent wealth brought on by the saltpeter mined along its banks. Saltpeter is known for its mystical and mineral properties and is called the

Mother of Gunpowder. Before the discovery of chemical explosives around 1900, saltpeter was glorified as an inestimable treasure and coveted by governments and militia around the world.

I made a tonic of carrots, ginger, turmeric, and orange juice to mix with the mushrooms. We toasted a great friendship and to destinations yet unknown, and trust was the most important aspect of the day. I was in an area I had never hiked before and desired to feel safe. Time purposely slowed my motion and revealed passages between the tall trees, not all the trees, just some of the wise old oak and hickory trees that have graced the landscape for generations.

As I gently approached the curtains of energy between the trees, I reached out to feel my way through to the other side. Each time, the opposing side seemed familiar but new. The vibrations of the forest were exuberantly alive, and their echoes whispered permission for my safe passage. Tom walked ahead for a while, which allowed me to feel alone but fully connected to my surroundings.

On our way back to the truck, we noticed a large, flattened boulder in the middle of the stream and took a cool but comfortable seat. As the songbirds joyfully announced our presence, the reverent water rose to the occasion. I had always heard the expression *"water seeks its own level,"* but now I was experiencing it. Two souls existing in the balance of nature. The glistening illusion was unmistakable.

As our mystical journey was coming to an end, we drove through some of the most spectacular farmland I have ever seen. The crazy part was that panic took control of my heart. I was scared as hell and grasped the door handle as if it were my last moment on earth. I tried hiding my fear because I did not want to ruin his enjoyment. He took notice of my fear and helped me to understand my reasons for leaving. He knew me beyond all others and reaffirmed my *Why.*

He stopped by a convenience store before dinner. I chose to stay in the truck as he put on a song he had been saving for me. Instantly, my fear turned to sadness, and a deluge of cathartic tears streamed down my face. As the forlorn artist sings of regrets and apologies, he makes it abundantly clear that he would *"go back to the start."* Listening to Coldplay sing about how it was never easy, but nobody knew parting would be this hard must have known Tom and I set each other apart from the rest of the world.

We had a delightful dinner on the backside of a restaurant set perched high above the river's edge. We spoke about life and, hopefully, trying to reach our potential. He said he knew I was destined for greatness and that staying here would thwart the process. Throughout all our trials and tribulations, we remained friends. As the sun set over our adventure, we rejoiced the day and all of our tomorrows.

At his house, I remember looking at a bunch of empty beer bottles and saying, *"Just so you know, you can't drown your emotions in alcohol; those little fuckers can swim."* Then we put a movie on and waited to fall asleep. It felt nice to relax in the arms of my best friend. I have never really been able to define our friendship but maybe that's the point. I don't have to. It just exists.

CHAPTER 8

JOURNEY TO A NEW WORLD

It's Time

Apparently, when I encouraged my children to be independent and adventurous, they listened. Both said they had never heard the message *to stay*. When they expressed interest in staying, I told them they needed to go out and experience the world. Then, *if* they decided they wanted to return, they could. If you don't leave after high school, you probably never will. It's not good or bad; it's just a mindset.

Life is an adventure, and you need to go live it. See what the rest of the world looks like. Eat the food of other cultures, listen to their music, experience their ways, and go hiking. Figure out how we are the same and how we are different. Learn what you need to learn and move along.

I always said, "*When you two go off in the world, I am out of here.*" Well, now it was time to listen to myself. The only problem was I did not know where to go and had nobody to go with.

In my quest to explore the unknown, I searched for a job that could transfer with me until I could figure out where or why to go someplace different. I accepted a position with a local company that was expanding. This was a great opportunity, and the skill set and the prestige were highly transferable. I was set to start in March 2020. Honestly, check the date; you can't make this stuff up.

I was so excited for my *birth month* this year. I celebrate a birth month instead of a *birthday* because it is just plain old rude not to allow all your friends and family to spoil you for a month. It is just disrespectful not to partake in various celebrations for yourself when people want to feed you and give you presents. Come on! This is purely altruistic. Believe me! Stop being selfish and share in the fun.

This year, my actual birthday dinner with my children and some friends was on a Friday night. I made my Parmesan crostini, topped with paté, tomatoes, and capers for an appetizer. Then, I broiled my lemon ginger salmon with a side of coconut chia rice and broccoli for the entree. We had sparkling water and my special blend of absinthe cocktails. We ate a scrumptious carrot cake topped with a delicate cream cheese frosting for dessert, and played board games. I was on top of the world.

Special Note: Everyone who loves Absinthe has an Absinthe Story. I suggest you try it out for yourself. Please be careful; it is very strong and was originally created for medicinal purposes. The main ingredients consist of wormwood, anise, and fennel. It has a bright green color and was considered taboo for many years because certain types of wormwood contain thujone. However, it has been researched, proven safe, and used for centuries for people and animals. Artemisia Absinthium is the scientific name which has it's origin from the Greek Goddess Artemis.

Secret Recipe: 2 Parts Absinthe + 1 Part semi-sweet, white Vermouth + Ginger Beer over a tall glass of ice. Shake and enjoy. It tastes like the licorice-flavored Italian ice we ate as a kid from Good Humor.

Now, back to reality, or should I say a newly imposed reality. The following Monday, a strange virus shut down the world. That sounds odd; what does that mean? Are we shut down for a day, a week, a month? The next day, I contacted my future employer and asked what I should do. He said, "*I don't know. Why don't you give me a call in the next week or so.*" I thought that sounded reasonable.

Two weeks later, I called and asked what I should do. Again, he said, "*I don't know. Why don't you give me a call in a few weeks.*" I was feeling rather apprehensive and unsure of my future, but I still had a glimmer of hope this would all pass and I could begin work. A month later, I called to check in as requested. He replied, "*I'm sorry, I just laid off all my staff. I have no idea what I am going to do now.*"

Although I was shocked and disappointed, I understood. The entire world was shut down, and very few people seemed to have hope. But there was a voice deep down in my soul. It kept getting louder and louder and would not go away. The voice insisted, "*It's time.*" My brain asked, "*It's time for what?*"

I have been busy all day, every day, my entire life. From the moment I woke up until the moment my head hit the pillow, I was busy. If I wanted to make time for something, I made it happen. My life was all about the schedule and everything I wanted or needed to accomplish. I kept a calendar with shapes and symbols depending on the type of event. It was color-coded by person and location of the event. It entailed personal and professional activities and kept track of various events I may desire to attend. I didn't skip a beat, and I was always on time.

Now, I had all the time in the world. Now, I had time to pack up my life and start over. I jokingly laughed inside my head, "*Really, God, did you have to shut down the world to make me listen? I know I am stubborn, but this is over the top.*" The incessant voice grew louder and louder, "*It's time.*"

In life, many view the concept of time as an objective fact. Humans create timelines for their lives their daily schedules, and delineate parameters of what they can offer or expend. People refer to time as if you can buy, invest, or spend more time. On the contrary, if you receive, lose, or invest less time in something, it is deemed less important.

However, from a shamanic perspective, time does not exist as an objective truth. Moreover, the concept of time refers to consciously experiencing moments as if they are timeless. Have you ever been to dinner with someone as an obligation? Time seemed like a burden and took much longer than expected. But, have you ever had dinner with your best friend, and hours later, you had no idea how time flew by?

I have never been overly concerned with real-time. Moreover, I have been concerned with how I experience the time I have. I have not had a television in my *living* room since I left the marital home. If I was going to have limited time with my children, it was going to be quality time. Our living room was connected to our dining room and meant for living, not *staring* at a television screen.

Our living space was warm and comfortable while the music played. The lighting was dim, golden, and interspersed with candles. Our time was spent communicating or just being together. This concept did not always go over well with my children and their friends because kids love to watch television and play video games, which can seem like a vast wasteland. However, there is time and space for that in my house. Just not here, in our sanctuary, which was filled with things that made the mind wander.

One day, I found an antique mantle clock with the hands and the internal parts removed. It looked like it belonged in a children's adventure storybook. So, I put it in the living room near my stained-glass window with candles behind it. It was a curious and gentle reminder not to focus on the hands of time. Rather, it was time to focus on the love in the room and the light emanating from within time.

Now, I needed to figure out the objective timeline of my life along with the philosophical concept of *"It's finally my time."* I had never had this much time and probably never would again. *"Ok! I will pack up my house, sell it and move. Where? I have no idea! With whom? I have no idea! Why? Because I need to heal fully and not just be content. I need to be the person I was meant to be in this world."*

All I knew was that I wanted to be someplace warm. I jokingly told everyone I was moving to Hallmark town. I would find the most picturesque small town and magically stumble upon the most incredible yet modest local guy. Then we would rendezvous at the local coffee shop and somehow make the holiday town festival a huge success. Then, of course, live happily ever after.

For the next couple of months, I cleaned, packed, organized, and purged while following my motto, *"If in doubt, throw it out."* Don't get me wrong, this was *not* an emotionally easy process, and there were several saboteurs and helpers along the way. Most importantly, I was hopeful. While Covid was spreading poison throughout the world, I was creating my panacea.

The Plan

"If in doubt, throw it out" has been one of my favorite concepts and sayings for many years. My mom loves to quote me as she is amazing at giving simple-sounding advice to some of the most difficult problems in life. You can literally pour your heart out for an hour, and her one-sentence response of pure hearted wisdom is exactly what you needed to hear to proceed successfully.

When I cleared the houses of older people who had passed, it brought great despair, knowing the things they cherished most in life had little or no value to the next person. Pictures of unknown relatives tossed aside. Children's artwork buried in obscurity. Calendars detailing years of activity. Dried flowers gathered from an unknown adventure, handmade blankets eaten away by moths. You name it, cherished items discarded as unwanted trash.

In turn, I learned to save things that brought me great joy or served a purpose. The monetary value of the item had no intrinsic value. How I felt about the item determined the level of value. Since I don't like clutter, I had to be selective and creative. I had two beautiful glass front display cases within my French doors leading to my dining room. The cabinets became a treasure trough of magical little items that occupied space in my heart.

I have a decorated jelly jar filled with tiny notes from my children. I have rocks and leaves I collected on hikes. There are mementos from strong women who encouraged me to be myself—trinkets to connect me to my real friends and a beautiful array of greeting cards from my mother. I have two of the four wine glasses from my wedding toast because some things last forever, even though they are not what you expected.

Joyfully purging or packing up the past allowed new thoughts to enter my mind. In life, I had always had a plan. So, if I was genuinely going to recreate my life, maybe creating a plan was counterintuitive. I did not know what I did not know, but I was determined to find out.

I decided not having a plan was *the plan*. I packed up all my cherished belongings and made everything else disappear. I kept what I wanted from my children's bedrooms and asked them to remove or discard the remaining items. Physically and emotionally, this was no small task and did create a ruckus.

Within three months, my ninety-six-year-old house was clean, empty and restored. The permanent artwork added a mystical charm. The real estate agent encouraged me to change the warm shades of gold that made my home glow to shades of modern gray to attract young prospects. My answer was steadfastly "No." My home was enchanting and unique and anyone who wanted to live in a clipping from a trendy magazine didn't deserve to live in my house anyway.

Sorting through a lifetime of memories was an incredible way to honor the light they had brought into my world and to say goodbye to the house I called my home. I bought this house entirely on my own, and it was the longest time I had lived anywhere besides my parents' house. Acceptance of a well-lived life coupled with the anticipation of starting a new one was an alluring concoction of controlled chaos.

Saying goodbye to friends and family members was different. Some people stick by your side while others walk away. Some encourage you, while others tear you down. The encouragement part is relatively easy but emotional. The ordinary negative reactions weren't easy, but I knew they were coming. The unexpected slaps across the face and punches in the gut from the saboteurs were brutal.

Those unhealthy relationships trying to stop my progress were terminated, and I was blamed. Whenever someone offered destructive criticism, laughed in jest, or flat out lied, I pushed harder toward my goal. These saboteurs actually helped to reiterate the importance of a phrase I developed long ago, "*I would rather have nothing than a bad something.*"

Personally, abandoning the voices of the Mitote telling me I was going to fail was laborious. I continuously mitigated the arguments and found resolutions. Loving and nurturing the voices inside my head telling me to follow my path was scary but offered hope. I just needed to have faith in *the plan*.

The moment the former dream ended, I was not anxious or fearful. My soul was at peace and the only voice I heard inside my head declared, "*It is finished.*" I quietly bowed my head and prayed, "*Thank you. Yes, it is finished, and I am ready. I know you are preparing me for something bigger.*"

I knew the next couple of months in Maryland would be my last. It was a time for my soul to celebrate. Each morning as I awoke, I felt the Spirit within me. My visions had not come to fruition, but that was the point. She was my faithful companion. When the sun was shining brightly, the Spirit beckoned me to lift my face into the sky and feel the warmth of her touch. The gentleness of her hand caressed my cheeks as she guided me with patience. As the skies darkened and drenched the earth with rain, the Spirit held my hand as we joyfully jumped through the puddles of water and mud that had covered the earth. As I crawled into bed each night in hopes of a restful slumber, the Spirit wrapped her arms around me and whispered sweet melodies into my heart. She sang soothing lullabies of a journey yet unknown and invited the moon to enlighten our nightly path. Proudly, the moon shone through my window and asked me to trust the process.

Sometimes, the moon comes out to play with the sun in the heavenly blue sky. Each time I see them co-exist in my presence, the Spirit fills my soul and brings a smile to my peaceful lips. Instantly, my children are walking with me hand in hand. We are finding freedom together, my babies. I love you.

Our Forest

I took a job in Maryland that allowed me to move to North Carolina and work from home. I felt fortunate to find a job during the shutdown, but it was honestly the most boring job I have ever had. The first several months in my new location were literally cold, dark, and rainy. Almost everything in town had shut down by five o'clock, and everyone was still wearing face masks. Meeting new people was not an option due to the strict rules from Covid. I had never been so bored in my entire life.

In fact, I have rarely ever been bored and loved to playfully ask, *"Are you bored or are you boring?"* when people couldn't figure out what to do to entertain themselves. Weather permitting, I found lovely places to walk and explore. Then, I set my sights on finding the story behind the story of the land.

I lived five minutes from Wrightsville Beach and loved to start at the island's south end, walk up to the second pier, and then back down in time for sunset. Watching the surfers ride the waves in their long black wet suits was a great escape, especially during high tide. Dusk was spectacular as the sun appeared to set on both sides of the island and cast beautiful colors near a large stone jetty.

I stumbled upon Abby Nature Preserve while traveling up *the sound*. It's a charming historic area that was originally a peanut farm. More recently, it was a blueberry farm. As you meander through the old farm roads, you will see a stream that used to house the old grist mill. As you cross the wooden bridge, you traverse the old-growth and new-growth forests and the bottomlands in the floodplain.

You encounter a huge field of wildflowers and new-growth trees at the far end. The first time I passed the barrier gate, I could have sworn I saw the figure of a man wearing brown trousers, a white shirt, and a leather hat. It was like he was waiting for someone. The second time I saw this figure, I was intrigued and did a little research. Unfortunately, I only came up with a few names and old photographs.

Sound: A long and wide channel of water that connects two other bodies of water, such as the ocean. These sheltered wetlands are formed by islands or reefs and experience less wind and waves than the ocean. North Carolina has over 5,000 miles of inlet waters and has more sounds than any other state.

Along the Cape Fear River was an intriguing area known as Fort Fisher. It was the last standing confederate stronghold before the end of the Civil War. This earthen fortress looked and felt different than other forts I visited along the east coast of the United States. As I approached the beach area, the energy of the land was powerful. Upon research, I came up with a few colonial and Native American names and locations, but nothing substantial.

There is a navigational marker for river pilots known as Big Sugarloaf Dome, which has aided entrance into the Cape Fear River for centuries. This point is in Carolina Beach State Park and is home to the Venus Flytrap Trail. I was excited to find a few of these endangered species on my own. There are several carnivorous plants indigenous to this area, but I was unable to locate any more.

The Cape Fear River, plus its tributaries, winds through more than 200 miles of the Coastal and Piedmont regions of North Carolina and flows into the Atlantic Ocean near the old seafaring town of Southport. The name Cape Fear originated in 1585 from an expedition out of Roanoke Island and is the fifth oldest surviving place name in the United States. The river was key to transportation routes for colonial pioneers who encountered several thriving Native American tribes, including a few whose origins have fallen into obscurity and are collectively known as the Cape Fear Indians.

Also, I hiked around a few of the remaining Bay Lakes in the area; the largest is Lake Waccamaw, which means *"People of the Fallen Star"* and is the oldest lake in North Carolina. The descendants of the Cape Fear Indians may have joined this tribe, which was most likely associated with the Siouan Tribes, or they could have assimilated into the Peedee in South Carolina.

Bay Lakes are elliptical bodies of water stretching from Delaware to Georgia and are abundant in North Carolina. The hundreds of thousands of depressions that grace the landscape are natural water reservoirs with the same shape and geographic orientation. The origin stories of these lakes are plentiful, and researchers cannot come to a definite conclusion.

Most scientists believe these lakes formed when glaciers waxed and waned and created pockets of water. However, as the Waccamaw name implies, many believe these lakes formed when meteorites crashed down to earth. Today, many of them are boggy or dry. Over the years, they have been overrun with vegetation or drained. Look up several aerial views of bay lakes, and you decide.

Even though I found these sanctuaries, the question in my mind was, *"Why?"* What made this seemingly sparse area so beautiful and coveted for many generations? As far as I can tell, too many people came to this land of prosperity and saw an overabundance of natural resources. After less than 200 years and the many avenues of opportunity, this seemingly *endless supply* of natural resources dwindled into a situation of *ending this supply* of natural resources.

We are aware of what happened to the native and enslaved peoples in this area, but I do not want to get into that topic. That is a book in and of itself, and I am certainly not an expert on the subject. However, I think what happened to the Longleaf Pine Ecosystem is a good metaphor. This mindset is currently transforming the coast and pushing out the current inhabitants who have cherished this land for generations regardless of socioeconomic status, religion, or ethnic background.

Developers have a lust for money. Enough is never enough. There is no connection to the ocean, the land, or inhabitants. *High-dollar cotton* isn't just expensive; it's out of reach on purpose. They want you to leave so they can fill in the swamps that clean the water, cut down all the trees to build their houses, and put signs up to direct all people they deem less worthy to get the hell out of town.

High Dollar Cotton is a Southern colloquialism that means being highly successful. It originated when the cotton crop grew high and promised a good profit and less arduous work.

Long Leaf Pine Ecosystem: from the Coastal Plain of the east down through most of Florida and over near the Mississippi Alluvial Valley, the ~90 million acres of this endogenous forest, which was integral to the body of natural resources in which all peoples cohabitate had been shrunk to ~3 million acres. This is not a mathematical mistake. Approximately 97% of *our forest* had been decimated.

At the entrance to the Green Swamp Preserve, where I was able to hike through a long-leaf pine ecosystem and see numerous varieties of endangered plant and animal species, there is a sign with these two quotes from just after the American Revolution to just after the Stock Market crash that helps to explain the devastation in such a short period of time:

In 1789, when the thirteen original colonies finally became independent states, William Burton stated:

> "We find ourselves on the entrance to a vast plain which is
> mostly a forest of long leaf pine, the earth covered with
> grass, interspersed with an infinite variety of
> herbaceous plants, and embellished with extensive
> savannas, always green, sparkling with ponds of water."

In 1932, when the stock market crash reached its lowest value in the 20th century at 89% below its peak, B. W. Wells commented:

> "Not one of these great natural wonders, worthy of
> the name forest, remains intact within the state's borders.
> It has been rooted out by hogs, mutilated by turpentining,
> cut down in lumbering or burned up through negligence.
> The complete destruction of this longleaf forest constitutes
> one of the major social crimes of American history."

Unfortunately, as I wrote this chapter, much of the Green Swamp Preserve burned in a wildfire, and the park will remain closed for at least a year. Fortunately, this ecosystem benefits from periodic controlled burning. So, we shall see what the future may bring.

What we do to the forests and the water of our world simply reflects what we do to ourselves and our communities. Next time you see an elderly tree, take a short respite beneath its mighty branches and breathe in the fresh air. Listen to the birds and the insects while you admire the mushrooms and the lichens, which communicate to keep everything healthy and alive.

Next time you happen upon a lake or a stream, remember that our faces are reflected in the waters of life and that our eyes are a reflection of our soul. The miracles of life and growth are contingent upon our waters; if they are polluted, we are, too.

I remember the first time I peered into the red and golden waters of Lake Waccamaw. The mysterious nature of these crystal-clear waters with a native hue transcended my journey. They were unlike the blue and green waters where I had seen my face before. I knew I was on an ancient and sacred land. The anticipation of the journey back in time was alluring.

I walked twelve miles that day in search of remnants of the past. But to my dismay, I was unable to find any clues. When I returned to my car, I slowly drove around the lake, hoping to find some semblance of a time gone by, hopefully not forgotten. When I reached the end of the road, there was a small dam where I saw an elderly man fishing. *"Excuse me, sir, are you from here?"* The answer was yes, and I was excited. *"Are there any hiking trails or historic sites where I can learn more about the area?"*

He shrugged his shoulders and said, "Nothing I am aware of around here." I could not describe his expressions as being sad. It was more like he was carrying around a bundle of sorrow and did not know where to lay it down. He politely nodded and turned towards the lake before casting his fishing line. I solemnly returned to my car and decided to head back to the house.

Patience

I had been living in North Carolina for over a year, but it did not feel like home. I had not seen my children, friends, or mom in such a long time. Talking to them on the phone or via video was nice, but it does not replace the physical connection of love in person.

Within that year, I had kept in touch with some people and let others fade into memories. The ones I held close were my real friends and felt more like family to me. They felt like family before my move, but now, my feelings had been validated. My communications were sporadic because I was purposely trying to detach and start over, but I did not want to lose what was real and enduring.

Love doesn't comprehend time and space; it just exists. Further, I make it a point to let people know I love and appreciate them. If I magically died tomorrow, would anybody need to stop and think, *"Does Amy love me?"* The answer is *No* because my love would already be written on their heart.

This was the first winter holiday season without my children, which was a difficult feeling to swallow. I was determined to make it a happy season despite having no plan. One morning, I jumped out of bed and knew exactly what to do. I was going to make my own version of Thanksgiving and started to text my friends to figure out their holiday schedules.

Within a few days, my route of gratitude had formed: 10 friends in 10 days, plus my mom. It was fabulous! So many familiar faces filled with love, laughter, and companionship.

During my Christmas route, I was able to see some of them again, as well as a few others I missed the first time around. Even though my heart was filled with joy and these people were very important to me, I knew I no longer belonged here. My love remained even though my life was someplace else. Even though this new place did not feel like home, I was there for a reason.

I was determined to learn what I needed to learn and then move along. In my mind, three to five years seemed to be the voice I heard telling me to be kind and patient. I know patience is supposed to be a virtue, but impatience can be a pretty amazing companion sometimes.

Let's pretend you are standing in a burning building and have seconds to escape with your life. Do you desire to be kind and patient? *Nope.*

Imagine you made a succulent feast and asked 40 guests to arrive by 2:00 pm, and one guest insisted on bringing an integral part of the meal. Then, that guest was nowhere to be found and frivolously and unapologetically showed up well after dessert was served. Would you be kind and patient? *Nope.*

What if you have ten monumental tasks you need to accomplish this week, and someone you need to accomplish the first task responds, "*Huh—no big deal. I'll get there when I get there. I may have some time at the end of the month. Just send a reminder.*" Does it behoove you to be kind and patient? *Nope.*

I could come up with a million reasons why being patient had not been virtuous in life, and now I was asking myself to be kind and patient for some unknown reason. If I had known *Why* and *When* it may or may not come to fruition, I probably would have been a little more patient.

Either way, I continuously told myself, "*Be kind, Amy. Be patient, Amy. Let life happen.*"

One of the best parts about being in a new place and cherishing your old friends as well as new acquaintances was that many of these voices told me the same things about myself. "*Look at all the adversity you have overcome. Look how much you are healing. You are stronger than you think you are. You are brave. Of course, you need to be patient. God has a plan.*"

In turn, I tried to let go of the forward-thinking motion of my brain and focus on thinking about right here, right now. This moment in time will never happen again. I need to cherish each moment as an opportunity to learn more about the overall plan.

Journey down every passage and peek inside every door. If it looks good, go for it. The moment you realize the chosen corridor is not destiny, be thankful. Then, turn around and start again. But this time, you will have more wisdom in your pocket. Each and every time a door closed in my face, I thought, "*Whew, one more down, who knows how many more to go. Yeah, me.*"

Initially, I felt uncomfortable. As time progressed and door after door closed in my face, I became disillusioned. This struggle to unravel the life I had created was a difficult task. Fortunately, at the end of the day, I still had myself. I knew who I was, and I just needed to figure out *where* I was going and *why*.

I longed to find a spiritually based community where I felt comfortable. I was under the impression I would find people whose belief system complimented mine, and I would be able to expand my knowledge base and my wisdom. I do enjoy being alone, but this experience was a bit much.

I remember reading, "*When the Student is ready, the Teacher will appear.*" Simply, we can only learn lessons when we are ready, willing, and able to learn. However, "*When the Student is truly ready, the Teacher will disappear.*"

I thought, *"Does this mean I am ready to be the Teacher? Does this mean I am the Student becoming the Master? Does this mean my hands are ready to help create the healing I wish to see in the world?"*

One notion biting at me was the elusive shark's tooth I desired to find. The megalodon teeth that were given to me by a fisherman were a lure to bring me to a place in life where I did not want to be. The second shark's tooth was actually a shell and led me to danger. So, I thought, maybe I had been looking in all the wrong places, not just for shark's tooth, but for a job to restart my life.

Through LinkedIn, I made a few local, national, and international acquaintances and explored opportunities within and outside my region. Technically, I thought this location could be my home base as I ventured out into a new vocation.

As I was settling into my new house, life took an unexpected and amazing turn. The elusive dream job was local and would be coming into fruition within the next few months. Then, I met a guy who seemed perfect for me, but his timeline in life was a little off-kilter and would most likely be realigned within the next few months. Maybe this entire situation was why I had been primed for *patience*.

As I enthusiastically walked around the lake near my house, I thought, *"Awesome! Count me in."* I had some time to fill, so I needed to figure out what to do to feel happy and productive until everything came to fruition. Many people during my life suggested writing a book. Was it finally time?

The Week Before Christmas

I felt my plan was set, and patience would guide me. I felt deep calmness and purpose in my solitude. Although there was lingering sadness, I was learning to be joyful by embracing my sense of sadness as I progressed. I had gained several months of life to devote to a respite from the busyness of life. I had time not to worry and rush around. I had time to share my knowledge and wisdom purposely. I had time to write a book in peaceful contemplation of a time gone by but not forgotten. This was my musing that started it all:

"The busyness of the world has sustained my existence for so long.
When I leave that world, the mountains and the sea fill
my soul for brief and fleeting moments.
I see beauty in God and in Nature.
But, when the light turns into dark, I am still alone.
Alone in a world of solitude without meaning.
Alone in a world I created and want so desperately to escape."
~Amy

Withstand the Storm

I knew I needed to make this quote more robust. The question was, how do I expand upon this quote and make it a story? I wanted to create something that felt intelligent yet mysterious. I did not want it to sound silly or immature. Properly engaging was of the utmost importance, and I had an idea.

It had been a long time since I experienced a healing ceremony, and I wanted to open new corridors. One corridor I wished to explore was my ability to write down the stories in my heart and guide them with my soul. A package arrived, and when I opened it, my adrenaline was pumping. The inside wrapper read, *Golden Teacher*. I smiled and thought, *"Of course, it is time to teach myself."*

To celebrate the new year, I made a safe plan to explore my inner thought processes with these mushrooms. I did not want to be confined to my house, and I did not want to confide in anyone else. Few people were aware of my healing methods, and I wanted to keep it that way. Why? Because the dreams of many overshadow the truth and judge others who choose an alternate path.

I wore warm clothes and set my chair up on the beach. I brought a blanket and a few bottles of water. This experience would take several hours, and I wanted to be comfortable. The sky was blue, and the wind was crisp as a few clouds started to roll in. After a short while, I felt a change in the energy of the tide. Within the next twenty minutes, most people on the beach were departing.

As the beach dwellers dissipated, an intensely large and dark cloud swept up the coast and covered most of the area. Soon, this ominous sky dragon grasped the wind with brute strength and enticed me to stay. The sand was whisking around like an hourglass suspended by the hands of time. Each grain of sand destroying manmade delusions of grandeur served a purpose as they pelted my exposed skin.

I secured my hat and sunglasses and wrapped myself in the blanket to ensure I would be safe. As I looked around at the few brave souls left on the beach, I thought, "*This is going to be absolutely incredible if I don't die. I am prepared to withstand the storm.*"

My view of the earth was of a flattened disc floating within the expansive universe. I was at the center of the disc, and it was not my time to venture any further. It was time to immerse myself in the deep and mysterious water and understand we are all waves in one ocean of life. I was neither in the water nor away from the water. I was simply, elegantly, and profoundly with the water.

I envisioned my children running up and down the beach while diving into the waves of divine turbulence. *"My sweet and beautiful babies, look at you so happy and carefree. I have been trying to share the beauty I see in the world with you for years."* These tumultuous waves are here to break the unhealthy cycles and restore balance and harmony within our worlds.

I cannot heal your wounds; I can only show you what I have learned. Then, you can heal yourself.

That Christmas, I bought both children a necklace as a spiritual symbol of my love. I wanted them to know I was always with them. I included a shell, a candle, and some Palo Santo in the package. My hope was that they could reconcile the past and build a new future. One version of the story must die for the next version to come to life.

As the rejuvenating ocean mist sanctified my soul, each intense burst of sunlight pierced through the menacing creature in the sky. As this messenger skillfully absconded back into the light, darkness subsided. Peacefully, I understood the storm was over. I sat with myself for a while and let the medicine continue its path. This juncture of my journey was coming to an end, and it was time to move along. Metaphorically, I did not know where I was going. All I knew was that I could not stay here.

That week, I discovered how to write my introduction post for LinkedIn. I sat down at the computer ready to go. But, only a few short frustrating sentences made it onto the screen. I was disappointed and needed to figure out how to approach this new corridor in a different way. That evening another storm was brewing so I went and sat near the pier on Wrightsville Beach where the surf is high.

I invited the Goddess of The Wind which embodies the song, dance, and chant to come, sit down, and talk story with me. *"He aloha mele, pretty Hoku"* cleanse my thoughts with the ebb and flow of the tide. As words and phrases entered my mind, I texted them to myself. I stayed until the cold became too much of a burden. I went back to the house and took a long hot shower. Before bed, I sipped on a fresh brew of sage and ginger root tea as the remnants of the storm sang me into a peaceful slumber.

The next morning, I awoke to the birds singing outside my window. The storm had passed, and it was time to begin a new day. After breakfast, I quickly transcribed my texts and completed my introduction post. I sent a copy of my musings to my children and received very positive feedback.

The following day when I hit *post,* I shed a few tears of joy as well as fear. Initially, my breath was controlling my fear but soon that pit inside my stomach turned to a sense of excitement coupled with a sense of uncertainty. Who knew this allusive little metaphor for life would receive over 12,000 views. My fingers and toes were numb as I responded to every comment for several days.

Uncovering the magic that had always been inside of me was such an amazing gift. Most importantly, a gift I had given myself. My brain was buzzing as I exclaimed, *"Ok! What do I do now?"* I received a lot of direct messages of praise as well as encouragement. I received an invitation from a man who read my post and invited me to be in his group. I had no idea what it was but it looked intriguing, so I explored his **BIZCATALYST360°** website.

I felt a whirlwind of joy, confusion, fear, and delight. Then, I thought, *"I am not a writer."* I am not sure how I will be able to hold my own with all these published authors. I was confused and apprehensive. I did not understand why or how I would fit into the group.

What I did understand is that I had met a brilliant man and along with his wife, they were on a mission. They created a platform to change the world and I had been invited to participate. One other thing that was elusive to me was that this community is not your typical networking group. Moreover, it is like a loom where you net-weave yourself into a community where you genuinely belong in the fabric of life.

Dennis J. Pitocco; Chief Reimaginator 360° Nation: *"If we are serious in our quest to rediscover humanity at its best, then our job is to "walk the talk" today and every day, doing our best to figure out what the world is trying to be — and then help the world be that, be better, and be even more. The world depends on every single one of us, showing up and being present, as best we can, in our imperfect radiance. We will be better humans, building a better future together, when we take stock not just of how we change the world, but how we treated each other and ourselves along the way."* Thank you for believing in me. You and your creation has significantly altered my life. I am eternally grateful. Below is my first short story and why we met.

The Unchartered Course to Discovering Magic

"The busyness of the world sustained my existence for so long.
When I left and ventured into the mountains, my soul was filled
for a few brief and fleeting moments.
Surrounded by people, I am alone in a world of solitude.
Alone in a world I created and want so desperately to escape.
The voices of the mountains chanted my name.
My heartbeat was but one instrument creating the wondrous
and magical songs of nature.
Trekking over jagged peaks and dredging through swollen
valleys was my refuge. The intrepid warrior living behind
my eyes continued.
My trials were a kaleidoscope of colorful passages opening
and closing before my eyes, eventually leading me to a brand new
but strangely familiar place—a place I did not want to be.
In another part of the world, the seal and the turtle
were creating new dreams. In my world, the hawk and
the heron beckoned me to the sea.

Discard your existence and breathe in the salty air.
Purify your thoughts and allow the power of the sun
and the tides to rejuvenate your soul.
The shark encouraged me to dive deep into the unknown
and warned the charts have long been discarded and the perils
ever abound. Follow your heart and the promise of the maiden
journey shall be golden and profound.
Stay true to the unchartered course.
Allow yourself to discover the magic."
~Amy

In Dis Life

Fourteen years after leaving my marriage, I sit at my computer contemplating my book. At the end of each chapter, I shed a few tears. The tiny droplets that fall from my eyes are solemn acceptance that we are supposed to suffer tragedies and God only asks us to carry what we can endure. When I look back into the devastation scorched earth caused, I realize the purpose was vast and wondrous.

I have returned to the person God intended me to be. However, I am richer, fuller, and wiser than I could have ever been if I would have stayed in my marriage. I know the day my love for my husband left me and I know it will never return.

When I hear our wedding song, I can see his face mourning from across that board room table when I presented the plastic business card from Couples Therapy we taught together. What a drastic change our relationship had endured as he undeniably knew my love for him had ended. What he didn't realize was that was the year I started to fully love myself. It was the year I wanted to be completely *Amy*. Unfortunately, his goal was to steal that from me. I still feel an intensity of fear deep inside my soul when I hear his name. The unfathomable torture he put me through changed me.

We will never be friends or speak to each other unless absolutely necessary and pertaining to the children. I am able to look back and cherish the memories and the amazing children we created together. I can look back and continue forward and remember Israel Kamakawiwoʻole sing, "*If it all falls apart I will know deep in my heart In Dis Life I was loved by you.*"

Some words that independently came out of the mouth of both my children on separate occasions haunted me for years. "*Mommy, you shouldn't have left, you could have saved Daddy.*" They were right in one respect, I love to fix things, all kinds of things. But, after years of abuse and neglect, I decided I couldn't or wouldn't continue to try to save him any longer. He needed to save himself.

In traditional Hawaiian hula, there is a guiding hand gesture called *Kekuhikuhialakaiʻi*, which means, "*Let me show you the way.*" Let me teach you what I have learned. Let me help guide you through the journey the universe intended for you to take and be the person you were meant to be. I cannot fix you. I can only show you the way.

Anybody can pick up a book full of words to *tell* you how to live a beautiful, brave, and authentic life. But how many people actually live those words? How many of those people can *show* you the way?

How many people have walked through hell and looked Darkness straight in the eyes and said "*Get the fuck out of my way*"… many I am sure. How many of these people have surpassed these events and come out happy, peaceful, and wise souls? Well, these are the types of people you want to follow. These are the people who have developed deep wisdom through experience, and who evolve our history.

Over the years, many people have inquired why I never sought revenge: the divorce, the accidents, the respiratory illness, and the working conditions. From my perspective, revenge would automatically make me a vengeful person. To seek out revenge and desire ill will towards another is counterproductive to leading a happy and healthy life.

Anger and revenge are ugly companions who rent space in your mind. If I desire those poisonous playmates to vacate the premises, I need to replace them with love and fortitude. I need to be courageous to overcome the pain of adversity. I need to embrace the journey, after all, it's mine.

This type of inquiry always reminds me of a discussion I was involved in about Dinah's story in the Old Testament. I do not think the story necessarily teaches this lesson, but this is what came to fruition in our group. So, I am going to retell it in my own condensed version and let you know why I refer to this emotional tug of war as a *Dinah Issue:*

Dinah went into the city and had intimate relations with someone of royalty. Her father, Israel and her 12 brothers were enraged and insisted they marry. This was customary for the time period. However, some of the brothers customarily *"turned the other cheek"* and looked the other way even though they did not feel vindicated.

On the flip side, some of the brothers sought revenge as afforded by custom, *"an eye for an eye."* This source of anger caused tremendous upheaval in the communities and the revenge permanently changed history. Ultimately, all of the brothers' minds were filled with dis-ease and they separated into 12 conflicting tribes.

So, when I am conflicted with the dilemma between *turning the other cheek* and *an eye for an eye*, I choose *None of the Above*. Why? Because I am not willing to live in a place of dis-ease. I am not going to ignore a situation nor am I going to seek revenge. I am going to step out of the situation and find alternative solutions. All this sounds quite wonderful and fanciful, but it is usually a burden in and of itself. Ultimately, this will make everything work out better in the long run.

For example, I worked with a woman whose position far exceeded her capabilities. Further, she learned how to work *the system* to avoid work as much as possible. She loved instigating a fight, and when her behavior was questioned, she immediately ran to human resources to report an incident *"against her."*

If her behaviors did not directly affect people's work, most chose to turn the other cheek and ignore her provocations. Initially, I did ignore her. But, when her antics got several very well-respected people into trouble, I took action. I kept a log of her behaviors to show her patterns and methods over time. I notified my superiors of the log. Why? Because I knew one day I would need it to protect myself. She was positioning herself to cause problems in my life.

When tempers rose and incidents occurred, it was a *he said, she said* battle of words and that was not something I wished to engage in. You do not have to justify the truth, but you do need to justify the lies. So, the day she entered my office without permission and closed the door behind her, I knew the moment had come. I listened to her abusive tirade and allowed her to physically threaten my space. Then, I ensured every word that came out of my mouth was 100% truthful and spoken with respect.

Instead of waiting for her to run to human resources with some bogus story, I went directly to the top. I sat in the corporate suite until someone was able to meet with me. I told my version of the story, and instead of attacking her, I stated, "*I do not feel safe,*" which was 100% the truth. I requested security and not revenge. From then on out, the only thing I needed to prove to get my desired response was to define why I did not feel safe. The remaining part of the story was left up to human resources and her next employer.

Strength with Grace

The only way to win is to step out of the game. I don't mean to step out of the game and surrender in defeat. I mean, change the game. Do the unexpected. Do the right thing.

Most games in life are power struggles. Physical, emotional, or spiritual games are a perpetual tug of war that causes internal and external strife. These uncomfortable or aggressive competitions for power guide many aspects of our everyday lives with or without our knowledge or consent.

In my quest to describe an extremely important concept of control, I discovered the word *hegemony*. This concept is indicative to all modern societies and has a gradual and pervasive harmful effect.

This system of control is dependent upon an imbalance of power and compliance is expressed as a mutual and reciprocal understanding of the perceived truth. However, it is the truth the other person has created and wants you to believe. Ultimately, this version of the truth benefits them, leaving you feeling disempowered, frustrated, and angry.

In my opinion, people are seldom controlled by an overt overriding and dominating force. Rather, the controlling factors are information and ideas made available and legitimized by those in power.

We seem to adhere to a specific set of norms and values and to reject others because we have been taught to do so since birth from our families of origin and external influences. Other forms of power such as the television, politicians and people of authority indoctrinate our minds through very specific ideologies. The overt and covert messages sent via schools, places of worship, corporations, the political and legal system, and mass media are integral to the plan.

To add insult to injury, conflicting or divergent ideas or plans of action are either ignored or discredited by the exact same sources who already possess power over us. It is easier to maintain the status quo when most people believe the status quo was developed with everyone's best interest in mind.

This indoctrination happens so frequently and from so many sources it catches many unsuspecting victims clearly by surprise if they ever acknowledge it at all. Without discernment, many believe their knowledge is common sense. As Benjamin Franklin remarked, "*Common sense is not so common.*"

Consider this analogy: When a doctor taps your knee with the rubber mallet, your leg automatically kicks out with a knee-jerk response. You don't have to know why or how, it just happens. You can see the same knee *jerk* responses when people divulge their viewpoints in an equally unthinking way.

Hegemon: the acknowledged leader. This person knows when to lead and when to assign roles of leadership to diffuse power struggles. The situation they create is still within their sphere of influence.

Hegemony: the ability to lead or dominate. A person in this position is perceived to be the strongest and most powerful and therefore able to control others. This position is contingent upon being proactive and charismatic. This type of leadership is dependent upon consent over coercion. The art of hegemony strives for the moment an individual relinquishes control and gives permission to the leader. Ultimately, the leader is viewed as an authority figure and is no longer questioned.

On a macro level, **Hegemony** can basically be broken down into three categories:

Hard Power: where one country has military dominance and resources over another country. On a micro level, this would be a power struggle with the *playground bully*. I am bigger than you. I am stronger than you. I am louder than you. This is my playground, so you better do what I say or else.

Let's face it, power struggles with the *playground bully* are boorish and obtuse. After all, I think we have progressed a bit beyond those survival of the fittest Neanderthal days. Haven't we? But be careful, some of these cave dwellers have evolved and learned to use modern tools instead of sticks and stones.

IE: In social media and television, there is a blurred line between news that follows professional and ethical standards of excellence and news entertainment. Institutions have an agenda and desire to be in control. If you challenge these institutions, they will destroy you through misinformation and disinformation. Controversy spreads like wildfire and can instantly destroy people's lives. But the bully doesn't care, and more views means more money and prestige.

I am sure you know a few people who love to run around and spread fake news about you in order to maintain their perceived control. What is their motivation? How do you handle it and why?

Structural Power: the economic prowess of a dominant country to create economically viable solutions to support the subordinate countries and maintain control. On a micro level, it is usually the person who has more money or is financing the situation. If they sign the checks, they are in charge.

Power struggles with the *rich kids on the playground* threaten your family structure, your job, and your life. It's a shame they do not see anything but their own perceived economic value. Honestly, I doubt if they care. They love to dangle rewards in your face to see how far they can suck you into the game.

IE: In the corporate world, many believe whoever has the most financial resources at the end of the game is the winner. They value progress over people and feel employees are expendable. If the overall purpose is to make money and you speak out against the person who controls the money, you will most likely get fired or set up to quit. However, if you buy into the system, ignore unethical behavior and maintain a dog-eat-dog mentality, you will receive personal and financial accolades and incentives.

When was the last time you kept your mouth shut at work, or better yet, when did you challenge the person with the finances? Either way, how did you feel when the situation occurred, and how were you forced to feel in subsequent encounters?

Soft Power: This is where the cultural institutions of the dominant country impose behavior control over the weaker countries that favor the social and economic interests of the dominant country. On a micro level, this would be the popularized social group norms. Powerful and seductive cultural movements where the *cool kids on the playground* can override entire systems.

The *cool kids* can be fun to hang out with. They wear trendy clothes, frequent global franchises, and dictate our music, movies, and media choices. They are the trendsetters, and jumping on the bandwagon with them may be exciting at first. But when agendas change and the sources of money shift, so does their mindset. Where do you think the money to support their lifestyles comes from anyway?

IE: Being considered a cultural icon consumes time, money, and energy. Every person at the top is just one step away from falling short and allowing the next person to move ahead. These influencers need to be highly vigilant and adaptive because they can be swiftly and assuredly stabbed in the back by friends, family, colleagues, and strangers. The agendas of those who want to see them rise or fall may vary greatly, but understanding that motivations always exist is of vital importance.

Consider any of your favorite celebrities in music, movies, sports, or television. What was their personal struggle to make it to the top? What types of hard power and structural power aided their struggle? Now that they are at the top, what cultural institutions covet their influence over the population? Do companies sponsor them to sell their products? Do clothing manufacturers dictate what they wear? Do politicians and economic leaders elicit their support?

Think back to high school. How were the cool kids treated differently, and why? Did the teachers call them out to put them down or make them rise to the occasion? What type of personal gain did the cool kids get as opposed to the type of personal gain the teachers got? Where are those kids now?

Hard Power and Structural Power walk hand in hand with Soft Power on the playground, whether you witness their behavior or not. These people love to create games that use subtle and covert methods to manipulate and maintain control over others. It is a skill they develop that is strengthened the longer they get away with it. Often, their entire lives.

Understanding Soft Power is packed full of charisma and may be used in a myriad of ways to bolster consent without awareness. It gives us insight into how we can respond to the antics thrown our way. It can entice your soul and stab you in the gut while whimsically decorating the playground equipment for the entire community to enjoy.

My outline of this aspect of interaction between people is certainly not a call to action to disrupt the structure of our society. Moreover, I am simply trying to stimulate your mind and ask you to consider the amount of control exerted over us daily on multiple levels of existence.

Now, close your eyes or draw a picture and imagine you are standing inside the eye of a hurricane:

The spiral where you stand is seemingly safe while the powerful winds twisting around you are exerting their control. If you want to remain safe, stay in place and be silent. Be aware you are in the eye of the storm and navigate the passages carved out by those who enforce control around you.

These forces will supply adequate food and clothing if you comply. They will provide adequate shelter and social activities if you comply. If you comply, they will help you raise your children and care for the sick. If you comply, these forces will help you live a life of constant disease and make it sound like a utopia. How does this compliance feel?

After you contemplate what I have shared and taken the time to observe the world around you, I encourage you to take a giant leap out of the eye of the hurricane. Understand the great beauty as well as the destruction that these winds of change continuously create. Most importantly, do not step out of the eye of the hurricane with Anger or Vengeance. It is best to step outside the storm with Love in your heart.

Once your awareness broadens or heightens, take a look around. Experience the world from the vantage point of Freedom. Through a newfound Love of Freedom, you can experience Strength with Grace. Just breathe deeply and admire the landscape. The rest will take care of itself.

Be a Good Human

When I feel the misuse or abuse of hegemonic power is directly affecting me, I am not willing to sit back and be in a position of subordination.

This is my personal territory, and if you cross the line, I will swiftly and assuredly knock you down. Many people have experienced the backlash of trying to control me as I stood my ground. Unfortunately, a positive outcome was not always the result.

Subordination is the opposite of hegemony: The act of ranking someone or something as less important. A subordinate is seen as less than the authority figure and ultimately deemed an inferior servant.

As a child, I was curious and respectfully asked questions. Then, when the statements did not make sense, I made observations to point out what needed to be considered. My inquiries came from a place of innocence. I was unaware I was challenging authority. I simply thought I was doing the right thing.

It isn't easy to give precise examples because I had great relationships with most of the adults in my life. However, one example happened repeatedly, and I had to point out the problem. When the teachers made seating arrangements, I had to sit by the boys who got into trouble. The teachers used me to help control the boys, but it was unfair. All my friends got to sit together and enjoy the day.

When I pointed out this situation to the teachers, some were bothered. I just wanted to be treated fairly, and they wanted to make their lives easier. In fact, this exact situation happened with my daughter in elementary school, and I had to speak to her teachers regularly.

As a teenager or young adult, I still felt inclined to do the right thing, but my observations were not always purely innocent. I knew my curiosity and line of inquiries made some people feel uncomfortable. I also knew many people agreed with me and remained silent. So, I felt I needed to learn when and how to express myself accordingly.

Sports became an appropriate outlet for my need to learn the art of being skillfully assertive. Basketball has always been my favorite sport; stepping out onto the court changes me. I feel graceful and elegant as well as strong and aggressive. The roll of the ball in my fingers and the crack of the net uniquely transform my soul.

The Biggie Under the Basket: This metaphor came to fruition for me at a young age and has stuck with me through adulthood. Before basketball games, the opposing teams, their coaches, and the referees sized up the opposition. I would do my regular warm-ups on my side of the gym as expected. Anytime I sensed the competition was going to be unsportsmanlike, I always knocked out a few three-pointers and smiled at the onlookers. Why? Because I knew what was coming and I was prepared.

Within the first few minutes of the game, the most aggressive opposing player would charge into me, attempting to intimidate and cause pain. Instead of trying to play the game fairly, they just wanted to hurt me and force me to cower in fear. If I did not stand up for myself, the physical abuse would perpetuate throughout the game, and I would suffer greatly. I did not allow anyone to see my pain. I held it inside.

In turn, I learned how to take the charge. I posted up when I knew the biggie under the basket was coming for me. Both feet were planted, shoulders in line, and arms crossed at my chest. BAM! Those players would hit me with all their might. Often, they hurt more than I did, and occasionally, they would fall. Then, I would look as if I was sorry we collided. It must have been an accident. Right? My skill set versus their brute strength. Oops again, sorry. It may hurt, but I am still going to win the game.

However, I will admit that sometimes, I purposely made observations that I knew would irritate the authority figure. It made me giggle because I had won the silly little power struggle they had created. Knowing that others agreed with me and joined in on my laughter was fun.

Once, I was in a pool hall with some friends, and I beat the playground bully and won control of the table. He was angry and started to run his mouth to instigate a fight. He intended to scare me and force us to return the table to him and his obnoxious friends. Two of my male friends were anxious to retaliate physically, but one stopped and said, "*Let her handle it,*" because he saw that look in my eyes.

I hoped to diffuse the situation by making an irritatingly simple but accurate statement. In my best playground voice, I exclaimed, "*You must have diarrhea of the mouth. It just keeps running and running and running."* Whew, boy! He was enraged, but his obnoxious friends became amused. The more he ran his potty mouth, the more his own friends laughed at him. Then, the other patrons joined in the laughter. Ultimately, he left the bar, and everybody enjoyed the rest of the evening.

On the flip side, when the subordination became abusive, I helped to diffuse the situation with facts. When the facts didn't obtain the desired result, my kind, respectful, and poised way of dealing with a situation became assertive and occasionally aggressive. Basically, when people trapped me in a corner, the only way to escape the power struggle was to *fight fire with fire*—doing the right thing transformed from more of a feminine methodology to more of a masculine one.

When I coached basketball, a player did not show up for practice for almost a month but showed up to the game with her father. All my players played 50% of the game most of the time, although I was only required to play them 12.5%. If there were open spaces, I filled them in with the players who exerted the most effort during practice. It was fair and logical and made our team successful. On this day, I allowed the player to play 25% of the game and explained it was due to attendance, and she accepted my answer gracefully.

After the game, her father initiated a verbal onslaught to attack me from across the gymnasium. I respectfully explained the situation, and his onslaught revamped history and brought up irrelevant issues. Then, my demeanor changed, and I aggressively told him he had one of two options: *"One, you can show up and help me coach my team. I am there twice a week for two hours with games on the weekend, and there is an open gym for three hours on Friday nights."*

He was infuriated and requested the second option. I replied, *"You can simply show up to open gym and play me one-on-one. Then we will see who has more skills."* Whew, boy! He was hot, *"I don't have time for that shit"* and stomped away. When he arrived Friday to pick up his daughter, I was standing near half-court. I could see him looking at me from the corner of my eye. I took a couple of dribbles, and BAM! Hit a three-pointer. At the end of the season, I firmly shook his hand and thanked him for allowing me to coach his daughter. He may not have liked me, but I gained his respect.

As an adult, I understand that provoking authority figures and giving rise to specific emotions or reactions is not advantageous to my goal of doing the right thing. I knew I needed to refine my skill set to gracefully step outside the eye of the hurricane and achieve my desired results.

Doing the right thing does not necessarily equate to more money, prestige, or popularity. Often, it means to stand alone. When you stand alone, others *do* notice, respect you more, and may join you.

In my opinion, about a third of the people will agree with you, while another third may disagree. Honestly, the last third doesn't care one way or another. I feel that most issues in the world fall into the same categories. So why stress yourself about a third of the people who may want to oppose you? You probably don't care for them very much anyway. So, it's no big loss.

I am absolutely sure my opposition thought I was a complete bitch, and often called me many such names. But really? Please. Come up with something original. Come up with something I don't already know about myself. Survival is a life skill, and it may look masculine at times. I don't care. I saw bitch as an art form, and if you want to go there, I am game to play. But don't run and cry when I win.

I am graceful whether I win or lose the game in fair play. A good game is a good game, and the winner earns their position. I would never take that away from anybody. In fact, I appreciate a great athlete and intense competition. After all, we are children playing a game. It is supposed to be fun and educational. Why in the world would anyone want to purposely hurt a young girl playing a game she loves the most? Why would anyone want to adulterate life lessons through a game for children?

After my second car accident, I no longer had the time, energy, or desire to be competitive. My body had been in pain for years, and the thought of any more pain made me panic. My go, go, go, be your best all day, everyday attitude transformed into a *just do what makes you happy* outlook on life. Pain, control freaks, and mean people do not make me happy. Being subordinate definitely sucks.

Again, I needed to redefine and refine what it meant to be a good human and do it without the pain and suffering of taking on the biggie under the basket. I was done taking the charge on the basketball court, in the boardroom, or in my personal endeavors.

If you desire to be a good human and are unsure how to take the first step, try this next exercise. I encourage you to ask others for descriptive words in each category. But, after you have the lists, I think it would be more advantageous to discover these energies within yourself, on your own, before you process them with others. Please ensure you interact with people who will add value and constructive comments to this exercise. Destructive comments will burden your self-assessment.

Visualize or sketch two balls of energy. Take those balls and elongate them into strands of energy with one strand on each side of you. Connect them together with perpendicular sections of life like a step ladder. Allow them to twist and turn around. Take what you need from each side and each step as you encounter each new experience. This is your own metaphorical DNA.

Masculine Energy refers to characteristics that *predominantly* describe men: strength, power, courage, bold, independent, assertive, competitive, daring, dominant, unemotional, aggressive, confident, etc.

Feminine Energy is characteristics that *predominantly* describe women: nurturing, kind, sensitive, sweet, supportive, gentle, passive, emotional, helpful, understanding, composed, distinguished, etc.

Human Energy *is a characteristic that describes being a good human and striving to do the right thing,* which requires attributes from both strands of energy. One strand is not better than the other, and they are not mutually exclusive. These attributes do not require special labels or terminology. They do not require protests or propaganda. Human energy is simply your desire to live the best version of your life.

Quick Question:

What adhesives are holding your metaphorical DNA together?

Just Be Yourself

What happens when contending against the perceived masculine hegemony does not transfer over to contending against the perceived feminine hegemony? It's a whole new ball game. The fight fire with fire mentality with men usually gave me a few points of respect or at least made them go away and stop the fight. But these types of interactions escalated situations with women in different ways:

The Pretty People: It genuinely amazes me how many times I have been told something like, "*Amy, you are never going to have a boyfriend because you are always you. Men love a facade. Let them believe they are in control of everything for about a year. Then, when you get your claws into them...*"

These seemingly pretty people are everywhere and are motivated by money or prestige. If you are not following their latest trends, you are perceived as less than others; to them, *everything* is a competition. I am so sorry to break the news. I am not in that competition. If a man thinks he loves me because I am acting stupid, helpless, or fake, I don't want him anyway. He is not worthy of my time.

They willingly relinquish control for a short period of time because they think they are gaining control. Further, they love to compliment other women so they can gain the upper hand and receive compliments in return. This seems to be a way for them to feed their own low self-esteem, which never improves from these interactions.

In my experience, when one of those pretty people pays me a compliment, I simply say, "*Thank you,*" and remain quiet. I am not attempting to be rude; rather, I am confidently stepping out of the game.

Take some time and look at some pictures of some genuinely beautiful women from cultures all over the world. The depth of beauty within their eyes and the smiles that adorn their faces can't be bought; they just exist. These are the women I admire and respect.

The Vagina Club: Please do not be offended. I coined this term in jest, but it has stuck over the years. I am sure you will understand.

As a young adult, I participated in team meetings for children living in a treatment center. The rules were the same across the board. It didn't matter if you were six or thirteen years old. It didn't matter about your background or level of intelligence. Nor did it matter what was the right thing to do. Everyone suffered the same consequences and received very few rewards.

There was an overarching initiative to revamp the entire system. In turn, I did some research every week and presented a few ideas. I suggested how to customize treatment plans according to age and skill levels, instill natural consequences, and bolster rewards. Each time I presented my research and suggestions, I was covertly or overtly chastised by a group of women who wanted to maintain control of the system. I inherently knew I would continue to lose every battle.

So, the question was, *"How do I present the right ideas and allow them to be accepted without a fight?"* In turn, I asked a male co-worker (who would one day be my husband) if I could tell him what I needed and teach him what to say, but only if he agreed with my suggestions. He graciously accepted my offer, and for the next month or so, all of my suggestions came out of his mouth as if they were his ideas. All the women thought his ideas were amazing and turned them into actionable items. Initially, he was in complete disbelief. The discrepancies and reactions changed his perspective on these leaders.

The experiences with these types of women are a great example of the challenges females face and the arduous task of being seen, heard, and valued in the workplace. I learned a lot about myself and how to bring the real Amy into the forefront without the fear and counterproductivity of being torn down.

The Debbie's: I created a basketball clinic when my daughter was in first grade. I allowed three different grade levels, and about thirty to forty girls participated each week. The girls had so much fun the first three years and made friends in other grades. Then came the fourth year. I sent out a letter stating I would still run the clinic for all the girls, but I was creating a travel team in addition to the clinic. Further, I made it very clear that I would have try-outs and only select ten girls.

I knew this team would be an issue. There was a group of women who desired to be in control of all the activities for all the girls. The biggest problem was that most of these women and their daughters were not athletic and desired to create a losing situation for everyone involved. This wasn't the first controlling initiative for the group I will collectively call The Debbie's. These women loved to complain about everything and caused problems for years. Sorry if your name is Debbie.

Regardless, my efforts to do the right thing for the ten girls who would ultimately make the team were proactive and justified. I asked three male coaches, one of whom was a very popular figure, to help me evaluate each player. I created a form with ten different skills and an area for sportsmanlike conduct to include the ability to be a part of the team.

I averaged all four scores in each category at the end of the tryouts. Out of the fourteen girls, there were four girls in question. One was an excellent player but was a year younger and smaller than everyone else. I encouraged her parents to put her in a younger league at the recreation center so she could showcase her skills and not get crushed by the older and larger girls.

Another girl was an excellent player but a year older than everyone else because she had transferred from another country. The older team in our school needed another player, so I encouraged her parents to transfer her up a grade for sports.

Then there were two. These girls refused to follow basic directions and received very low scores from all four evaluators. I contacted The Debbie's and received exceptionally poor feedback. They called all the other women in the controlling cohort to persuade them to issue complaints about me. Over the next few weeks, I received many overt as well as covert statements and had various forms of control and manipulations waived in front of my face.

Ultimately, every member of the Athletic Association backed my decision 100% and thanked me for amicably executing the process. I did not argue. I did not complain. I simply did the right thing and did not succumb to the participation trophy mentality.

If you are an advocate for rewarding team players for simply showing up, I do not want to offend you. But I disagree entirely. Everyone is born with gifts bestowed on them by God. Be uniquely you. Forcing people to serve your perceived purpose in life or forcing others to live something that does not match their life purpose deters them from their greatness.

If someone possesses a gift, be open to receiving it. If your receptors are warped or broken, fix them. Think about this: What if the greatest violinist in the world never touched a violin? What if the greatest basketball player in the world never set foot on a court? What if the greatest philosopher in the world never learned to write? What if the greatest mother in the world was never allowed to conceive? What if the greatest father in the world died in battle before his child was born?

What if you lived your entire life and never realized your full potential because the world is forcing you to be something or someone else? Stop the facade and realize how amazing it would be just to *be yourself* and find people who love you for it? Now, create a list for the following two inquiries:

In your entire life, who has permitted you just to be yourself? A family member, a teacher, a coach, a friend, a spouse, a child? Is the list long or short? Do these people know how important they were to your growth and self-affirmation? If not, go thank them; in person is preferable. If they are deceased, speak to them in your mind when you are about to fall asleep. They will hear you.

Now stop and think or create a list of everyone you have permitted to be themselves. Is your list long or short? If it is long, keep going. This means you are on the right path to genuine relationships. If it is short, do some serious soul-searching and ask yourself, *Why?* Then, figure out *How* you can begin down that much-needed path in life.

My Home

I was on the precipice of my new life. It was like standing on the edge of a cliff with a parachute on my back and peering into the distance. I felt as though the fog was lifting off the mountains, and soon, clarity would rise with the dawn of a new day. The thought of jumping was exciting but also induced a sense of peace in my soul. I was progressing with confidence.

However, there was a strange feeling deep in my gut. I surmised I missed my children. There wasn't one day or moment when I didn't miss them and long to be by their side. I knew they were doing what they needed to do on their own. Right now was not our time to be together.

For several months, I had been engaged in a series of meetings with my potential future employer for a job I thought would be perfect. At the end of a three-hour in-person meeting where I was tasked with writing my own job description and outlining a regional program, I confidently stated, *"If this job is mine, the first thing I am going to do is jump on a plane and visit my children in Hawaii."*

Instantly, our eyes met, and we smiled in confirmation, *"I would get that ticket as soon as possible. I will need you to start within the next sixty days."*

I was overjoyed. I went back to the house and bought my plane ticket to Hawaii. I planned to stay for a few weeks and experience the magic of aloha with them. I was going to embrace my babies and feel *my home* once again.

In this new area of the world, the spiritual feeling of home had eluded me from the start, and initially, that was understandable. The longer I stayed, the feeling grew more and more ominous. This house did not look, smell, or feel like my home. The people around me did not make me feel at home or afford me the comfort of feeling like myself. The city and surrounding area were flat, and the land had been stripped of life. It wasn't easy to find sanctuary and feel *my home*.

I felt a little more comfortable when I considered my potential job and relationship. I reminded myself that my life was still in transition, and nothing was actually real just yet. However, I wholeheartedly believed it was going to be. Not only had I been praying, but I had also been doing *the work*. As a child, my mother always said, "*God helps those who help themselves*" and now it was finally my turn.

For years, I diligently worked and made as much space as possible for my new life. I wanted and needed to feel *my home* before taking that giant leap off that rocky cliff, safely parachute, and land on the ground. I knew this new area would not be my home forever, but I believed it was a good option for the next three to five years. Therefore, I was determined to make it the best.

In my view, Heaven is not a mystical place beyond the clouds; it is the people and the places we are destined to find right here on earth. When we experience these treasures, we feel home.

This notion reminds me of my favorite movie. "*What Dreams May Come*" starring Robin Williams and Annabella Sciorra and a spirit guide, Cuba Gooding Jr. This 1998 movie is not a comedy. It is based on a book written by Richard Matheson in 1978. Philosophically, this movie is intriguing on multiple levels, and the cinematography is outstanding. I have only watched a few movies more than once, and this is one of them. I see, feel, and learn something new every time I watch it.

In the movie, Chris (Robin) and Annie (Annabella) are soulmates destined to meet each other on Earth. Chris is a doctor, and Annie is a painter. Together, they create a wonderful life until tragedy strikes again and again. Finally, Annie gives up and takes her own life, and Chris enters the depths of hell to save her, along with the wisdom from a few other important souls.

The cinematography is absolutely incredible because Annie's version of Heaven and Hell look somewhat the same and are both located in her version of *home*. Heaven is filled with love, light, and vibrant colors, while Hell is decrepit, miserable, and filled with shades of gray.

I used to think I was slightly more aligned with Annie's character because I could never imagine my life without my husband and children. Nobody can create a plan of action for losing their most valued treasures in life. On the flip side, nobody should have the right to judge another person for their responses to such tragedies. But the last time I watched it, I realized I was both Chris and Annie.

Yes, my life seemed gray, and I was determined to save myself. Nobody was going to do it for me. If you would like to know the story's outcome, I suggest you pick a time to sit down and absorb yourself into the movie. One other thing, pay attention to the red scarf. It shows up in some unexpected places, and I have often imagined Robin Williams looking at it from a distance when his own life ended far too soon. Depression is a tough demon to conquer, and nobody should battle alone.

Whew, that was a heavy place to visit, but I felt alone, and I wanted that feeling to leave me. This concept of home is essential before we move on to the next chapter. Now would be a great time to find a place you feel is sacred. Your bedroom? A spot down by the river? A place of worship? Driving in your car? A hike in the mountains? Your dad's workbench? Your mother's grave site?

Now, look around and contemplate: Who and where is *your home*? What do you see, and how does it make you feel? Do the people in your version of home present as themselves, or can they ascend into their heavenly form?

Here is a problem I have with my vision of *home*. My entire life, I had the same vision, but due to the circumstances of my life, I will probably never have that version of home come to fruition. I am not really sure I want that version of home anyway. It doesn't match my personality very well.

The real problem is that I do not have an updated vision of my home. I know plenty of things I *do not* want and some things *I do* want. But, in actuality, my vision of home is a work in progress.

So, if your vision of home is still in-formation, no worries. Just keep track of the things you want and don't want. Most importantly, stay true to yourself. Do not let others be in charge of your destiny. Please do not mistake my sentiment and deem yourself entirely in charge of all aspects of life. That would mean controlling others.

Find people whose dream of home compliments or adds to your vision. If your loved ones discourage or criticize your vision, maybe you need to consider a few deep heart-to-heart discussions before progressing. There is no sense in giving up who you are just to please somebody else. Find common ground and nurture it, or go your own way. I believe the soul knows when it has found its way home. Please pay attention to your instincts; they will be your guide.

CHAPTER 9

❧⚜❧

SOLITUDE ON THE CAPE FEAR

I was so excited when I stepped off that plane. I was going to spend some time in paradise with my babies. This would be our first real vacation as a family in fifteen years. Due to their work schedules, I would have some time with my son and my daughter alone and time together. My anticipation of the journey was a fanciful combination of old memories alongside new memories meant to satiate my soul.

My son had obviously been surfing, and it was great to see him in action. The tides of *Waikiki* definitely called his name. *Wai* meaning freshwater springs, and *kiki*, meaning to spout, was once home to numerous streams and taro (food staple) patches. Before the landscape was significantly altered to create the harbor, waves could reach up to thirty feet or more in this area. Now, the metropolitan city and the beaches are relatively calm and make a great spot for him to play beach volleyball. The courts are regularly set up by a man who wants to give young people something productive to do on the beach.

I was pleased my son learned how to communicate in *Pidgin* (pronounced pigeon) as a sign of respect to the locals. The term originated in Chinese and referred to the language of business within various cultural groups speaking different languages. When I lived there, I had to learn to communicate effectively with my neighbors and clients. Fortunately, my linguistic ability clicked back in.

Pidgin is slang, but in my mind, it goes deeper into the community's mindset. *Honolulu*, meaning Fair Haven, situated next to Waikiki, was a vibrant international harbor hundreds of years before Europeans arrived in the 1700s. Since then, it has been noted as a famous global port for trade and tourism. In 1850, it became the official capital of this kingdom. Surprisingly, before world trade was a way of life, the almost 1 million inhabitants on the island of Oahu were healthy and self-sufficient. Now, the same number of inhabitants import over 80% of their required goods. This situation makes them highly vulnerable to a strategic attack. Consider, the infamous battle at Pearl Harbor is only 8 miles away.

When we went to my son's baseball game, I thought I saw a sign for my favorite Chinese restaurant, Fook Yuen, in Honolulu. I couldn't believe it, so I went inside to inquire, "*Excuse me, sir, I used to live here twenty-five years ago, and I was just wondering if this is the same restaurant and if you are the same owner?*" The man looked very serious and gently closed his eyes as he tilted his head and said, "*Unfortunately... Yes!*" Just then, a smile burst upon his face, and he started to laugh.

At least the local food was still tantalizing to my taste buds. For breakfast one day, I had an egg sandwich with the best tomatoes on top. Remember how tomatoes used to taste before large corporate farms got a hold of them? Well, these scrumptious little bite-size morsels from *Ho Farm* were over-the-top delicious. I tried a coffee drink made with *Kava* powder. This additive made my tongue and lips tingle and gave me a sense of euphoria. It wasn't like the high of coffee; it was much more subtle.

Kava root is originally from the island of Fiji but is currently popular all around Polynesia. Traditionally, when somebody is invited to a welcoming ceremony or another's house, they should bring the root with them as an offering. This is similar to how etiquette prompts us to bring a bottle of wine or flowers as a host gift. Kava root is ground into a liquid concoction daily and strained before drinking. In ceremony, sharing this beverage helps to bolster peace and settle disputes in the community.

However, like many indigenous practices. The Food and Drug Administration has cast a dark cloud over this root, and it is difficult to find. It is often equated with people living on the fringes of society, and those who partake in this beverage may be looked down upon. I suggest you try it for yourself. It is rather bitter, so learning how to prepare and drink properly would be very beneficial.

Last but not least, there was an array of places making homemade *acai* bowls (pronounced ä-ˌsä-ˈē). These tasty berries that will stain your mouth purple come from the Amazon Forest. They grow on long branches from atop certain palm trees and are harvested much like coconuts. Traditionally, the men and women tie leaves around their feet, climb to the top of the tree, and chop down what is needed with a sharp blade. Today, this super healthy fruit is harvested and turned into powder for easy transport and preparation. If you desire this delicacy, be careful; some put an overabundance of sweeteners in to make it more like ice cream or gelato. Either way, you will be hooked once you try a bite topped with fresh coconut flakes, local pineapple, and other exotic fruits.

One day, we drove to two different remote spiritual sites and had to hike a short distance to see them. Upon arrival at the first location, a police officer was posted and blocking the entrance. He did not speak and motioned for us to continue on. At the second location, we approached with a family of four who lived a few blocks away their entire life. Again, the entrance was blocked, and the officer made us leave without explanation. We were all confused, and I asked the family if they had any suggestions.

On our way to a third location, my daughter got a terrible headache. Fortunately, this site was located within a local community and was open. However, the trail was long and not an option at this point. I went over to a man selling dried meats out of his house. "*Excuse me, sir, is there a shorter trail than the one at the top of the hill to see the heiau?"* He looked confused and asked me why I wanted to go there. I replied, *"Well, my daughter and I have been trying to find places to hike to that have a lot of energy, and they are all closed. She suffers from headaches, and I want to help her get rid of them."*

He was pleasantly surprised and asked me a few more questions before he went to get his sister. Their grandmother was a *kahuna,* medicine woman, and their family lived on this land for generations. After I explained that I had worked with a shaman from Peru and that my intentions were pure, they took us over to a green plant with long leaves. The sister showed my daughter how to choose and prepare the correct Ti leaf for medicinal use. She showed us the path and asked us to stay to the right of the hills as the left side had bad energy. As we had hoped, my daughter's headache vanished within minutes.

After the hike, I wanted to learn more and asked to speak with them again. The woman showed me an enormous mango tree she had planted as a child and told me the story of the land. This valley used to be the wettest valley on Oahu. It housed 350 families, and they were self-sufficient. In the early 1980s, the government tried *"to help protect"* the native lands and allow the locals to keep their homes. The community was offered money, and their land became a protected preserve. However, months after the deal was executed, all of the water resources were intentionally diverted to the other side of the island to use for development. Today, this valley is able to house about 30 families sustainably.

As I expressed my sorrow, she politely nodded and explained that it was a recurrent theme and a few other themes I was aware of, but it completely broke my heart anyway. Besides not having access to spiritually significant areas, the local people have been forced off their land. The entire coastline was filled with people who could no longer afford to live in a house. I can't call them homeless because Oahu is their home, and they still exist there. However, they can no longer pay the yearly taxes on the houses they have owned for generations, nor can they afford to move. The lifestyles of the rich from other areas of the world changed the entire landscape, and there was no shelter from that storm.

Trying to be happy and carefree was a burden. The paradise I once embraced felt like an elaborate deception. Many things appeared the same, but the people and the land felt different. The energy had changed, and so did the meaning behind, or should I say lack of meaning behind my experiences. This feeling prompted me to find another ahi fishhook necklace Hawaiians call *makau*. I bought one made of curly koa wood from a local carver over 25 years ago. When I wore it, I felt powerful. Unfortunately, it disappeared. By the way, I bought it years before Disney made it a cool tourist thing.

When we visited the Bishop Museum, they had a local hand-carved makau for sale in the showcase. There was also an exhibit to explain the real meaning behind such a sacred object. I will need to go strictly by memory because much of the research I currently found provides a water downed meaning. Basically, a person would need to select the proper tree and make a dedication, much like the surfboard discussion. Then, the person would need to know how to carve the wood according to family tradition, the type of catch (fish) desired, and the location of the catch in the ocean.

Next, the fisherman would need to make an offering to the gods for a bountiful catch. In turn, this fisherman would be able to provide for himself and his family. His family is a contribution to the fishing village and the village takes care of each other. Proper fishing means you are a community leader and contribute to the circle of life. I was proud to wear my new fishhook necklace and bought one made of bone for my son.

Although The Polynesian Cultural Center is a huge tourist attraction, the indigenous villages representing all of Polynesia are a great immersive learning experience. The people who work there make their own money to pay for college, learn the ways of their elders and maintain their cultural heritage. We ate traditional food, participated in games and ceremonies, and listened to the origin stories and various forms of hula and chant. I saw the magical glow in my children's eyes as if they were young again, and I was their mommy, showing them the way.

A man played the *ukulele*, a small four-stringed guitar that means little jumping bug at Kapi'olani Park during a craft market. He was giving away *leis*, flower necklaces, that had passed their prime from his family business. He explained they had supplied leis for tourists for generations. I listened for a while and requested my favorite song. When "*He Aloha Mele*" came out of my mouth, he looked surprised. I explained that I lived on the island 26 years ago, which meant a lot to me. I could hear in his voice that it also meant something to him. The spirit of aloha was still alive; it just took extra time and effort to uncover it.

Just before my departure, my son helped me out of the car and gave me a huge hug as I melted into his arms. I didn't want to let go. Even the frantic traffic control people at the airport ignored our extended embrace. As he leaned down and kissed my forehead, I started to cry and eventually laugh because we knew everyone was looking at us. Just then, he looked deep into my eyes and said, "*Mommy, nobody could ever love me more than you do.*"

I hope the various peoples now known as Hawaiians intentionally educate and nourish the souls and spirits of the islands. Our future as a nation that cares for its people depends on it. The truth is that we should all be *keiki o ka'aina*, children of the land.

The Land of Promise

My flight back had delays, and I was in transport for over twenty hours. Between the journey and the time zone change, I was exhausted. After acclimating back at my house, I took a ten-mile hike to rejuvenate. It felt good to process my feelings in solitude. The following evening, I went to dinner with the man I was dating but felt rather blah. The next day, we discovered we had Covid.

I was isolated for ten days and slept quite a bit. I was thoroughly convinced the unwanted flu vaccine I was forced to endure in 2018 gave me Covid before it was an international crisis. The only good part was that I already had the antibodies, so it was far less detrimental this time. The crazy part was that I lost an incredible amount of hair, and my intestines were not cooperating with me.

Amazingly, I found my original Ahi fishhook necklace. It had been hiding in a box in my dresser, and now it had a new companion. I just laughed because I figured there was a reason for my discovery, but I did not know why just yet. Hmm, ancient wisdom combined with my old life and my new life.

For the remaining part of the summer, I focused on completing my current projects and designing the new program for my permanent position. It was all about meeting new people, seeing what existed, and deciding what to develop next. I absolutely loved it. The man I was dating had several business trips, and his children were visiting, so I took the opportunity to take a few overnight trips myself.

Everything seemed to be on track, although I still felt uncomfortable in my gut. This place is *not* my home. I tried to convince myself, *"Come on, Amy. This is only for the next few years and is perfect for you. You have done this all before, you can do it again. Trust the process."*

People started to betray me one by one, and I looked deeper into myself. I ruminated over the relationships and the process. With each betrayal, I accepted yet another closed door and thanked God for allowing me to focus better on what I genuinely wanted. I thought, *"Thank you for letting me find out who you really are before I invest too much time and effort into your bullshit."*

When I described these betrayals to a wealthy business owner on the other side of the state, he said, *"Ha! We call New Hanover County the Land of Promise. I promise I will do this and will do that, but without explanation, you never see or hear from them again. Don't worry about these people; you far exceed them. Being in any type of relationship with you is like winning the lottery."*

He was right. I attempted to plant my seeds in the dirt when I really desired soil. But that didn't take away my suffering. I needed to determine how to fix the situation and move forward. Unfortunately, the only common denominator was *me*. I felt defeated and confused. I was tired of people telling me I was great and wonderful while their underlying intent was to use me selfishly.

I repeatedly thought, "*I would rather hear ONE truth than a thousand false praises.*"

The feelings I was experiencing cannot be appropriately described as depression. It was more like a moratorium of life. I wished to live a happy and productive life, but I felt like I had exhausted all possibilities. I had purposely given up my entire life and trusted the process. Now, I had to start all over again. I just wasn't ready.

Amelia Earhart once commented:

> "*The most difficult thing is the decision to act. The rest is mere tenacity. The fears are paper tigers. You can do anything you decide to do. You can act to change and control your life and the procedure. The process is its own reward.*"

The paper tiger is a metaphor suggesting that fear and anxiety may appear fierce but are fundamentally weak. Paper tigers are *empty threats* to the survival of your mind, body, and soul. Most importantly, they can be defeated. Usage of the term dates back to the 14th century Ming Dynasty.

Here is an interesting task. Make two origami paper tigers. Keep one in an obvious place as a reminder to face your fears as you progress through the day. Put it on your mirror, your desktop, or your refrigerator. Be creative. Others will inquire. Create your own version of the story for the response.

For the second, create your paper tiger and label your fears and anxieties. Say quiet prayers of contemplation as you destroy your fears and anxieties. Burn them in a fire, shred them by hand or with scissors, or drench them in water and let them disintegrate into nothing but mush.

Would you like to know what prompted this exercise? Well, it is twofold, no pun intended. First of all, I love another quote by Amelia Earhart, which I have playfully stated for many years,

"Proper preparation is 90% of the journey."

However, we all know her fate. So, I say it to kind of make fun of myself when I try to plan every detail and hope for success.

The second prompt was much more tangible. About ten years ago, I had some gingerbread people paper cutouts from a group project for children at Christmas. There were a few left over at the end, and I took two home. I wrote a bunch of positive words to describe myself on one of them and hung it on the refrigerator that winter. On the other one, I wrote a bunch of words to describe the part of myself I needed to improve upon. Then, I used it as a bookmark for books concerning self-improvement. Apparently, I forgot about it, or it forgot about me—poor little cookie.

Either way, in the middle of writing this chapter, I opened a book and my gingerbread cookie fell out and surprised me. Initially, finding such an old piece of joy made me laugh. But then, as I embraced the memory, it brought a little sadness. Some of my fears and anxieties had been overcome, but some were still sprinkled on my cookie, waiting to be baked. So, the following evening, I made a fire in the backyard and threw my paper cookie into the burning flames. This was not a punishment; it was an offering. I'm pretty sure God loves warm gingerbread cookies baked with love.

If I am a Healer

Over the next couple months, I kept to myself except for a few friends I had made in the area. Reconciling who I am supposed to be in this world at this point in my life wasn't going to be easy, and I needed time to think and explore. If I am supposed to guide people in their journey to heal and use my hands as an instrument of light, what would be the most effective use of my time?

I attempted to make some connections with people in the healing arts professions. I wanted to find people whose philosophies complimented mine and who may potentially want to share wisdom. I thought if I told them about my work with a shaman and the people I have helped to heal, they may welcome me into their cohorts. Unfortunately, I ran into a bunch of people who wanted to charge me $180 per hour for a *"get to know me session"* or they wanted to cleanse my energy over Zoom. *"No thanks."*

Don't get me wrong, I understand people need to run a business and make money. But I was looking for *genuine* relationships that could be nurtured and reciprocated. I thought if I started to tell more people about my gifts, I may feel more comfortable, and possibly, new doors would open.

A woman had been limping for months after an arduous relocation from another state. She expected it would eventually get better, but it progressively worsened. Finally, she sought traditional physical therapy, which didn't seem to help.

One night, I asked if I could help, and she reluctantly agreed. I bought some almond oil and CBD gummies from the store to prepare for the healing. Both help with pain, swelling, and relaxation. I had her lay on the bed comfortably as I lit candles and incense while playing songs for a cleansing meditation. Her body was very stiff, and relaxing was almost impossible.

Progressively, I worked the energy below her knees, but from the shins down, everything felt lifeless. Since I knew her quite well, I gave a funny but official diagnosis: *"stuck in the mud"* and *"a blocker."*

She laughed and asked, *"What does that mean?"* I explained, *"The healing process is reciprocal. I can offer you my energy, but you need to accept it. You are blocking me. When you are ready to accept what I have* to offer, we can try again." She inquired, "When will that be?" I smirked and replied, "I don't know. That is up to you. I guess it is when you are ready to be unstuck and get out of the mud."

A few weeks later, we were having dinner, and she had a cocktail. She seemed in good spirits, so I asked if she was ready to try again. She agreed, and again, I prepared her for healing. This time, I had her drape her legs over the side of the couch. This position seemed to be more advantageous for releasing the dis-ease. I lowered the lights and lit some candles.

Again, I moved the energy down to her skin and closed my eyes. I was waiting to see the metaphor for the blockage. I saw a foggy gray cloud, "What does gray mean to you?" She replied, "I see a butterfly. No, wait a moth. Lots of moths flying around." As my hands penetrated her leg, I could feel the energy fluttering slowly and then rapidly. I massaged it down and squeezed it out of the bottom of her foot. I could tell she was in pain and said, "If this is too much, I can stop." She nodded, "No, keep going." Eventually, the fluttering chaos dissipated, and I threw the energy away and sent the spirits back into the light. I covered her with a blanket as she drifted off to sleep. Within two days, she never limped again.

Another woman suffered through a divorce and accidentally broke her arm by falling off a small ladder. She thought she needed to let go of the bad energy of the divorce and asked if I would help. She had a couple of glasses of wine and was relaxed, so I thought this would be an appropriate time to try. As I felt the places in her body that I thought would need attention, they seemed to be healing properly. I shut my eyes and gently touched her cheek as I saw and felt her falling to the side, "Tell me about falling."

She recounted the story about her recent fall but that was not it. I could see she was a small child and said, "No, not this fall. Tell me about when you were young." Her demeanor changed, and she started to cry. She told me about falling out of her playpen and the subsequent interactions with her mother and sister. She confided she had never spoken about this incident before, but there was a strong correlation to the current situation. As the healing ended, we hugged, and I thanked her for trusting me.

I was telling a male acquaintance about *my hands,* and he chuckled and asked if I was a witch or something. I assuredly replied, "No, *I live in the light.*"

Again, he chuckled, "*So, I am just supposed to believe this hocus pocus works or something?*" I shrugged and replied, "*I don't care if you believe me. I am telling you something from my experience I know is true.*" He looked somewhat curious and asked, "*So, you think you can fix me?*"

Then, I laughed, "*That's hilarious, nobody can fix you! But I will certainly assess you and tell you what I see and feel. But you have to trust me. I do not control the experience; I can just communicate it to you.*" He thought about it briefly, "*Ok, I'm in. But I don't want any gummies or anything. Just tell me what I have to do.*" I looked at him, motioned up and down at his reserved demeanor, and replied, "*The most important thing you have to do is to learn to relax.*"

Later that day, I lit some candles and encouraged him to relax. I rubbed almond oil down his shoulders and spine. They seemed to be just fine. Then I asked permission to rub his chest and abdomen, and again, everything seemed fine until I felt a distinct line connecting his upper abdomen and heart. It sent a very uncomfortable jolt of dark energy through my body. I said, "*Tell me about your chest.*" He looked slightly irritated and confused. So, I asked, "*Did you ever have an injury to your chest?*"

He became bothered and restless. He said he was uncomfortable and wanted to change the music. I felt as though I had trespassed into his private territory, so I backed away. He mumbled a few things about a job he used to have and said he would tell me some more next time.

A few weeks later, we met for dinner, and he divulged a string of traumas he had endured. He would not look me in the eyes, and his voice was agitated. Ultimately, this set of communications ended our friendship. The best indication of his silent suffering came when he said, "*You got to go to Peru and drink ayahuasca, and all I got was a hospital bed and some ketamine drips.*" According to his version of the story, he was physically and emotionally sabotaged at work, and in the same time period, his former wife had a miscarriage. Several life-altering encounters pushed him over the edge.

Whew, that was a surprise. Honestly, I had to research ketamine because I didn't know what it was. I felt bad that he was suffering, but all I did was point it out. I did not like being the messenger, nor did I like being the brunt of his anger. I did warn him. It's not my fault he didn't believe me.

Regardless, I was still stumbling around the question, "If I am able to help heal people, what should I do next? Further, if healing is my purpose in life, how do I uncover the layers holding me back and progress in the proper direction?" It has become apparent that I need to be me and be able to share my gifts.

I Need 5 Minutes

I hiked, cooked, and built fires in the backyard during this time. For the most part, I wanted to be left alone except for one friend going through his own version of hell. Since the beginning of our friendship, Jerry has always felt like a brother to me. Genuine, down to earth, and no pretense coupled with a desire always to do the right thing. He is a great human.

Occasionally, speaking with him about his pending divorce made me feel like I was talking to myself so many years earlier. He was being dragged over the burning coals by a selfish person who was unable or unwilling to see the big picture. I was amazed to see how calm and respectful he remained throughout the entire ugly process. I was humbled that my advice made a difference in his heart.

When we were done talking about all the bad stuff, our little exchanges were filled with laughter and appreciation for life. Jerry is attractive and in good physical health, which makes him look quite young for his age. He always looks for the bright side of a situation and loves to tell his famous dad jokes.

On the flip side, being around him was a reprieve from the misery I was experiencing. There were plenty of days when all I thought was, "Whew, I need a good long nap!" One day, when Jerry told me about a period in his life when he took a lot of naps, I ran this thought by him to reframe his need for rest and rejuvenation:

Autumn days are perfect sleeping weather. The air is cool and crisp as the sun warms your soul. "If this were your reason for an afternoon slumber, nobody would question you, right?" What if your body needed to rejuvenate because something completely knocked you down or out of whack?

You lost work. You lost love. You lost trust. You lost faith. You lost hope. You lost family. You lost friends. You lost yourself.

Think about this for a few minutes. For a bear, hibernation is a necessary part of the life cycle and serves a great purpose. Has anybody ever questioned the process? No, it is what bears do to exist. Now, consider this circumstance. If you wake a bear up early from its hibernation, it isn't just an inconvenience, it can be a disaster. Emerging from hibernation requires a lot of energy and depletes reserves that are key to surviving the winter.

If loss symbolizes winter in your heart, wouldn't it make sense to sleep through the long cold nights and blustery winds? Wouldn't it make sense to purify your mind and body in the comfort of your sanctuary? Think about who you really are so when you wake up from the much-needed rest, you will be refreshed and ready to go.

Unfortunately, some people choose to fill up their emptiness with the busyness of life. If you feel the urge to do that, stop and take a moment to reflect. Consider listening to your body calling for deep rest. Find solitude and detach from the rest of the world in a healthy and respectful manner. When you arise, take a long hot shower, nourish yourself, go for a long walk and breathe. Then ask yourself and decide, "Am I in need of deep rest or am I depressed?"

If you are depressed, this method may work but I encourage you to seek companionship and don't forge through this season alone. Resting may leave you feeling vulnerable and that is OK. Learning to lean into and let go of your feelings will help you through the winter.

Learning how to explore the methods of deep rest may seem difficult and unproductive, I assure you, they are not. If you want to pretend you are a big brown bear, go out and forage a bit so your tummy is full and find yourself a comfy little spot for hibernation. Nestle inside that big furry blanket and let your mind be at ease. Think, "This is where I am supposed to be, and the rest of the world can wait."

Another story I wrote in this time period resonated with Jerry and strengthened our friendship. Essentially, it is code for I really need to talk to somebody, or I am going to explode. I actually took a therapeutic intervention I learned many years ago and coupled it with a Hawaiian legend from one of my favorite goddesses, Pele. All you need to say is, "I need five minutes." and the rest is history:

Hawaiian Mythology will have you believe eruptions from within the Earth are caused by the Goddess Pele when she is angry. She who is known to shape sacred land can cause earthquakes by stomping her feet and volcanic eruptions by digging her magic stick into the ground. Pele is the Goddess of fire, lightening, wind, dance, and volcanoes while her elder sister, Namaka, is the Goddess of the waves and the majestic sea. Like many sisters, they have had a many disputes.

The spirits of the chants and hula still talkstory about how the vast chain of islands were formed when the sisters were engaged in volatile arguments. Altogether, there are 137 islands while the 8 largest are the most well-known. Technically, the Hawaiian Islands were formed by a hot spot in the middle of the tectonic plate located in the Pacific Ocean. The hot spot is fixed while the plate is moving. So, as the plate moves, various seamounts and islands formed over millions of years and are still forming now.

When your *hot spot* is filled with anger or disgust and your feelings intrude on your ability to relax or be productive, ask permission to erupt with emotions. Why? Because running around and randomly throwing hot embers on people and progress can really burn. Basically, all you need to do is let it rip from your gut for five uninterrupted and cathartic minutes! Here is how it works:

1. Find someone you trust and ask permission to explode for five minutes.
2. Recipient agrees to listen or agrees to ask for a little more time to prepare themselves to listen fully.
3. If the recipient interrupts the five minutes, you automatically get one more minute.
4. If the explosion is long or involved, you can ask for a maximum of two more minutes.
5. Remember, this explosion is not an attack, it is a release… like letting all the air out of a balloon.
6. You can erupt like you are screaming at the universe; the recipient should just listen.
7. The recipient should not judge what you are saying, question you, or correct you in any way.
8. When you are finished, it is over. Let some time pass while you eat, drink, or engage in an activity.
9. When the emotion has dissipated, the recipient can provide feedback, ask questions, or offer advice.
10. Thank each other for trusting each other and trusting the process.

This process can rid you of the poison you have been collecting in your body and allow you to feel a sense of freedom. It can allow you to turn a potentially stressful meeting, event, or dinner into a happy, productive and trust building situation. Learning to extinguish the fiery molten lava together will help your friendship flourish and not falter.

After I wrote this section, I thought back on my life to some of the people who allowed me to use this technique before I actually defined it. A couple of people stood out in my mind but one was by far the best. The only real rules we had were, "*Are you alone and do you have a few minutes to talk?*" The rest was automatically implied by the tone or infliction of my voice. He instantly knew I needed my friend. He admires the unfiltered version of Amy as he has known me since I was a freshman in college.

Kenny was in one of my friend groups in college, and we dated off and on for the years I was in school. He has always been unfiltered and proud of it. After I graduated, we went our separate ways. Here's a funny story about how we reunited our friendship. I enrolled my daughter in middle school, and they sent home a list of all the girls and their families with contact information. As I casually perused the list, one name jumped out at me. I couldn't believe it. After all these years, his name was touching my name on the paper. I literally laughed out loud and wondered what he had been up to. A few weeks later, I found out he transferred his daughter to another school so I believed I would never find out.

A couple of years passed and I was divorced. As I was rummaging through some old papers, I found the contact list so I decided to reach out. After all, our college years were significantly defined by our music and every time I heard some of my favorite songs, I fondly thought of him. Our friendship instantly returned like we were in college drinking and dancing once again.

Alternative Rock in the early 90s defined *our* generation. Every time I hear the Ramones blast out, "*20, 20, 24 hours to go, I want to be sedated, nothing to do, nowhere to go-oh...*" I want to jump up, look around, and find my friend, nicknamed Money, on the other side of Poor Richard's Pub. It was our favorite little dive bar, where the music was loud, and the atmosphere was hot. As soon as those lyrics permeated the air, we jumped up in a *hurry, hurry, hurry* to get to the dance floor before we went *insane*. I can see Lap and Craiger waiting to jump in after finishing their final game of pool.

The world was changing, and we were going to be the ones to make it happen. We were intelligent yet rebellious and our non-conformist standards took the world by storm. We craved authenticity on our own individual paths. As the band Modern English helped us realize, "*The future's open wide*," I looked around and joyfully danced, "*I'll stop the world and melt with you*." We had all seen the difference and our friendships were definitely getting better all the time.

Some of us became wildly successful while some settled into ordinary life. Down the road, our socioeconomic status didn't matter because we were *friends* who loved to dance our way through challenges in life. The literature calls us disillusioned but I prefer to say we were creating our own illusions outside of mainstream thought. We didn't necessarily need to release our emotions with words, because INXS could simply sing, "*I need you tonight*." and we all show up to dance our frustrations away and decide, I'm just "*gonna live my life*."

So when I needed to erupt with emotions, there was no judgment, and Kenny always reminded me, "*You are my sunshine*." If I was broken down in the middle of nowhere, I can assure you he would drive to the end of the world and back to save me because that is what real friends do for each other. Then, he would buy me a drink, and we would reminisce about old and new times.

Now, I would like you to think back to a time of great social transformation. These shared experiences bond people in *mysterious ways*. I remember the first time I was alone on the dance floor in the middle of Hammerjacks, a huge music venue when U2 insisted I saw "*the man inside the child*." All of the best up-and-coming bands frequented this spot to get noticed, and Amy #2 (although she insisted she was Amy #1) kept track of their play dates in The City Paper. What a wild ride to learn, "*If you want to kiss the sky, better learn how to kneel…*"

Have you come up with a time period yet? Maybe? Well, figure out a time when the only thing that exceeded your desire to have fun was your energy to be on the stage, the field, the court, or the classroom. Who were your friends? What music did you listen to? Where were you living? What social activities did you engage in? Who was your sunshine?

I encourage you to reach out to some of these people if you have lost touch over the years. Face it, we aren't getting any younger but we sure are getting wiser. I'd be willing to bet communicating with some of your friends from a time gone by but not forgotten will enrich your soul. Shared experiences can be a blessing in disguise. Until then, when you are in a funk and there isn't anyone to listen, turn the music on and turn it up loud and just let your heart feel gloriously free and rock!

Time To Prune

I thoroughly enjoyed writing one-page posts for LinkedIn. Not only was I helping others pay attention to nature and to my wisdom, I was also helping myself. I would have never imagined writing could be this therapeutic. Everywhere I ventured seemed to be a new lesson I wanted to learn. As I was walked through the forest, I noticed how the passageway between pine trees with furrowed rough bark opened up a new universe. These majestic beauties could withstand the harshness of winter as well as the heat from summer wildfires. There is a great word in Japanese philosophy which exemplifies how the forest can help to heal your body and soul through immersion. **Shinrin-yoku** literally means *forest bathing*.

One day, as I was wandering through the woods, a wise old tree beckoned me to sit down and talk story. The mystical branches swayed with the wind so beautiful and proud. The roots danced their way through the soil so courageous and strong. In turn, I found a bench for a quiet respite. Suddenly, I heard the music of the land sing a song as I watched the fire ants leave their earthen fortress and scurry into the folds of the dense bark. You see, the trees provided sanctuary for weathering the storm.

The wise old tree beckoned me to pay close attention. The art of pruning starts before my seed is planted in the ground. If you plant the right seed in the right place, you will intrinsically avoid unnecessary obstacles. Be sure to consider the true nature of the tree you want to grow and understand its intended form. Contemplate how pruning is necessary but can create damage and stress for me and my community as we all live here together. We need each other.

A vulnerable tree is more susceptible to insects, disease, cold, and drought. Ensure you take all necessary steps to minimize our risk. Choose the proper tools, time, and technique to prune.

I asked, "*Why are you telling me all of this? The trees in my yard are healthy and bear beautiful flowers and sweet fruit.*"

"*Come, my dear, listen a little closer. Have you ever met someone who has cut off time and resources to their employees and hoped they would thrive anyway? Do you know someone who has kept a job that caused so much dis-ease but they were afraid to quit? How many people stay in a destructive marriage because they think it's better for the children? Do you know someone who is unhappy and stagnated because they have denied their true passion? Am I making sense?*"

"Well, yes." I replied. Then, the wind roared as the clouds encroached upon my blue sky. Then, I realized why the ants had taken cover. It was time for a healing rain. As I peered down the path, searching for direction, I heard the tree whisper into the distance, "*Continue on through the forest, my beloved, and leave our land a better place than you found it.*"

Great, it's time to prune, again. I was not sure how much more I could remove from my life. Replacing lost objects is easy. Replacing lost fragments of my mind, body and soul was extremely difficult. The best question was, "*Where should I start?*" I surmised to begin with the one thing that drives me absolutely crazy. Lies. I can feel lies throughout my body like when a speaker is too loud, and the vibrations drive you insane. Sometimes sensing a lie is helpful, like when somebody didn't complete a task and you call them out on it. At other times, sensing a lie is infuriating especially when it is being used against you.

Purging the Lies

I was desperate for the energy of the multitude of lies I had trapped inside my body to leave me. I couldn't wait any longer. Besides, my idea on how to extract this poison from my body was deeply personal and I wasn't exactly sure what I was doing. Except, I had watched my shaman perform a healing on a lady who had fallen from a burning building which left me in a state of awe.

I waited until I had an entire day to be alone in the house so I could eat some medicine I had been saving for quite a while. I *prepared the garden* in my mind and body that week, so I was mentally prepared to *operate* on myself for lack of a better term. If this big ball of anxiety and self-doubt had entered my body and found a home in my stomach, I was determined to extract it.

I mixed the mushrooms with some vitamin powers and orange juice then waited an hour for the medicine to take effect. I was determined to have a completely internal journey and not allow the outside world in for a peak. I purified the *surgical* space and my body with sage and candles. I asked the spirits to show me, teach me, guide me. I chose some enchanting music to accompany my work.

The air was cool, and the fireplace was hot. I took a few deep breaths and started my meditation while sitting on the floor. The energy was churning through my body like a beautiful and turbulent waterfall. The last time I tried to extract this energy, it kept coming to the surface and taunting me. Then when I expected a release, the energy went back inside laughing all the way to win the game. This time, I was determined to win.

I laid down and envisioned a bright surgical instrument opening my abdomen and slowly extracting the negative ball of energy. The music swirled through my veins as the passing of time wavered. The perceived extension of the songs coupled with my heart rate mysteriously kept me alive while portions of me were dying off. The release was curiously painful, but I continued on. Finally, the procedure felt like it had come to an end, and I analyzed each portion of my body to see if it had been cleared.

Apparently, I needed to be more aggressive. I got into the shower and let extremely hot water run down my body. I demanded the energy to, "*Leave me now! Go back to the light where you belong.*" several times. I knew a common side effect of the medicine is to regurgitate or purge the emotions. But I had never had that experience. However, I remembered how I spit out the PTSD from my car accident many years earlier and my body began to dry heave. Once again, I decided to spit and felt a huge release. I asked aloud, "*Are you actually gone or are you just hiding from me?*"

I dried off and rubbed almond oil all over my body. When I looked into the mirror, I felt a yearning for more. More? "*Is there more energy stuck inside my gut?*" I don't think so. I decided to meditate looking into the mirror so I could see myself from a distance and figure out what remained. The energy that left me felt masculine while the energy that remained felt feminine yet oddly aggressive.

Instinctively, I knew I needed to satisfy my feminine urges as they were calling out in celebration of our victory. I laid down and unleashed the waterfall in peaceful ecstasy. As I wrapped myself up in my blanket, my entire body was tingling as I smiled. The Amy who was being suppressed began to sparkle. I felt beautiful, vibrant, and alive. When I returned to the mirror, my arms were more prominent, and my hands were glowing with translucent *flux lines* surrounding them.

The word flux is similar to the word flow in terms of energy. To understand what I was experiencing, imagine placing your hand on top of water and watching the ripples flow around you. However, those ripples are short lived and dissipate quickly. If you prefer to imagine a little deeper into my flow of energy, look up a picture of magnetic flux lines on the internet. Notice how the diameter of each flux line extends out in a complimentary position, do not intersect, and form a closed loop. Those lines are what I saw encompassing the parts of my body that had suffered extensive damage years earlier.

As the medicine wore off, I wandered around the house for a little while in search of any lingering energy. Then, I fixed myself a light snack and went to bed. I took comfort in my healing.

The Soil

I was introduced to a farmer and thought his methodology would fit perfectly into the regional program I was designing. I asked if I could come and learn firsthand as I believed our endeavors would be mutually beneficial. He was a gracious host and invited me to stay for two days. The moment I stepped out of my car, I thought, *"How am I going to get through two days with this guy?"* The energy exuding from him was immense. Unbeknownst to me, his grandfather had been an indigenous medicine man and he had inherited some spiritual gifts. Most importantly, his gifts were complimentary to mine.

When he spoke, I could perceive his thoughts and said them aloud even though I did not know it at the time. He told me in subsequent conversations and said the observations were uncanny. As we were touring the property, I stepped onto hallowed ground and instantly felt energy run down my spine and into my legs. I could feel myself vibrating in unison with the earth. I had not felt energy this strong since I had been in the mountains in Peru.

Just then, he looked into my eyes and asked, *"Are your eyes always that green?"* I bashfully responded, *"Only sometimes, I think it is the land."* We were definitely communicating on another level. His demeanor softened as he let down his guard and asked, *"You can feel it, can't you?"* I got a little nervous. It was rare for anybody to call me out like that, and I had only known him a few hours. I hesitantly replied, *"Yes, I can feel it all through my feet and legs."* He explained he felt it on his back and down his spine. The rest of the tour heightened our spiritual closeness.

After dinner, we talked about his back story and his method of healing his own PTSD. He had seriously contemplated suicide many times over and had learned how to save himself as well as others. Apparently, twenty-two retired military veterans commit suicide every day, and the problem needs to be addressed. Let me reiterate: Twenty-two people per day, totaling over 8,000 per year, who served and protected our country die due to negligence. We need to provide necessary services instead of overlooking or exacerbating problems with "*cocktails*," the laundry list of medications provided for those suffering.

We discussed how we could use plant medicine and move energy in people with our hands, although neither had formal training. Our hands were a conduit for healing, but it was a secret very few were allowed to know. I was in awe—finally, somebody who understood me.

He suggested we try to perform a healing ceremony for each other and I agreed. We ate a moderate dose of psilocybin mushrooms, hydrated with a proper amount of fluids, and wrapped ourselves up in blankets on the front porch for several hours. His music selection was mesmerizing coupled with the sounds of nature. As we watched far off lights in the sky, we talked about our pasts and how our tragedies were being transformed into triumphs for all to share.

The area was remote, and you could hear sounds far into the distance. Mostly, I felt comfortable, but I knew the darkness he had experienced far exceeded mine. I had an ominous feeling about what else was out there with us. Twice, when he was recounting the hell he had endured, I had to stop and reset my train of thought and ask to change the subject. He completely understood.

When it got too cold to be outside, we went inside and sat down on opposite sides of the living room. Then came something neither of us expected. We decided to try our healing technique on each other. We agreed to lay our hands upon the dark energy we felt in the other person. So that you understand, this was not a sexual experience; it was spiritual. I decided to go first. I could feel his dis-ease in his mid to lower back. When I placed my hands upon him, it felt like my hands were inside his torso. As I moved my hands, I saw a flowing blue and black body of water ripple through my fingers. I asked what this meant. He replied, "*That is where I am from. I grew up on the water, and it was my life.*"

As my hands submerged deep into his water, I saw two objects and inquired. He could see exactly what I was seeing and named the objects. I was focused on the one to the right, which he described as a conch shell. I said, "*Tell me more about the shell.*" He hesitated and replied, "*I am not sure what else to say.*"

Just then, his back became extremely hot as my hands rapidly swirled up and down his spine. Inexplicably, I pulled the shell out of the right side of his back, and at that exact moment, a huge flash of white light illuminated the entire room. I immediately removed my hands and jumped back. We were both in awe and sat down on our respective couches.

In total dismay, he questioned, "*What just happened? Have you ever done that before?*" I replied, "*Well, I guess a little bit but nothing that extraordinary. What about you?*" He nodded in disbelief, "*No, nothing that intense.*"

After some time passed, he offered to try and heal me. As his hands massaged my shoulders and neck area, I explained the memories he was bringing into consciousness. I could tell his hands were experiencing pain, and I taught him to *throw my pain away*. Pain is energy; if he moved it out of me, it could get trapped in him instead. So, he needed to discard it.

My neck was stuck out of place, but he put it back into alignment. But there was something else inside my esophagus. He found two spots and was able to pull one out by the use of our breath. Our lips never touched, but I inhaled as he exhaled into my soul. As he inhaled my breath out of my soul, I exhaled. The energy transformed as our breathing meditation reciprocally aligned, and I gasped for air. He held onto my shoulders for support as I coughed, allowing one spot to dissipate. *Something* left me, and I felt different in an obscure and undefinable way.

We discussed how neither of us had ever experienced anything that powerful. It felt strange saying good night as I entered my room and prepared for bed. It was difficult to go to sleep because I felt like all the synapses in my brain were rapidly firing. Also, I couldn't help but think something unsettling was waiting outside. Eventually, I closed the curtains and drifted off to sleep.

The next day, I learned more about his program and listened to some of the stories of those who helped him along the way. We performed a soil test in multiple locations and learned firsthand how soil is not dirt. Dirt is dead. Soil has health and is considered a diverse living ecosystem that sustains plant, animal, and human life. It contains fungi, bacteria, algae, and other living organisms that help create the system's foundation. Sustainable farming can revamp our environment and make the world a more inhabitable place to eat, live, and grow.

Before I drove away, he gave me a hug and a small kiss goodbye. We knew we would never see each other again. We came from and exist in different worlds. But we met for a reason. Why? I believe we were sent as divine messengers to help each other move on to the next phase of our journey. We were not made to go on this journey together.

As far as the conch shell goes, it is a call to action. Blowing it initiates a ceremony or special occasion. My occasion or his occasion? Probably both. Within weeks after my journey to the farm, I was betrayed three more times. The three main aspects of my life keeping me in Wilmington were lies. No disagreements, arguments, or apologies, just not the truth. Being betrayed by people you have known for a short time is terrible. Being betrayed by someone you have trusted your entire life is unfathomable. This place was not fertile ground; it was dirt.

Call to Action

In my mind, a call to action meant I needed to get out of this town. During the day, I diligently worked towards an indistinct goal in some other part of the world. I usually walked five to six miles in the afternoons to refocus my brain. Starting over again was frustrating, but at least I had a renewed sense of joy within myself, although I still felt detached from the rest of the world. The next step in life had never taken this long or used this much effort. If you are revamping your entire life, there are no easy answers. Maybe one day, somebody will send me an easy button. I'd love to use it.

I mentioned this strange feeling of detachment in a 360° NATION group discussion, and one of the participants offered to talk more outside the group setting. I had been familiar with Roger for about a year, and he was always kind and thoughtful. He had endured great adversity, and I found his perspectives grounded, loving, and insightful, so I agreed to meet with him via Zoom the next day.

The same afternoon, I walked the path around the lake by my house. The body of water is natural, but the border of the lake and the surrounding walking trail were man-made and can be used for bikes and golf carts. It is relatively peaceful and has several species of birds and a couple of alligators living in the habitat. It is a good choice if you do not want to pay attention to where you are going.

As I rounded the third loop, I stopped in my tracks. Right in front of my foot was a shiny black shark's tooth. I thought, *"Impossible!"* I had been searching the beaches for a shark's tooth for two years without any luck. I was convinced finding a shark's tooth would symbolize something important. I tried to block out the voices, *"No. No. No. I do not want to hear that message."*

Apparently, my work here was unfinished, and something in the universe prompted me to pay attention. *"Ugh. Stupid shark's tooth! I don't want to listen, nor do I want to stay."*

The next day, Roger and I had an incredible conversation for hours. The sadness, as well as the love and laughter, was cathartic. He has a unique way of hearing and reframing what I say. I do not usually trust anyone like I trusted him with my feelings. But hey, he lives almost 4,000 miles away, so who could he possibly tell anyway? Then, we decided to keep the conversation going via direct messages to help me explore further possibilities.

The first response from Roger: *"This question came to me after our conversation yesterday. It may not help, but I thought I'd share on the off chance that the opposite may be true, too. If we truly believe God is within and outside us (non-duality,) yet we so easily, understandably, and innocently forget this (and live from duality,) doesn't finding the answers we seek simply involve remembering the former?"*

After a few more exchanges, I replied: *"A huge part of my emotional connection to God is my connection to people I love. When they hurt me, it affects my connection to everything else. Yes, I feel disconnected. I'm trying to understand and break apart my definition of love so I can hurt less intensely and for a shorter period of time."*

After a few more exchanges, Roger said: *"It struck me that the whole thing wasn't about me or others. Nor about what I wanted to have in life. Nor about analysis and intellectual concepts. It was much bigger than that. Connected more to a feeling about how I wanted to "be" in the world, irrespective of the obstacles I will continually encounter."*

I liked the freedom to directly message my feelings at any point in time and not expect an immediate reply. Much care and thought were put into our exchanges. Often, I would wake up in the middle of the night and have little epiphanies. Apparently, my brain thinks it is brilliant at 2:00 am, and being able to type out these thoughts in the moment was extremely helpful.

As our exchanges continued down an unknown path, I felt my companion by my side without judgment. Although I knew all the truncated opportunities were happening for a reason, I had difficulty believing the truth. Confiding in Roger helped ground me and afforded me a helicopter view of my experiences.

One more point Roger highlighted: *"You already have everything you need to turn your life around. It's just that you can't see it. You're understandably caught up in what life has put before you thus far, which makes access to your innate qualities of resilience, creativity, and compassion trickier than might otherwise be the case."*

I thought it was not about me or any people I come in contact with or my experiences. This whole dilemma was redirecting me to think, *"Who am I supposed to be in this world?"* My entire life, everyone, including my mother, has told me I should write a book. But how do you write a book about finding the light when you feel stuck in the dark? Further, how do I reconcile my feelings and find the time to accomplish this task? So many things didn't make sense.

Then, Roger encouraged me to remember that *"things do not have to make sense."* To me, that is a tough notion to swallow. My brain has difficulty letting go of things *until they make sense.*

Just a side note: Roger wasn't always encouraging everyone to use this technique. He suggested that when we stop fighting or contending against our current knowledge and become comfortable in our state of unknowing, paradoxically, clarity often appears in alternative ways. If you would like to know more about how Roger contemplates life and our current struggles, check out his Substack on how *Helpful Questions Change Lives.* https://hqcl.substack.com

I imagined a bunch of cows in a pasture ruminating on thoughts and ideas instead of grass. Each beautiful little blade of grass was literally food for thought. Yum. Yum Yum. Think about it: cows, deer, elk, giraffes, and camels (plus a few more mammals) have a unique four-compartment stomach, a part of their complex digestive systems. The way they process food, absorb nutrients, and obtain energy is different from other animals.

They chew on their thoughts and ideas, swallow, and regurgitate all day long. Guess what? They also co-ruminate, which means they share their thoughts and ideas with the other animals in the pasture. Just imagine how much these thoughts and ideas can mutate and transform within and around this entire rumination process. Eventually, the grasses make their way through the digestive systems and exit the cows by the same normal excrement process.

More importantly, am I really a cow who wants to endlessly ruminate and hang out with excrement from my past? No, I am not, and neither should you be. Trying to break apart, analyze, and make sense of the excrement may not be the best answer. This whole forgiving and forgetting thing is not for me. I am more of a remember what happened, understand the why and how, and then, let it go because staying angry at somebody impedes a genuinely loving relationship.

Here is some more food for thought. In general, rumination (repetitive thoughts) tends to lead to depression about events that happened in the past. Worry leads to anxiety about future uncertain events (potential threats). These are not separate entities; they are intertwined and cause dis-ease. My biggest barrier to progressing was making sense of it all.

Love Versus Cathexis

Most of the time, I make statements that do not exemplify comparison through competition. I prefer to make observations that allow people to uncover differences respectfully. A simple way to express those differences is to say, "Your definition of (blank) doesn't match my definition of (blank)." When presented this way, nobody is right/wrong, good/bad, or superior/inferior; it simply means we are different.

I find conversations amusing when one person is set on making their definition the correct one. They desire to prove they are right and everyone else is wrong. Some people try to be covert, while others are more overt. They usually start out the same way. The person appears uncomfortable and sifts their position or fidgets, often interrupts or talks over people, and then gets loud or aggressive as if we cannot hear them. Hilarious, I heard you the first time. I just disagree.

For example, my definition of a great day may entail hiking ten miles with my best friend, having amazing food and beverages, and listening to live music. While someone else may define a great day by cleaning the house, going to the grocery store, and watching a movie at home on the sofa. Neither one is bad, wrong, or inferior, just very different. However, at the end of the day, that person may say my activities were a complete waste of time, or I should choose to be more responsible. Ha! Thanks for the feedback. If these types of interactions allude to your version of a happy life, you may not be a good match for each other in the long term.

One big question I ask myself is, "*Why do people define love so differently?*"

Observing the world around me, I hear people say, "*I love you.*" But then, they want to change, control, abuse, manipulate or neglect you. That combination just doesn't make sense to me. I have always considered *love* to be an *action verb* as well as a *state of being.*

If I love somebody, I have a feeling of connection, which is my state of being. But if I simply sit around and do not take any action or choose to be abusive or indifferent, then how can my love continue to exist? If I take improper action in the relationship, then love should cease or should not have existed at all.

For example, have you ever heard somebody say they love someone because they have potential? Well, what does that mean? Are they on a path to success, and they have invited you along? That sounds cool. But what if they are on a path to nowhere, a dead end? Then you think, "*If they could only move into a new house, find a different job, get new friends, and stop drinking so much, they would be perfect!*" Sorry honey, wake up and smell the coffee. That is not potential. That is poison going both ways.

Don't you find it disturbing to think you are falling in love with someone or you supposedly have a loving relationship, and then one day, you wake up and feel nothing but disgust? It's like spoiled milk. Once your milk sours and you open that container and take a whiff, whew, there is no turning back. You are done. The milk should be poured down the drain. So, when your relationship sours, why do you keep trying to drink sour milk, otherwise known as poison?

Now, on to my next big question. If you love somebody, and some adversity occurs, why wouldn't you want to mend the relationship with a proper apology? In my mind, if an adequate apology is accepted by the other, the relationship remains on common ground and perpetuates accordingly. If an improper or no apology exists, the relationship is unbalanced and causes friction. Ultimately, this friction weighs down a relationship, causes resentment, and perpetuates poison.

If you initiate a relationship and elevate your standards of interaction, make sure you are doing it for yourself and not the other person. Why? Because you should desire to be the best person by yourself and the other person should have the same perspective. If you make changes for another person, you will eventually tire and return to your former self because it is human nature and is much easier.

Evolving into the person you wish to be in the world takes great effort, and there are no guarantees. If your relationship ends, you won't get your time, money, and efforts back, even if you save your receipts. The process of elevating your standards for yourself is worth much more. In fact, it may be priceless. The next time you need to move along, don't tally up your expenditures and begrudge your losses; be grateful for the life lessons. Be thankful you realized *it is time to go* and be grateful for the good times you experienced.

"Yeah, this sounds good, but what about real life?" Thank goodness you asked! Because the last two questions led me to my next question or should I say dilemma. Why am I unable to forgive certain people in my life who I supposedly have love for? If I think their version of love sucks and they refuse to take responsibility and apologize for abusing me, then how on earth am I supposed to forgive them? Do I really love them, or am I simply *attached* to the relationship? Big difference.

This dilemma had been weighing heavily on my mind for a long time. Forgiveness is supposed to set you free, and I didn't feel free of the emotional burden, although I had been trying. Why was I retaining this burden inside my heart?

Energy Retention: Thankfully, this wonderfully young but wise woman led an intriguing discussion on *cathexis,* which is currently defined as an investment of emotional energy into a person, idea, or object, especially when it reaches an unhealthy level of conscious or unconscious thoughts or behaviors. Joan's heartfelt discussion stuck with me for days, and I could feel *something* brewing.

Energy Release: It was 2:00 am, and I woke up with a *cathartic* jolt. Not only was I awake, but I was also wide awake, and *not making sense was making perfect sense!* I discovered how to let go of the emotional burden during my discussions with Roger and Joan. I wanted to write it down because I knew I would forget the intricacies by morning. I rummaged through the bedside table and found a book with some blank pages. I ripped out one of the pages and drew a basic diagram. I scribbled a bunch of words around the diagram to remind myself of my own little, or possibly large, epiphany.

Fortunately, I figured out how to turn a normal learning diagram into four different types of energy retention cards resembling Shamanic Oracles Cards. Like an orator, the Latin origin of the word oracle means to utter predictions. Turning over these cards will help to foretell what your relationships may look like and help you decide whether or not you would like to keep them. After all, we choose our own cards which means we can also discard them before the game ends.

Note: The two cards (A & B) on the top require a lot of emotional energy and retention. These images are clear and bold because I am sure they are easily recognizable in your life, or at least they should be. The bottom two cards (C & D) require far less emotional energy and retention unless the relationships start to evolve over time. I feel most people have probably experienced relationships in all four categories throughout their lives. It is just human nature. The only one I recommend you completely avoid or at least do your best to avoid is The Toxic Mirror. The other cards are perfectly acceptable in given situations.

The Sacred Scale (A) *(Loving Reciprocity)*: These relationships are emotionally balanced, not neutral. They entail a mutually beneficial and loving exchange. They are not always in perfect alignment, but continuous effort should be made to restore that alignment. Not everyone is always happy, healthy, and productive. Each person has their unique gifts to offer. These relationships learn to compensate and complement one another to create a harmonious life balance.

The scale is comprised of the sun, as seen through the key to eternal life, which dates back to antiquity, and the moon, as seen through the dichotomy of death and rebirth. All of these are necessary components of the energy of the universe.

Cathexis coupled love is an enticing and perpetual struggle for our existence. Many people confuse being drawn to someone and being in love with them. These two distinctions may start in the same area, but the cathexis part should only be in the initial phases of love. Once the emotional investment has a genuine foundation in love, you should feel comfortable with your emotions. The investment has paid off twofold. In the emotional commitment or offering of love, you give and receive love just like your partner. It is a choice you are willing to make, and you freely give love without expectations in return. Wisdom will intricately weave your bonds together.

In *The Road Less Traveled* by M Scott Peck, he emphasizes two factors concerning love I have always ascribed to:

> *"We are incapable of loving another unless we love ourselves"*
> *and "Two people love each other only when they are*
> *quite capable of living without each other but choose*
> *to live with each other."*

The Toxic Mirror (B) *(Look What's Wrong With You)*: These types of relationships are one-sided and leave you feeling emotionally drained and overwhelmed. The toxicity of that relationship often spills over to other relationships, which ultimately perpetuates your feelings of discomfort with yourself and with others. The unhealthy person is continuously forcing the mirror in front of your face and demanding you fix what is wrong with you in order to improve the relationship. That unhealthy person doesn't understand that the mirror is facing the wrong way. The toxic person must look at their reflection and ask, "How can I fix myself." But I think we can agree that will never happen unless something drastic occurs to alter their life. Usually, by then, it can be too late.

Cathexis, coupled with hate, incurs tremendous energy for both participants. However, one feels superior and the other inferior. If you are not comfortable with my word choice, you can replace it with other dark emotions that may exacerbate fear and anxiety. Either way, this relationship takes as much or possibly more of an emotional investment than love. A genuinely loving and compassionate person will often take physical and emotional action towards loving and caring for somebody they dislike or feel uncomfortable around. These interactions are emotionally intense and draining. What do you receive in return? Certainly not love, most likely some burden, no matter how large or small, perpetuating your soul's dis-ease.

What Is Love: Creating a set of words to define love could be infinitesimal and may not completely convey the message in your heart. Creating your own definition can be difficult so here are a few examples to help you out:

M Scott Peck defines love as:

> "*The will to extend one's self for the purpose of nurturing one's own or another's spiritual growth.*"

I thought it would be advantageous to give you this definition since his ideas somewhat prompted this discussion. This is the reciprocal nature of love, which means if both parties practice this definition, both will individually succeed as well as the relationship.

Socrates suggests love is:

> *"a form of divine madness and a pathway to understanding*
> *the nature of reality."*

I love how he calls it divine because love is a gift from God. However, the way he throws in madness is great because when you find love, sometimes you must question your own sanity. Could this actually be true? Why am I acting like this? Oh, my goodness, I must be crazy in love.

1 Corinthians 13:4–8a:

> *"Love is patient and kind; love does not envy or boast;*
> *it is not arrogant or rude. It does not insist on its own way;*
> *it is not irritable or resentful; it does not rejoice at wrongdoing*
> *but rejoices with the truth."*

Ahh, the truth, that is music to my ears. If you genuinely love somebody, your relationship should have a truth-based foundation. There are some truths you can only share with your loved one. Sharing certain emotions outside that relationship could be considered unfaithful.

Buddhism:

> *"Unselfishly wishing others to be happy; to be delighted to be in*
> *their presence; to offer our affection and smiles and hugs and*
> *help freely without wanting anything in return."*

Lama Zopa Rinpoche explains:"Love is wanting someone to be happy. Attachment is wanting it to be me that makes them happy." We have all experienced somebody getting horribly jealous when someone or something besides them makes you happy. Then, their goal is to selfishly take that happiness away from you and then somehow make you feel better. This is securing their position in your life, not love.

Buddhism believes attachment is a form of delusion and thus one of three root causes for our mental suffering. This philosophy believes attachment is a mistaken belief system and can make one ignorant to the facts. If a person believes their inner source of happiness is contingent upon another person, place or thing, then they would also believe this entity would solve their own feelings of being incomplete. Possibly, they do not understand that true love comes with no strings attached. Curious to know the other two root causes for our suffering? The first would be a combination of greed, lust and desire while the second involves hatred and anger.

Let's say your mother passes away, and your father is devastated. Initially, you and your father create a strong bond in remembrance of your mother. You console each other and create new memories because it makes you both relatively happy. Eventually, time passes, the sadness starts to dissipate, and your father meets another woman. This woman makes your father very happy, and you are filled with anger and jealousy. You want that woman gone. She is a menace and doesn't belong in your father's heart. You try to control and manipulate the situation because you love your mother and father. But is that fair? Is that really love, or is something else going on here?

What Isn't Love: I will tell you what words should not be included in your definition of love because these words should never coexist in a loving relationship: abusive, controlling, hurtful, neglectful, degrading, malicious, abandoned, etc. It's when one forces you to drink their poison and then expects you to enjoy it. Then, when you don't enjoy their poison, they give you more. Ultimately, the poison will infiltrate your relationship and cause dis-ease in your mind, body, and soul.

Suppose the definition of love you have experienced throughout your lifetime is filled with dis-ease. In that case, you may not notice because the initial stages of the new relationship will make you feel comfortable. You know, like wearing an old pair of shoes. They may feel great at the moment, but once you get going, they should be discarded. I believe this is why people end up in relationships that mimic or recreate prior relationships and ignore or do not comprehend the warning signs.

Red flags are not pretty banners commending your new relationship. They are warning signs you need to pay attention to, or else. Ignoring them means you value the hope of a relationship over the hope for yourself to be happy. Fear and anxiety weave their way into the patterns of your existence, and it is incredibly difficult to unwind them and start again, even if you desire to do so.

Have you ever seen a vibrant, intelligent, and charismatic person enter a relationship and just not seem like themselves anymore? Eventually, they may get sick or avoid social situations because they are too tired. Then, as the relationship progresses, they drastically alter their personality as if it was their choice. When you question the changes, the person defends the one they love because they have stuck by their side. Are the changes healthy and made by a loving choice or changes due to attachment?

How many people are aware of the subtle or not-so-subtle changes that occur inside of them when in a relationship? The self-awareness part comes into play when you ask yourself, *"Is this emotional investment of my time based in the light or the dark?"* You will feel free, although connected, if it is based in the light. Most importantly, you will feel like yourself and smile at that person in the mirror. You will continuously feel overwhelmed and undervalued if it is based in the dark. You are investing emotions, and the recurrent payback in the mirror is hell.

The Parasol (C) *(How's The Weather)*: Using a parasol to shade ourselves from the heat and rays of the sun dates back to at least 3500 BC. Imagine walking alone through a crowd of people on a sunny day. You can smile and wave, say a few polite greetings, or cheer on a fanciful game or novel entertainment. A crowd may surround you, but essentially, they are acquaintances or strangers. Of course, most of these people passing you by also have a parasol to shade themselves from the sun. Oh, and don't forget, it is always sunny, and everyone is seemingly "fine." When you return home and put your parasol away, your house is empty.

The small emotional investment of an acquaintance does afford you a certain amount of fleeting joy. Maybe you work in the same building, or your kids play soccer together. Maybe a street musician plays a song to greet you, or the bartender perfectly makes your specialty drink. Do you really know these people? No. Not knowing their name or not recognizing them out of context doesn't make you a bad person; it makes you human. Would it change your life if you saw them every Thursday for years or never again? Maybe, but probably not for more than a few moments.

However, this may be a place to start if you want to make new friends. Remember to use your intuition. If these acquaintances make you feel comfortable, try something new. Invite the person from work to lunch sometime. Have an end-of-the-year soccer party at your house. Ask people at the music festival what they enjoyed most. Strike up a conversation like sitting in the sitcom *Cheers,* where everybody knows your name. Speaking up first to make new connections will amaze you.

But listen up! Don't get caught up in *"The Let's Get Coffee Sometime (Syndrome)."* Many of those acquaintances hanging out under their parasols wish to stay alone. If the conversation goes beyond modern niceties, they will agree to coffee with you because it is a nice thing to do. I will tell you right now, they have no intention of going. So, don't take it personally, expect it. After all, it is sunny, and sometimes, we need to jump over a few lingering mud puddles.

The Carriage Ride (D) *(Stuck In The Mud)***:** Before the invention of the automobile and paved roads, people used a horse and carriage to travel. The carriage driver had to pay attention to the people, the supplies, and the schedule and attempt to be on time. When riding in the back of the carriage, there is no way to have a genuine, in-depth conversation. Your acquaintance with them could be a few days or a few years, but you do not know much about them personally and most likely on purpose. They wish to remain unfamiliar and emotionally distant from those around them. Their demeanor may be pleasant or unpleasant, but you never know what is happening inside them.

If the day goes smoothly, everyone will have a pleasant journey. But, if the roads are muddy and impassable, or if there is a diversion, there is a problem. The driver has a lot of work to do to get everything and everyone up and running again. Surely, getting stuck was a great inconvenience, and the driver was very busy and uncomfortable. But look out! Here comes your intuition again, and you feel the urge to create a relationship with the driver because you think they just might need a friend.

These emotionally detached and unavailable people can potentially learn to live in the light if they choose to learn and grow. They are not necessarily bad or undesirable; they are guarded. When they let their guard down and invest some emotional energy into the light, they can open themselves up to love. However, if their guard dissipates and the darkness gets darker, it's probably time to run the other way. Get back into that carriage and keep your mouth shut. You will reach your destination eventually and can say a fond farewell.

Don't take this notion too far or be overly pessimistic. Some relationships need to be emotionally distant. I would venture to say most of your superiors at work or school don't openly share their emotions, which is all right. If you are working on a serious project with major deadlines, you won't have much time for personal stuff. Possibly, you live in a neighborhood where everyone likes to keep the peace and stay to themselves. Just trust your intuition. You know that feeling in your gut and assess the next step.

Good luck in this game of cards. I wish we could whisper our utterances about people; it would cause our hearts much less misery and more peace and prosperity.

Maybe you are asking yourself why I am telling you all of this information and why I describe my diagram as an epiphany. Again, I am so happy you asked because *something* genuinely left my body that night, and I felt absolutely amazing.

I concluded that I only needed to forgive people I loved to perpetuate the loving relationship. This does not mean the relationship is perfect. It just means I want that person in my life. People say you can't pick your family, but you can pick your friends. Well, I decided many of my friends are my family, and I get to define my family. So, why can't I choose? You know what? I can. It's my life.

Let's consider my epiphany a basic mathematical logic problem:

If I love somebody, then I need to forgive them. Therefore, I am perpetuating the relationship.

If I don't love somebody, I don't need to forgive them. Therefore, I am not perpetuating the relationship. To solve the equation, I just need to let go of the attachment to the relationship.

Remember, attachment is not love; it is emotional energy. When I let go of the attachment, God shall judge that person and allow the natural consequences of life to occur. Here is a little secret: this concept of letting go led me to the name Daniel. I no longer have to judge him; God will.

Here is an important caveat: letting go. If you choose to leave a relationship and the other person does not want to let go, that person can perpetuate the relationship negatively. They may harass you for your time, energy, and money and/or negatively impact people close to you to cause friction. They may promise to 'change" to rekindle the relationship, or they threaten you personally or professionally when you decline. They may make you feel guilty and blame you for losing the perceived love.

Listen to me very carefully; *a negative relationship is still a relationship*, and they are receiving emotional energy by keeping you trapped. The opposite of love is not hate because both contain an emotional investment. The opposite of love is indifference, which is a lack of interest or concern, including a lack of empathy towards that person.

Unemotional silence may be best if words cannot diffuse or terminate the relationship respectfully and peacefully.

With that being said, if I get to choose my definition of love and I get to choose my family, then that is all I need. If someone does not love me the way I want to be loved, then I do not have to love them and I do not have to wish for forgiveness. I do not have to forgive the darkness because I choose to live in the light. I must simply wish for and work towards the emotional energy to leave me. When that energy finally leaves, and I am not emotionally invested, my suffering should end.

This concept may leave a bad taste in the mouths of many spiritual leaders, mentors, and guides. However, I do not believe everyone can *get over it or pray to get past it*. I can come to terms with understanding the situation and letting the emotions dissipate. The feelings may never fully leave, but they don't have to linger in your everyday thoughts. If you are genuinely able to fully forgive a person who has purposely and permanently infiltrated darkness in your life, then your brain is wired a little differently than mine. I am curious, though. How did you do it?

One thought could be that you have learned how to forgive yourself, and that's a big one. If you have let go of all the shame and doubt you have gathered throughout your lifetime, you are on the right track. I will assume that churning up all your thoughts and ideas about people may be more productive when you can assign your interactions with them into one of these four quadrants versus ruminating over them in one of your four stomachs. So, get a pooper scooper and use that cow excrement as fertilizer for the soil in your new garden of life.

Santa is Real

As the winter holidays drew near, I felt an internal shift emerging, but I wasn't quite there yet. The thousand voices of the Mitote had quieted a bit, but not enough. I still needed to be alone with my thoughts. *"If I am a healer, then what should I do next?"* I was determined to find out.

Attending the group discussions I was involved in via 360° NATION was a great help because every group member was unique and eloquently described their perspectives. Whether listening or actively participating, I was gaining much-needed wisdom. Surprisingly, a man who runs a podcast invited me to be a guest on his show.

I was a bit nervous but decided it was a great idea. However, I was distracted by the holidays and my pending visit to see my daughter. So, I asked if we could record our conversation at the beginning of the new year. I wanted to be calm, confident, and prepared. He politely agreed and wished me well.

A few days before my departure, I went hiking through Abby Nature Preserve because I heard the surrounding area and a large portion of the trails had been sold to a land developer, and we all know what that means: total demolition. When I arrived on the far side of the trails upon the entrance to the open fields, the spirit who stood by the gate was not there anymore. I smirked and said, "*I guess they kicked you off the property, but don't worry, this is where the wildflowers grow. I'll remember you.*"

On the opposite side of the field, I was trying to identify some dark bluish berries growing on an extensive line of bushes and saw an older man walking towards me. "*Excuse me, sir. Are you from around here?*" He looked a little confused and replied, "*Yes, I grew up just down the road.*"

I was excited because I had many questions and thought he might have answers. "*Do you know what types of berries these are? My nature app can't seem to identify them.*" He did not know about the berries but was curious about the app. I told him it was a free download called "Seek" from National Geographic, which helps you identify plants, animals, and insects and correlates your findings by geographic location. "*Plus, you get points and attain levels when you find a native species.*" as if I was a child looking for a gold star sticker on my worksheet. I explained, "*I love it!*"

We continued our conversation for a while because he knew much about the area. Then, I told him this preserve was one of my sanctuaries and that I was very upset because it would all be gone soon. The owner had sold the property. *"Before they demo this field, I want to come and dig up some of the passion flowers I found. They are so beautiful, and I have never seen anything like them before."*

Just then, he looked down to the ground, and sadness filled him, *"I am sorry. It's me."* as he pointed to his chest. It took a few seconds to sink into my brain, *"Are you Bob?"* I asked. *"Yes, my family owned this land for over two hundred years, and I really didn't have a choice. Fortunately, the developers will keep the nature preserve open to the public."*

Then, I described the spirit at the entrance gate and how I researched the people and the property over a year ago. He clearly said, *"It has to be Nemrod Nixon. He was a tenant farmer on this land his entire life. The old water well used to be by the entrance, where he would take breaks from working and cool off. He and my grandfather mentored me as a child."*

"Is he buried around here?" I inquired. Bob shook his head and replied, *"No, he is buried in Pollock's Cemetery, a historically black burial ground across from Scott's Hill Loop Road. Why do you ask?"*

I replied, *"The second time I saw him, I distinctly felt like he was trying to tell me something. So, I went home and researched, hoping to find a photograph or something to identify the spirit I saw."*

Bob replied, *"He was probably watching over you to make sure everything was all right."* Suddenly, a strange chill went down my spine as a faint swirl of dust caught my eye in the distance. It was getting late, so I said, *"Hey, I will be out of town until next year, but if you would like to hike sometime, I would really enjoy it. I am looking for new trails and would love to learn more about Nemrod."* Bob was pleasantly surprised as we exchanged phone numbers and parted ways.

Within a few days, I was heading to Oregon. My daughter had only been there a few months and was excited for me to visit and explore. Unfortunately, I had a layover in Denver, and when the plane landed, the temperature was -15° Celsius, and my winter outerwear was packed in my suitcase. I was one of thousands of people stranded at the airport, but I kept a smile on my face. Nobody wanted to be stuck there, and I certainly wasn't going to add to the burden.

I felt calm and peaceful even though I walked 10 miles due to multiple cancellations and gate transfers. Several people even asked me why I appeared so happy, and I simply replied, "*It's my only choice.*" Finally, my flight got canceled, and I closed my eyes in disbelief. I thought, "*This isn't over yet.*" as I traveled to the end of the customer service line. People were everywhere, and the airlines offered free snacks and water. I took some but eventually gave it to a woman whose child would not stop crying. She apologized for the commotion, but I assured her we all felt the same way.

In my mind, I prayed, "*Please God, all I want for Christmas is to hold my daughter in my arms.*" If I was meant to be in Denver for Christmas, I sent several SOS messages and had a few options if the airlines could not accommodate me. Having so many friends to contact in my time of need was comforting. Grace would surely set me free.

After waiting four hours, I got to the front desk and handed the lady my ticket information. After a few minutes of her clicking away on the computer, guess what? I literally got the last seat on the last plane to Oregon, and boarding was in three hours. My eyes instantly filled with tears of joy as I wished her a Merry Christmas and a Happy New Year. Thankfully, I slept most of the way to Oregon.

On that silent and holy night, all was calm and magically bright. I sat in front of a blazing wood-burning stove with my daughter nestled in my arms. She was my tender and beautiful baby once again. I brushed her hair back and glided my fingers gently across her face. The warm scent of the fire took me back to a simpler time. I reminisced about baking cookies and decorating ornaments with my children. Just as a vision of reading Christmas stories by candlelight popped into my head, she looked into the fire and said, "*Look, Mommy, the flames are dancing for us.*"

The first time we sat in front of a candle and watched the flames dance was when we lived in Georgia, and I was pregnant with my son.

Having a new little brother would be a big deal, and while she was excited, she was understandably a little anxious. So, I wanted to make our relaxation time together special forever. *"No matter where you go and what you do, we can always light our candles together and watch them dance."*

As I nestled into bed that night, I watched tiny snowflakes freeze into sparkling patterns on the windowpane. I could see the moon trying to peak through the clouds in hopes of illuminating the land for Saint Nick's mystical and magical journey. I whispered my favorite Christmas song and prayed that the world would be sleeping in heavenly peace like me. By the way, Santa, I know you are real.

CHAPTER 10

❧✦❧

THE LAND OF MILK AND HONEY

Unearthing the Past

Throughout the next couple of weeks into the new year, we contended against the rain and mud. Accepting you will get wet and dirty is part of the plan. We traversed snow and ice-covered mountains, bathed in hot springs, and found secret gardens along an old mill stream. My daughter seemed different, but I couldn't quite place my finger on what different meant. All I knew was that I loved it and anticipated even more miracles.

As we ventured up the coast, we ate in a seafaring town where sea lions barked at the wind, explored mysteriously foggy beaches, and saw stunning cliffs with layers of intense color. I knew saying goodbye was going to be difficult. But, when she gave me a huge hug and her sweet little voice said, *"Thank you for coming to visit me. I don't know when I'll see you again,"* a deluge of tears ran down my cheeks and warmed my heart. I knew I had received my Christmas wish.

Fortunately, the plane rides back were uneventful, and I made it home safe and sound. Moreover, I made it home, ready to take on 2023. Over the years, I learned that stepping out of current reality and experiencing genuine love in the abundance of nature are the best ways to prepare for the future.

Like traveling by plane, you get an aerial view of the world and all that is occurring. Your feelings and emotions and a small carry-on bag are all you have. You choose the experience. When you land, you are ready for the next adventure. Within days, every ounce of me wanted to find a path to the river that had been eluding me. Coincidence? I think not. On my next outing, I discovered the trails to the area of the Cape Fear River I had been looking for. I just felt like I was supposed to be there.

It was low tide, and the landscape was distinctively different. During high tide, these secret pathways vanish, and everything blends in with the river. I saw a land bridge to the other side of a small tributary. I was hesitant to crossover because I did not know the depth of the mud beneath the surface.

As I slowly approached the stream bed, I saw a grayish rock the size and shape of a marble flattened on one side with a distinctive hole in the center. It was relatively interesting, but I tossed it aside. Then, I found another and another, identical in form. I was so excited I had found fossils! I had no idea what they were, but I had a small bag with me and collected as many as I could carry.

This discovery gave me a purpose and made me feel overwhelmingly alive. The fossils were intriguing pieces of the past that had been lying dormant for years. Now, I was bringing them back to life, just like I wanted to bring myself back to life. I thought I was doing a great job, but something was still eluding me. It's something obviously important but apparently not so obvious to me.

I wanted somebody to see the real Amy and just say, "*Hey, I want you by my side.*" Personally or professionally, there must be somebody out there who wants me. *All of me.* Picking somebody to experience life with isn't like going to a buffet dinner where you can pick and choose which portions you like and discard the remaining ingredients. It may be a 12-course meal *without substitutions,* but I know I am well worth the price. Basically, I want somebody who wants all of me and vice versa.

Day after day, I went down and gathered many varieties of prehistoric fossils and tried to identify them in the evenings. Finally, the moment I had been waiting for! I found a medium-sized, shiny jet black shark's tooth dating back over 38 million years. The triangular crown of the auriculatus tooth with side cusps are usually smaller than the popularized megalodon teeth, dating back about 5 million years. However, the auriculatus is larger than current day shark teeth, and due to evolution, the side cusps no longer exist.

Countless hours spent in solitude unearthing the past brought back the Amy I knew in childhood. She was quiet because she did not want anyone to see who she was on the inside. Being alone in search of treasures buried deep inside brought calmness to my soul. I love being alone. I did not want anyone to intrude on my privacy until I figured out what to do next on my path to redemption by unearthing my past's positive and intriguing aspects.

My path to redemption surpassed being saved from sins, evil, or errors in my ways. Moreover, my seemingly lifelong path to redemption included regaining my words, thoughts, and actions from the Amy I had lost or possibly misplaced. I knew I had made amends with everyone I had purposely or accidentally wronged, whether they accepted my gestures or not. As far as I was concerned, my debt had been paid and now, I needed to shift my focus from what was wrong with Amy to what was right with Amy. This was necessary if I wanted to continue to heal, help my children, and ultimately help many others for the rest of my life.

During the low tides of my newly found sanctuary, I uncovered the Amy I once knew. However, I inextricably wanted her back better than before, better than ever imagined.

I learned to listen to the tides changing, which can only occur when you cherish the silence. On the Cape Fear, when low tide shifts to high tide, the water is fast and furious with a distinctive sound. Ignoring the sounds of the river calling you for a few brief and fleeting moments can transform your safe journey into a treacherous maze through the marsh. It can literally take your life.

During high tides, I continued my job search. Along the way, I met someone who owned a consultation agency and was offered a personality survey. Out of curiosity, I agreed. The administration of the survey was quick and easy. The paper report seemed to be relatively on target. Ok. Cool. Thanks. Often, I think those surveys spout out what people want to hear and can be passed on to numerous participants.

However, when it came time for the principal consultant to synthesize my data verbally, I was overly delighted with his feedback. This man, with only one prior Zoom meeting, was telling me intricate and accurate details about myself. It was wonderful that almost a complete stranger validated my introverted and extroverted personality traits. He had been assessing people and company structure for a multitude of years, and it showed

Yes, I am both. I am an introvert, but I actually prefer to call it my cute and quirky side. My brain never stops thinking, usually in multiple tangents simultaneously. But I am also an extrovert with a love for connection and communication. Both sides working in tandem satiate my curiosity, at least for a while. The absolute most hilarious part of our conversation about the real Amy was this portion of the assessment and my score:

"This person thinks so far outside of the obvious pattern; they aren't aware of what's "normal." They are the epitome of thinking outside the box. There is no box. Whether they work with concepts or objects, this person can find rare solutions that may bend business in unexpected directions. Be prepared for suggestions that may or may not be profitable, but always be innovative. Ingenuity is enhanced by experience and education."

During this portion of the feedback, he illuminated additional criteria and explained that the majority of the population scores were between 40 and 60. I had no idea what that meant and inquired. He laughed and exclaimed, *"I will say this is the most constructive way possible!"* I assured him I was ready to hear the news. *"You scored a 70, and that makes you a complete freak!"*

We both burst out into laughter because the characteristics he described and the inquiries I confirmed completely delineated his assertation. In other words, I am a freak of nature! I can work for exceptionally long periods and have the complete mental stamina to kick ass at the same time.

My counterargument was that I absolutely do not want to do that all day, even though I can. Why? Because that characteristic behavior can lead to an extremely boring extracurricular lifestyle. I make sure to take a break and be human for a while. Work hard, play hard. Get some rest. I added the get some rest a few years back. Why? Because I desired to be happy and healthy in the latter years of life. And by the way, if you do not listen to your body, it will insist on it.

My Podcast

It was finally time to record my Podcast with Mac. I was excited yet nervous, but felt relatively confident. I thought the best scenario was to stick to four main obstacles I had overcome and keep them as objective as possible. I felt bridging into the emotionally based aspects concerning the trauma would be too much. Mac was a gracious host and allowed me to feel proud to just be myself. He is one of the best group leaders I have ever met, and his wisdom transcends into all of his endeavors.

If you would like to check it out, please go to any of the Podcast platforms and enter: **back2different by Mac Bogert.** Once there, find my name *Amy Olmedo, Versions of the Truth* (Season 3; Episode 67).

I thought putting this one hour episode into the world was an entertaining way to call myself as well as others into action, and hopefully not cause too much of a ruckus. I was ready to tell my story, and I was not going to keep my suffering and subsequent healing a secret any longer. It was time to heal together with those I love, and those I have yet to meet. Just like this book, my hope is to be able to bond with people on common ground and progress.

I received very positive feedback from a wide variety of people. I also sent it to some of my friends and family. Some responded quite well, and others never responded. I have no idea what any non-responders are thinking, and that is fine. Their thoughts are not my business. Both of my children said they fully supported me and my opinions, but they were not ready to listen. I understood their hesitation and appreciated their honesty and candor. I let them know they could listen when ready.

Between my fossil sanctuary, and all the recent events leading up to this Podcast, I felt ready to take on the world. I made a playlist on Pandora which signified this portion of my life. I listened to it on my way to and from the sanctuary most days. I had always considered myself more of a mountain person, but there was definitely an energy making the river satiate the tides within my soul.

When the band Caamp sings *"Feels Like Home,"* I felt like I was living the song's lyrics. There was something in my heart that felt like a burning fire and the yearning of the river made those burning embers feel like I was home. Every day when I took myself down to the water,

I intrinsically knew I needed time to continue on my journey. I beckoned the river, *"Please give me some more time."*

I was always alone except on a few occasions when I saw this guy drive by on his dirt bike. The first two or three times, we simply nodded to each other and finally on the fourth time, we gestured a wave. Obviously, we were both here to get away from something, but we found ourselves sharing this remote sanctuary. The next time I saw him, I was sitting on a large log and changing my shoes. He stopped and spoke to me for a while. He told me he had lost his mom from Covid along with a few other things going on in his life. He was innocent and kind, and just seemed to need a *mommy* to talk to.

After several conversations down by the river, he told me his father was a beekeeper. I told him I was very interested in learning about the bees and the medicinal purposes of honey. I was willing to exchange work for knowledge if his father was interested in teaching me. I love to learn things through hands on knowledge. When I can see something in my mind, it sticks with me. Ha! No pun intended.

So, we exchanged phone numbers and communicated a little bit. Occasionally, I sent him pictures of my fossils, and he sent me pictures of his elaborate fish tanks.

About a month went by and I had not seen him, nor had I heard from his father. I thought, oh well, another missed opportunity, and I continued on. However, one day as I was walking down to my sanctuary, I saw a huge bulldozer knocking down over a mile worth of forest. The destruction was so fresh, all the trees were weeping resinous red tears of sorrow. I started to cry, and desperately wanted to share my sorrow with somebody who would understand. I immediately texted the guy on the dirt bike, *"Have you seen what they have done?"*

After a few messages back and forth, he rode his dirt bike down to the river to meet me and brought me one of his favorite drinks: a Sun Drop soda. We sat on a log for a while and talked about how the developers have destroyed this area's natural beauty. We could not figure out how or why *anybody* could believe you need to *destroy* everything to build something new except the almighty dollar. Money controls the world, and developers only care about the bottom line.

I had not shared my fossil gathering with anybody, but felt this was an appropriate moment. We were both sad and needed to uncover amazing things from our past. We walked up the coast, and crossed over the tributary. A short distance up was a secret campsite I would have never discovered without him. Before we parted ways, he inquired if his father had contacted me. I replied, *"Nope, not a word. I really am interested in learning, and I know how to fix stuff and follow directions."* He said he would contact his father when he got home. I halfway expected to meet someone named Bubba who wore tattered overalls while magically whispering to bees.

I took a few pictures of the bright orange sunset over the river as I started to head back to the house. I laughed and thought, *"Ha! I think I just made a deal with another alux."* But, this mischievous bearded woodland creature just didn't disappear into the forest, he rode his dirt bike home with some fossils in his pocket for his fish to hang out with. Seeing the joy in his bright green eyes reminded me of my children. I longed to have them by my side. It was nice to bond with someone who understood me.

When I returned to the devastated forest, it looked like the Sahara Desert. I saw a small band of trees in the distance they had left to separate the two development sites. It appeared as though several thousand homeless birds were perched upon a small hand full of trees. The screeching mournful cries were piercing as they sat unsheltered from the storm. It is one of the worst gut wrenching sounds I have ever heard. As I gently closed my tearful eyes, my broken heart encouraged my mouth to speak, *"I am so sorry they destroyed your homes; I do not know where you will go, but my heart goes with you."*

I hung my hiking sandals upon a few of the leftover trees lying on the ground. Their long life had finally come to an end. I noticed their tiny white and purple baby trees lying by their side who never had a chance to flourish. There was something in the orange of the sky that seemed mysteriously old and new all at the same time. I bowed my head and prayed for finding beauty in devastation. I prayed all the creatures of the forest would find a new home. I wished the newcomers to this land happiness and prosperity. Possibly, they were coming here to heal as well.

When I got home, I made dinner and took a hot Epsom salt bath before bed. I thought maybe it would be better if I initiated the conversation with his father so, I sent a text message, *"Hello, this is Amy, I met your son down by the river. I don't know your name except, Dad."* Within minutes we had a few exchanges and Ken offered to tell me anything and everything I wanted to know about honey. I assumed he was a tough cookie, so I offered some information about myself. I wanted him to trust me.

Ken was responsive and communicated quite well. He had a witty and charming sense of humor. Ken explained he was a master bee keeper and had been extracting honey for twenty years and currently had around 160 colonies. He offered some information about bees that was interesting, but I wanted to learn firsthand. I decided to send him my Podcast and thought, *"He will either think it's amazing or he will run the other way."* Either way, I was going to cut to the chase and figure out if he was willing to work with me or not. Fortunately, my plan was a great success because my honesty and candor was met with kindness and respect.

The Compass

A week before my birthday, I watched the movie, *"Out of Africa"*. I knew it was an old movie, but it popped up on my Netflix as a top suggestion. It was two hours and forty minutes long, so I did not expect to get through the entire movie in one sitting. However, once I started, I couldn't stop. The scenery was stunning, and the story resonated with me on so many levels.

The movie starts in a dreamlike state with a fiercely independent woman recalling, "*I had a farm in Africa at the foot of the Ngong Hills. I had a farm in Africa.*" As the beautiful and determined Meryl Streep rides a train across the grasslands, the musical composition is intense and thought-provoking as the sun rises over a hopeful day. The movie is based on a memoir written by Isak Dinesen, whose real name was Baroness Karen Blixen, in the mid-1930s. Although Meryl was thirty-six years old and had two young children in real life, her character appeared quite young and relatively sheltered by her prestigious upbringing in Denmark.

She did not want to marry her suitor out of obligation, and be stuck in a boring austere life. She agreed to marry an adventurous and handsome gentleman who promised to take her to Africa, and possibly see the world. However, the husband she enticed with money and prestige failed to hold up his end of the bargain, and ventured out into the world without her for months at a time. When he did return, it was for a short and lonely period of time. Ultimately, she thought he stole her ability to feel whole.

However, she accomplished more than most men could ever dream in her relative solitude. When it was time to embark on her own adventure, a lofty admirer reprimanded her and insisted she return to the farm. On the other hand, an intriguing and life-loving man who cherished the land just as she did offered her a gift. It was a beautiful compass to help guide her through the untamed grasslands of Africa. The moment this gift was bequeathed upon her journey, I had to stop the movie and cry. I longed for that mysterious and delightful gift to be bestowed upon my heart.

The next day, I had promised to go on a hike with Bob. I could tell he was trying to reconcile his past, and find peace in this world. Throughout his lifetime, his high profile job and family situation did not allow him to feel his feelings. After his wife passed onto the next realm, he became involved with another woman who wanted to emotionally control him. She did not allow him to speak about his wife of over 40 years or go out with his friends without intense interrogation. Apparently, my friendship with him allowed him to start paying attention to everything in between point A and point B.

As I hopped into his truck, I asked, *"Have you seen the movie, Out of Africa?"* He looked a bit bewildered and replied, *"Yes, several times. It was Tuulikki's favorite movie."* When they met, she was a young and beautiful airline hostess from Finland who loved to travel to exotic places and collect artwork. Africa was her favorite destination. Eventually, we got to our hike at The Green Swamp Preserve. It was seemingly untouched by the outside world as though we had stepped back in time.

During our hike, we talked about the immense love he has for his family, and what he endured while his wife was sick. I told him about some things I had been working on, and my desires to write a book and create a retreat. Apparently, what I described definitely piqued his interest. Along the way, I identified and took some pictures of native and carnivorous plants. Thankfully, we found our way back from beyond the preserve, and did not run into any black bears as this is *their* sanctuary.

Afterwards, he asked if I would join him for dinner. We found a restaurant situated on the water, and the view as well as the food was outstanding. He asked some additional questions about my book and the retreat. After dinner, he dropped me off at the house and thanked me for the adventure. The next day, I texted him a couple of pictures and thanked him for his kindness. He replied, *"No, I need to thank you. Yesterday was the anniversary of my wife's passing, and you made me the happiest I have been in a long time."* Whew, I had no idea. Beyond being surprised, I was deeply humbled. I noticed he still wore his wedding ring, and hearing this gave me a little insight into his emotional state of mind although I did not ask him about it. I thought I would be intruding on his privacy.

A few minutes passed, *"Please let me pay for your book. You have declined my offer multiple times, but hear me out. You have given me a present, and now I would like to give you one as well."* I was blown away. How on earth can somebody say no to a man who has been so kind and generous, and is finally starting to pay attention to the beautiful side of life once again. I accepted the delightful gift he had bestowed upon my heart, *my dream.* I will finally have time to write my book, and hopefully create a retreat center for those who have suffered great adversities in life. Further, I knew he had helped several other people he cared for to follow their dreams.

Within a week, a whirlwind of events were set into place to transform my dream into a reality. Well, maybe I shouldn't call it a dream. I have had these ideas swirling through my mind for over thirty years, and were actually the reason I started the real estate investment company with my former husband. Unfortunately, we all know how that turned out. After raising two children on my own, and being knocked down by accidents, illnesses, and poor relationships, I had no idea if I would be able to return to my intended calling. Furthermore, I knew I couldn't do it all alone.

Miraculously, I found out I wasn't alone. I discovered my ideas were greatly needed in the world, and there were a bunch of people who wanted to support me in various ways. Fortuitously, I found myself at a writing convention in Tampa thanks to the gracious invitation from my newly found friend, Eileen, and to Bob who was ready for another adventure.

The unconventional writing convention allowed me to meet so many wonderful people I had met online through 360° NATION. The physical connections perfectly complimented the virtual connections, and most importantly, the hugs were real. I thoroughly enjoyed the speakers as well as the activities, and it gave me a chance to look deeper inside myself. The self honesty of this group astounded me. I contemplated how this group may be the spiritual enclave I had been searching for.

On the way back from Tampa, we stopped at Lochloosa Wildlife Management Area because I had always been intrigued by the song's namesake sung by JJ Grey and Mofro. The depth and power of his voice, and the lyrics to this song are insanely powerful. I needed to visit the area that inspired this creation. JJ was homesick for her as he so eloquently calls the lake and it's majestic surroundings. Lord, he needs her and she's slipping away to all the damn developers tearing her heart out. As we four wheeled through dirt roads leading to nowhere but everywhere beautiful, I wondered why anybody would want to destroy this mystical habitat. I could feel his voice and Lochloosa pulsating through me.

Apparently, JJ Grey was not the only person inspired by the rare beauty of this area as we discovered Marjorie Kinnan Rawlings homestead was just a few miles away in Cross Creek. She brought the area abundant with orange groves into international fame with her book, "The Yearling" in 1938. Upon our visit, Bob and I toured the grounds, tasted wild oranges on the outskirts of the area, and walked the trails her many affluent visitors traversed almost a hundred years ago. At the approach stands a sign with a quote from Marjorie dating back to 1942.

"It is necessary to leave the impersonal highway, to step inside the rustic gate and close it behind. One is now inside the orange grove, out of one world and in the mysterious heart of another. And after long years of *spiritual homelessness, of nostalgia, here is that mystic loveliness of child-hood again. Here is home."*

I wondered if she was looking down from Heaven and understanding that is how I feel when I find a place of raw beauty and where I feel closest to God.

As we pulled down branches and picked a few wild oranges in the depth of the woods, we expected a sweet treat. However, these juicy little pieces of sunshine were so bitter, we instantaneously burst in laughter, and I thought, *"This place is truly enchanting. I am sure this lady would more than comprehend my true north. Now, I need to go find my compass."*

Oh Honey

Three days before my birthday, it was finally time to meet Ken. We planned to get some coffee at a local restaurant. My sister did not know who I was going to meet, and asked if it was a date. I replied, *"I'm not sure."* She looked confused. I explained I originally intended on meeting him to learn about honey, but our conversations seemed to be going in a different direction. I had a tinge of excited nervousness which is not my typical reaction to such an invitation.

When I walked into the restaurant, Ken politely stood up from the table to greet me. As I sat down, I saw a book about love languages we had been discussing via text and a beautiful jar of golden wildflower honey. My heart skipped a beat, and I bashfully smiled; this must be a date. *"Thank you"* didn't seem to cover how I felt at that moment. This man must be incredibly brave or crazy. I picked brave because the kindness exuding from him made the rest of the world disappear.

About three hours into our conversation, I asked, *"Can I tell you something that may sound a little strange?"* As he agreed, I took a deep breath, and explained I rarely Google people. But, something inside me insisted I look up your wife. As I read the obituary, *"Those blessed to have her touch their lives and hearts will never forget her quirky sense of humor and infectious laugh, as it lit the room."*

Further, I explained when I was reading the passage, I distinctly heard feminine laughter. But, when I got up and opened my bedroom door and inquired, "*Hello, is anybody here?*" nobody answered. I am almost positive I heard Karen laugh, and I haven't been able to get this cheerful laughter out of my mind. Ken calmly looked at me and replied, "*Yep, that sounds like something she would do.*"

After five hours of talking and laughing as if we had known each other forever, the servers put up the chairs and turned off the lights. I guess we needed to leave but neither of us wanted to. He cordially walked me to my car and shook my hand goodbye. My heart smiled as I watched him fade beyond the streetlight. I felt like our souls had gently embraced as a sweet, yet imaginary kiss lingered on my lips. The sensation felt so real. I was filled with delight as he turned back to look at me one last time.

Upon my return, my sister asked, "*So, was it a date?*" My usual response to such questions starts with a "*well*" and interjects with a "*but*". On this occasion, I simply replied, "*I think I just met the nicest man I have ever met in my entire life.*" I got into bed with an overwhelming sense of peace in my soul. Ken texted to thank me for an enjoyable evening, and asked if I would like to meet for dinner after I got back from Tampa. I graciously accepted. As you read above, Tampa was a great success.

Ken invited me to his favorite Mexican restaurant. We talked and laughed about a multitude of things for hours. This time, I asked if I could tell him about my dream which was right in line with the angelic laughter I heard a few weeks back. After he agreed, I explained I was in a bright, large hospital room with long, flowing curtains. There were two women in sheer white gowns who needed to tell me something important. The one on my left was standing and silent while the one to my right was seated with her hands on the arm of the chair. She wanted me to convince Ken that this dream was real.

As I looked around, I said, "*I need something to prove you are real.*" She held a key ring filled with a multitude of keys all belonging to the hospital except one. It was silver with a green plastic top, and it belonged to an old Volkswagen Passat. She said, *"Tell him about this key. Then, he will believe you."* As I reached towards her, I woke up and jotted down the information so I would not forget by morning.

Without trepidation, Ken replied, *"I think I know exactly which key you are talking about. I'll look for it when I get home."* Whew, what a relief. I thought for sure he would think I was crazy as hell. But now, he would find the key and hopefully unlock the mystery. I had a distinct feeling Karen had brought us together, and he did as well. I assumed she wanted him to be happy and continue with his life. As the evening ended, he walked me to my car and invited me to visit his bee yard. He was planning on heading down there on the coming weekend. I excitedly agreed to go.

On Saturday morning, we went to two of his bee yards, and I watched him re-home a swarm in his shorts and t-shirt. I had never seen so many bees in my life, and I opted to stay in the truck. Again, I thought this man must be incredibly brave or crazy. Again, I chose brave because of the huge smile across his face. I loved the way his mustache curled up at the end of his smile as his eyes glowed. This seemingly mysterious man experienced the world with the innocent and curious eyes of a child, but the wisdom and knowledge of an elder. The combination of the two was distinctively warm and inviting, unlike anything I had felt before. The emotional closeness was intense.

I thought our last stop was Shelton Herb Farm. This magical century year old farm grows over 800 varieties of culinary and medicinal herbs. It looks and feels like you are in an old story book filled with plants, animals, insects and of course, green anoles which are lizards native to coastal North Carolina. When the male anoles are trying to allure a mate, a large red protrusion with white dots pops out from under their chin, and they bounce up and down like they are dancing. One was definitely flirting with me near some orchids in bloom. Yes, I am talking about the lizard, not Ken, in case you are wondering.

As we toured the greenhouses and surrounding area, we rubbed leaves to get the essence on our fingertips. The scents were as amazing as my company. Every time I wanted him to smell something, he closed his eyes, and took a deep breath before pausing to describe the nuances of the aroma. Ken asked me to close my eyes so I could experience the wonder with him. Occasionally, my brain was like, "Is this guy real?" Honestly, nobody can fake this stuff, and he was a perfect gentleman.

We shared a scrumptious dinner at a restaurant back toward my house. Minutes turned into hours, and it was time to take me home. I invited him in to talk, and before we knew it, it was after midnight, and he went home. Fourteen hours had flown by, and I was sad to see him go. We agreed to go for a hike the next day, which turned into another twelve-hour day. All of this seemed too good to be true.

Finally, on the third consecutive day we only spent eleven hours together because we both had to get up early the next day. As we stood by the front door, we closed our eyes and gave each other a small kiss. Wow. I could barely breathe as we leaned in for one more kiss goodbye. I watched him drive away as I seemingly floated up to my bedroom. I was too happy to be tired, and my whole body was tingling.

Ken is intensely peaceful, unlike any other person I have ever met. Initially, I did not know why I felt this strongly about how or why he was different. After hearing his life story, it started to make sense. It felt like he had been my best friend forever. He understands that adversity creates the man; it does not define him. I felt safe from external sources because of his demeanor and lifelong choices. I also felt safe from internal sources because he had intentionally chosen peace. If he were not capable of aggression, he would be considered harmless. In today's world, that may be regarded as weak. However, if he is capable of aggression and purposely chooses peace and love, he is indeed a wise warrior and master of life. I feel intensely comfortable and loved by his side.

Days turned into weeks, and one night we drove down to the end of the road at Fort Fisher where the ferry rides arrive and depart each day. It is a great place to watch the sun set over the horizon because it creates an illusion of setting over all three sides of the peninsula. The uninterrupted remoteness carries the promise of a new and glorious adventure for those who journey to this historic destination.

Ken looked rather pensive as he held my hand. His voice was soft and eloquent as well as vibrant and brave when he spoke three words we had both longed to hear, "*I love you.*" However, Ken is definitely not a man of few words. I wished I could have recorded what he said that evening because it was unlike any romantic gesture I had ever heard before. It was beyond extraordinary. When he was done speaking, I replied, "*I love you, too*" as we tightly embraced. He exhaled a sigh of relief, and with a slight quiver in his voice he laughed, "*I was sure hoping you would say that.*" It was extremely powerful and real, a feeling I had never felt before awakened inside my soul.

After the universe seemed to calm itself down from the excitement, I started to laugh, "*You are the most vulnerable and genuine man I have ever met. First, you show up with a jar of honey and a book about love, and now you sound like Hemingway.*" He burst into laughter and replied, "*What I lack in courage, I make up for in tenacity.*" We couldn't stop laughing and just then, a car filled with teenagers pulled in, and parked about two feet away from my car door as if there weren't thirty other available spaces away from our romantic rendezvous. "*Ha! I guess we are like school children and got caught. We should go. But what do you mean I sound like Hemingway?*"

The next day, I sent this quotation, and explained I had this quote inserted in the front of my yearly calendar for two years atop an antiquated world map. I felt only a man who truly understands *genuine love* could conceive of such a notion. I thought maybe one day I would meet that man, and now I have. What Ken said was better than this quote, but it will have to suffice.

"All men fear death. It's a natural fear that consumes us all.
We fear death because we feel that we haven't loved well enough or
loved at all, which ultimately are one and the same.
However, when you make love with a truly great woman, one
that deserves the utmost respect in this world and one that makes
you feel truly powerful, that fear of death completely disappears.
Because when you are sharing your body and heart with a great
woman the world fades away. You two are the only ones in the
entire universe. You conquer what most lesser men have never
conquered before, you have conquered a great woman's heart,
the most vulnerable thing she can offer to another.
Death no longer lingers in the mind. Fear no longer clouds y
our heart. Only passion for living, and for loving, become your s
ole reality. This is no easy task for it takes insurmountable
courage. But remember this, for that moment
when you are making love with a woman of true greatness
you will feel immortal."
Adapted from Ernest Hemingway's literary style and quoted
from his character from Midnight in Paris.

Within a few weeks, we discussed becoming intimate, and took a walk down to the pier to listen to the frogs mating songs. As the moon rippled blue streaks into the dark water, the sweet sounds of nature drowned out the rest of the world. It was just the two of us. I was quite nervous because he had been happily married, and made love to the same woman for 40 years. His life was here in Wilmington, and I was looking to move elsewhere. I asked if we would be compatible in the long run.

He softly took my hands, and intently looked into my eyes, "*Everything in your life, and everything in my life has brought us to where we are today. I would not change one thing about you, and you have not tried to change one thing about me. If I desired to change you, control you or abuse you, I would not have the person I love. Ultimately, you would grow to despise me. Then, our love would cease to exist. I insist you do what you need to do in life, and we will figure everything out together.*" Ken has a unique and satisfying way of making difficult things in life seem pleasant and tolerable.

We had both been blessed. We had both chosen to live in solitude while our souls healed from our own personal tragedies, and now we had found each other. We were both independent and self-sufficient so we did not *need* each other. We *chose* each other, and we were in it for the long haul.

Oh yeah, the real honey. I didn't forget. I wanted a sustainable product for my retreat idea, and honey is actually the perfect product. Was it a coincidence I met one of the few master beekeepers in this region? No, I think it was meant to happen. God was simply smiling upon us. Ken understands the passion, love and life sustaining relationship behind wildflowers and honey bees. He admires and appreciates their heavenly beauty, and their life lessons that grace our Earth.

Have you ever walked through a field of wildflowers, and admired their adorning faces peering into the sun? Next time, take a closer look. Each one of those mystical wildflowers sends out energy signaling the honey bees to fly in and collect pollen and nectar. *Pollen* is one of the richest and purist natural foods consisting of up to 35% protein. It can independently exist within the cells of the hive and is an essential component of the raw honey.

Nectar is a sugary substance secreted by plants that rewards pollinating insects. Upon collection, the bees convert complex sugars in their honey stomachs into the two principle sugars that ultimately create honey. Most of the honey we consume is made from flower nectar. Both of these food sources provide all of the necessary nutrition for the entire colony of bees.

In ancient times, pollen was referred to as ambrosia which in Greek literally translates as *immortality*. Along with nectar, they are regarded as an immortal food and a regenerative substance. In Egyptian mummification ceremonies, honey was offered at various points and certain incantations refer to the dead person going about the afterlife like a bee thus symbolizing *ka*, a person's vital life force.

For thousands of years, bees have been collectively creating honey with perfect accuracy, and people have been extracting that honey as well as the other products created by bees for culinary and medicinal purposes as well as offerings to the gods all over the world. Through my research, I discovered the purple passion flowers I love are equated with the Passion of the Christ.

The Bible mentions honey in twenty-three books, including sixty-one verses, and is often associated with prosperity and abundance. When God called Moses to lead his people out of Egypt to a land flowing with milk and honey, it was not a coincidence, it was a promise.

The Quran clearly discusses rivers of honey flowing in *Jannah*, one's final home in paradise. *"There comes out of their [bee] bellies a drink of different colors, wherein is a cure for mankind. Surely in that is indeed a sign for a people who meditate." 16:69 Quran.* The Prophet Muhammad believed eating honey allowed for a thousand remedies to enter your stomach and a million diseases to be let out.

Depending on traditions, Buddhist monks are only permitted to have one or two meals a day; however, the Buddha named honey one of five foods that can be consumed at any time. Therefore, it is celebrated as a daily ritual and in annual ceremonies. *"Just as a bee, without hurting the flower, its color or scent gathers its nectar and escapes, so should the sage roam in the village."* Dhammapada 4:49. We should take what is necessary in life without causing destruction.

Don't forget about the honeymoon. Traditions say couples were given a honey supply for one month after their nuptial ceremony so both may be vibrant, healthy, and hopefully conceive. But don't worry. The only thing I want to conceive at this point in my life is a retreat center, and I want to create it with those I genuinely love. Oh honey, wouldn't that be so sweet!

My Book

Ironically, I started to write my book the year before all these changes occurred. When I tried to access my files, about 60% of the internal documents had been translated into Chinese, and could not be reverted to their original format. I assumed this happened when my LinkedIn account was tampered with. I had the initial ping of *"Ugh! I am going to explode!"* Then, I remembered I wrote those sections of the book when I distinctly felt something very important was missing in my life.

Now, I had permission from myself to start from scratch with more wisdom. Many of the voices inside my mind that had been guiding my way faded into the past. It was time to compare the story I had pre-written for myself with the story that is still being written today.

The best part is that this is *my* story, and it will forever belong to me. Plus, I have two amazing children to show for it. Hopefully, my story will help many people create a better tomorrow.

Fortunately, my timeline and names of sub-chapters still existed in English. So, I was able to recreate some of my efforts in organizing the structure of my book. Each day, I woke up ready to take on the world, and emotionally re-live my life through each of the sub-chapters. As expected, it was an amazingly cathartic experience. However, strange things were manifesting in my life that I did not expect. Initially I thought, "*Hmm, strange coincidence.*"

Sometimes, I needed to clarify things in my mind and put them down on paper. I would call or text many of my friends or family mentioned in this book. They are keepers of my wisdom. By far, the best discussions were with my children and Ken. They know me and my vantage point. They were able to help me process my thoughts, feelings, or actions in alternative ways. Their wisdom, combined with my experience, often shifted the outcome's energy.

I loved writing down my ideas and casually throwing them out to others to surmise their responses. It helped me gauge what my potential readers might be thinking. I wanted my words to be as understandable as possible, and not be written for a select few individuals who may already agree with my system of beliefs. Remember, I do love words. Using the right word at the right time can make a huge impact. I attempted to select the best words to inspire, not discourage people from continuing on.

In the middle of my book, I returned to physical therapy. I had been limping in pain since the end of last year, and my leg was not healing. I was referred to a woman whose hands instinctively found the pain. Jacky could not leave any of those pesky little dis-ease laden demons behind. Her methods were deep and painful, but I knew the pain was productive. I trusted her form of healing. At the end of our sessions, she said a prayer over my back as she cleared the energy so it would not be able to return to my body or relocate into hers.

Jacky has a beautiful soul that lives between her Native American Lumbee heritage and her Christian belief system. I do not know much about her life, but I can assure you she is a testimony to the word "survivor." Every Lumbee I have met has a distinctive quality about them that I admire. I am not sure how to label this feeling, but I believe it has something to do with overcoming the continued adversity this tribe has faced from both sides of the social spectrum.

One day, I asked Jacky about life energy, and she gave me a small lesson on Chakra rocks. Up until this time, nobody had really shown me how to use them, they just asked me to believe. "*Umm, believe what? You are swinging a rock over me and asking me to make intentions.*" However, Jacky changed my knowledge and perception. After our session was over, I purchased my own Chakra rock from a holistic store nearby. I simply picked the one that felt right.

The white Selenite stone at the bottom was semi-transparent and crystalline. It had several other small stones of various colors up the chain. I showed Ken my findings, and we tested the energy of multiple things at the dinner table: our body parts, batteries, copper bracelets, glasses, cans, rocks and the dogs, all with different results. We were determined to figure out the energetic connections. Between his knowledge of electrical theory and my curiosity behind the healing properties, we sketched our own theory. The next day, I did some research, and our pictures aligned quite well with ancient philosophy. Obviously, we have a lot more to learn but understanding the origin of the healing properties was tantamount to using them. I have been practicing ever since and love sharing my findings.

The world is in need of healers who originate and heal in the light. Jacky is one of those healers and knows her true calling in life. Her hands of love and light will continue to shape my healing as well as many others until her hands finally lay to rest. In my opinion, we all need to proactively walk away from those who live *of this world* and join with people who live *in this world*. I wonder how many people know the difference, and how many actually care about the difference.

When *"world"* is used in the Bible, it is translated from the Greek word *"cosmos."* The cosmos usually refers to the earth and its inhabitants in this spiritual arena. If the inhabitants are *"of this world,"* they have their backs turned to love, light, energy, and God, which means they face toward and follow darkness. Darkness represents sin, poison, and dis-ease.

If they choose to turn their backs on darkness and follow love, light, energy, and God, they will live *"in this world."* Basically, we are an *integral* part of the natural world and life cycle. When one follows the light, they experience freedom. Remember, we have a choice, and darkness as well as light can be quite alluring.

The scientific term *cosmonaut*, Russian astronaut, literally translates to *kosmos*, universe and *nautes*, sailor. So next time, you are sailing through the world looking for something to heal your mind, body and soul, check out who or what is already on board and soaring with energy from light.

The more I sailed into the light, the more I realized something very important. Those who live in and perpetuate the light usually endure great adversity. This feeling had been nagging at me for months: *"The further you go into the light, the more the darkness will pursue you."* Why? Because the more I wrote in the light, darkness seemed to find a way to manifest itself into my current life. Initially, I thought it must be a coincidence but literally every sub-chapter brought on past traumas in a new way.

Then came Chapter 8. If you listen closely, you will hear Beethoven's 5th Symphony play *"Da Da Da Dunn."* This sting is widely used in movies to indicate a moment of suspense, and is appropriate when introducing this manifestation. At the beginning of the chapter, there was a prescribed or controlled burn that was conducted near the Green Swamp Nature Preserve. These types of fires are necessary for the environment to thrive and have been conducted since ancient times.

However, this controlled burn jumped its designated barriers, burned for over a week and encompassed almost 16,000 acres. The sky was dark, gray, and heavy for well over a week and ash covered the ground like fallen snow. Most outdoor activities were canceled in the region, and very few people were outside due to air quality levels. It was like a wild beast had finally been unleashed.

Besides my sadness, this man-made disaster triggered my respiratory system and put it on high emergency alert. I could barely breathe, and my coughing returned in full force making it almost impossible to sit still or sleep. Ironically, it correlated with the writing I was immersed in. It was the first time I became so distracted I had no idea what to write. Possibly, there was something I was supposed to be paying attention to or searching for to add to my personal healing. All I could think was, "*What else is going to happen to me?*" Whew boy, I am sorry I asked.

Manifestations

As I mentioned, the words I was writing seemed to be manifesting their way into my current experiences. Many sub-chapters allowed specific anxiety to reemerge that had somewhat dissipated. I thought, "*Well, that is to be expected.*" The sub-chapter about my body knocking over the telephone pole made my arm and hand ache like it happened last week. I believed it was a bit odd, but I accepted it. Unbelievably, the pain vanished every time I turned the chapter in to my editor. Hmm, that is much more than a coincidence. The sub-chapter about my brain trauma caused severe migraines for two weeks. I thoroughly believed this was over-the-top ridiculous. But, just like my arm, the pain vanished upon submission.

Then, an extra-ordinary and undeniable event happened which completely overhauled my life for three anxiety filled months. Initially, I was not going to include these manifestations in my book. But after several discussions, I realized I needed to address the metaphor and ask myself, "*Why is this happening for me?*" instead of "*Why is this happening to me?*" This is absolutely 100% disgusting, and I will probably not be able to laugh about it until next year.

Here it goes: As I was writing the section on hegemony, I became agitated and angry. I was not unaware of all the control being slammed upon us every day. But, writing it down clearly and concisely significantly triggered my emotions. I hoped everyone would understand how macro and micro control is one of the primary sources of dis-ease we encounter almost every moment of the day whether we know it or not. Remember, emotional dis-ease left unresolved leads to physical disease, and hegemony depends on our *consent* to thrive.

In my opinion, the other primary source of dis-ease during our life is common sense. Often, people may glaze over it, laugh it off, or roll their eyes instead of constructing a resolution. Incongruent, misdirected, or confusing communication left unresolved puts us in a place of dis-ease. Over time, if these conversational *"mistakes"* continue, the dis-ease will perpetuate and may ultimately cause physical disease. How often have you engaged in an argument only to find out you weren't really arguing about the same thing, or somebody just didn't understand what you were expressing? Honestly, it happens way more often than you think. Next time, take a step back and think before you reply.

For instance, when Amelia Bedelia *"draws"* the curtains and *"dresses"* the chicken, we are delightfully taught to have patience with people who think differently. That is a very nice way to say *"misinterprets"* our intended meaning. But what if you had to live and work with someone who could not comprehend what you were talking about most of the time? The interactions would be frustrating on multiple levels and cause dis-ease in your relationship even if there was no mal-intent. These interactions would not be delightful even if Amelia served her famous lemon meringue pie.

Philosophically, if you imagine an ethereal cocktail filled with control and lacking common sense, would you want to drink it? No! It would poison your system. As my mind was bouncing around these notions in my sleep, I was awakened at midnight by something crawling across my face. I pinched it off, and squished in between my fingers.

The smell was absolutely vulgar, which prompted me to jump up and turn the lamp on. There were hundreds of tiny brown bugs all over me and my bed! My hands and wrists were covered with itchy red dots. Panic mode was attempting to take control.

I ran into the bathroom and looked into the mirror. Then, the metaphor dawned on me. These wretched creatures symbolized every single person or entity who had tried to control me in my life, and I was enraged. I wanted revenge. I got a bottle filled with alcohol, and ran back to the bed to exterminate them. Fortunately, it killed them on contact. Eventually I ran out of alcohol, and researched other methods of extermination. Lemon grass oil kills on contact so I filled up a bottle of water, and added ten drops of the essential oil several times. I was determined to destroy these horrible little beasts.

Eventually, I thought the traumatic event was over and laid down on my couch. I could not fall asleep because I kept killing the imaginary bugs crawling all over my skin. That morning, I called Ken. He came over with his son to remove my mattress and box springs. The wicked pests that looked like apple seeds were bedbugs, and they had destroyed my king-size bed beyond repair. I immediately made an appointment with a professional extermination company.

My PTSD kicked into full gear. I did not sleep for the next three weeks. Each time I began to drift off to sleep, the imaginary bugs returned for another attack. Fortunately, Ken was by my side. He calmly held my hands and expressed, "You are safe. There are no bugs. We are in this together." as he helped me breathe and relax. He never once insinuated I was crazy or insane. He simply loved me.

The exterminator directed me to completely clear my bedroom and most of the house, including everything except the furniture, within two days. Pathetically, all of the other people directly involved in the situation exacerbated my trauma. I have absolutely no idea why some people purposely add more trauma to traumatic events. I find their trauma-stacking behaviors to be absolutely repulsive and reprehensible. I will never forgive their audacious display of naive and selfish behavior, complete disrespect, and judgment. Every ounce of my body was experiencing rage. I had no idea how to release it. Of course, the Trauma Stackers just blamed me anyway.

Then came writer's block. Actually, I blocked out almost everything except my children and Ken. I did not want to add this subchapter to my book, but after three months of an uphill battle against control and lack of common sense, I knew I needed to "come clean."

After four professional treatments, I finally passed the inspection. They said they had never seen an infestation so widespread and difficult to treat. They thoroughly believed the moving company was responsible due to the extent of damage, and the time intervals of my travels. The moving company transferred me a multitude of times to people supposedly in charge of incidents. They never followed through with any communications or accepted any responsibility. Ultimately, this fiasco cost me over $7,000, some personal trauma, and some relationships. Oddly, within a few months some cities shut down for the same infestation. I wonder if I was to blame? Not.

Ken and I cleaned every tiny little nook and cranny with wood soap, and then used alcohol swabs on every screw hole. Next, I cleaned and waxed all the furniture while Ken repaired several other mistakes made by the movers. There were actually 15 screws missing that were supposed to hold my bed together. I guess if the bugs weren't going to get me, eventually gravity would. It was humbling to have my best friend by my side. He made the entire situation suck less.

I was standing in line at the grocery store and saw this question: Do you love or like your partner more? I contemplated and thought, both. I love him and like him the most. Ken pondered the question for a moment and replied, "Love seems to be the easy part. You can fall in love with somebody just as easily as you can fall out of love with somebody. However, when you like somebody, love will grow and not fade away because you were friends first." I smiled, "You are the best friend I have ever had."

Eventually, my writer's block went away. The best thing I can say about stupid Chapter 8 is that it gave me some additional time to collect wisdom concerning hegemony. I have been paying much more attention to how control and common sense are intricately woven into our lives, and surmising how to counteract the dis-ease and poison.

When I walked through Tampa, I looked down at the bricks on the boardwalk by the river across from the university. One of them read:

"I know God will not give me anything that
I can not handle.
I wish he didn't trust me so much."
Mother Teresa

Whew! When I agreed to write this book, I had no idea what journey I would endure. I am sure I am meant to write this book, not just for myself, but for my children and you. I cannot make a significant impact on the world all alone. But I can make an impact on a select few. Then, hopefully, the rock I have tossed into the water shall ripple with courage and respect. I suggest you keep a few rocks in your pocket and feel the energy. When you are ready, let them fly and bask in the glory of the light shining upon the rock, the water, and you.

Just a side note: As long as my writing is manifesting things into this world, I heard the lottery jackpot is up over a billion dollars, and I may go and buy my second lottery ticket ever. The first one I bought was when I turned 21 but obviously, I didn't win. Who knows, maybe I will tonight! Wish me luck. I hope you are asking yourself what I would do with a billion dollars. Well, my retreat has been brewing in my mind for over 30 years, and now it is my time to create it. Stay tuned, there is more to come.

Freya

I had been searching for an illustrator and wanted to find an artist with a complimentary style to what I was seeing in my mind. As I was walking through a small craft festival, I saw a young woman selling artwork she had created with wood and a *Pyrography Tool Set*, wood burning instruments. Her artwork intrigued me, and we struck up a conversation. Almost immediately, she told me about the adversity she suffered in her youth although I did not inquire. Then she spoke about her work with a shaman to restore her health because the medical profession had given her a dismal outlook for the future. I told her about my book, and asked for contact information because I thought we would be a great match.

After a several exchanges and a bunch of excuses, I surmised she was blowing me off. I was rather baffled because I thought, "*You are an artist, and you want to sell your artwork. I am giving you an opportunity to make money during your down time, and you are not interested. Strange to me.*" For the next couple months, I looked around for another illustrator with no luck. I felt a little discouraged.

Then, I felt intensely drawn to join a 6-hour meeting over Zoom. Ha! I know, right? Who is drawn towards a 6-hour meeting? In case you are wondering, I am not into inflicting pain upon myself. The meeting was broken into one-hour sessions with a speaker for the first fifteen minutes of each session. You can listen to and participate in as many sessions as you like. They are similar to TedTalks, but fierce guidelines do not dictate these 360 Nation, InsteadTalks 360°.

I made it to the second session, which discussed mythology as a therapeutic intervention. I was fascinated because I had just finished and received feedback about "*The Legend of The White Heron.*" One of the participants asked a question, and I noticed an intense image of a goddess on the wall behind him. During the break, I inquired if that was his artwork, and he replied, "*Yes, that is Freya, a Norse Goddess. I actually won an award for this drawing.*" In turn, I sent him a connection request on LinkedIn. After a few messages back and forth, I sent him a copy of my legend, and he absolutely loved it. Then, I offered him to read the entire manuscript because I wanted his artistic and youthful opinion of my work. In the meantime, I did some research on Freya.

Serendipitously, something extraordinary happened I did not expect. As we discussed my words and experiences, symbolically our communications wove together the pages of the book as if it was bound in antiquity, and meant to come alive right now. Our in depth exchanges helped to transform the devastation lingering inside my soul into something undeniably beautiful. On the flip side, something amazing transformed inside of his soul as well. I believe it brought him closer to his purpose in life. But, that is his story to tell, and hopefully it will come to life one day soon.

Guess what else is really cool? Freya, The Goddess of Love and War, is the most renowned Norse Goddess in the Pantheon. *Freya*, whose name means *"The Lady,"* is associated with love, splendor, and fertility. But she is also associated with war and death. She epitomized beauty and used her insatiable attraction to get what she wanted. She has been equated to Aphrodite, Venus, and The Mother Mary throughout history. Freya embodied her people's penchant for the magical arts of divination and symbolically has two distinct phenomena indicative of her irresistible attraction.

Penchant is strong inclination or instinct, and is derived from the Latin *pendere*, to weigh. She and her people practiced a form of magic or sorcery called *Seidr*, which involved discerning and influencing fate, otherwise known as the future.

According to legend, when Freya cried, her teardrops fell to earth, transforming the ground into pure gold and the oceans into amber stones. Therefore, gold was referred to as *Freya's Tears*. Most importantly, these tears rained down in sadness after her husband abandoned her.

Here is an odd twist to the story. Freya was married to Ódr (Od or Odur), the Vanir God of ecstasy, longing, passion, and rage. His name means *The Frenzied One* in Old Norse. Little else is known about him because he mysteriously disappeared from the oral and written traditions. However, there has been scholarly speculation Ódr is either the same God or the twin brother of Odin, the King of Æsir. Either way, their marriage produced twin daughters, and both of their names translate as *treasure*.

Freya's most prized possession was a necklace created from the elements of her tears. The Brísingamen (*gleaming torc* or *amber torc*) was made by dwarves who gathered the treasures and forged them with fire into a mystical and magical work of art. Freya guarded the coveted necklace with a fiery passion. The dichotomy of her personality lends itself to the colors associated with her power: black and red. You may think, "*All right, these are cool colors.*" But there is more behind the story.

Also, please do not confuse Freya with her twin brother, Freyr, the God of Peace and Prosperity. He is a composite of Zeus who controls the rain, Helios who controls the sun, and Demeter who controls the harvest. Their father was Njörd, the God of the Sea while the story of their mother faded into antiquity.

If the sound of Freya and Freyr ring familiar, it is because the base of the word is currently used throughout the Germanic languages. For example, *Fräulein* means young, unmarried woman and is diminutive to "*Frau*," meaning married woman. While Führer (ˈfjʊərər), sometimes spelled Fuehrer, is a German word meaning *leader* or *guide*.

Unfortunately, an extremely prominent figure chose the name *Führer* to anoint himself as "The Leader" of the Nazi Party in 1921. He delegated himself as the sole source of power, and absolute authority figure in efforts to unite the *Nordic-Germanic Master Race.*" Coincidence, I think not. He was aligning himself with the gods, and chose black and red for his insignia. In today's world, the individual word is usually avoided due to its connection with World War II. However, the suffix -führer is used in conjunction with words such as *Geschäftsführer* (manager), *Spielführer* (team captain) and *Bergführer* (mountain guide). Horrible how something good transformed into something evil.

If we jump back to before Christianity starting spreading across Europe, black and red were associated with many symbols of power and prosperity including ladybirds. The beautiful yet aggressive heavenly creatures necessary for a bountiful harvest were called *"freya-fugle"* in Old Norse, meaning *Freya's bird*. The name *Ladybird*, or Lady Bug in America, originated during the Middle Ages. The red or sometimes yellow insects with 2-7 black spots were known as the *Beetle of Our Lady*. They were named after the Virgin Mary, who was often depicted wearing a red cloak in early Christian paintings. Followers believed the spots symbolize The Seven Joys and Seven Sorrows of Our Blessed Lady.

As soon as I discovered this, I shed tears of sweet sorrow. I saw my children's grandmother in my mind just as I saw her in my dream many years ago. Her face and her hand appeared as though it was yesterday. Her death signified the end of my marriage, and now I know why she was consoling me. This discovery actually occurred during the last seven pages of my book and took me from *believing to knowing the truth*. If you recall, Grandma signified the ladybug in our family since we visited her grave site, and she landed on Daniel's shoulder. The presence of the Ladybug symbolizes love and joy for my children.

Let me explain the bittersweetness of my emotions. In my mind, belief is a form of doubt. In its simplest form, if someone asks, do you know your name? I do not reply, *"I think my name is Amy."* Instead, I reply, *"I know my name is Amy."* I used to *believe* Grandma came to console me upon her passing. Now, I *know* she came to console me until I was ready to learn the truth, accept it, and act upon it. I *know* she wants me to end the cycle of abuse in our family and to help other families do the same. Both grandmas always parted ways with the same message, "Love one another."

Last Friday, most likely a *portmanteau*, in conjunction with Freya's Day, this discovery prompted a strange yet validating set of emotions. On one hand, I was grateful Grandma fully supported my efforts to end the cycle of abuse, but I was also sad. She knew I would endure suffering after she ascended into heaven. I was also sad because she endured much suffering throughout her life. I have always felt that if she had been still alive, the adversity in my life would have been much less. We can't change the past; we can only strive to impact the future. In Old Norse, þökk fyrir, with gratitude in my heart, thank you, Freya, for helping to validate my book and all that I have expressed. My passion for love and life continues despite the wars within and around us.

Know Thyself

I knew I needed to create a landing page for my book and a landing page for creating my retreat center. The first task would be a little more objective while the second would be much more subjective because I do not own the land yet. Further, I do not have a specific location selected for my retreat. I found a few options for web designers. They were either too busy, arrogant, or technical to be bothered with my creative endeavors. I needed someone who could be highly creative and highly technical to give my website the love and passion it deserves.

While looking for a match for my website, I met a guy named Michael. After our first individual Zoom meeting, he reminded me of The Oracle, played by Gloria Foster from "*The Matrix*" movies with Neo, played by Keanu Reeves. When Neo first meets The Oracle, she is smoking a cigarette and baking cookies. She prompts Neo to sit down and eat the cookies, but initially, he declines. The camera flashes over a Latin expression, **Temet Nosce, Know Thyself,** on a placard hanging over her kitchen door. Then, her unconventional wisdom begins to flow.

Temet Nosce originated from the temple of the Greek god Apollo at Delphi. This ancient religious sanctuary was erected in the 8th century BC. It was home to the Oracle of Delphi and the priestess Pythia, known in the ancient world for divination seeing the future. Knowing yourself and your purpose in life was of the utmost importance over 2,800 years ago, as I am sure it was well before that.

Michael can energetically connect with the past and does not confine himself to labels or titles. He came to me because I was searching for answers, and I am a *"fiery yet gentle soul filled with courage and curiosity.*" He is a wealth of knowledge and wisdom but proclaims the only gift he can provide for others is to be a living example. Through his unconventional work and calling in life, he hopes to guide people to understand that they are the greatest gifts they can give unto themselves. I haven't eaten all his cookies yet, but they smell delicious.

Michael's universal wisdom is stimulating my brain in new and enticing ways. He believes, "*You have to love every flaw, every wart, every hair, everything you have in your life. You must fully and unconditionally love every aspect of yourself and your weaknesses. Then, your flaws become your greatest strengths.*" Probably the most profound thing he stuck in my brain is that we (meaning all of us) choose our parents before we are born. I pondered this thought and the next during a long walk.

Michael encouraged me to embrace and love that big ball of anxiety fully, which I have been holding in my tummy for years. This was the complete opposite of what I had been trying to do. I fully desired that big ball of negative energy to leave me. I needed to convince it to stay and love it unconditionally. Ugh. I thought I would try it because the thought had never really crossed my mind. After a few days, some thoughts occurred to me, and I felt a little different. I guess we will see.

Michael introduced me to a new word, *clairsentient*. I guess you can tell by now that I love new words, especially if they help describe me. It's funny how I never learned that one because I know the others. The concept can be broken down into avenues of intuition known as *"The Four Clairs."* However, I included another one about smell because it happens to me quite often. The examples I offer may seem like brief and fleeting moments, but they are actually filled with purpose and passion.

Clairaudience (hearing) is the ability to perceive or *"clearly hear"* auditory sounds or voices in the spiritual or metaphysical realm. Some may call it psychic hearing, extrasensory perception, or that little voice in the back of your mind. Spiritual deafness would entail the opposite, meaning that one is incapable of hearing or blocking out those messages unless they come directly out of the mouth of another human.

Hearing sounds beyond our ordinary experience can be confusing and intimidating. I can assure you they are well worth the time and energy to discern and integrate them wisely throughout life. We all have all of these abilities. Some people are just more tuned with the energy.

During an extremely difficult turning point in my life, my grandmother appeared to me. Her auditory message was clear and simple, "Don't be afraid anymore." Within one day, my perception and method of dealing with the situation entirely changed. It was as though her words opened a passage in my heart.

Clairvoyance (seeing) **is** the ability to see things beyond our normal range of sight. Many may call it intuition or *"clear sight"* into the past, present, or future. Observing paranormal activity may prompt someone to dismiss the vision as a shadow or their imagination, which is a distinct possibility. But what if I told you many of those visions are real? Learn to pay attention; you will feel the emotions and impact of the reason they exist. You are not crazy. You have a gift, so learn to accept your truth and the messages within. No crystal ball is necessary, although they are pretty to look at.

One second, before an SUV jumped the curb and made multiple intrusions on the sidewalk less than 5 feet to my left, Ken clearly saw it in his mind. Instantly, he pulled me out of the way and pushed me into the grass as he watched the SUV recklessly skid and drive away. Without a doubt, he saved my life.

Clairsentient (recognizing) Many people in this category are labeled empathic. The word itself means *"clear feeling"*. They can perceive emotional energy that is not necessarily perceivable to our basic set of senses. In my opinion, being an empath seems like a curse as well as a blessing. Sometimes, the emotional energy of the room or a person is so strong it becomes a huge distraction. Beyond that, the energy involved in an interaction may be emotionally draining. Learning how to filter out unwanted distractions purposely proves beneficial. On the other hand, perceiving emotional energy can perpetuate relationships, help solve interpersonal problems, and process situations effectively. Learning to feel your feelings is essential for self-protection and preservation.

When I worked in the treatment center, I clearly recognized a boy's father walking down the hallway and immediately called security. I had never seen him before, and he was supposedly in prison for multiple crimes. I felt darkness and security was able to respond to the pending crisis swiftly.

Clairolfactance (smelling) This extrasensory perception of smell may be classified as synesthesia, where smells translate directly to something else. Synesthesia is a fancy name for when you experience one of your senses through another. You may hear instrumental music but see colors. You may smell rose-scented soap, but you may also feel the presence of your grandmother. Another form of this heightened perception is when one smells scents not in their current environment. Memories may trigger these internal smells or come from an unknown energy source. The sweet scent of victory or smelling danger lurking is more than in your head; it's in your nose.

The perfect gift had been alluding me for weeks. While strolling, I distinctly smelled Agua de Florida from my ceremonies. I searched for the precise origin, but alas I found nothing except the perfect gift. I could chalk it up to coincidence, but I have serendipitously followed this mystical scent before.

Claircognizant (knowing) means *"clearly knowing"* or perceiving information outside the parameters of knowledge or wisdom. Your gut instinct is keenly aware and in tune with people and places in your surroundings. Learn to listen and discern when your tummy is telling you something. You cannot confirm or deny what you have experienced, but it is real. Discounting your perception or the perceptions of others is a recipe for destruction. Acknowledging and understanding your instincts will hopefully add some sweetness to your life.

For over 30 years, I have known I am supposed to write a book and create a retreat. However, life always seemed to get in the way. Every time I stepped toward my goal, I was forced to take two steps back. Obviously, it was not my time. However, over the past couple of years, I had no choice but to follow my calling. Life, love, and happiness spoke my name. I clearly know what I am supposed to create, and it is my job to paint this image in the minds of others so they can comprehend the message in my heart. We are all here together for a reason, and I know the overarching reason is love.

My Sanctuary

I introduced you to The Legend of the White Heron at the beginning of this literary adventure. I told you about growing up and venturing out into the world. I described the family I created and subsequently transformed. I described a mystical sanctuary filled with wildflowers only to rediscover my life's purpose. Then, I left you hanging along with all those woodland creatures. Finally, I am ready to introduce you to my magical sanctuary, possibly our sanctuary.

Ever since I was a young girl, I have seen this plot of land in my mind. I have not seen it in real life, but when I step onto this hallowed ground, I will *know it*. I see my house beside me and other structures in the distance. I feel the energy of the land penetrating my body and the air blowing my hair in the breeze. I hear birds and bees soaring through the air and the dogs running up to greet me. I smell the alluring scent of tall grasses blowing off the edge of the lake and the freshly cut cedar wood waiting for me in the workshop. Walking down to the pier to take a break after a hike, I taste the fresh herbs and honey from my garden of life. The bright sun is warming my skin as I bask in the glory of each passing day. I am *home* with *my family* by my side.

How does this plot of land fit into my retreat idea? Well, this is my home and my retreat, a sanctuary for all to enjoy. The primary purpose of this retreat is to help any ordinary person who has suffered an extraordinary event and needs time to detach, heal, and prosper. The second purpose of my retreat is to invite various artisans to detach from the reality we are forced to live in and allow them to be in an environment where they want to live—giving everyone the freedom to create their masterpieces.

Grab your shovel, and let's dig deeper into my dream that will become a reality. Will it look exactly like my description? I have no idea. What I do know is that all dreams are open to interpretation. Why? As I mentioned, I am sharing this dream with my family and those I love. If I genuinely love them, their dreams will also become my reality. Remember, loving relationships are reciprocal; maybe it will turn out better than I could have ever imagined. God definitely works in mysterious ways.

The Big Picture means if I win that billion-dollar lottery I was talking about in the last chapter, my retreat center would tentatively look like this. I guess I need an interpretive center to make all these elements make sense. Just kidding, they weave a beautiful pattern of healing, creativity, and powerful energy designed to enhance love, life, health, and happiness. To me, genuine health is a harmonious balance of all these elements.

The earth is fertile, and all structures shall follow the traditional songlines of the land. The concept of songlines, also called dream tracks, originated with the Aboriginals in Australia. When erecting structures, the least amount of intrusion possible will be afforded to the natural environment. I want all visitors to be able to feel the energy of the land. This is not some kind of mystical fantasy. Honestly, land that has been relatively untouched or at least not destroyed or completely reconstructed by humans feels vibrant and alive.

At its core, a **songline** facilitates the listener in two distinct ways. First, the songs are like an auditory and visual map to help navigate the land. Second, the songs are a repository of cultural knowledge to teach individuals about particular landmarks, water resources, naturally occurring features, and their spiritual significance. Many of these songs transcend linguistic barriers and facilitate cross-cultural communication. If you look at an image of a songline, you will notice they are created with many dots. Essentially, these *"Footprints of the Ancestors"* or *"Creator Spirit Tracks"* is a painting technique that represents poking holes through the veil of truth. Meaning that you can only engage with the knowledge and wisdom you are prepared to receive.

The water feature, whether a lake, river, or stream, follows the lay of the land and provides quiet respite and recreation for visitors. The animals will have equal access, and consideration shall be taken when making the surrounding areas safe and productive for all. I would like to have a pier and specialized equipment so the natural water resources can be enjoyed in various ways. The view shall intrinsically be yours whether you are standing near or floating in the water.

The element of fire shall be central when the day turns into night. However long your stay may be, let the fire warm your hands and your heart. Cook your food over the open hearth, and allow the sweet sounds of music to entice your soul. As you watch the flames dance high into the sky, you will feel the wonder of this magical journey. Alternatively, for those nights when the food must be prepared inside, you can peek through the window of a modern-day Basque Country **Txoko.** In this gastronomical society, people come together to eat, drink and socialize. Gastronomy is the art and science of selecting the proper ingredients, cooking food according to customs, and serving a feast for the senses—basically, the art of good eating.

Jumping back to the music aspect of these experiences, fireside concerts are a must. If you dance and play to the beat of a different drum, what better place can you showcase your skills than beside other artists who can help you in your endeavors? I figure if you can *wow* an audience with an acoustic version of your favorite song, you will undoubtedly be able to make it happen in the studio. Additionally, when you chill out and warm up, your next song may magically come to life.

Since the natural elements wax and wane in seasonal cycles, I would like to have a few greenhouses that contain hydroponic systems to maximize the health and taste of fresh herbs, mushrooms, and vegetables. This way, we can all learn to eat our way back to health in a delicious and satisfying way. Growing and eating food how nature intended it to look, feel, and taste will make our taste buds and tummies happy. Our honey bees and butterflies will stay busy.

Tiny Homes: Living spaces where spirits and creative energy from all over the world shall dwell. Every continent shall be represented through its mythological folklore and traditional teachings. These immersive experiences are a cross between a bed and breakfast and a therapeutic retreat. These are not highfalutin cabins whose novelty will wear off by the end of the evening. Moreover, they are simple but elegant, thought-provoking destinations for your overnight journey. *The Dragon House* may be my first tiny home endeavor. Wouldn't it be amazing to feel its tough and leathery skin?

Tiny Workshops: Where workspaces come to life through curiosity and experience. The primary workshop in my sanctuary shall be a "living classrooms" beehive. Imagine being immersed in a life-size honeycomb and learning lessons from the queen and her servants. Straight from the Royal Jelly all the way to the honey in your mouth, every moment will be sweet, healthy, and oozing with wisdom. Taste the honey right off the comb and learn to contribute to the cycle of life.

The next workshop shall be for woodworking because this is how much of the imagery will come to life. Whether it is a table, a chair, or artwork, the woodcarving elements will enhance the view. Close your eyes and imagine drinking a refreshing local brew in an old-world public meeting house. Sit back and wonder if *Sasquatch* is waiting outside to greet you. This craft pub shall tame those wild woodland people by teaching them to brew their own concoctions and enjoy them at the fireside.

Another workshop I would love to create would be a blacksmith shop. I can hear the ting ting ting of the hammer and anvil forging our creations to life. This is a perfect adjunct to the woodworking shop. I would love to keep old-world traditions alive and merge them with our new world ideas. I want all of my activities to be fun and affordable. Obviously, I cannot create and maintain all of these ventures on my own. My concept is big, but it is achievable within the proper community.

I am fully aware that my many ideas will take a considerable amount of time, energy, passion, love, and money. Hopefully, my wealth will manifest itself through the lives I touch every day.

When I was in college, I went to a festival and saw a magnificent pendant. It had a tree on it and the inscription read, *"Everything she touches she changes."* It was too expensive to buy then, or maybe it just wasn't my time yet. Either way, the sentiment has always stuck with me. I looked for that vendor over the years but never found them. I like to think the message signifies me and my intentions in life. I desire to make a difference in my world. I know I cannot change the world as a whole; nobody can. However, I feel my world is getting ready to expand!

One Big Question: Are you curious about what has transpired since the conclusion of my book? Yay! I was hoping you'd say yes. I'll admit, I was a bit surprised because it all happened so quickly. Here it goes! Ken and I bought a reforested 10 acre farm for our home, retreat center, and honey bee farm. It is only 15 minutes outside of Wilmington and centrally located to so many natural sites I refer to in my story. It is a perfect sanctuary to build our dream. I am so excited for you to join us on our journey. Hand in hand and heart to heart. We are in this together.

Please go to my website and sign up. You can follow us through the various stages of building. Contribute or participate in creating various fundraisers and structures, especially in our living classroom. Most importantly, you can become an integral part of the magic awaiting inside. I am excited to spend some time with you.

Website: **WhiteHeron.us**

It is difficult to comprehend that I am concluding my book. I have invested so much time, energy, and emotion. Part of me wants to hold on, while the other part wants to let go. But we all know I can't, and as my grandmother said, "*Don't be afraid and let go.*" I am ready to take the next step forward, leave the past behind me, and be the light I wish to see in the world!

I hope you will walk away with a little more wisdom in your pocket and find answers to some of your life's trials and tribulations.

When you close your eyes this evening, think about our journey and how you will start living your life to the fullest. It may be difficult, but you deserve it. If you need me, I am simply a phone call away. I would love to start a relationship with you. Don't leave just yet! One more section to go.

Book of Magic

Before I highlight some of the characters that made my book of magic come alive, I would like to thank all the people who closed the door-ways I opened. If life in those passages had been more comfortable, I may have overstayed my time and missed out on opportunities to thrive. I would also like to thank all the mischievous spirits who caused havoc in my life. All of you coerced me into new and creative endeavors I would have missed if suffering ceased to exist. May God bless you and keep you safe from harm. Now, onto the good stuff!

First and foremost, I would like to thank everyone who has con-tributed to my life and the creation of this book. I am eternally grate-ful. A few of those people wish to remain anonymous, while others have retired or moved on in this life or into the next. However, some of those amazing people are available if you want to reach out. They are here to help.

A special thank you goes to my children and my mom. I love you all more than you could ever comprehend. You are the eternal light that keeps my heart alive. Not a day goes by when I do not think of you, and long to be by your side. Thank you for loving and trusting me to follow my dreams.

Another special thank you goes to Bob for being my business partner. Your objective and passionate outlook helped to transform my dream into a reality. Working together has been a distinct pleasure I will never forget. Our concerted efforts will help a multitude of people now and in the future.

My last special thank you goes to Ken, the best friend and lover I have ever had. Everything I have endured in life has led me to you. Your love and companionship helped to make my story my masterpiece. Your version of love perfectly matches my version of love. Together, we will rediscover the world.

I look forward to creating our new home, our sanctuary where love will grow and prosper.

Dennis Pitocco, 360° NATION: Thank you for creating a rich and vibrant community where all voices matter and are respected. The Friendship Bench has been my faithful companion throughout this entire endeavor, and the participants feel like family. The world needs more leaders like you. God bless.

Eileen Bild, OTEL Universe: Thank you for allowing my voice to be my gift and for introducing me to people who will help my voice extend out in unexpected and enriching ways.

Matt Maes, Quantum Keyhole: Thank you for helping me to unwind and weave together the images of my life. Your hand and your heart created beauty in the darkest hours.

Roger Martin and **Michael Padurano:** Thank you for extending your hands and hearts in sincere companionship when I was looking for answers to questions I had not yet asked myself.

The Oasis of Ladies in My Heart: Thank you all for creating such a loving and supportive group of friends to make Wilmington home. Your refreshing springs of joy sprinkle magic in my soul.

Teresa Velardi, Authentic Endeavors Publishing: I do not know where to start, or shall I say, end because there is so much more to come in our journey together. Thank you for upholding my words and my book to be authentically mine. I am delighted you saw a beautiful vessel when I came to you as clay. You allowed God to be the potter for my life's work; for that, I am truly blessed. You and your team of experts brought my imagination to life better than I expected.

Doreen DeJesus-Harper, Ambicionz: Thank you for creating my interactive website and for having the business savvy to understand and create what I was extrapolating in my mind.

Aljon Comahig, Inertia Illustrations: Thank you for impeccably capturing the image, style and essence of the pictures in my soul. The stylistic elegance of your contributions elevated The White Heron.

A Closing Acknowledgment and thank you goes out to **YOU.** Don't look beside you or behind you to see who I am speaking to. Get up, go look in the mirror, and *know* I am talking to you. This is the end of my book, but definitely not the end of my story. I am looking forward to the next chapter and the next book. I hope you are as well. The cover is on my website! For now, my companion and hopefully one day friend, I must say, "Goodbye or *possibly until we meet again.*" *Peace & Love Always ~ Amy*

ABOUT THE AUTHOR

Amy Olmedo is on a mission from God.

Amy's life story is an intriguing mixture of spirituality, mythology and teaching points to help you embrace her appreciation for life. Amy invites you to experience triumph over tragedy in *White Heron: A Creation Story*.

Peruse her website and sign up to be a part of the dream. www.whiteheron.us

The website will allow you to delve into her magical world. Let nature become your sanctuary as you immerse yourself in the healing powers of nature and rediscover wisdom from within. Somewhere in between the mystical woodland trails and the honey bee farm, you will be able to rest, reconcile the past and recreate your future.

COMING SOON

White Heron: A Companion Workbook

Let this companion be your guide as you explore the book and explore yourself. This intriguing workbook is filled with life lessons, immersive activities, and coloring pages that align with the magic and mystery of what's inside.

This workbook would be great alone, with a friend, or as an integral part of your next book club experience.

White Heron: Companion Journal

In quiet contemplation, write down the messages emanating from your heart while listening to music that stimulates your soul. Allow your hand to gracefully transform the pages from black and white to the colors you see and feel on the page coming into formation.

Let wisdom walk by your side, and guide you to unspoken questions, and allow the answers to call you by name. Discover unique ways to unlock the mystery and magic of your story waiting to happen. These words will endure the test of time, your time.

Come on, I am waiting for you.

Alexander: Unearthing An Immortal Love Story is an extraordinary adventure in discovering how to fall in love and stay in love with the worst parts of yourself.

This mysterious and alluring romance allows The Magician to live a genuine and authentic life filled with love, laughter, and wisdom, ultimately serving her purpose in our world.